child psycho-pathology:

behavior disorders and developmental disabilities

2nd edition

MARILYN T. ERICKSON

virginia commonwealth university

prentice-hall, inc.
englewood cliffs, new jersey 07632

Erickson, Marilyn T.
    Child psychopathology.

    Includes index.
    1. Child psychopathology. 2. Child psychiatry.
I. Title. [DNLM: 1. Mental disorders—In infancy and
childhood. WS 350 E67c]
RJ499.E63 1982   618.92'89   81-8660
ISBN 0-13-131094-1   AACR2

editorial production/supervision and
    interior design: barbara kelly
cover design: lee cohen
manufacturing buyer: edmund w. leone

Printed in the United States of America

10 9 8 7 6 5 4 3 2 1

ISBN 0-13-131094-1

Prentice-Hall International, Inc., London
Prentice-Hall of Australia Pty. Limited, Sydney
Prentice-Hall of Canada, Ltd., Toronto
Prentice-Hall of India Private Limited, New Delhi
Prentice-Hall of Japan, Inc., Tokyo
Prentice-Hall of Southeast Asia Pte. Ltd., Singapore
Whitehall Books Limited, Wellington, New Zealand

to Eric
for loving and caring

contents

11

conduct disorders 222

12

anxiety and other emotional disorders 251

13

disorders affecting physical functioning 273

14

preface

The purpose of this book is to introduce students to child psychopathology and developmental disabilities and the clinical methods for assessing and treating children's developmental, behavioral, and emotional problems. Although the information contained in this book is derived primarily from research conducted by psychologists, also included are the contributions of other disciplines, such as education, medicine, social work, and speech pathology, with respect to theory, research, and clinical practice.

My primary goal has been to present an overview of the field that relates past and present trends to future directions. To that end, the book contains a variety of the theoretical and clinical approaches to child psychopathology and developmental disabilities. The somewhat heavier emphasis on behavioral approaches reflects the current research productivity, which promises to have an increasing impact on future clinical practices.

A second goal has been to develop an understanding of how information about children's behavior disorders is obtained and the problems associated with the evaluation and interpretation of this information. The third goal had been to familiarize the student with the major categories of child psychopathology and developmental disabilities and our knowledge with respect to their assessment, etiology, and treatment.

The first half of the book contains general information about assessment methods, theories and research on etiology, and approaches to treatment or intervention. The second half contains comparable specific information that has been obtained about children with certain types of behavior problems. The student should be aware that the population of children with behavior disorders may be subdivided in a variety of ways; the diagnostic and labeling system used in this edition is based primarily on the *Diagnostic and Statistical Manual of Mental Disorders*, 3rd edition (DSM-III).

Most books require an extended period of devotion by the author, and the two editions of this one are no exception, having been written in parallel with the many other activities of academic life. In a larger perspective, however, an author's product is the result of a much longer history of contact with the research literature and interactions with specific individuals. I am particularly indebted to Lewis Lipsitt, Judy Rosenblith, Donald Baer, Lucie Jessner, and Harrie Chamberlin for their lasting influences as teachers and colleagues, and to my students and clients, who have continued to challenge and teach me.

introduction

1

The study of children's behavior disorders is largely a twentieth-century phenomenon. Before modern times children's status in society precluded the possibility of substantial concern about behavior disorders; first, because the odds against physical survival were very high and, second, because children were perceived as sources of amusement for adults and as property of relatively little value. Descriptions of children's abnormal behavior did appear sporadically in the writings of the eighteenth and nineteenth centuries, but disordered behavior was viewed as primarily reflecting some inherent evil in the afflicted person (Kanner, 1962). The role of early childhood experience in the etiology of behavior problems was not formally recognized until the advent of psychoanalytic theory. With the exception of mentally retarded children, concentrated study of children with behavior disorders did not occur until the 1930s. Many changes in society very likely contributed to the new focus on children's problems: greatly decreased mortality rates, the development of educational opportunities for all children, the introduction of psychological treatment for adult problems, the development of methods for measuring human behaviors and the accumulation of data describing children's growth and behavior.

Knowledge of the behavioral repertoires of children at different ages was a crucial prerequisite to the study of child psychopathology. The child development researchers of the 1920s and 1930s initiated the first large-scale studies of behavior using both longitudinal and cross-sectional approaches. The longitudinal approach involved the observation of the same children periodically throughout their development period beginning in infancy. The cross-sectional approach utilized different groups of children at each age level. Both approaches have presented a variety of advantages and deterrents to researchers (Nunnally, 1973) but nevertheless have provided a critical foundation for judging the normality or abnormality of behavior.

Reliance on the norms of behavior has not been universally accepted by professionals who deal with children's problems. Some clinicians prefer to use personal standards for judging whether or not a behavior is abnormal, and some rely almost exclusively on the judgments of the adults complaining about the child's behavior. Lack of reference to norms, however, can result in a child's behavior being diagnosed as abnormal when it, in fact, is not significantly different from that of same-aged children.

the clinical professions

In modern times a number of professional disciplines have been involved in the assessment and treatment of children's behavior problems. In the early child guidance clinics three professionals, the child psychiatrist, the clinical child psychologist, and the social worker, provided the services for the child and the parents. Initially, their activities were complementary: the psychologist administered and interpreted tests, the psychiatrist interviewed the family members and later treated the child, and the social worker counseled the parents. Through the years, changes in the training programs have created an overlap in the clinical skills of these professions. Clinical psychologists, for example, are now trained to conduct the diagnostic interview as well as to administer and interpret a broad spectrum of tests; much of the psychologists' training also focuses on treatment techniques. Thus, to a large extent, the skills of clinical psychologists and psychiatrists in assessment and treatment are comparable. The principal differences between psychiatrists and clinical psychologists lie in the medical training of the former, which prepares the psychiatrist to diagnose physical problems and to use medication in treatment.

training programs

In this section we describe the characteristics of training programs and educational requirements for psychiatrists, clinical psychologists, and other professionals involved in the assessment and treatment of children's behavior problems.

Psychiatry. Psychiatry is one of the medical specialties; intensive training in psychiatry begins only after the student completes undergraduate and medical school programs, each of which takes about four years. In medical school the student is given a curriculum in the basic sciences and small amounts of supervised clinical experience in many of the medical specialties, including psychiatry. Intensive training in a medical specialty is called a *residency* and is usually based in the appropriate clinical department of a medical school. Many residency training programs affiliate with community facilities, such as clinics, hospitals, and institutions, and these settings are thereby also available for the training of residents.

Residency training programs in psychiatry require two years of supervised experience working with adults. Those trainees who are interested in focusing on the problems of children spend from one to three additional years gaining supervised experience with children and their parents. Departments of psychiatry typically employ clinical psychologists and social workers who also contribute to the training of residents.

The goal of the residency in psychiatry is to train the student to provide diagnostic and treatment services for a broad spectrum of behavioral problems. The goal is achieved through seminars and direct experience with a variety of patients. Supervision of the resident's activities with patients usually involves the trainee's describing the interactions during a session or playing a tape recording of portions of the session and the experienced clinician (supervisor) commenting and making suggestions about the resident-patient interactions. Occasionally, the resident may have the opportunity to observe experienced clinicians conducting interviews or providing treatment or doing both. Supervision may be conducted on a one-to-one basis, or several residents may meet weekly with a supervisor to share their training and experiences.

After a year of diagnostic and treatment experience following the residency training program, the psychiatrist becomes eligible for the written examination for certification in adult psychiatry by the American Board of Psychiatry and Neurology which is followed by an oral examination. After successful completion of these examinations, the psychiatrist may take the examination for certification in child psychiatry. This procedure is in addition to the examination required by state medical licensing boards, which permit physicians to practice medicine.

A small number of psychiatrists supplement their therapeutic skills by enrolling in a psychoanalytic institute. Completion of the course of study, which is usually pursued part time over a number of years, allows the therapist to be called a *psychoanalyst*. The training includes seminars, the psychoanalysis of several patients under the supervision of an experienced psychoanalyst, and a personal psychoanalysis. A few psychoanalytic institutes accept candidates who do not have medical training. A person without an M.D. degree who has completed training in psychoanalysis is called a lay analyst; the most prominent lay analyst working with children is Anna Freud, the daughter of Sigmund Freud, who has directed the Hampstead Clinic in London, a major training center for lay analysis.

Clinical Psychology. Clinical psychologists are trained in university departments of psychology and receive the Ph.D. degree upon completion of the program, which usually takes about five years. During this time the graduate student takes courses in the theoretical and applied aspects of psychological principles and receives supervised experience in assessment and treatment. Most of the clinical psychology training programs prepare students both to do research and to provide clinical services.[1] Research training is considered to be necessary for several reasons: (1) to provide the clinician with the skills to evaluate the research literature, (2) to emphasize the importance of research in the advancement of the field, and (3) to encourage and provide the background for conducting research on clinical problems. A large number of Ph.D. clinical psychologists are employed in positions (community clinics, institutions, private practice) involving the delivery of assessment and treatment services to clients. Other clinical psychologists join the faculties of university psychology departments, where they teach courses, supervise students' clinical work, and conduct research.

As in psychiatry, the training programs in clinical psychology emphasize clinical work with adults and vary greatly in their training resources for students who plan to work with children and their parents. Only a few programs specialize in the training of clinical child psychologists or have close relationships with child development programs whereby the student can acquire a comprehensive understanding of children. The student interested in working with children may obtain the necessary clinical experiences during practicum or internship assignments, or both, although occasionally such experiences may be postponed to a postdoctoral internship lasting one or two years.

Doctoral training programs in clinical psychology may be accredited by the American Psychological Association (APA). APA accreditation indicates that the training programs meet certain requirements. In 1980, 112 doctoral training programs held APA accreditation. During the period of graduate study, one year is devoted to a clinical internship; APA accreditation is also available to facilities (that is, psychiatry departments, clinics, and institutions) offering internship training.

Doctoral level clinical psychologists are not the only professional psychologists offering clinical services. Counseling and school psychologists, whose training programs (also eligible for APA accreditation) may be in either departments of psychology or in schools of education, also provide assessment and therapeutic services. In addition, a large number of master's degree level professionals in clinical, school, and counseling psychology are employed by agencies, clinics, and schools. The APA does not grant full membership to master's level psychologists or accredit master's degree programs.

Other Professionals. In addition to psychology and psychiatry, members of other professional disciplines provide services for children with behavior problems. Social workers, for example, have a long history of helping parents to cope with children's

---

[1] Several training programs offer a Doctor of Psychology degree instead of the traditional Ph.D.; these programs emphasize the practitioner role and deemphasize training in research.

problems. The master's degree in social work is the principal academic degree and is awarded after two years of course work and supervised clinical experience. A few universities offer the Ph.D. in social work, but the recipients of the doctoral degree usually go into teaching, research, and administrative positions.

Other specialists in medicine (pediatricians, neurologists, and general practitioners, for example) are often called upon to evaluate and recommend treatment for children with behavior disorders. Physicians are trained primarily in the physical aspects of children's problems but are also expected by parents to provide advice on a wide variety of behavior problems. Medical school and residency training programs vary greatly in the emphasis placed on normal and abnormal child behaviors, and many physicians must rely heavily on their own clinical experience with children to provide advice to parents on behavioral problems.

Most of the remaining professions providing services for children with developmental and learning problems require at least master's degree level training. Other professionals currently involved in some aspect of assessment or treatment, or both, of children's behavior disorders include special educators, physical therapists, occupational therapists, nursing specialists, nutritionists, speech pathologists, and rehabilitation counselors.

research approaches to understanding children's behavior problems

It is generally agreed that the goal of behavioral science is to acquire knowledge that would enable us to predict and control behavior. In the specific case of children's behavior disorders the ultimate goals are to develop effective treatment procedures and to prevent problems through a complete understanding of the factors that cause these problems. As you will learn in the remaining chapters of this book, our knowledge falls far short of these goals, although significant progress in some areas has been made.

The quality of scientific knowledge depends both on the creativity of the investigator and the research strategy employed in the collection of data. The creative component of this equation is not well understood but basically consists of ideas or hypotheses about relationships among variables. The sources of these hypotheses may be determined by previously acquired knowledge in one area or in more than one related area of study and direct observation of phenomena. The highest level of scientific creativity is reflected by theory that states general principles about relationships among variables and provides testable hypotheses. While relatively few scientific investigators have created theories, most of them work within a theoretical system and design their research to test specific hypotheses. Creativity is often also a significant component in research methodology (for example, in choosing measuring instruments, apparatus, and specific procedures). It is through the continuous interweaving of creativity and research strategy that new knowledge is acquired.

Our understanding of children's behavior disorders has come from a variety of sources ranging from descriptive studies to experimental research. Each of the research strategies has made unique contributions to our knowledge, but each one also has certain disadvantages or problems associated with it. The history of psychology suggests, in addition, that the various research strategies are mutually dependent on one another and that no single one could provide all of the necessary information.

descriptive studies

Fundamental to the acquisition of scientific knowledge is description of the phenomenon of interest. Descriptions of behavior, normal and abnormal, may take many forms. For example, the earliest sources of information about the developmental progression of young children may be found in the "baby biographies," which are narrative descriptions of individual children's behaviors, in most instances recorded by their psychologist-parents (Kessen, Haith, and Salapatek, 1970, pp. 299ff). Biographical accounts of behavior offer a richness of description not attained by other methods of study and have provided a fund of information for investigators who have subsequently applied more systematic research methods in the collection of data. For instance, the early baby biographies depicted the regularity and timing of developmental changes and most probably contributed to later studies on the development of large groups of children. The biographical approach, however, does present serious problems for the researcher seeking general principles of behavior. The reliability of the biography is questionable in that the parent-biographers might have biases that distort the data. Moreover, the biographers vary their organization of the data and attention given to specific behaviors and, in that way, preclude any direct comparisons among the biographies. These particular problems have been solved to a large extent by the development of standardized procedures in the collection of behavioral data.

The studies that have provided us with normative data on the developing child (behavioral abilities of children of different ages) have used several variations of the descriptive approach, including narrative accounts by parents during interviews, description based on observed behavior, ratings of behavior by parents, teachers, and researchers, and scores on specific tasks or tests. Statistical analysis of narrative descriptions requires the intervening step of someone rating the written description on a psychological dimension, such as aggression.

In order for investigators to make statements with reference to groups of children and to compare individual children to other children of the same age, all data have to be classified or quantified (reduced to numbers), or both. A variety of methods, therefore, have been developed for translating narrative description into numerical description. At the simplest level, a child might be scored on whether a particular behavior is present or absent. Since observers do not necessarily agree on the definitions of specific behaviors or concepts encompassing multiple behaviors, investigators began to use *operational definitions*, which are exact descriptions of the behavior or characteristic being assessed. Operational definitions of behavior are exemplified in tests in which each item or task is administered in a predetermined manner and the criteria for passing or failing clearly designated in the test manual. Operational definitions ensure that each child is being rated or scored on the basis of the same criteria, thus making it possible to discuss average or typical levels of response.

Describing the performance of groups of children usually involves two statistical measures, a measure of central tendency, which represents all of the scores in the group, and a measure of variability within a set of scores. The most frequently used measure of central tendency is the mean, the arithmetic average of the scores. Among the available measures of variability, the standard deviation is most often reported in psychological research studies. The standard deviation is particularly useful because it provides an objective method for determining whether an individual score is unusually high or low by showing how far it is from the mean.

In general, descriptive studies have focused on the assessment and comparison of behaviors as a function of the child's age, sex, or socioeconomic level. These demographic variables, of course, cannot be designated as having caused differences in behavior and are better conceptualized as correlates of behavior differences. Behavioral differences between males and females, for example, are as likely to be a product of differences in child-rearing patterns as the direct result of genetic and biological differences.

While descriptive studies of behavior rarely provide direct evidence of cause-effect relationships, they have been invaluable for providing hypotheses and theories regarding factors that cause differences in behavior. In many ways, the clinical assessment of a child with behavior problems parallels descriptive research. The clinician accumulates a large amount of information about the child and subsequently forms hypotheses about the factors that may be responsible for the problems. The clinician has no way of knowing with certainty what the critical factors have been and, therefore, relies on a combination of previous clinical experience, knowledge of the research literature, and descriptive information about the child to derive hypotheses about the nature of the problem and the treatment methods that might be effective.

correlational studies

Correlational studies represent a second approach to the understanding of behavior. In comparison with descriptive studies in which behavior is simply described or presented as a function of demographic variables, correlational studies measure the extent to which two or more variables may predict one another. In the typical correlational study, data on at least two characteristics or variables are collected from or about each individual within a group. Examples might be test scores on two types of tests, parents' attitudes on child rearing and on children's social behavior, or ratings of problems during pregnancy and child behavior ratings at three years of age. The sets of scores are subjected to statistical analysis, which summarizes the relationship of these scores in a correlation coefficient that may range from +1.0 through 0 to –1.0. A +1.0 correlation indicates a perfect positive relationship between the two sets of scores—a high score on one variable is invariably related to a high score on the other variable. A –1.0 correlation indicates a perfect negative relationship between the two sets of scores—a high score on one variable is invariably related to a low score on the other variable. In both of these instances knowledge of a person's score on one variable permits optimal prediction of that person's score on the second variable. A correlation coefficient of zero indicates that there is no relationship between the variables. In practice, it is rare to find either perfect positive or negative correlations between psychological variables. Rather, the majority of correlational studies reports values that are less than perfect but greater than zero. The size of the correlation is evaluated in terms of the probability that it could have been obtained by chance. The statistical significance of a correlation is substantially influenced by the number of subjects from whom the data were obtained; that is, relatively low correlations (closer to zero) may reach statistical significance when large groups (several hundred or more) are involved in the study.

Unfortunately, correlational studies frequently lend themselves to misinterpretation. The greatest misinterpretation is that a high correlational relationship necessarily implies a cause-effect relationship between the variables. It is important to remember that correlational studies only reflect the extent to which two variables are related; they *may* indeed be causally related, but there is always the possibility that a third (unmeasured) variable is causing the changes in the two measured variables. In many psychological studies, no decision with respect to these alternatives can be made without further investigation.

Correlational studies have provided us with a substantial amount of our knowledge about children's behavior disorders. They have been particularly valuable in providing hypotheses regarding the variables that may be implicated in the etiology of behavior problems. In addition, correlational research provides the foundation for many of our assessment methods. For example, the reliability of psychological tests may be measured by correlating the scores obtained on the first administration of a test with scores obtained on a second administration (test-retest reliability) or correlating scores on one half of a test with scores on the second half of the test (split-half reliability). Since tests must be reliable to be useful, high correlations (0.8 to 0.9) are required for a test to be considered reliable. Another example of the use of correlation in evaluating assessment methods is the determination of the amount of agreement between ratings of behavior by two observers. Just as in the case of psychological tests, behavioral ratings must be demonstrated to be reliable by high correlations, that is, the independent ratings of two observers must be in agreement before that method of assessing the behavior is considered to be reliable.

experimental studies

Experimental studies also examine the relationships among variables, but they possess the asset of giving us better information about cause-effect relationships.

In the simplest case, an experimental study evaluates the relationship between an independent variable and a dependent variable. The *independent* variable is usually some aspect of the stimulus environment (for example, type of treatment) which the researcher varies or manipulates and includes two or more levels of the experimental conditions. Subjects are randomly assigned to the different levels of the independent variable. The random assignment of subjects to the levels of the experimental condition essentially counterbalances the individual differences among the subjects due to biological factors and prior history. That is, random assignment tends to make the goups more similar or comparable to one another at the beginning of the study. After the subjects have experienced their respective levels of the experimental condition, the researcher obtains data on the *dependent* variable, a measure of the subjects' response or behavior.

Let us consider an example in which a researcher wishes to evaluate the effect of two forms of treatment on children with a specific type of behavior disorder. In this example, the researcher would probably include what is called a *control group,* that, is a group that did not receive either of the two forms of treatment. The independent variable, then, would be type of treatment and would include three groups of children: two groups receiving different forms of treatment and one control group. Individual children with the behavior disorder would be randomly assigned to one of the three groups. After the treatment phase had been completed, the same behavioral measure of the dependent variable would be obtained for each child in each group. The dependent variable in this case could be a direct evaluation of behavior through observation or ratings of the child's behavior by parents or teachers. The scores or ratings for the children within each group would be combined and described in terms of means and standard deviations. Statistical analysis of these data would determine the extent to which any differences among the groups were due to chance or random variability. In psychological research, differences among groups that might occur by chance five or fewer times out of one hundred are considered to be statistically significant. That is, when the probability is very low (5 percent or less) that the differences among groups occurred by chance, there is general consensus that the differences in group scores were most likely due to the different experimental conditions.

There are many possible variations of the basic experimental design. For example, more than one independent and/or dependent variable may be included. In addition, experimental designs are not confined to groups but may be used with individuals. Chapter 3 will provide a description of the experimental designs currently being used to evaluate the treatment of individuals.

Experimental studies require a number of safeguards or precautions to prevent the validity of the data from being jeopardized. Expectations or hypotheses on the part of experimenters or observers may, for example, influence the accuracy of the data. It is often necessary, therefore, for the person collecting the data not to know the group to which the subject has been assigned because such knowledge may bias the behavior ratings in favor of one group or another.

Because experimental studies involve doing something to or for subjects, they lend themselves to greater concerns about ethical issues. Much experimental research on the causes of children's behavior problems, for example, cannot be conducted because injury or potential harm to the subjects might be forthcoming. In some instances, similar experimental research might be conducted with animals, but in other instances our information is necessarily confined to the findings of observational and correlational studies. Both alternatives often result in knowledge that is incomplete.

Most experimental research cannot be clearly divided into "harmful" and "beneficial" categories. Although the researcher may believe that a particular treatment could be of benefit to clients, it may well not be. For this and other reasons, researchers usually submit their research plans to ethics committees for appraisal and also obtain "informed consent" from research subjects. Informed consent involves the subject's signing a paper that designates that the subject has been informed about the procedures and goals of the study. In the case of children, informed consent is obtained from the parents or guardians.

Conclusions

A variety of professional disciplines provide services and conduct research on children's behavior disorders. Although there is some overlap in their clinical skills, the various disciplines tend to complement one another in their capacities to assess and treat children with behavior problems.

Our knowledge about children's behavior disorders has been derived primarily from descriptive, correlational, and experimental research studies. Descriptive and correlational studies have been invaluable in providing hypotheses about cause-effect relationships with respect to the etiology and treatment of children's behavior disorders. Experimental studies provide the direct tests of these hypotheses and are our best source of understanding causal relationships.

assessment and diagnosis: the interview and standardized tests

2

Assessment refers to the collection of information about a child's behavior problem and the evaluation of that information to determine the possible relevant factors with respect to its cause, or maintenance, or both aspects of the problem. Diagnosis refers to the labeling of a child's behavior problem after the formal assessment procedures have been completed. In practice, diagnostic labels are sometimes changed after the initiation of treatment when additional information suggests that they are not accurate. That is, most clinicians do not consider assessment to terminate with the choice of a diagnostic label but rather to continue throughout the course of treatment.

A variety of methods have been devised to assess the behavior problems of children. The range of available techniques reflects the fact that professionals from several disciplines have been responsible for the assessment of children's behavior problems. The professionals most often called upon to assess these problems are physicians (particularly psychiatrists, pediatricians, and neurologists), psychologists, and educators. Members of some disciplines are more competent than those of other disci-

plines in the use of specific assessment procedures. While most children with behavior problems are examined and diagnosed by a single professional, there has
been a strong movement toward interdisciplinary diagnosis, a procedure involving
the combination of information derived from the assessment methods of two or
more disciplines. The typical child guidance clinic, for example, usually has a
child psychiatrist, clinical psychologist, and social worker on each diagnostic team.
A number of federally funded training programs affiliated with universities have as
many as a dozen or more disciplines represented on a diagnostic team. These larger
diagnostic teams are able to assess in greater depth the child's physical, neurological, developmental, and psychological status as well as the effects of past and current environmental factors.

There is considerable controversy regarding the efficiency of assessment methods
and the problems resulting from the labeling of children. The principal goal of
assessment and diagnosis is to determine what form of treatment should be initiated
to alleviate the problem. Unfortunately, a system that accomplishes that goal has
not yet been developed for children's behavior problems. Clinicians have not been
able to agree on the diagnostic labels that are appropriate for children's problems
or the exact criteria for the use of particular labels. Much of the difficulty resides
in the inconsistency of labels; some describe an assumed internal psychological
state, others describe current behaviors, and still others describe etiological factors. In recent years, several attempts have been made to improve the diagnostic
criteria used in the labeling of children's behavior problems.

You may ask why labeling or formal diagnosis is necessary. Your question is
shared by a growing number of psychologists who feel that the labels currently
used, such as mental retardation and neurosis, do not facilitate the choice of treatment and may, in fact, result in psychological harm to children due to the reactions of other people in their environment, such as relatives, teachers, and friends,
to the labels. On the other hand, clinicians need labels for purposes of communication, a kind of shorthand in lieu of extended descriptions of behavior and etiological factors. These abbreviated descriptions have been used as a way of grouping children with behavior disorders and of separating children whose problems
are believed to be of different origins.

Most clinicians agree that the primary purpose of classification is to improve
communication among clinicians rather than to facilitate the understanding of a
particular child's problems. Clinicians are aware that no one label can adequately
describe all the nuances of a particular child's behavior or environment. Although
labels are meant to group children according to common characteristics, they are
sometimes used incorrectly to draw inferences about other characteristics. That
is, the usefulness· of labels has tended to be undermined by those who make inferences about children's characteristics that are less than perfectly correlated
with the particular diagnostic label. For example, a diagnosis of mental retardation
could be inferred to mean that the child is incapable of learning to read, and reading instruction may be denied to the child. The inference would probably have
been drawn from there being a higher percentage of retarded than normal children

who do not learn to read with conventional instruction. Such an inference would be incorrect for several reasons. One reason is that many retarded children do, in fact, learn to read. A second is that the technology of teaching is continually improving and will no doubt result in greater numbers of retarded children learning to read in the future. Third, inferences focusing on lack of performance tend only to ensure that the performance will continue to be lacking (this is the self-fulfilling prophecy).

The available diagnostic or classification systems used by clinicians tend to delimit the available choices. Although it is possible to defer diagnosis or to conclude that none of the labels is appropriate, clinicians tend to choose the one label in the system that best fits the child's problem. This situation deserves careful consideration because some children may be labeled inaccurately if no adequate label is available in the system.

This chapter reviews the procedures typically used by traditional clinicians in the assessment of children's behavior disorders: the interview and standardized psychological tests. It concludes with a description of classification or diagnostic systems currently in use.

referral information

The assessment process usually begins before the child is seen. Children are typically referred to clinicians or community clinics by other professionals or by parents who have recognized the possibility of a behavior disorder. During the preschool years the general practitioner or pediatrician has frequent contact with the child and may observe problem behavior in the context of routine physical care of the child. If parents are concerned about a behavior problem during this period, they often bring it to the attention of the child's physician. Thus, physicians are likely to be responsible for most referrals to clinicians during the preschool years.

Physicians vary in the amount of information they provide in their referrals, but they almost always offer their hypotheses with regard to the nature of the problem and possible etiological factors. In addition, physicians will provide relevant information when it is requested by the clinician. Most clinicians want a report on the child's physical history and current physical status and their possible relevance to the behavior problem. Screening tests for vision and hearing are also highly desirable before the initiation of psychological assessment procedures. Thus, the physician may contribute a significant amount of information about the child and the family that may be useful to the clinician.

After the child enters school, teachers become an important source of referrals, although physicians continue to refer their patients (who are seen less frequently for routine physical care). Most of the less severe children's behavior disorders either occur after the age of school entry or are recognized only in the context of a large peer group. The teacher, then, may become aware that a particular child's behavior is atypical or inappropriate in comparison with the behavior of other children. The child's teacher, by describing the behavior problem in the school setting, also contributes relevant referral information.

If parents refer the child, the clinician will attempt to secure relevant information from other professionals familiar with the child. Permission to obtain such information from other professionals must be given by the parents in writing. Occasionally, parents withhold permission or do not inform the clinician about earlier contacts with other professionals. In these instances, it is often discovered that the parents have been unable to accept the previous diagnosis and are "shopping" for another opinion. Discovering that their child has a serious behavior disorder with a poor prognosis is difficult for most parents to accept readily, and unfortunately, these parents are only too willing to invest themselves and their financial resources in any program that promises cure or complete rehabilitation.

Information from other professionals who are familiar with the child may help the clinician to conceptualize the problem and to design a more efficient assessment procedure. The interview may be more quickly focused on the problem, and the selection of standardized tests to be administered more efficiently determined.

the interview

Interviewing is the diagnostic technique used most often by professionals in the assessment of child behavior disorders. Interviewing consists of talking with the parents and the child with the goal of determining the nature of the problem, its etiology, and the situations in which it occurs. Clinicians of various theoretical persuasions differ in the amount of information they seek in any one area of inquiry. In general, diagnostic interviews are fairly structured in that the clinician is actively seeking information and has delineated those areas in which information is needed. This section on the interview describes the primary aspects of the clinical interview as conducted by most professionals.

In most cases, the clinician depends primarily on the information obtained from parents in making the diagnosis. Children often do not possess the verbal skills to provide the necessary information or are reluctant to discuss their problem with the clinician. Kessler (1966) has pointed out that children may be reluctant to speak freely about matters such as hostility toward their parents because they are afraid that the clinician will share this information with the parents. Interviews with parents also present problems for the clinician in that parents may feel guilty or may be afraid that they will be blamed for the child's problem and thus distort the information given to the interviewer.

In a child guidance clinic, the diagnostic interview with the parents is usually conducted by a social worker or a child psychiatrist, although it may also be conducted by a psychologist. The interview usually begins with the clinician's request that the parents describe the problem that caused them to seek help. It should be kept in mind that parents do not always initiate the diagnostic process. While most parents are earnestly seeking help for their child, some of them have been "forced" to obtain professional aid and may not be optimally motivated. Often, for example, a community agency, such as the school or juvenile court, advises parents to seek help for their child when the child is presenting a problem behavior outside of the home environment. It is understandable, therefore, why some parents feel ambivalent and helpless under these conditions, particularly if they are having no problems with the child at home.

After the parents describe the problem for which they are seeking help, the clinician explores with them the circumstances under which the problem occurs, the frequency with which it occurs, and the length of time it has occurred. The parents are asked to recall when the problem was first brought to their attention and what the circumstances were at that time. The clinician then frequently inquires about other problems that might have occurred in the child's history.

Early in the interview many clinicians attempt to secure a developmental history on the child. The parents are asked about the pregnancy, labor, and delivery of the child to determine whether organic factors might have been involved. The possibility of organic factors is also explored by inquiring about illnesses and accidents occurring during infancy and childhood. If the clinician has a psychoanalytic orientation, the parents will be asked to recall experiences involving feeding and toilet training. The clinician in this instance is seeking evidence for unusual or traumatic circumstances surrounding these psychologically important events. An attempt is also made to describe developmental milestones, which include the ages at which the child sat alone, took the first step alone, said the first word, and combined two words when talking. These milestones give the clinician a general impression of the child's early rate of developmental progress. It is difficult for parents to remember when these milestones occurred, particularly if they have had more than one child. If parents have kept a baby book or other records of the child's developmental achievements, they are requested to bring them to the interview.

In addition to the review of the child's developmental progress, information is sought regarding the child's social behavior. The clinician is interested in the child's social interactions with peers, siblings, and parents. During the interview the clinician is attempting to assess the parents' attitudes toward the child and their potential role in the development of the behavior problem. Parents are questioned about their own histories including physical, developmental, learning, and psychological problems. The rationale for this inquiry is that behavior problems are sometimes repeated in successive generations, and this repetition of occurrence may alter a parent's perception of the problem. For example, a father may report that he also had great difficulty learning to read when he was in school and was able to overcome the problem (that is, has a job which requires only minimal reading ability); in this instance, the father may not perceive his child's inability to read as a significant problem. If the clinician suspects a hereditary etiological factor, the parents will also be asked if other blood relatives have had the same problem or one similar to it.

Depending on the nature of the problem and the age of the child, many clinicians find it useful to conduct the interview in whole or in part with the parents and child together (Krill, 1968; Granger and Wanberg, 1967; Kaplan, 1969). With this arrangement the clinician is seeking to assess the family interaction patterns and their possible role in the development of the behavior problem. The clinician observes which members of the family do most of the talking and who looks at whom during the interview; some clinicians draw inferences from these behaviors. For example, if the mother speaks most of the time during the interview and tends to answer questions directed toward the husband or child, the clinician may infer that she is the dominant parent and is presenting an inappropriate model for the child. (As can be seen in this example, inherent in some inferences is the assumption that the clinician knows what the correct interaction pattern should be.)

Although cognizant of the difficulties, many clinicians attempt to interview the child alone in the hope that the child's behavior will reveal information that will enable the clinician to understand more thoroughly the nature of the problem. Initially, the clinician asks questions that require relatively brief answers, such as the child's name, age, and the school attended. The interviewer gradually moves into areas that are related to the problem behavior simultaneously attempting to secure the child's confidence and ease in the situation. The clinician often asks the child why he was brought for the interview; the answer to this question will frequently reveal information regarding the child's perception of the problem as well as the source of knowledge leading to the perception. Sometimes, parents never openly discuss the problem with the child and do not prepare the child for the interview. In other instances, the parents may present the visit to the clinician as a negative experience, as punishment for the problem behavior. Lack of preparation or presentation of the interview as punishment may result in a child who is unresponsive or hostile, or both, to the interviewer. It is then the clinician's task to communicate to the child the reasons for the visit and to assure the child that help will be forthcoming.

As the child's confidence develops, the clinician begins to inquire about relationships among family members. Such relationships are considered by clinicians with a psychoanalytic orientation as being primary etiological factors to be explored in considerable depth. The interviewer may ask leading questions to encourage the child's expression of emotion and disclosure of usually unacceptable thoughts. For example, the clinician may encourage a child to express hostile feelings toward his father as a way of examining the characteristics of the father-child interactions. The clinician would be particularly interested in the extent to which the child's responses reflect accurate perception of reality.

The child's behavior during the interview is often interpreted by the clinician as being characteristic of the child's behavior in general, and the clinician may interpret the child's behavior toward adults in general. Given the unique qualities of the conditions surrounding the clinical interview, it may be incorrect to generalize to other situations; but the behaviors presented during the interview may well provide hypotheses about the variables controlling the child's behavior:

> While the child may well be able to block the assessor by diversion or negativism or tears from getting direct statements, these attitudes and other interview behaviors constitute in themselves data about the child. (Palmer, 1970, p. 116)

When the child to be interviewed is young, below the age of nine or ten years, some clinicians utilize doll play as a substitute for the direct oral interaction between the interviewer and the child. That is, a doll is introduced into the situation and serves as a mediator between the clinician and the child. In the doll play interview, the clinician asks questions about the doll, and the child answers for the doll. In using this technique, it is assumed that the child, in answering for the doll, is answering for himself. With the doll as mediator, the child is presumed to be less anxious about revealing feelings and thoughts.

The clinician may add other dolls, which are presented as members of a family, and ask questions about these dolls. Again, the clinician is attempting to secure information about the child's perception of interactions among family members. The play interview may also include a wide variety of other toys with which the child is permitted to play as he wishes. The play interview technique is frequently used by psychoanalytically oriented clinicians who believe that children act out unconscious conflicts, defenses, and wishes in a symbolic manner during play. Noyes (1948), for example, stated:

> The toys given him represent all the common interests of childhood; dolls representing the family, animals, blocks to build houses, etc. The use which the child makes of these toys offers insight into mental mechanisms or gives clues regarding the child's unconscious. In the child play may be regarded as the speech of the unconscious. The child may use the imaginary characters of his play to express his own disturbed feelings. . . hiding behind the anonymity of a of a doll he may tell of death wishes directed toward a parent or sibling. (p. 505)

The clinician may in this way view play behavior in the child as analogous to free association in the adult.

During the play interview the clinician asks questions about the child's behavior with the dolls or other toys and observes which toys the child chooses to play with and which toys the child chooses to exclude. The clinician is also interested in the child's emotional responses to the various toys—particularly responses indicating distress. Many clinicians believe that these emotional responses and the toys that evoke them may provide valuable insights regarding the source of the child's problems.

In summary, the aims of the clinical interview are to identify the type of psychological problem presented by the child and to determine the source of the underlying conflict. In pursuit of these goals the clinician collects information from the child and parents through verbal interaction, occasionally using the play interview to facilitate the interaction with young or fearful children.

standardized tests

A wide variety of tests have been designed to assess the behavioral characteristics of children. A standardized test is one for which data from a large number of children have been collected, and information is provided regarding the average performance of children at different ages. The test results obtained from a particular child are then compared with those of the standardization group with the same chronological age. A standardized test also provides information about the reliability and validity of the test. The most important measurement of test *reliability* is the amount of agreement in the test results when the test is administered on two occasions separated by an interval of time. A reliable test is one that yields similar results on both occasions; an unreliable test is not an acceptable assessment tool. *Validity* refers to the test's ability to measure what it purports to measure. In the case of intelligence tests, for example, the validity of a new intelligence test is measured by the extent to which its results agree with the results of other intelligence tests administered to the same individuals.

Standardized tests are administered primarily by clinical and school psychologists who have been trained in their proper use in graduate school programs and during internship. In the administration of a test the psychologist is seeking an optimal performance from the child while following precisely the appropriate instructions developed for the test. To ensure getting the most accurate results on a test, the examiner must take certain precautions, which include being assured that the child is not physically ill, that the child's principal language in English, and that the child is not excessively anxious or fearful. Many psychologists request that the child receive a general physical examination and tests for vision and hearing prior to the administration of psychological tests. Physical problems and sensory defects can seriously impair performance on psychological tests and can, therefore, lead to inaccurate interpretations of a child's behavioral functioning.

Anxiety or fear in the testing situation can also result in depressed performance on a test. Young children are particularly susceptible to anxiety in strange situations. To decrease the possibility of reactions based on fear, it is usually advisable for a parent to accompany a preschool child during test administration, although exceptions may be made when there is reason to believe that the presence of the parent may interfere with the child's performance. Young children are often reluctant to talk spontaneously or to respond verbally in novel situations, and examiners, therefore, tend to begin testing sessions with tasks not requiring verbal responses, such as drawing a picture. A useful technique is to engage the parent in conversation for the first ten minutes or so of the session and made no demands on the child. Having the child seated in the lap of the parent during testing frequently prevents young children from reacting strongly in fear, although the examiner must instruct the parent not to participate in the testing (that is, not to help the child by repeating the instructions or manipulating the test tasks).

Many different types of test are available to the clinician. The clinician's choice of specific tests is determined by the information obtained from the referral source, interviews, and observation of the child's behavior during the interviews. Because many behavior disorders reflect or are accompanied by problems in development, intellectual functioning or learning, intelligence and achievement tests are usually administered during the assessment procedure. Personality tests are also frequently administered to determine the type and possible causes of certain behavior problems (which may or may not be accompanied by intellectual problems). Tests for special functions (for example, language, visual perception, visual-motor integration) may also be administered, particularly when the clinician suspects that specific deficits may be hindering a child's performance on the more general tests or in learning at school. Some of these tests for special functions will be described in later chapters dealing with specific behavior disorders.

Psychological testing is completed in one or several sessions depending on the clinical setting, number of tests administered, and the age of the child. Blau (1979) has suggested that children tend to be overtested in educational settings but undertested in community mental health centers and child guidance clinics. Preschool children tend to become fatigued and uncooperative after about one hour of testing, while older children continue to be cooperative for several hours. Most children, particularly those of preschool and early elementary school ages, enjoy the testing procedure and the challenge of the "games."

intelligence tests[1]

The first intelligence test was developed in 1905 by Alfred Binet to identify French school children whose abilities would prevent them from progressing adequately in the regular public school program. Since that time, the original Binet scales have been revised periodically, and other intelligence tests have been developed.

The principal intelligence tests are administered individually by master's or doctoral level psychologists. Intelligence tests which are given to groups of children have also been developed, and they may be administered by school teachers and other professionals with lesser amounts of training in test administration and interpretation.

Individually Administered Intelligence Tests. The success of Binet's original test prompted two American psychologists at Stanford University, Louis Terman and Maud Merrill, to develop an English-language edition of the test for use with school children in the United States. This American edition of the test is called the Stanford-Binet Intelligence Test. The Stanford-Binet has been revised several times to update some of the items and to improve the sample of children upon which the norms are based.

A well-standardized test is based on a sample of children that reflects the population of children for which it will be used. In order for a test to have accurate norms, the characteristics of children in the normative sample should be representative of those characteristics of children in the whole population. For example, if 40 percent of the children in the United States come from families in which the parents have less than a high school education, the normative sample should in-

---

[1]The concept of intelligence and the use of intelligence tests have stimulated much debate among psychologists, educators, and the public. For a review of these issues, see Cronbach (1975) and Wechsler (1975).

clude approximately 40 percent of children whose parents have less than a high school education.

The latest revision of the Stanford-Binet, called Form L-M, was published in 1960 and is the edition most often used today (Terman and Merrill, 1960). The norms for the Stanford-Binet have recently been updated by Thorndike (1973) and more accurately reflect the performance of the U.S. population of the 1980s. An interesting finding is that the scores of contemporary preschool children, measured in the form of an Intelligence Quotient (IQ), are about ten points higher than those obtained by children of the same age forty years ago.

The Stanford-Binet has been standardized for use with children from the age of two years and with adults. The IQ score takes into account the child's chronological age, mental age, and the variability of performance in the standardization group of the same chronological age. Mental age reflects the child's performance on the tests that have been arranged by age level. Each age level contains six items or tasks and one alternate item in the event that the examiner makes an error in the administration of one of the six regular items. During the preschool ages, the Stanford-Binet age levels are presented in six-month steps. At the two-year level, for example, six items are presented, and each item completed successfully is worth one month of mental age. Beginning with the six-year level, the age levels are presented in one-year steps with each of the successfully completed items being worth two months of mental age. The age levels on the test reflect the performance of the children in the normative sample; six-year items, for example, are items which the average six-year-old child in the normative sample was able to complete successfully. Thus, the performance of a child being assessed with the Stanford-Binet is compared with the performance of children of the same age in the normative sample.

In administering the test, the examiner usually begins by presenting items that are at an age level immediately below or the same as the child's chronological age. Information derived from the interview or from school records affect the examiner's choice. The examiner's first goal is to establish the child's *basal mental age,* which is the age level on the test at which the child passes all six items. If any items are failed at a particular age level, the examiner proceeds to the next lower age level until the basal mental age is established. When a basal mental age is established, it is assumed that all items at lower age levels are also passed. The examiner then continues to present items at higher age levels until a level is reached at which the child fails all six items; this level is called the ceiling mental age. The examiner will have administered all items within each age level between the basal mental age and the ceiling mental age and recorded the number of successes at each age level. Mental age is determined by adding up the number of months of credit received for each successful item. A sample test summary is presented in Table 2-1.

Note that the basal mental age is placed at the three-year six-month level. Since all items below that level are also assumed to have been passed, the child is given credit for three years and six months of mental age. After the mental age is determined, the examiner usually refers to a table in the Stanford-Binet manual to obtain the child's IQ score.

Table 2-1 Sample test summary from the Stanford-Binet
          Form L-M Intelligence Test

	Years	Months
II		
II-6		
III		
III-6	3	6 Basal mental age
IV		5 Five items passed—one month credit for each item passed
IV-6		4
V		3
VI		4 Two items passed—two months credit for each item passed
VII		4
VIII		0 Ceiling mental age
IX		
X		
Total	3	26
Mental Age	5	2

The Stanford-Binet is particularly useful for assessing the intellectual functioning of children because of its wide age range of items and high levels of reliability and validity. In addition, procedures have been developed to determine a child's strong and weak areas (Sattler, 1974, pp. 142-164 and 508-509; Kaufman and Waterstreet, 1978). The reliability of the Stanford-Binet has been reported as follows:

Since reliability is a function of both age and magnitude of IQ, it was necessary to compute reliability coefficients for the ages separately. At ages 2½ to 5½, the reliability coefficients range from .83 (for IQs 140-149) to .91 (for IQs 60-69). At ages 6 to 13, the range is from .91 (for IQs 140-149) to .97 (for IQs 60-69); and at ages 14 to 18, the range is from .95 (for IQs 140-149) to .98 (for IQs 60-69). (Terman and Merrill, 1960, p. 10).

The validity of the 1960 revision of the Stanford-Binet is derived from several sources. The items on the test have been demonstrated to measure the same thing that was being measured by the original scale. In addition, increases in mental age correlating with increases in percentage of children passing from one chronological age to the next were compatible with those of the earlier scales. And, finally, the items chosen for the scale were highly correlated with the total score.

The Wechsler Intelligence Scale for Children - Revised (WISC-R) (Wechsler, 1974) is an individually administered test designed for children six through sixteen years of age and is a revision of the original WISC (Wechsler, 1949). In contrast to the Stanford-Binet, in which the items are arranged by age level, the WISC-R arranges items according to subtests with the items within each subtest arranged according to difficulty. The twelve subtests are equally divided into verbal and performance categories. Verbal and Performance IQ scores are calculated in addition to the Full Scale IQ score which is based on the sum of the scores from the verbal and performance subtests.

The primary advantage of the separate IQ scores is that children with specific deficits may be more readily identified. Children with certain motor or visual perception problems, for example, are likely to obtain considerably lower Performance IQ scores than Verbal IQ scores, and an overall IQ score could, in some cases, mask important diagnostic information. In general, differences between the Verbal and Performance IQ scores that are 15 points or greater are considered to be significant and call for further investigation. The construction of the WISC-R permits the examiner to identify strengths and weaknesses of intellectual functioning.

A measure of mental age is not used with the WISC-R. Rather, a score is obtained for each of the subtests using the scoring criteria in the manual. This raw score is then converted to a standard score,[2] where the mean has been set at 10 with a standard deviation of 3. The conversions from raw scores to standard scores are given in the manual for the various chronological ages. The standard scores are then added and converted into Verbal, Performance, and Full Scale IQ scores where the mean has been set at 100 with a standard deviation of 15.

The WISC-R contains six verbal and six performance subtests that are administered in alternating order. The examiner has the option of administering four, five, or six subtests of each type. A short description of each subtest is presented below.

WISC verbal subtests.

1. *Information.* This subtest consists of questions that cover general information that the child acquires at home and school.
2. *Comprehension.* In this subtest the examiner presents the child with situational problems orally. The aim of this subtest is to measure practical judgment.
3. *Arithmetic.* In this subtest the examiner presents the child with arithmetic problems that must be solved within a certain time limit without the use of pencil and paper.
4. *Similarities.* This subtest requires the child to explain how pairs of objects or concepts are alike and measures the child's conceptual skills or abilities to perceive relationships.
5. *Vocabulary.* The child is asked to define a series of words that vary in difficulty.
6. *Digit Span.* The examiner presents increasingly long lists of digits, and the child must repeat them forwards or backwards. This subtest measures short-term memory.

WISC performance subtests.

1. *Picture Completion.* In this subtest a series of pictures with line drawings of objects is presented to the child who must identify the missing part.

---

[2]A standard score, or Z-score, is a unit of measurement that allows the results of tests of different lengths to be compared by reducing their raw scores to a common scale. A standard score is computed by the following formula: $\dfrac{\text{raw score - mean score}}{\text{standard deviation.}}$

2. *Picture Arrangement.* Sets of pictures are presented to the child who must arrange them from left to right in an order that reflects a sensible story. This subtest measures the child's ability to put visual stimuli in a sequence to reflect temporal relationships.
3. *Block Design.* Cards with geometric patterns are presented to the child who must reproduce the patterns with colored blocks. The child obtains extra points for reproducing the design faster than the allotted time. This subtest measures visual discrimination and the ability to perceive spatial relationships.
4. *Object Assembly.* Pieces of increasingly more difficult puzzles are presented to the child who must assemble them within a certain time limit. Extra points are given when the child assembles the puzzle in shorter time periods. This subtest measures object recognition, the ability to perceive spatial relationships, and perceptual-motor skills.
5. *Coding.* The child is required to draw symbols that correspond to other symbols as quickly as possible. The score is determined by the number of correctly drawn symbols completed within a certain time limit. This subtest measures perceptual-motor abilities.
6. *Mazes.* In this subtest line drawing mazes are presented to the child through which a continuous, unobstructed path must be drawn. The Mazes subtest measures spatial perception.

Within a subtest, the examiner presents items in order of difficulty until the child fails a certain number of consecutive items. The criteria for reaching the ceiling vary for each subtest. When this ceiling is reached the examiner discontinues the presentation of items for the subtest and begins presenting the easier items on the next subtest.

The WISC-R manual reports average split-half reliability coefficients of .96 for the Full Scale IQ, .94 for the Verbal IQ, and .90 for the Performance IQ. The average split-half reliability coefficients for the individual subtests range from .70 to .86. These results are comparable to those obtained for the 1949 WISC (Gehman and Matyas, 1956).

The validity of the WISC-R has been evaluated by examining its relationship to the Stanford-Binet. The average correlation between IQ scores on the Stanford-Binet (1972 norms) and the WISC-R Full Scale IQ was .73, the Verbal IQ .71, and the Performance IQ .60. A comparison of the mean scores on the WISC-R Full Scale and the Stanford-Binet revealed that the Stanford-Binet IQ is about 2 points higher at ages 6, 9½, and 12½; the WISC-R Full Scale IQ is about 2 points higher at age 16½. Such small differences indicate that the WISC-R and the Stanford-Binet IQ scores for normal children are similar.

The Wechsler Preschool and Primary Scale of Intelligence (WPPSI) was designed for use with children ranging in age from 4 to 6½ years old (Wechsler, 1967). The basic format of the WPPSI is similar to that of the WISC and provides Full Scale, Verbal, and Performance IQ scores. The verbal subtests of the WPPSI include: Information, Vocabulary, Arithmetic, Similarities, Comprehension, and Sentences. The performance subtests include Animal House, Picture Completion, Mazes, Geometric Design, and Block Design.

The reliability coefficients (correlations between odd and even items) for the Full Scale, Verbal, and Performance Scales are .96, .94, and .93, suggesting that the reliability of these scales is excellent. The reliability of the individual subtests, however, may not be adequate enough for the interpretation of individual subtest scores (Oldridge and Allison, 1968). Validity studies have indicated that the WPPSI has moderately high correlations with the Stanford-Binet, although it tends to give lower IQ scores, particularly to above-average children. The WPPSI has been well standardized with a representative sample of children, but its usefulness is hampered by a restricted age range and a long administration time.

The McCarthy Scales of Children's Abilities (1972) were designed to measure the strengths and weaknesses as well as the general intellectual level of children from 2½ through 8½ years of age. Six scales are used to assess a variety of cognitive and motor behaviors. Scores for each of these scales are based on three or more specific tests.

1. *Verbal Scale.* The five tests for this scale assess children's abilities to express themselves in speech and the maturity of their oral concepts. They are asked to respond with one word answers, phrases, and sentences to items that examine memory, thinking, and reasoning functions.

2. *Perceptual-Performance Scale.* The seven tests for this scale consist of tasks that assess children's reasoning ability through the manipulation of materials (for example, copying designs, drawing, and assembling puzzles); these tests do not require the child to speak.

3. *Quantitative Scale.* The three tests for this scale measure children's facility with numbers and their understanding of quantitative words. An attempt was made to avoid items of the classroom test variety.

4. *General Cognitive Scale.* This scale is composed of all the tests in the Verbal, Perceptual-Performance, and Quantitative Scales and provides a measure of overall cognitive functioning.

5. *Memory Scale.* The four tests for this scale assess the child's short-term memory.

6. *Motor Scale.* The five tests for this scale assess coordination on a variety of gross and fine motor tasks.

The McCarthy Scales manual reports average split-half reliability coefficients of .93 for the General Cognitive Scale, .88 for the Verbal Scale, .84 for the Perceptual-Performance Scale, .81 for the Quantitative Scale, .79 for the Memory Scale, and .79 for the Motor Scale. Test-retest (after one month) coefficients indicated a high degree of test score stability that ranged between .69 and .91 for the six scales. Minimum score differences of 11 to 15 points between scales are necessary for clinical interpretation of strengths and weaknesses.

The validity of the McCarthy Scales has been evaluated by examining their relationships to the Stanford-Binet and the Wechsler Preschool and Primary Scale of Intelligence (WPPSI). The correlation coefficient between scores on the General Cognitive Scale and the Stanford-Binet was .81 and .71 with the Full Scale IQ score on the WPPSI. The McCarthy Motor Scale was not correlated with the WPPSI

Verbal, Performance, Full Scale IQ scores or the Stanford-Binet IQ scores, while the other McCarthy Scales showed a wide range of positive correlation coefficients. It may be concluded that the General Cognitive Scale is moderately valid when the WPPSI Full Scale and Stanford-Binet IQ scores are used as the criteria; the individual McCarthy scales may not be considered interchangeable with WPPSI and Stanford-Binet IQ scores.

The Cattell Infant Intelligence Scale was standardized for use with children from two months to thirty months of age (Cattell, 1940). It was designed as a downward extension of the 1937 edition of the Stanford-Binet. The items are grouped by age levels that are spaced at one-month intervals during the first year, two-month intervals during the second year, and three-month intervals during the third year. Stanford-Binet items are included among the test items placed in the latter half of the second year. If any thirty-month Cattell items are passed, testing is continued with the Stanford-Binet. The administration takes about thirty to forty minutes, and its scoring is essentially the same as that of the Stanford-Binet.

The items on the Cattell are primarily of a sensory-motor type because of the relatively restricted behavioral repertoire of the infant. Also included are items evaluating social responsiveness, verbal development, and short-term memory. The Cattell Scale was standardized during the 1930s with a group of 274 children from middle-class families; the size and characteristics of the standardization group are considered inadequate by today's criteria.

Test scores on infant tests are not as reliable as those on tests for older children, primarily because the behaviors of infants are more variable from day to day. The validity of infant test scores has been the subject of considerable discussion. In general, the research studies suggest that infant test scores are not good predictors of later IQ scores for samples of normal children. Several studies, however, have demonstrated substantial validity for children who receive *low* scores on infant tests (Illingworth and Birch, 1959; Erickson, 1968b).

The Bayley Infant Scales of Mental and Motor Development include the age range from one month to two years (Bayley, 1969). The standardization sample for the Bayley is the most comprehensive and representative sample achieved for infant scales.

The items within the Mental and Motor Scales are arranged in order of difficulty. The items on the Mental Scale evaluate the infant's social responsiveness, vocal and verbal behavior, simple problem-solving abilities, and reactions to environmental changes. The Motor Scale items evaluate the child's gross motor and sensory-motor development. The child's performance on each of the scales is calculated by adding up the number of passed items and converting these numbers to standard scores that are based on the distribution of scores for children of the same age. These scores are converted to developmental quotients of which the mean is 100.

The Bayley Scales are particularly useful in clinical diagnosis because of the larger number of items at each age level, the separate evaluation of mental and motor functioning, and its superior standardization. Its administration time, however, tends to be lengthy (about one hour) and fatiguing for many infants.

With the more recent focus on the identification of children with behavioral and developmental problems at the earliest age possible, there is a renewed interest in infant tests and early behaviors that might be predictive of later problems. In general, sensory-motor functioning appears not to predict later intellectual abilities, except perhaps for children who perform very poorly. Vocal and verbal abilities, on the other hand, may well be the best available predictors of later intellectual functioning.

The Slosson Intelligence Test (SIT) has been standardized for use with adults and children beginning in infancy (Slosson, 1963). The SIT is an age-scale test that provides mental ages. Most of the items were taken from the Stanford-Binet and the Gesell Institute of Child Development Behavior Inventory. The majority of the items are presented orally and require a spoken response from the child. None of the items has a time limit. The SIT takes only approximately twenty minutes to administer, in contrast to the forty-five to sixty minutes required by the Stanford-Binet and WISC tests. The SIT has been designed to permit its administration by relatively untrained examiners. Because of its practical advantages the SIT is becoming a popular test in school settings for screening children for special education programs.

The Slosson manual reports a test-retest reliability coefficient of .97. The validity of the SIT with the Stanford-Binet is reported in the manual as ranging from .90 to .98. These high correlations are to be expected when two tests contain a large number of the same items. In general, scores on the Slosson are similar to those on the Stanford-Binet. Like the Stanford-Binet, the SIT correlates more highly with the Verbal Scale of the WISC than with the Performance Scale.

Himelstein (1972) has urged that the SIT not be used without reservation as a substitute for the Stanford-Binet. He cites as criticisms the inadequate descriptions of the test construction and standardization sample in the manual. For prekindergarten pupils, test-retest reliability has been reported as between .7 to .8, and predictive validity with achievement test scores as the criteria have been described as only moderate (Klein, 1978).

The Peabody Picture Vocabulary Test (PPVT) was designed to provide an IQ score that is based on receptive language skills (Dunn, 1959; 1965). The test consists of a graded series of plates each of which includes four pictures. The examiner presents a word, and the child is requested to indicate which picture depicts the word. The test is designed for children between the ages of 2½ and 18 years. Administration time is about fifteen minutes.

The manual presents alternate form reliabilities ranging from .67 to .84 with the highest reliabilities being obtained from the oldest children and the lowest reliability from the six-year-old children. The validity of the PPVT with the Stanford-Binet has been reported to range from .22 to .92 with a median correlation of .66 (Sattler, 1974, p. 237). For mentally retarded children, scores on the PPVT tend to be higher than Stanford-Binet scores. IQ scores on these two tests are also not comparable for children from ethnic minority groups (Milgram, 1971).

The PPVT is a reliable and moderately valid instrument, but it should not be used as a substitute for the Stanford-Binet or the WISC. It is particularly useful as a screening test, because of its short administration time and ease of scoring, and as a test for children with expressive language problems.

The tests described in this section are only a sample of the available individually administered intelligence tests that are used for screening large numbers of children or for assessing children with certain types of handicaps which preclude their being given the Stanford-Binet or the WISC. The reader is advised to consult Buros' *Mental Measurement Yearbooks* for additional information about these or other tests.

Use of Individually Administered Intelligence Tests in Diagnosis. Psychologists administer intelligence tests to the majority of children referred for the diagnosis and assessment of behavior problems. The frequent use of intelligence tests in the diagnostic process reflects the important role that level of intellectual functioning plays in the complex array of behaviors manifested by children. Mischel (1968) has suggested that intelligence may well be the only characteristic or trait of persons to remain stable over relatively long periods of time.

Securing an IQ score is rarely the only goal of the psychologist administering an IQ test (Rabin and McKinney, 1972). The assessor observes very closely the child's responses to each item and records the child's answer to each question. The content of children's answers often provides hypotheses regarding specific problem areas. Bizarre or very unusual responses, for example, would have a different meaning than would vague or imprecise responses. A child's answers could also suggest the presence of a hearing deficit or a lack of understanding the meaning of certain words. The assessor is also particularly interested in describing the child's strengths and weaknesses in the various areas of intellectual functioning. Knowledge of strengths and weaknesses provides a beginning point for the development of a therapeutic program in many cases.

The assessor also seeks an understanding of the child's approach to problem situations. For example, is the child concerned about the correctness of his answer? Some children seem not to care about whether they are right or wrong in answering questions, while others ask the examiner about their performance quite often during the administration of the test. Does the child answer the questions or approach task items impulsively without adequate reflection? For some children, tasks that are timed are performed more poorly than items without the imposition of time limits. The examiner notes the child's response to complex tasks. Is the task approached in a systematic or disorganized way? In puzzle tasks, for example, the child may move several pieces around at a time in a random fashion or move one piece at a time.

The examiner also observes how the child responds to the increasingly difficult items. Some children will simply state that they do not know the answer, while others will present elaborate rationalizations. Perseveration, or giving the same answer without regard to the question, is also a possible response when the correct answer is not known. Does the child give up easily or become upset when the items become difficult? The behaviors of children while taking tests should not be freely generalized to other situations, but they do aid the examiner in understanding the relationships among the behaviors being observed. They may further provide hypotheses regarding variables that control the child's behavior in other settings, particularly the contingencies which have been used in the past for problem-solving behaviors.

Group-Administered Intelligence Tests. A number of intelligence tests have been developed for administration to groups of children particularly in school settings. These tests enable school personnel to assess large numbers of children for the purpose of describing the general level of intellectual functioning of a group (for example, class, grade, school). Group tests are also frequently used to screen children who should receive individual assessments. The administration and scoring of group tests do not require trained professionals, as do most of the individually administered intelligence tests. They are usually administered by teachers who follow the instructions in the booklet.

Group intelligence tests have certain disadvantages in comparison with the individually administered intelligence tests. The greatest disadvantage is that the examiner is not able to monitor the behaviors of the children taking the tests. In other words, group tests usually result in scores and nothing more. The scores that are derived from group tests also tend to be misused or misinterpreted. That is, scores on group intelligence tests are sometimes erroneously used to make decisions about individual children. Some of these decisions, such as placement in special educational programs, have profound influences on the child's future and must be based on the more reliable and valid data derived from individually administered tests. Group intelligence tests, relying heavily on reading and pencil-and-paper skills, may greatly penalize children with specific learning disabilities by giving IQ scores that are considerably below those that would be obtained on the individually administered tests that sample a broader spectrum of skills.

A number of group-administered intelligence tests are available for use. A few of the better ones have been selected for description. The California Test of Mental Maturity (CTMM) is a group-administered intelligence test widely used in schools for the purpose of screening children with intellectual deficits. The CTMM (Sullivan, Clark, and Tiegs, 1957) consists of twelve subtests designed to assess functioning in the areas of memory, logical and numerical reasoning, spatial relationships, and language. Mental ages and IQ scores can be determined for the whole test, language, and nonlanguage abilities. The CTMM is designed for measurement at six levels: preprimary (kindergarten), primary (grades one through three), elementary (grades four through eight), junior high (grades seven through nine), secondary (grades nine through thirteen), and advanced (grades ten through college). Two forty-five-minute periods are required for the administration of the CTMM, and all subtests have time limits.

The reliability of the CTMM has been reported as satisfactorily high for whole test, language, and nonlanguage scores. The validity of the CTMM has also been considered as highly satisfactory when its scores are correlated with those on the Stanford-Binet and WISC (Horrocks, 1964, p. 249).

Another popular group-administered intelligence test is the Otis-Lennon Mental Ability Test (1969). Various forms of the Otis test have been published since 1918; the Otis has the distinction of having the longest continuous existence among the group tests of intelligence. The latest edition has six levels ranging from kindergarten through grade twelve. The standardization sample was chosen to be representative of the U.S. educational system with controls for geographic location, size of school, family income, and type of school (public, private, church related).

Test-retest reliabilities over a one-year period were in the .80s and .90s. The validity research on the Otis was extensive and demonstrated high correlations between the Otis and other measures of scholastic aptitude.

achievement tests

Like intelligence tests, achievement tests may be administered to either individual children or groups of children. School systems frequently administer group achievement tests to all pupils on a regular basis, such as once a year or every two years. Individually administered achievement tests are given by psychologists or teachers who have received specific training in the diagnosis of learning problems. Children who are given individual achievement tests have usually been identified on the basis of poor performance on the group tests or have been referred by their teachers on the basis of poor classroom performance.

Achievement tests are oriented toward performance in school subjects, such as reading and arithmetic. The scores obtained on achievement tests are given in terms of grade equivalent; for example, a score of 3.5 on a reading achievement test indicates that the child's reading performance is equivalent to that of the average child in the fifth month of the third grade.

Individually administered achievement tests. The diagnostician chooses an achievement test on the basis of the problem presented by the child. In some instances, a child may be referred for a behavior problem, but the clinician may want to determine whether the child's academic achievement may be a factor in the development of the behavior problem. In cases for which the clinician wants a global measure of achievement in the principal school subjects, the Wide Range Achievement Test (Jastak and Jastak, 1976) could be used. The Wide Range Achievement Test (WRAT) provides tests for reading, spelling, and arithmetic. Each test has two levels, one for children between the ages of five years and eleven years eleven months and the other for persons from twelve years through adulthood. The three tests require about twenty to thirty minutes to administer. Time limits are used for some of the items. The reliability of the WRAT is reported in the manual as being very high. The correlations between the WRAT scores and those on other tests measuring ability in the same school subjects are also very high.

In those cases for which a deficiency in a particular school subject has been demonstrated through screening tests or teacher assessment, the clinician will choose a more comprehensive test that will evaluate the various skills underlying the specific academic ability. In other words, the clinician attempts to identify the areas of strength and weakness within the school subject area.

Since reading is the school subject most often associated with learning problems, an example of an individually administered reading achievement test will be discussed. The Spache Diagnostic Reading Scales (Spache, 1963) consist of a series of tests to evaluate oral and silent reading skills as well as auditory comprehension. The test battery includes three word-recognition lists, twenty-two reading passages varying in difficulty from grade levels 1.6 to 8.5, and six supplementary phonics tests. The word recognition lists evaluate the child's sight vocabulary and reveal the child's methods of word attack and analysis. The supplementary phonics tests aid in the classification of errors made by the child. The comprehension scores for the oral reading passages provide an estimate of the most appropriate level for instructional reading materials. The Spache also provides a score for the child's independent reading level that designates the grade level of reading materials that can be read silently with satisfactory comprehension. A potential reading level score, which designates the maximum level that may be expected with remedial or classroom training, can also be determined. The child's potential reading level indicates the ability of comprehension when passages are read to the child. Both the reliability and validity coefficients for the Spache tests have been reported as being high (Spache, 1963, pp. 7-9).

Group-Administered Achievement Tests. The Iowa Test of Basic Skills (Lindquist and Hieronymous, 1955-56) is designed for children in grades three through nine. It provides scores in vocabulary, reading comprehension, language, work-study skills, and arithmetic. The Iowa Test has been very well received by professionals because of significant improvements in its development compared with that of similar tests. The authors have thoroughly researched school curricula and have provided superior validation of the items.

The split-half reliability coefficients range from .84 to .96 for the major tests and from .70 to .93 for the subtests. The latest edition of the Iowa Test provides norms from a representative sample of children drawn from public schools across the United States. The predictive validity for the latest edition of the Iowa is not described in the manual but is claimed to be comparable to that of previous editions that very adequately predicted status in high school and first-year college courses.

The Stanford Achievement Test (Kelley, Madden, Gardner, and Rudman, 1964) has five batteries of tests for children in grades one through nine. The Primary 2 Battery, for example, is administered to children in grades 2.5 through 3.9 and gives scores for word meaning, paragraph meaning, science and social studies concepts, spelling, word-study skills, language, arithmetic computation, and arithmetic concepts. The Stanford Achievement Test has probably been the most frequently used group achievement test since its first edition appeared in 1923.

Split-half reliability coefficients are generally quite high (in the .80s and .90s), although reliability for a few of the single tests is low enough to preclude their use as individual tests. The manual for the latest edition reports neither test-retest reliability coefficients nor validity studies comparing Stanford Achievement Test results with those of other achievement tests.

personality tests

Many clinical psychologists, particularly those with a psychoanalytic orientation, have been trained in the administration and interpretation of personality tests. A number of assumptions are implicit in the use of personality tests, the foremost of which is that individuals have traits that are fairly stable across situations. The goal in personality testing is to assess these traits and to determine their role in the development of the behavior problem. Two types of tests have been devised to assess personality characteristics in children: inventories and projective techniques. The inventory consists of a series of items or questions to which clients respond. Clients may rate themselves on a series of attributes or answer questions about themselves with regard to their feelings, attitudes, and interests. Projective tests consist of series of pictures, inkblots, or statements upon which clients must impose meaning, such as describing what is happening to the people depicted in a particular picture.

Inventories. Personality inventories have been designed primarily for adult clients, and only a few of them provide norms for children. One inventory that does have norms for adolescents (fourteen through seventeen years of age) is the Minnesota Multiphasic Personality Inventory (MMPI). The MMPI, devised by Hathaway and McKinley, was first published in 1943 and revised in 1951. It contains 550 statements covering many areas of life experience to which the client responds "true," "false," or "cannot say." Administration time is usually one to two hours. Responses are counted and yield scores on four validity scales and nine clinical scales. The validity scales assess the client's tendency not to respond to the items, to give socially acceptable answers, to be defensive, and to misunderstand the items. Scores on the validity scales are taken into consideration in the scoring and interpretation of the clinical scales. The most recent description and review of the MMPI have been published by Dahlstrom, Welsh, and Dahlstrom (1972; 1975).

The clinical scales were designed to discriminate among various types of patients receiving diagnostic labels from psychiatrists. The names of the scales reflect the more commonly used psychiatric diagnostic labels. Each of the nine clinical scales of the MMPI is described briefly:

1. Hypochondriasis Scale (Hs). A measure indicating abnormal concern about bodily functions.

2. Depression Scale (D). A measure of the feelings and behaviors associated with depression.
3. Hysteria (Hy). A measure of symptoms related to the loss of sensory and motor functions of psychogenic origin.
4. Psychopathic Deviate Scale (Pd). A measure of the client's inability to experience deep emotional responses, to profit from experience, and to conform to social mores.
5. Masculinity-femininity Scale (Mf). A measure of the tendency toward traditionally masculine or feminine interests.
6. Paranaoia Scale (Pa). A measure of suspiciousness, oversensitivity, and delusions of persecution.
7. Psychasthenia Scale (Pt). A measure of phobias and compulsive behaviors.
8. Schizophrenia Scale (Sc). A measure of bizarre and unusual thoughts and behaviors.
9. Hypomania Scale (Ma). A measure of excessive productivity of thoughts and actions.

The test-retest reliability of the MMPI has been acceptable with correlations ranging from .46 to .93 with an average of about .76 (Horrocks, 1964, p. 550). The validity of the MMPI, however, is highly questionable. The primary problem appears to be its use of psychiatric diagnosis as the criterion for validity. Psychiatric diagnostic labels themselves lack adequate reliability except for the major psychiatric categories, such as psychosis and neurosis. No testing instrument can achieve high validity with a criterion that is unreliable.

The California Test of Personality (Thorpe, Clark, and Tiegs, 1953) is an inventory designed for both children and adults. Five yes-no questionnaires cover the age range from kindergarten through adulthood. Each questionnaire provides scores for two major categories: personal adjustment and social adjustment. Each of these two categories is further divided into six subtest categories, yielding a profile reflecting scores on twelve subtests. The subtests under personal adjustment are self-reliance, sense of personal worth, sense of freedom, feeling of belonging, withdrawing tendencies, and nervous symptoms. The subtests under social adjustment are social standards, social skills, antisocial tendencies, family relations, school or occupational relations, and community relations.

The reliability coefficients for the whole test and the personal and social adjustment categories appear to be moderately high. The reliability of the subtests is below an acceptable level, however, suggesting that the subtests should not be used for individual diagnosis. The validity of the California Test of Personality is difficult to evaluate quantitatively because the variables that it purports to measure are different from those of other personality tests. Its validity is strongly supported in the manual and rests primarily on the theoretical orientation of its author (Thorpe, 1945).

The Children's Personality Questionnaire (Porter and Cattell, 1963) contains for each of the two forms of the test seventy pairs of items for children between the ages of eight and twelve years. Within each pair the child chooses the one that best describes him or her. The reading level of the test is third grade. A time limit is imposed on the child, and the average time taken to complete the questionnaire is one hundred minutes. The test is scored on the basis of fourteen primary personality traits.

The short-term test-retest correlations for the individual subtests ranged from poor (.47) to borderline acceptable (.72) for Form A. Because the combination of the two forms resulted in reliabilities that were higher (up to .80) than those obtained for each form separately, it has been recommended that both forms be administered. The validity of the subtests was assessed within the context of Cattell's personality constructs and ranged from poor (.33) to moderately high (.83) for Form A.

The Personality Inventory for Children (Wirt, Lachar, Klinedinst, Seat, and Broen, 1977) uses data from *parents'* responses to "True" and "False" items. It contains thirty-three scales among which are validity scales and clinical scales, such as Depression, Delinquency, Anxiety, and Hyperactivity. The standardization involved nearly twenty-six hundred children between the ages of three and sixteen years. The manual provides considerable evidence of the inventory's reliability and validity.

Projective Tests. Projective tests are frequently used by clinical psychologists in their assessment of children with behavior problems. Many of the projective tests can be used with both adults and children, and a few of them have been designed primarily for children.

The most widely used projective test is the Rorschach Inkblot Test (Rorschach, 1942). The Rorschach consists of ten inkblots printed on individual cards that are presented to the client one at a time. The client is asked to look at the card and tell what is seen or represented on the card. No time limit is given. When the client has responded to all ten inkblots, the examiner inquires about each response in order. In this inquiry the examiner is attempting to determine what part of the inkblot elicited the response and what perceptual cues were involved. The Rorschach is administered to clients of all ages, although it is more commonly used with adolescents and adults.

Each Rorschach blot is scored for location, determinants, and content. Location designates whether the client's response refers to the whole blot or specific parts of it; determinants include all references to form, color, shading, and movement; content refers to the type of object depicted by the response, such as, humans, inanimate objects, plants. A variety of scoring procedures have been devised for the Rorschach, but that described by Exner (1974) is becoming the most widely used. The interpretation of the Rorschach is based on the absolute as well as relative scores in the various categories and subcategories. Norms for children and adolescents have been published (Ames, Métraux, Rodell, and Walker, 1974; Ames, Métraux, and Walker, 1971). Test-retest reliability on Rorschach responses for children has been quite low; these poor results have been attributed to children's lower attention span, varying motivation, and changing personality (Zubin, Iron, and Schumer, 1965, p. 189).

Several thousand articles and books have been written about the Rorschach, and yet the validity of the test has not been demonstrated to the satisfaction of research psychologists. The research studies that have reported high Rorschach validity have been strongly criticized as having major flaws (Eysenck, 1959). Clinicians, on the other hand, maintain that the interpretation of patterns of scores on the Rorschach is based on substantial experience with clients and is, therefore, clinically valid.

The Thematic Apperception Test (TAT) is the second most often used projective test. The TAT was developed by Murray and his coworkers at Harvard University (Murray 1943) to assess the drives, emotions, and conflicts of personality. The test consists of thirty pictures, some of which are primarily for men, women, girls, or boys, and others for everyone. The client is instructed to make up a story for each picture the examiner shows. The client is asked to tell what led up to the event in the picture, what is happening in the picture, what the people in the picture are feeling and thinking, and what the outcome will be.

The basic assumption underlying the TAT is that the stories created by the client will reveal inhibited tendencies that the client will not or cannot describe. Interpretation is based on the central figure in the story who is assumed to represent the client. The examiner attempts to characterize the central figure in each story, noting similarities in characteristics across stories. The examiner then determines the general nature of the situations confronting the central figure, again attending particularly to those features that recur. The examiner lists the traits recurring among the people with whom the central figures interact. Murray has developed a list of types of environmental situations that are classified according to the effect they have on the central figure, and the examiner uses this list as the framework for the interpretation of the test results. Examples of these kinds of environmental situations are Affiliation (the central figure having close personal relationships with others), Dominance (other persons trying to force or prevent the central figure from doing something) and Physical Danger (the central figure being exposed to danger from nonhuman sources). In analyzing the reactions of the central figure, the examiner usually uses Murray's list of needs or drives to assess the client's motivational patterns. Murray's list of needs includes drives, such as Achievement, Nurturance, and Destruction.

The reliability of the scoring and interpretation of TAT protocols appears to be quite satisfactory. Research studies on the validity of the TAT have yielded contradictory findings.

The Children's Apperception Test (CAT) was designed for use with children between three and ten years of age (Bellak and Bellak, 1949). Believing that children identify more readily with animals than with people, the authors designed twenty pictures of animals in humanlike situations (for example, a rabbit alone in a crib in a dark room). The pictures are planned to elicit responses related to oral, anal, and genital activities, sibling rivalry, and parent relationships. No research studies investigating the reliability and validity of the CAT have been conducted. The most recent review of the CAT may be found in Bellak (1975).

classification and diagnosis

After the tests are administered, they are scored and interpreted by the clinician. A detailed report based on all of the assessment data is then written. This report usually includes information obtained from the referral source, the interviews, and the test results. The later portions of the report provide the clinician's diagnosis of the problem, probable etiological factors, and suggestions for types of treatment or specific treatment plans.

If the assessment procedures have been conducted by a team of professionals, each of them writes a report based on the individual's findings, but the formal diagnosis and treatment plan is deferred until the team has a conference and members exchange information. The combined reports and clinical opinions are then used as the basis for a group determination of diagnosis and treatment plan.

The classification and labeling of children's behavior problems have a long history with origins in both education and medicine, particularly psychiatry. The principal classification system in use today is contained in the *Diagnostic and Statistical Manual of Mental Disorders* (DSM-III) (1980). The DSM-III recommends that each client be classified on the basis of five axis:

Axis I Clinical Psychiatric Syndrome(s) and Other Conditions	Axis III Physical Disorders
	Axis IV Severity of Psychosocial Stressors
Axis II Personality Disorders (adults) and Specific Developmental Disorders (children and adolescents)	Axis V Highest Level of Adaptive Functioning Past Year

The major categories of Axis I, Clinical Psychiatric Syndromes, include the following:

Disorders usually arising in Childhood or Adolescence (except Specific Developmental Disorders)	Somatoform Disorders
	Dissociative Disorders
	Psychosexual Disorders
Organic Mental Disorders	Factitious Disorders
Substance Use Disorders	Disorders of Impulse Control not Classified Elsewhere
Schizophrenic Disorders	Adjustment Disorders
Paranoid Disorders	Psychological Factors Affecting Physical Condition
Psychotic Disorders not Classified Elsewhere	Conditions Not Attributable to a Mental Disorder
Affective Disorders	
Anxiety Disorders	

In addition to the disorders usually arising in childhood or adolescence, the categories more likely to apply to children and adolescents are: Substance Use Disorders, Schizophrenic Disorders, and Anxiety Disorders.

Specific Developmental Disorders coded in Axis II include the following:

Developmental reading disorder
Developmental arithmetic disorder
Developmental language disorder
Developmental articulation disorder
Mixed specific developmental disorder
Atypical specific developmental disorder

Under each of the major categories for Axes I and II are listed subtypes of the disorders. For example, the major category, Disorders Usually Arising in Childhood or Adolescence, includes the following subtypes:

Mental retardation
Pervasive developmental disorders (for example, infantile autism)
Other disorders of infancy, childhood, or adolescence
Attention deficit disorders
Conduct disorders
Anxiety disorders
Eating disorders
Stereotyped movement disorders
Other disorders with physical manifestations

Within each subtype, specific conditions are labeled and assigned a five-digit code number. For example, under the subtype, Specific developmental disorders, are represented the following conditions:

315.60 Specific reading disorder
315.10 Specific arithmetic disorder

315.32 Developmental language
         disorder
315.39 Developmental articulation
         disorder

Axis III is used to indicate any physical problem that may be relevant to the understanding or management of the client. The classification system used for Axis III is the latest revision of the *International Statistical Classification of Diseases* (1978).

Axis IV is used to indicate specific psychosocial stressors that are judged to be contributing to the client's problem; in addition, a rating of the severity of the stressor or stressors is made. In considering psychosocial stressors, the clinician considers the following areas: conjugal (for example, separation, death of spouse), parental (for example, becoming a parent, friction with child), other interpersonal (for example, problems with boss, friends, neighbors), occupational (including work, school, homemaking), living circumstances (for example, residence change), financial, legal, developmental (for example, puberty, menopause), physical illness or injury, and family factors specific to children and adolescence (for example, poor relationship between parents, inadequate parental control). Guidelines are provided for assessing the severity of the psychosocial stressors as follows:

code	term	child or adolescent examples
1	None	No apparent psychosocial stressor
2	Minimal	Vacation with family
3	Mild	Change in school teacher, new school year
4	Moderate	Parental fighting, change in school, illness of close relative, birth of sibling
5	Severe	Death of peer, divorce of parents, arrest
6	Extreme	Death of parent or sibling
7	Castastrophic	Multiple family deaths

Axis V is used to describe the client's highest level of adaptive functioning during the past year. Adaptive functioning is reflected in a composite of social relations, occupational functioning, and use of leisure time. The overall level of functioning is rated on a 6-point scale ranging from superior to grossly impaired. Examples of each level are provided in the *Manual* to assist the clinician. For instance, a rating of Fair (4) would be assigned to a child who was doing poorly but who had adequate peer and family relations.

Interrater agreement for the diagnostic categories of the DSM-III ranged from 20 percent to 100 percent with a mean of 54 percent for child referrals (Mattison, Cantwell, Russell, and Will, 1979). The higher levels of agreement were found for mental retardation, psychosis, conduct disorder, and hyperactivity, while the lowest levels were obtained for anxiety disorders and the subtypes of depression. Validity was examined by comparing the classifications of referral children with those of "experts" (Cantwell, Russell, Mattison, and Will, 1979). The average agreement between the experts and the raters was less than 50 percent and highest for mental retardation, psychosis, hyperactivity, and conduct disorder. Although the authors of these studies appeared to find these results supportive of DSM-III, the levels of reliability and validity are far short of those expected for psychological instruments.

Conclusions

Most clinicians rely primarily on the interview and standardized tests for the assessment of children's behavior disorders. The clinician must be aware that adults do not always remember historical events or report current behaviors and events accurately. In spite of its possibly low reliability and validity, the interview is of paramount importance because children's behavior problems occur in the context of their interaction with parents and other relevant persons. Standardized intelligence and achievement tests are particularly useful in comparing an individual child's performance with that of same-age peers and may be useful in determining the type of treatment needed by the child. Many clinicians also find that data from personality tests are useful in planning treatment programs, but other clinicians challenge their utility for a number of reasons, including low or unavailable reliability or validity, or both. Formal classification or diagnostic systems have also presented problems with respect to their reliability, validity, and utility, but research that is being conducted in the 1980s offers some hope for improvement in these areas.

Recommended Readings

Hobbs, N., *The Futures of Children: Categories, Labels, and Their Consequences.* San Francisco: Jossey-Bass, 1975. Summarizes the implications of the diagnostic and classification procedures currently in use with children.

Hobbs, N., ed., *Issues in the Classification of Children.* San Francisco: Jossey-Bass, 1975. A two-volume treatise on diagnosis and classification of children's behavior disorders.

Jensen, A. R., *Bias in Mental Testing.* New York: Free Press, 1980. A research review indicating that standardized tests of mental ability are not biased against native-born minorities.

Palmer, J. O., *The Psychological Assessment of Children.* New York: John Wiley, 1970. An excellent coverage of the rationale for assessment and the specific assessment technique and methods utilized by clinical psychologists.

Sattler, J. M., *Assessment of Children's Intelligence.* Philadelphia: Saunders, 1974. A thorough description of the principal intelligence tests, their administration and interpretation, and their role in the assessment of children's behavior disorders.

assessment and diagnosis: behavioral approaches

3

Bijou and Peterson (1971, pp. 63-64) have stated that the basic reason for assessment is to secure information that can be used to plan a treatment program. Behavioral assessment is composed of two parts: (1) delineation of the problem that caused the child to be referred and (2) an evaluation of the child's behavioral repertoire. In general, delineation of the child's problem by a behavioral clinician involves referral information, completion of a behavior problem checklist by the parents or teacher, interviews with relevant adults and the child, and, occasionally, testing with standardized instruments. Evaluating the child's behavioral repertoire requires direct behavioral observation either in a clinic or in the child's natural environment.

Behavioral approaches to assessment have some features in common with the more traditional approaches. For example, both approaches usually include the collection of referral information and interviews with relevant adults. The behavioral clinician typically emphasizes the collection of data about current behaviors and events and gives relatively little attention to searching for the origin of the problem or to documenting the past history of the child. Standardized intelligence and achievement tests are sometimes administered by behavioral clinicians, but they interpret the test results primarily as a reflection of the child's current behavioral repertoire. (Personality tests are seldom used by behavioral clinicians for reasons that will be described later in this chapter.) The principal assessment methods, developed and refined by behavioral clinicians, include both direct and indirect techniques. A recent survey of the four major behavioral journals *(Behavior Research and Therapy, Behavior Therapy, Journal of Applied Behavior Analysis, and Journal of Behavior Therapy and Experimental Psychology)* revealed that 71 percent of the assessments utilized direct observational procedures, while 29 percent utilized such indirect methods as interview, self-report, and rating by others (Bornstein, Bridgewater, Hickey, and Sweeney, 1980).

This chapter reviews the assessment methods utilized by behavioral clinicians and discusses the behavioral alternatives to traditional diagnoses. An increasing focus on this area has been indicated by the publication, which began in 1979, of the journal *Behavioral Assessment.*

indirect assessment methods

referral information

In obtaining referral information the behavioral clinician focuses on reports from adults who have observed the problem behavior. These preliminary data allow the clinician to plan more efficiently for the subsequent assessment procedures. A referral by the child's teacher, for example, may indicate that the teacher should be interviewed and that the child should be observed in the classroom setting. Referral from a juvenile court, on the other hand, may indicate that assessment should involve a number of people and a number of settings (for example, home, school, job).

ratings by others: checklists and rating scales

A number of behavior problem checklists and rating scales have been designed to facilitate the assessment process. A typical list enumerates behaviors or characteristics to be checked if they occur or have occurred in the referred child. Certain behaviors must be judged and designated in terms of their frequency, such as "sometimes," "less than average," "frequently." Some checklists have also been developed into scales in which the scores from particular items are added together.

The available checklists and scales vary on several dimensions: number and kinds of problems covered, specificity of behavior, specificity of the setting in which the behavior occurs, and the age range of children for which the checklist applies. Some checklists contain items related to one kind of behavior problem, such as hyperactivity, while others are considerably more comprehensive in their coverage. The comprehensive checklists are particularly advantageous in clinical or institutional settings where they may be used as the initial assessment or screening devices prior to having interviews with the child's *mediators,* that is, significant persons in the child's environment. While the checklists clearly emphasize observable behaviors, the items within the checklists vary in their levels of abstraction ("hits other children" or "aggressive") and to the extent to which items require judgment by the responder, the person completing the list.

Some items are relatively straightforward in that the decision involves only presence or absence of the behavior, while other items require judgments that are considerably more difficult. For example, items such as "too few friends" and "excessively late" rely heavily on the personal experiences and value system of the responder. Having three friends might be an adequate number in the judgment of one teacher but "too few" to another teacher.

Specificity of the setting for the behavior may also affect the ease or difficulty of judgment. Items without reference to setting may be interpreted in various ways. For example, "overactive" may be checked by one mother only if her child is overactive in most settings, while another mother might mark that label although her child is overactive only on shopping expeditions and in church.

These characteristics of behavior problem checklists very likely affect their reliability and validity, but extensive research in this area has not been conducted. The available research suggests that items specifying behavior and setting are more likely to be reliable than the more abstract items. Similarly, validity would be expected to be higher for the most clearly specified behaviors. Other factors have been found to affect the data obtained from checklists. For example, the two parents may not agree on the items checked. This finding is not particularly surprising since parents rarely spend an equal amount of time with their child in the same settings; in addition, each parent's experience and knowledge about children are unique, and these are often used as the basis for judging whether a problem is present.

One factor that appears to influence the validity of checklist data is a possible "placebo" effect of treatment. One study showed that a significant percentage of parents whose children had been treated in a counseling center reported that their children's school attendance had greatly improved, when, in fact, attendance had decreased. This study and several other studies suggest that ratings of improvement by parents may not be accurate measures of change and, therefore, should not be used as the only measure for treatment evaluation.

You may be wondering how items on the behavior problem checklists are obtained. There has been a long history behind the development of behavior problem checklists beginning in the 1920s and 1930s when researchers became interested in describing both normal and abnormal behaviors and characteristics of children at different ages. Several of these early investigators developed lists of behaviors, which other researchers subsequently modified and used as the bases for collecting normative data on the incidence of behavior problems in normal children, the most well-known study being that by Macfarlane, Allen, and Honzik (1954). Both early and more recent investigators have derived items for the checklists from an examination of clinical case files describing referred children's behavioral histories and symptoms.

The development of behavior problem checklists has also led to an interest in the relationships among behavior problems. In some instances, items have been grouped together because they have common features or seem to occur together in individual children. A more refined method for grouping items has been reflected in the use of a statistical technique, factor analysis, which determines the correlations among all of the items and permits groupings of items that appear to be measuring the same factor. A factor, then, comprises several items that are measuring the same entity. The label given to a factor is assigned by the investigator on the basis of what the items appear to be measuring. In a factor analytic study, a large number of children, either a normal or an abnormal group, are evaluated with the same checklist.

The Behavior Problem Checklist (Quay and Peterson, 1967) is a widely used instrument that has been factor analyzed. It consists of fifty-five common behavior problems, and the rater indicates whether each problem is absent, mild, or severe. The factor analyses of these items have identified three dimensions of children's behavior problems: Conduct Disorder, Personality Problem, and Inadequacy-Immaturity. Research with older children has indicated a fourth dimension, Socialized Delinquency. Ratings have been done by parents, teachers, psychiatric aides, and correctional personnel. Norms are available for samples of children in public schools, special education classes, institutions for delinquents, and child guidance clinics. Reliability has been measured primarily by correlating the scores of two raters. The agreement in parent's ratings has generally been found to be higher than those of parent and teacher.

Achenbach (1978, 1979) has developed a more comprehensive checklist for children between the ages of six and sixteen years. The checklist contains 112 items that parents rate as being true, somewhat or sometimes true, or very or often true. Factor analysis revealed seven or nine factors depending on the age and sex of the children. The factors for normal or nonreferred boys aged six to eleven were Schizoid, Depressed, Uncommunicative, Obsessive-Compulsive, Somatic Complaints, Social Withdrawal, Hyperactive, Aggressive, and Delinquent. Test-retest reliability is quite high over a short period of time. Interparent agreement ranged from .67 to .74. Samples of children referred to clinics received scores that were significantly different from those of nonreferred children.

Miller (1972, 1977) has developed the School Behavior Checklist, which is completed by teachers. Two forms are available, one for ages two to six years (A1) and the other for ages seven to thirteen (A2). Form A2 has ninety-six items that are rated as either "true" or "false." Six main factors were identified for both forms. The factors for A2 were: Low Need Achievement, Aggression, Anxiety, Academic Disability, Hostile Isolation, and Extraversion. The standardization sample involved more than 5,000 children in the Louisville, Kentucky area. The test-retest reliability of the checklist was adequate or better for all scales except Hostile Isolation. The validity of the checklist has not yet been adequately examined.

Checklists and rating scales are particularly useful in the preliminary assessment of referred children, but their major contribution may be in the area of screening for early identification of behavior problems. Because they take relatively little time to complete, teachers and parents are more likely to be willing to cooperate with their use.

Wahler and Cormier (1970) have presented examples of checklists that focus on the environmental circumstances as well as the behavior problems. Their ecological approach includes having the parents designate the setting, the social consequences, and the appropriate behavior desired for each of the behavior problems presented by the child. These data provide the foundation for the behavioral clinician's interview with the parents.

In general, the behavior problem checklists focus primarily on the negative or defective aspects of children's behavioral repertoires. That is, they describe those kinds of children's behavior that cause concern to adults, but they do not present data with regard to the behavioral assets or strengths of those same children. Based on the idea that good adjustment is more than the absence of poor adjustment (Ross 1963), Ross, Lacey, and Parton (1965) incorporated items related to good adjustment in their checklist that was administered to elementary school boys. Their results indicated that these items formed a separate factor and thus gave support to the inclusion of positive behaviors as being a meaningful component of assessment procedures with children.

The importance of including positive behaviors in assessment brings up the issue of the basis for most referrals. Most of the complaints about children's behaviors revolve around behavioral excesses, that is, behaviors that occur too often. If viewed from a normative perspective, it is also apparent that behavioral deficits should be of equal concern. Such deficits could certainly be as detrimental to the child's future functioning as behavioral excesses. The development of comprehensive behavioral checklists that include behavioral excesses and deficits as well as positive behaviors would likely result in assessment that clearly delineates which behaviors should be increased and which behaviors should be decreased during the treatment or intervention program. These newer checklists would have to be designed with reference to behavioral norms and evaluated in terms of their reliability and validity, just as are contemporary intelligence and achievement tests.

the behavioral interview

Like the traditional interview, the behavioral interview consists of verbal interactions between the clinician and persons concerned with the child's behavior problem. The primary aims of the behavioral interview are to describe the behavior and to develop hypotheses about environmental factors that may be maintaining the behavior. In the behavioral interview, then, the parents are questioned extensively about the behavior problem itself, the conditions under which it occurs, and what the parents do when the behavior occurs. The behavioral clinician will also ask what attempts the parents have made to change the behavior and what results were obtained.

In those instances in which the child's behavior problem does not occur in the home, the behavioral clinician will conduct an interview with the primary adult in the other setting (for example, the school). The important point to note is that the behavioral clinician does not view the parents as being primarily responsible for the origin and and maintenance of all behavior problems. Behavior problems can and do develop in settings outside of the home, and it is those settings that the behavioral clinician will explore for the factors that cause the behavior to continue.

The behavioral clinician is generally less interested in historical factors than is the traditional clinician and tends not to interview the parents in depth about the child's early developmental history. Although the behavior problem is recognized to have originated at some point in the child's history, the behavioral clinician is more concerned with discovering the environmental factors currently maintaining the behavior than with determining the circumstances under which the behavior originated.

There are, however, instances in which a knowledge of historical factors might contribute some important information. When the presenting problem involves large deficiencies in the child's behavior, the clinician would want to know when the problem was first observed and what the child's behavioral repertoire was at different ages during development. In these instances, the clinician is attempting to determine whether behaviors were acquired and then lost or whether behaviors had not been acquired at all.

Children, of course, do not refer themselves for help with their problems; adults have the primary responsibility for determining whether a child should receive professional attention. One of the problems faced by clinicians is determining the validity of the problems described by adults in the child's environment. The behavioral clinician attempts to secure an accurate description of the problem from the adults, realizing that the description may be erroneous in some cases. In addition, there are situations in which an adult will describe as a serious behavior problem a behavior which is a common occurrence among children of that age.

The behavioral clinician, too, must be sensitive to the stress affecting parents seeking help for their child. Their experiences with the child or the complaints they have heard from other adults, or both, can be expected to influence their description of the child's behavior. A child who has created considerable problems, including social embarrassment, is more likely to be perceived in a negative way. Moreover, coming to a professional for help may indicate to many parents that they have failed in their parental responsibilities. This response is somewhat overdetermined by society's general assumption that parents are to blame for most inappropriate behaviors manifested by children.

Parental stress may affect the behavioral interview in a number of ways. First of all, parents may deny that the child has a problem and claim that they were "forced" to come to the clinic against their better judgment. This situation tends to occur when the behavior problem is specific to a setting outside of the home or when parental norms for behavior are at variance with those of other adults. Denial is understandable under these circumstances because the parents have not experienced the problem directly. This denial may be damaging, however, if their reaction also extends to attributing blame to the adults responsible for the referral, that is, denying that the behavior problem occurs in other settings. Other persons may, in fact, have some role in the maintenance of the behavior, but parents' direct knowledge of the relationship is sometimes slight, thus suggesting that their assignment of blame to others might be done to protect themselves from blame.

Second, parental stress may be responsible for a less than accurate description of historical events as well as current behavior and environmental factors. For example, parents may omit certain information, such as previous clinical contacts or complaints by other adults about the child's behavior, because they want an "objective" opinion about the child's status. They may also omit relevant descriptions of their own behavior with respect to the child's behavior because they feel that the clinician would not approve of it; they might, for example, omit reporting their use of physical punishment. The child's behavior problem itself may be magnified or diminished relative to its actual occurrence depending on the parents' perception of the overall situation. If they are not convinced that the child has a problem, the child's inappropriate behavior may be underestimated or played down. On the other hand, if the parents are overwhelmed by the problem or convinced by others that it is serious, they may overestimate its occurrence in their attempt to obtain the clinician's help for both themselves and the child.

Because of these distortions, clinical experience has suggested that the validity of data obtained by interview may be questionable. Several research studies have corroborated these clinical impressions for parents of "normal" children. In a monograph focusing on the research utility of retrospective parental report, Yarrow, Campbell, and Burton (1970) describe the relationships of data obtained from interviews with mothers to data collected three to thirty years earlier from nursery school records, pediatricians' reports, and psychological test results. The interview data revealed that mothers tended to describe their children's nursery school years in a more positive light than was described by the data collected earlier. In addition, the mothers' recollections were modified to be compatible with general social expectations of behavior for children of that age. Such studies suggest that mothers may not remember very accurately all of the events in their children's lives or their own perceptions about their children's characteristics. Under relatively neutral interview circumstances, mothers may tend to "remember" events and perceptions more positively than they were actually experienced at the time. Such findings should probably not be generalized to interviews with mothers whose children have been referred for behavior problems. Mothers of referred children may well "recall" more of their children's negative characteristics both in response to their child's current behavior problem and as a pleas for help from the clinician. While the behavioral clinician can be reasonably certain that the interview data may not represent optimal accuracy, the clinician does not usually have adequate resources for determining the type and direction of the distortions in parental interview data. Usually the clinician chooses to perceive the interview data primarily as a current reflection of the child as seen by the adults in the child's environment.

Another problem faced by the behavioral clinician in the interview is that adults are accustomed to using vague terms in describing children's problems. Adults often use such labels as "nervous," "lazy," or "bad" to describe adults' traits, and they also use these labels to describe children's. The behavioral clinician must attempt to determine exactly what behaviors have been occurring to warrant the trait label. The clinician cannot readily make a translation from the trait label to specific behaviors because people tend to use trait labels to refer to a wide variety of behaviors. The label "nervous," for example, could refer to sweating hands, faltering voice, overactivity, temper outbursts, or any combination of symptoms and behaviors. Furthermore, the same label might be used whether the behavior occurs in one or many settings.

The behavioral clinician, therefore, must direct inquiry during the interview toward a description of the behaviors that are the basis for the complaints from people in the child's environment. The clinician then inquires about behaviors the adult wishes to have as replacements for the problem behaviors. The adult is also asked to describe those situations in which the problem behavior occurs; these situations are called the *antecedents* of the problem behavior. Antecedents include all stimulus factors present immediately before and during the occurrece of the problem behavior. For example, a preschool child may be described as having temper tantrums only in the home and only when the mother is present. The antecedents then would include the presence of the mother and the home environment.

The behavioral clinician asks the adult what usually happens immediately after the behavior occurs; these occurrences are called *consequences.* Consequences include all stimulus factors present immediately after the occurrence of the problem behavior. For example, a mother might say that when her son has a temper tantrum she ordinarily approaches him and tries to calm the child by talking to him. In this instance the consequences for the temper tantrums include the mother approaching and talking to her son. Adults usually try several methods for changing the problem behavior prior to consulting a clinician, and clinicians inquire about what methods were used and the consistency with which they were used.

The behavioral interview also includes asking the adults what objects and experiences the child enjoys. In securing this information, the clinician is seeking stimuli that may serve as reinforcers for the acquisition of appropriate behavior. While certain types of food almost always serve as reinforcers, other reinforcers are preferable in terms of ease of administration. The clinician will ask how the child spends free time to determine the relative reinforcement potential for various activities. Children vary greatly in terms of what environmental stimuli may serve as reinforcers. Adults sometimes make mistakes when they designate potential reinforcers for children. Giving an article of clothing to a child who has no interest in his appearance, for example, is not likely to serve as a reinforcer. On the other hand, presenting the same item to a child who spends time looking at clothing in stores may well be an effective reinforcer. Asking the child what objects he would like to have or what activities he enjoys is one efficient way of determining potential reinforcers.

The interview also serves the purpose of permitting the clinician to evaluate the parents' and other adults' potential for optimal involvement in a behavioral intervention program. Consideration must be given to a variety of reality factors, such as the amount of time the adult has available or is willing to make available for the child's treatment. Similarly, this evaluation must include an assessment of the adult's receptivity to behavioral approaches to treatment. Since most behavioral intervention programs take place in the child's natural environment, rather than in the clinic, the responsibility placed on adults for direct implementation is considerably greater than that imposed by the traditional treatment programs. Many adults are not prepared to make major commitments of time and effort; they expect instead that the problem will be solved in the clinic during periodic visits to the therapist.

The extent to which adults expect to be involved, of course, is based, on their personal knowledge and experience. The average parent or teacher can be expected to be more familiar with the traditional approaches to helping children with problems because of their longer history of use. Moreover, adults' histories of coping with the behavior problems often convince them that they cannot help the child themselves, and referral is tantamount to giving the problem to someone else (that is, the clinician) for solution. Both of these factors tend to develop in adults an expectation of relief from responsibility.

The behavioral clinician thus has the difficult task of convincing the adults that their direct and continued involvement is crucial to the success of the intervention program. This persuasion must also include the behavioral clinician's successful handling of the adults' feelings of blame. To some extent, assessing and treating the behaviror problem in the natual environment strongly imply that the adults in that environment have created or caused the problem, and adults tend to be particularly sensitive to that possible relationship. Some adults come to the interview with the conviction that they are indeed responsible for the child's problem and fully expect that they will be blamed and made to suffer accordingly. A few of these individuals are disappointed or sometimes question the clinician's competence when they are told that the original cause of the problem is unknown or, at any rate, is not a critical piece of information with respect to behavioral assessment and treatment. Other adults are equally convinced that they are *not* to blame, and any suggestion, direct or indirect, that they participate in the assessment and treatment process tends to produce a lack of cooperation and a statement about who is to be blamed. Both of these reactions, the complete acceptance of or complete rejection of blame, represent extremes that are rarely encountered. Most adults are somewhere between these extremes, deeply concerned about their possible contribution to the problem and searching for other contributing factors.

The behavioral clinician often includes an interview with the child as part of the assessment procedure. Although beset with the difficulties described in the previous chapter, children's interviews can contribute useful information with respect to the child's understanding of the problem and the factors implicated in the maintenance of the problem behavior. At the very least, an interview with the child can provide the child's perception of the reasons for the referral and identification of reinforcers that may contribute to the intervention program's effectiveness. Although the child's views may not match those of the mediators, they are likely to exert a significant influence on the child's behavior. For example, if a boy reports hating his father, the father's effectiveness as a social reinforcer may be questionable, whether or not the father "deserves" the child's hatred.

standardized tests

Standardized test results are not usually an integral part of behavioral assessment. The primary reasons for this omission appear to be related to the behaviorist's rejection of traditional clinical methods and past misuses and misinterpretations of test data. The "medical model" of mental illness has historically emphasized the importance of underlying psychic conflict and the identification of "personality" characteristics in the assessment procedure. Behavioral clinicians have seriously questioned the utility of this model and have rejected personality tests on the basis of their poor reliability, validity, and utility with respect to facilitating the planning of treatment programs. Behaviorists maintain that behavior is situation-specific and, therefore, that trait labels cannot accurately describe people. Mischel (1968, 1979) has suggested that apparent consistencies in behavior reflect similarities in stimulus environments rather than personality traits.

The rejection of personality tests by behavioral clinicians has perhaps been overgeneralized to other types of standardized tests. Mischel (1968) has presented a strong case for the use of intelligence tests on the basis of their reliability, validity, and utility. Nevertheless, these tests are probably underused by behaviorists because in some instances the use of scores on these tests has had negative consequences for children. For example, low scores have sometimes resulted in inferior or no treatment. The stability of IQ test scores over time unfortunately has been misinterpreted by some professionals to mean that treatment programs can have no effect on later test performance when, in actuality, the stability may reflect that children's general environments tend to remain similar over time.

From a behavioral point of view, intelligence tests may be conceptualized as a sample of tasks for which norms have been developed. A low score suggests that the child's rate of learning these tasks is lower than for other children of the same age. Knowledge of a child's status relative to that of peers can aid in the decision as to whether the child's behavioral repertoire is indeed deficient. Low scores on intelligence tests do not indicate, however, the reasons for the behavioral deficiencies.

Intelligence tests can also be utilized as assessment tools in the evaluation of treatment programs that aim for comprehensive skill development through a comparison of scores obtained before treatment with scores obtained after treatment.

Achievement tests are more often used by behavioral clinicians because they assess more clearly defined skill areas. They include only a sample of the possible specific behaviors comprising the skill area and provide an estimate of the child's performance relative to that of peers. If a child is referred for learning problems in school, an achievement test would be used to assess the current level of skills in the various school subjects. Behavioral clinicians also use achievement tests to assess the effectiveness of remedial programs by comparing pretreatment and posttreatment scores and determining whether the rate of learning the academic skills was significantly higher during the treatment phase.

It should be kept in mind that a number of the training programs for behavioral clinicians, particularly those for master's level psychologists, do not provide courses or supervised experience in the administration and interpretation of standardized intelligence and achievement tests. Nevertheless, many research studies on behavioral treatment programs include scores on standardized tests in their descriptions of the subjects. In some of these cases, the tests were administered by traditional clinicians for other purposes, and the extent to which the behavioral clinician utilized the information derived from testing is unknown.

It is likely that behavioral clinicians will utilize standardized tests more frequently in the future for several reasons. First, behavioral clinicians will increasingly have to make decisions about whether children's behavioral repertoires are abnormal, and these tests provide norms for the behaviors that are assessed. Second, standardized test results can often save the clinician time during the behavioral assessment process by pinpointing the developmental or mental age level for a broad range of behaviors; that is, they may reduce the total number of behaviors to be assessed more thoroughly.

direct behavioral assessment (observations)

self-observation

A number of studies have examined procedures whereby children assess the quality and quantity of their own behavior. Although many children can be trained to collect accurate data on themselves, self-assessment procedures have inherent problems that reduce their reliability and validity. Namely, requesting children to record their own behaviors may lead to changes in those behaviors. Reports of these reactive effects have led to the use of self-assessment as a treatment procedure by some behavioral clinicians. Several studies have suggested that self-assessment of appropriate behaviors is associated with an increase in their frequency, while self-assessment of inappropriate behaviors leads to decreases in the frequencies of these behaviors.

behavioral observation by others

Direct behavioral observation is the principal assessment procedure used by behaviorally oriented clinicians. Behavioral observation is the method of choice because the data are considered to be more valid than data obtained by the traditional assessment methods. That is, because behavioral clinicians regard psychological problems as behavior problems (and, therefore, subject to the laws of learning), the direct observation of the behavior problem has been assumed to be more valid than the other, particularly the traditional psychometric, assessment methods. Since abnormal behavior is believed to be developed and maintained by environmental stimuli, the direct observation of the relationship of the behavior problem to the environmental factors should provide the most valid hypotheses about changes that would lead to improved behavior.

The behavioral clinician's first task in behavioral observation is to identify and delineate the target behaviors to be observed. The choice of behaviors is based on the information obtained from the referral sources, the behavior checklists, and the interviews with the mediators and the child. The second task is to determine the frequency with which these target behaviors occur and the environmental factors that are associated with the occurrence of the behaviors.

The initial period of observation is called the *baseline* observation period and focuses on the behavior as it normally or naturally occurs. The data obtained during the baseline observation period is later used in the evaluation of the intervention or treatment program. One of the important assets of direct behavioral observation is that it permits a continuous assessment of behavior, thereby allowing the clinician to know the child's status with respect to the target behavior at any point in time during the assessment and treatment phases.

settings

Behavioral observations are usually conducted in the setting in which the problem behavior occurs. Thus, if the problem occurs in the home, direct observation of the child would likely take place in the home. Research investigators have reported the recording of behavior in a wide variety of settings, such as schools, homes, and institutions. Studies have also been conducted in which behavioral observation takes place in a setting that is not part of the child's natural environment, such as a clinic office or in a research laboratory.

The diversity of settings in which behavior problems occur presents difficulties for the behavioral clinician. Permission for observation must be obtained, and observers who can work in that setting must be secured. For example, not all teachers are receptive to observers in the classroom, and few schools have personnel whose specific duties include the type of behavioral observation being discussed here.

Many different types of behavior have been observed and recorded. In general, the kinds of behaviors to be recorded are determined by the child's particular clinical needs. A number of behavior codes have been developed, however, for use in particular settings, such as the school, and these codes have been used frequently in the research literature. The clinician or researcher who designs a behavior code attempts to describe each behavior as precisely as possible, including examples both of its occurrence and instances that would *not* be considered part of the response class. This description of positive and negative instances of the response class is called an *operational definition*. While the same label may appear on several behavior codes (for example, playing), their operational definitions may, in fact, vary. Let us now examine a few examples of behavior codes.

In 1970, O'Leary, Kaufman, Kass, and Drabman reported a study on the effects of loud and soft reprimands on the behavior of disruptive students. Two children from each of five classrooms had been selected as subjects because of their high rate of disruptive behavior. In this study college undergraduates were the observers. Each child was observed for twenty minutes each day during the arithmetic lesson. A time-sampling technique was employed in which the child was observed for twenty seconds followed by ten seconds for recording the disruptive behaviors that occurred during the observation period. Disruptive behaviors were categorized into nine classes as follows:

1. Out-of-chair: movement of the child from the chair when not permitted or requested by teacher.
2. Modified-out-of-chair: movement of the child from the chair with some part of the body still touching the chair (exclude sitting on feet).
3. Touching others' property: child comes into contact with another's property without permission to do so. Includes grabbing, rearranging, destroying the property of another, and touching the desk of another.
4. Vocalization: any unpermitted audible behavior emanating from the mouth.
5. Playing: child uses hands to play with own or community property so that such behavior is incompatible with learning.
6. Orienting: the turning or orienting response is not rated unless the child is seated, and the turn must be more than 90 degrees, using the desk as a reference point.
7. Noise: child creating any audible noise other than vocalization without permission.
8. Aggression: child makes movement toward another person to come into physical contact (exclude brushing against another).
9. Time-off task: child does not do assigned work for entire twenty-second interval. For example, child does not write or read when so assigned.

The investigators used as their primary behavior measure the mean frequency of disruptive behavior. The mean frequency was calculated by dividing the total number of disruptive behaviors by the number of intervals observed. They might have used the frequency of disruptive behavior each day, but unavoidable circumstances, such as assemblies, occasionally prevented them from observing the children exactly twenty minutes each day.

Some studies in classroom settings have focused on a broader range of behaviors. For example, Werry and Quay (1969) were concerned with three general categories of behaviors: inappropriate pupil behaviors, pupil attending behaviors, and teacher-pupil interactions. Each category had various subcategories. In their definition inappropriate pupil behaviors included:

1. Being out of one's seat (without permission or when the acitivity, though permitted, is prolonged)
2. Physical contact or disturbing others
3. Making audible noise

Attending behaviors included:

1. Attending (the child must have eye contact with the task or teacher for not less than fifteen out of twenty seconds)
2. Irrelevant activity (not the assigned task)
3. Daydreaming (more than five seconds out of twenty)

The last category was teacher contact and included:

1. Contacts the teacher initiated positively
2. Teacher-initiated negative contact
3. Pupil-initiated positive contact with teacher
4. Pupil-initiated negative contact with teacher

Behavior was observed during twenty-second intervals followed by ten-second intervals for recording.

methods of assessing observed target behavior

There are several types of objective methods for observing and recording behavior. Since behaviors are observed in a variety of settings and under a variety of circumstances, specific methods of observation are usually designed for individual situations. Observations may be recorded every day or only on certain days when the child is in a particular situation. On the days of observation, the behavior may be observed for a relatively brief period, such as fifteen minutes, or for all of the hours that the child is awake. The important feature to note is that the observation period (the time of initiation and length) remains constant throughout the baseline and treatment phases. The specific period should be chosen because it is most probable that the behavior problem will occur. That is, observation is scheduled at a time when the child is most likely to engage in the problem behavior.

The most common methods for quantifying behavioral observations are counting the number of times the behavior occurs, counting the number of time intervals during which the behavior occurs, or measuring the duration or the amount of time the behavior occurs.

Frequency. Frequency measures involve counting the number of times that the behavior occurs within a specific period of time. Response rate is determined by dividing the frequency of the behavior by time. Response rate is a particularly useful measure when the behavior can be clearly delineated, and each occurrence of the behavior takes about the same amount of time. Examples of behaviors that lend themselves to counting are number of words spoken, number of classroom assignments completed, and number of times a child hits another child. A mechanical counter or a tally sheet on a clipboard is the only necessary equipment.

Interval Recording. With interval recording, each observation session is subdivided into small time units, such as fifteen or twenty seconds, and the observer indicates on a data sheet those units or intervals during which the behavior was observed. This method is also called *time-sampling* when the observer takes time away from observing the child to record behaviors occurring during the previous interval. A typical time-sampling procedure would involve the clinician's observing the child's behavior for twenty seconds and then recording the behaviors that occurred during the next ten seconds. Behaviors occurring during the ten-second recording period would not be recorded. The sequence of twenty-second observe and ten-second record is then repeated throughout the session; if the sessions are lengthy, observers are given brief (predetermined) rest periods during which they neither formally observe nor record the child's behavior. Interval recording would appear to have the disadvantage of not providing an accurate measure in that one instance of the behavior during an interval is considered equivalent to several instances of the behavior occurring during an interval. That is, for many studies utilizing interval recording, only presence or absence of the target behavior during each interval is indicated on the data sheet. However, having the precise frequency of the behavior appears not to have great utility for many behavior clinicians in that their programs focus on the direction and relative amount of change in the behavior as a function of intervention rather than on the specific number of behaviors occurring before and after treatment. When a serious, but infrequent, behavior problem is being assessed, a frequency, rather than an interval recording, method would probably be used.

The interval recording method has likely gained favor because of its usefulness in situations where the clinician wishes to observe a number of behaviors during the session. In these cases, the observer records the presence or absence of each form of behavior at the end of each interval. It would be very difficult to record the frequencies of more than a few behaviors simultaneously. Table 3-1 shows an example of an interval recording data sheet for seven behaviors. Circling a + indi-

table 3-1. example of an interval recording sheet for several behaviors

		Intervals												
		1	2	3	4	5	6	7	8	9	10	11	12	Total
Behaviors	1	+0	+0	+0	+0	+0	+0	+0	+0	+0	+0	+0	+0	
	2	+0	+0	+0	+0	+0	+0	+0	+0	+0	+0	+0	+0	
	3	+0	+0	+0	+0	+0	+0	+0	+0	+0	+0	+0	+0	
	4	+0	+0	+0	+0	+0	+0	+0	+0	+0	+0	+0	+0	
	5	+0	+0	+0	+0	+0	+0	+0	+0	+0	+0	+0	+0	
	6	+0	+0	+0	+0	+0	+0	+0	+0	+0	+0	+0	+0	
	7	+0	+0	+0	+0	+0	+0	+0	+0	+0	+0	+0	+0	

Session Number   Date

Child's Name   Therapist's Name

Time Started   Time Concluded   Name of Observer

Setting

Activity

cates that the behavior occurred during the interval; circling a 0 indicates that the behavior was absent during the interval.

The observer using an interval recording method usually has a stopwatch fastened to the top of the clipboard, which also holds the data sheet. After the watch is started, the observer's activities (observing, recording, or resting) are determined solely by the clock. In this manner, every session is structured in the same way.

Duration. Response duration involves measuring the interval of time between the onset and termination of the behavior. This assessment method is particularly useful when the amount of time spent engaging in the behavior is the criterion upon which appropriateness or inappropriateness is based. The difficulties involved with this method are that the onset and termination of the behavior must be defined such that observers could readily agree on when the behavior began and ended. Either a stopwatch or access to a clock is required by the duration method.

assessing antecedents, consequences, and setting events

In addition to determining the frequency or duration of the target behavior, the behavioral clinician must secure additional information regarding the stimuli that might be involved in the maintenance of the behavior. Some of this information has been derived from the interview and will be used to determine those aspects of the environment that will be included for assessment during the baseline phase.

As mentioned before, antecedent stimuli are those events that take place immediately before the behavior occurs and may thus serve the function of signaling to the child that reinforcement will be forthcoming if the behavior occurs. For example, mother's coming into a room may be a signal that attention will be forthcoming if a temper tantrum occurs. During the baseline phase, then, the observer records any change in environmental stimuli that precede the occurrence of the behavior.

Consequences are those events that occur immediately after the behavior occurs and may serve as reinforcers that strengthen the behavior. The observer also records the stimulus events that follow the behavior. The recording of both antecedent and consequent stimuli will provide information to guide the clinician in the selection of an intervention program, since these stimuli have a high likelihood of having a role in the maintenance of the behavior.

Setting events are those stimuli that appear to alter the effectiveness of reinforcement. For example, a mother's reprimand may serve to punish a given behavior in one setting and to reinforce it in another. The role of setting events has not been adequately explored in the research literature on abnormal behavior, but its importance in certain instances may be considerable. When clinicians are aware of the role of setting events in behavioral control, they are able to design more effective intervention programs. If the period of behavior observation includes setting changes (for example, home, park, grocery store), the observer may be able to detect differences in the effectiveness of reinforcers in the various settings.

Formal procedures for assessing the role of stimulus events are not as well developed as those for assessing target behaviors. Often, the assessment of stimulus factors is conducted in a casual fashion, rather than recorded and quantified. Preliminary behavioral observations during which setting events, antecedent stimuli, and consequent stimuli, as well as the target behavior, are recorded, are usually helpful. In addition, the inclusion of written descriptions about stimulus events during the recording portions of an interval procedure also provides descriptions of functional relationships.

observers

Since behavioral observation requires substantial amounts of time, use of professionals for this purpose is usually precluded. Fortunately, research studies have demonstrated that a wide variety of people, including parents, teachers, undergraduates, and peers, can be taught to observe behavior. Most of the research studies utilize paid observers or undergraduates who are earning course credit for participation in the research. Many clinical practitioners do not have access to such resources and have to rely more heavily on "volunteers" from the child's environment. To a large extent, the design of the behavioral observation procedure is determined by the availability and skills of the observers available to the clinician.

The data collected should not be influenced by the observers. Independent observers collecting data in natural environments are instructed not to interact with the children, since such interactions would not be part of the children's typical experiences and would interfere with the observers' attention to the observation and recording tasks. Observers are told to be as inconspicuous as possible while maintaining a position that permits them to see and hear. In the classroom, for example, observers usually position themselves in the back of the room. After a few days of observation, children in classroom settings cease to give more than minimal attention to the observers. Turning around and looking at the observer is handled effectively by the observer's avoiding eye contact with the child.

A behavioral assessment procedure for an individual child usually involves two or more observers, with the number depending on the amount of time required and the availability of observers. If one person is able to observe during all of the sessions, that person becomes the primary observer whose data are used. A second observer participating in some of the sessions is necessary for establishing interobserver agreement.

interobserver agreement

Because behavioral observation data may be influenced by a number of factors, notably the observers's interpretation of the behavior categories and the demands of the observation task, certain procedures are carried out to make possible the replicability of studies using human observers. One such procedure involves measuring the extent to which two or more observers agree that certain behaviors have occurred. Before the initiation of the baseline phase, the observers are trained in the behavior code and practice observing and recording the behaviors simultaneously, but independently of one another. The observers then compare their ratings to determine the amount of agreement. The most commonly used formula to compute interobserver agreement is number of agreements divided by the sum of the number of agreements and the number of disagreements, and the ratio is expressed in terms of percent agreement. Instances of agreement that a particular behavior did not occur are usually not included in the computation of interobserver agreement.

During the practice sessions, the observers compute their agreement and discuss each instance of disagreement, arriving at a mutual decision about how that behavior should be rated in the future. Training and practice sessions are continued until the observers achieve an agreement level of 80 percent to 85 percent or greater. Interobserver agreement continues to be monitored throughout the study to ensure continued agreement on the definitions of the response classes and the instances of occurrences of the response classes.

the baseline observation period

Ideally, the baseline phase should be continued until the behavior becomes stabilized. In practice, it is difficult to determine when the baseline phase should end because children's baselines rarely reach the stable levels found in the animal research literature. The greater variability in children's session-to-session behavior is no doubt due to the greater variety of environmental changes experienced by children. Thus, behavioral clinicians and researchers either decide that the baseline period will be of a particular length prior to the initiation of behavioral observations or arbitrarily terminate the baseline phase when it is apparent that the data reflect reliable high and low points. The general consensus is that a minimal baseline period should include one week (or five days in school settings) of data collection.

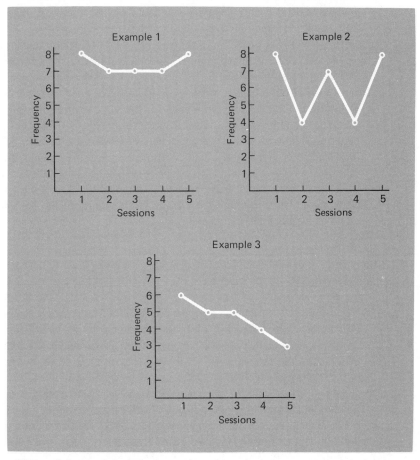

Figure 3-1 presents three examples of baseline data. In Example 1 the child engaged in an inappropriate behavior during either seven or eight intervals out of a possible eight intervals. The data reflect a high and fairly stable rate. The data in

Example 2 show more variability, such that on some days the child's rate of inappropriate behavior is very high, while on others the rate is moderate. The data in Example 3 would be considered unstable in that it shows a strong directional trend, the limits of which are more ambiguous than those in Examples 1 and 2.

reliability and validity

Only in recent years has attention been directed to the reliability (as separate from interobserver reliability or agreement) and validity of data obtained through direct behavioral observation. In one perspective, session-to-session variability in behavior may be viewed as an indication of reliability when the measuring instrument, setting condition, and observer training level are held constant. Perhaps statistical methods will eventually be used to measure this reliability and provide guidelines for determining the appropriate number of baseline sessions for individual clients. The validity of behavioral data poses greater problems because there has been no agreement about adequate validity criteria. One view is that the criterion is the data collected on a continuous time basis for the same sessions in which time sampling was utilized (for example, Powell and Rockinson, 1978). Another view is that behavioral data are samples from a behavioral domain or class of behaviors and, therefore, behavioral assessment methods should be examined for their content validity, namely, the extent to which a particular assessment procedure measures the class of behaviors it was designed to sample (Linehan, 1980). Behavioral clinicians are clearly beginning to question the assumption that behavioral assessment methods require no validity testing.

diagnosis and classification

For the behavioral clinician, diagnosis is essentially the description of the behavior problem and hypotheses with respect to the environmental stimuli that may be maintaining the behavior. The problem behavior may also be classified as an excess or a deficit, thereby specifying the use of behavior principles for decreasing or increasing the behavior, respectively (Ross, 1974). Behavioral classification systems for children's problems are still in an early stage of development, but it appears that the technique of factor analysis offers considerable potential for the ultimate development of an efficient classification system.

Conclusions

The most salient feature of the behavioral approach to assessment is its reliance on observable behavior and environmental events. This approach reflects the major assumption that behavior is largely controlled by environmental stimuli. The collection of behavioral data is subject to many of the same types of methodological problems found for the more traditional assessment techniques–namely problems of reliability and validity, and intensive research is currently being focused on these problems. Trends in the early 1980s also suggest that behavioral assessment methods will be used more frequently in the future by traditional clinicians. Similarly, behavioral clinicians are beginning to examine the possible utility of some of the more traditional assessment methods.

Recommended Readings

Gelfand, D. M., and Hartmann, D. P., *Child Behavior Analysis and Therapy*, Chapters 1, 2, 3, 7, 8 (Part 1). Elmsford, N.Y.: Pergamon Press, 1975. A comprehensive description of direct behavioral observation methods.

Jones, R. R., Reid, J. B., and Patterson, G. R., "Naturalistic Observation in Clinical Assessment," in *Advances in Psychological Assessment.* Vol. 3. Edited by P. McReynolds. San Francisco: Jossey-Bass, 1975. A review of the methodological problems associated with behavioral observation in natural environments.

Mash, E. J., and Terdal, L. G., eds., *Behavior-Therapy Assessment.* New York: Springer, 1976.

O'Leary, K. D., and Johnson, S. B., "Psychological Assessment," in *Psychopathological Disorders of Childhood,* (2nd ed.), pp. 210-246. Edited by H. C. Quay and J. S. Werry. New York: John Wiley, 1979.

Wahler, R. G., House, E. E., and Stambaugh, E. E., *Ecological Assessment of Child Problem Behavior.* Elmsford, N.Y.: Pergamon Press.

etiology: genetic, prenatal, and perinatal factors

4

This chapter describes some of the genetic, prenatal, and perinatal factors that are believed to have a causal role in the development of children's behavior disorders. Later chapters describe the roles of these and other factors in the etiology of specific behavior disorders.

genetic factors

Our understanding of the role of genetic factors has derived from a series of studies focusing on pedigree descriptions (that is, incidence of abnormalities in generations of families), culminating, more recently, in the direct visual examination of chromosomes and biochemical analyses of genetic material and enzymatic processes. Historically, Gregor Mendel is responsible for the postulation and demonstration of hereditary factors through his hybridization experiments with plants. Identification of the physical basis of inheritance, the chromosome, was the next, most salient discovery. The contemporary phase began with attempts to work out the chemical mode of gene action and the discovery of the detailed role of the enzymatic processes. Watson and Crick's (1953) description of the structure and replication of DNA initiated the science of molecularbiology and thus the possibility of understanding genetic processes at their most fundamental levels.

Until 1956, it was generally thought that the human cell had forty-eight chromosomes. Improved techniques for human tissue culture and for promoting and arresting cell division made possible Tjio and Levan's (1956) finding that the human cell has only forty-six chromosomes (twenty-two pairs of autosomes and one pair of sex chromosomes). The better visualization of the chromosomes also made it possible to observe their size and morphology (that is, form and structure) and to arrange them in a particular order. Being able to count the number of chromosomes and to examine their gross morphology has led to the discovery of a number of chromosome abnormalities.

The forty-six chromosomes contain approximately fifty thousand genes. In the last decade great progress has been made in the knowledge about chromosomes, because new methods for laboratory staining of the chromosomes (called "banding techniques") and other chromosome mapping methods have permitted parts of the chromosomes and their locations on the chromosomes to be clearly identified. A recent gene map (McKusick and Ruddle, 1977) shows that at least one gene locus has been identified for each of the twenty-two pairs of autosomes. For example, it is known that the Rh and ABO blood group types are located at particular loci on chromosomes 1 and 9, respectively. Future applications based on the mapping of chromosomes include the possibility of prenatal identification of individuals who will not manifest serious hereditary disorders until later in life; such applications will also be dependent on the study of the parents' chromosomes and knowledge regarding the relationship of genes that are located close together on the same chromosome.

chromosome abnormalities

The first clinical syndrome found to be associated with an abnormal number of chromosomes was Down syndrome or "mongolism." Lejeune, Gautier, and Turpin (1959) discovered that chromosome 21 was represented in triplicate (trisomy) instead of duplicate, thus increasing the chromosome count in each cell to forty-seven instead of forty-six. Trisomies of other autosomal chromosomes (for example, 13, 15, 17, and 18) have subsequently been described in the research literature. Many of the possible chromosomal abnormalities have been found only in unviable fetuses, suggesting that certain abnormalities in the number of chromosomes are incompatible with life.

In the normal human, sex-chromosome constitutions are XY in the male and XX in the female. Considerable research on the sex chromosomes has become possible through the relatively inexpensive sex chromatin test that identifies the number of X chromosomes. In one large-scale survey of newborn infants, 11 out of 4,400 were found to have abnormalities in the number of sex chromosomes (Leonard, Landy, Ruddle, and Lubs, 1974).

Approximately 50 percent of pregnancies end in spontaneous abortions during the first trimester. A high proportion of these aborted fetuses have chromosomal abnormalities, although the principal causes of this loss may be environmental; that is, the chromosomal abnormalities may be secondary to environmental factors (Douglas, 1975). About one out of two hundred live-born children has some type of chromosomal abnormality.

A large number of inherited metabolic disorders have been discovered, and some of them have been found to be associated with behavioral disorders. These conditions are almost always autosomal recessive or sex-linked and due to one defective gene. In general, the abnormalities may be broadly classified into errors of carbohydrate, lipid, or protein metabolism and are detected by means of urine and blood tests that evaluate amino acid levels. A number of the metabolic disorders can be treated by restricting or providing particular foods, chemicals, or drugs.

psychological studies of genetic factors

The area of behavior genetics encompasses a variety of approaches for determining the hereditary basis of behavior. Animal studies, which utilize selective breeding techniques, have yielded the most direct measures of the influence of heredity. Studies with humans, being necessarily correlational in design, have measured the contribution of heredity indirectly as a function of the genetic relationships among the persons examined.

Pedigree Analysis. One of the earliest techniques for evaluating the hereditary contributions to behavior involved the initial identification of an individual (proband) who had the behavior (or trait) and the tracing of the incidence of this trait in the proband's ancestors, siblings, and children. Galton (1869) used this method in his study of the families of eminent men. Pedigree studies have a number of methodological shortcomings, not the least of which is the confounding of hereditary and environmental influences. Galton's eminent men, whose abilities he believed were due to hereditary factors, were also raised in an intellectually stimulating environments. In addition, reliable descriptions of family members beyond a few generations are seldom possible. The chances of locating hereditary abnormalities are more likely, however, when families with more than one defective person are studied. Out of an institutionalized population of three thousand people, Wright, Tarjan, and Eyer (1959) found sixty-one families with more than one inmate, and nine of them had identifiable hereditary disorders. Investigators seeking to discover additional types of hereditary abnormalities might increase their chances by focusing their research on the remaining families.

Twin Studies. The most popular research approach in behavior genetics involves the comparison of identical twins, whose genetic endowment is identical because they result from the splitting of the same fertilized egg, and same-sex fraternal twins, whose genetic relationship is essentially the same as that of nontwin, same-sex, siblings. Specification of identical and fraternal twin status is not a simple matter; obstetricians and parents are incorrect in their designation about 10 percent to 15 percent of the time (Lykken, 1978). All of the earlier twin studies contain some error in the designation of identical and fraternal twin status. The more recent twin studies have tended to employ a series of twenty or more blood tests to discriminate the types of twins. When the results of every blood test are the same for a set of twins, they are considered identical; if the results of any one or more of these blood tests differ, the twins are considered fraternal.

The results of several dozen twin studies have suggested that heredity is the primary factor in determining the differences among people with respect to intellectual functioning, accounting for about 80 percent of the variance among the persons studied. In a longitudinal study of twins tested at intervals from three months to six years of age, identical twins were found to become increasingly concordant with age, while fraternal twins became less concordant as they became older (Wilson, 1978). Such studies have often been misunderstood to mean that intelligence is fixed or predetermined, when, in fact, they are only a description of the contribution of heredity under the environmental conditions experienced by that particular group of subjects. There is nothing inherent in the attribution of heritability that precludes a specially designed environment from increasing intellectual abilities. Theoretically, if all people lived under environmental conditions that best used their potential, then all remaining individual differences would be attributable to heredity. Scarr-Salapatek (1971) has presented data that support this idea. She found that heritability of intelligence was considerably higher for children in the upper socioeconomic groups than for children from lower socioeconomic environments.

Kallmann's family and twin studies (see, for example, 1950) contributed strong evidence that the likelihood of schizophrenia increases with the nearness of a blood relationship to a person diagnosed as schizophrenic. In the general population, the incidence of schizophrenia is less than 1 percent. Among relatives of schizophrenics, the percentage expectancy figures are: parents, 10 percent; siblings, 13 percent; fraternal twins, 12.5 percent; children, 16 percent; identical twins separated for more than five years, 78 percent; identical twins who have not been separated, 91.5 percent (Slater, 1953). Kallmann's studies of schizophrenia have been the focus of controversy for both methodological and interpretive reasons. This research has also been subjected to close scrutiny by theorists who have been strong advocates for a psychological-environmental etiology in schizophrenia.

In criticizing the twin studies, it is important to recognize that some of the deficiencies can be remediated, while others cannot. The main objection to the twin method has questioned the assumption that the environments of identical and fraternal twins are similar. In a sense, this argument is not a very strong one, since (1) the environments of twins raised together is likely to be as similar as could be found in nonexperimental situations, and (2) differences in the environments of twins reared together have a higher probability of being related to behaviors resulting from genetic differences than of being due to random environmental variations. That is, environmental differences are more likely to be dependent on the idiosyncratic behaviors of each twin than on differences in the environment per se.

Since heredity and environment are confounded beginning with conception, and perhaps prior to conception (Erickson, 1967), heritability figures should be considered rough estimates. In twin studies, all concordance is attributed to heredity, while discordance is considered to reflect the influences of environment. It is possible that not all concordance is due to the direct influence of the genetic constitution. For example, a particular complication during pregnancy could affect identical twins similarly and fraternal twins differentially, since fraternal twins are more likely to be at different embryologic stages at the time of the complication. In these instances, the prenatal factors may be of primary importance in terms of prevention. Some of the discordance found in identical twins may also be due to pre- and perinatal events that affect only one of the twins (for example, lack of oxygen during a difficult delivery).

Generalizations to the population from the data of twin studies have also been criticized on the basis that twins differ from the population. They tend to weigh less at birth and have shorter gestation periods. Older mothers are more likely to have twins than are younger ones (Penrose, 1961), and twins have a higher probability of being institutionalized.

Problems in the criteria used for diagnosis have also been mentioned in the criticisms of twin studies. That is, the criteria for diagnosis are neither consistent nor always precisely defined. Twin studies also have not always used some of the controls now deemed necessary in research. For example, some investigators have utilized observer-interviewers who were familiar with the hypotheses of the studies, possibly biasing the results in favor of the investigators.

Experimental Studies with Animals. Experimental behavior genetics utilizes the selective breeding of insects and higher animals to examine the effect of heredity on behavior. In addition, the environments in which the animals are raised are controlled. Behavioral differences among breeds of domestic animals have long been recognized. Studies by Fuller and Scott (1954) have shown some breeds of dog to be more independent than others, some to be more excitable, and others to be more easily taught.

Tryon (1940) and Heron (1941) used an experimental procedure that is considered to be a classical approach in animal behavior genetics. A group of laboratory animals is observed and measured for a particular behavior or trait. Animals that have the highest scores are interbred, and the animals with the lowest scores are interbred. The offspring of these matings are measured for the trait; again the highest scorers are selected for interbreeding, and the lowest scorers are selected for interbreeding. This procedure is continued for a number of generations. The studies of Tryon and Heron demonstrated that this method could be used to breed selectively for maze-learning ability in rats. Their maze-bright animals, however, were not necessarily superior in other learning tasks.

Inbred strains have been shown to differ in a wide variety of characteristics, such as alcohol preference, activity level, hoarding, emotionality, and social behaviors (Fuller and Thompson, 1978, chap. 9, 10, 11). Animal studies lend support to the thesis that a variety of behaviors may be governed to a significant extent by genetic constitution.

prenatal factors

A number of prenatal factors have been implicated in the etiology of behavioral disorders, but it should be stressed that much of our knowledge comes from correlational research that permits only hypotheses regarding cause-effect relationships. Although experimental studies have been conducted with animals, generalizations to humans must be made with extreme caution. For ethical reasons, experimental studies with humans are rarely done.

A primary source of correlational information has been the determination of those prenatal factors that have been associated with an increased infant mortality rate. Several researchers have suggested that the factors that cause death in some infants are also likely to cause physical damage to other infants that may be manifested in learning and behavioral problems. Such a "continuum of reproductive casualty" has been proposed by Lilienfeld, Pasamanick, and Rogers (1955).

Most of the available information in this area has been derived from retrospective studies. Children with particular physical or behavioral characteristics are identified, and their prenatal histories examined for evidence of detrimental conditions. There are a number of possible weaknesses in this approach, especially the reliance on poorly documented medical and hospital records. The errors involved in the poor recordkeeping are often those of omission, which reduces the chances of identifying a significant factor. When retrospective studies are carefully designed, however, they do add substantially to our statistical understanding of the role of prenatal factors in the etiology of developmental and behavioral problems. It should be emphasized that such knowledge does not permit the specification of etiology in the individual case. When a prenatal event known to be detrimental on a statistical basis has occurred, its causal role cannot be assured because very few complications of pregnancy, labor, and delivery uniformly affect all children. In other words, while certain pregnancy complications increase the mortality rate of the infants who experience them, most of the infants survive, and a substantial number of them will show no adverse effects.

Because of the expense and length of time involved, prospective, longitudinal studies are rare events. One substantial study, the Collaborative Perinatal Project (Hellmuth, 1967), has involved fourteen institutions of higher learning and twenty thousand children whose mothers were studied during pregnancy. The children received physical and psychological examinations at regular intervals from infancy through eight years of age. This project has already begun to provide information regarding the impact of prenatal events, and it will likely continue to generate significant findings during the coming years.

As will be seen below, the child is most vulnerable during the first trimester (three months) of gestation. During some of this period the mother is frequently not sure that she is pregnant. Many women are not even under a physician's care until near the end of the trimester. Prevention of adverse conditions during this period would, therefore, necessitate a comprehensive public education program.

nutrition

The mother's nutritional status has long been recognized as one of the most important determinants of the infant status. The condition of the child at birth depends not only on the mother's nutrition during pregnancy but also on her whole nutritional history. If the mother has been poorly nourished during her development, her physical condition during pregnancy will be less than optimal and increase the probability of adverse conditions for the child *in utero*. Even optimal nutrition during pregnancy will not counteract the deficiencies of a malfunctioning mother.

Next to genetic factors, nutritional history most strongly determines differences in height, weight, physical development, and morbidity rates. In the United States, the adolescent girl is likely to be the most poorly nourished member of the family. This problem is at least partly due to the culture's emphasis on slimness and the preponderance of easily available but relatively nonnutritious foods. Unfortunately, poor dietary habits developed in adolescence may continue into adulthood. Since approximately 25 percent of mothers having their first child are less than twenty years old, adolescent nutrition is an important factor.

Experimental studies with lower animals have shown that nutritional deficiencies are capable of producing serious disturbances in the growth and development of the embryo and fetus. Experimental research involving the deprivation of particular nutritional substances prior to conception and during pregnancy has demonstrated an increased rate of fetal death and congenital abnormalities (absence of eyes, small eyes, harelip, cleft palate, underdevelopment of lungs and kidneys). The timing of the nutritional deficiency during pregnancy is also important in determining whether or not a specific congenital defect will result. Genetic factors are also involved, however, because these studies show that different strains of the same species will respond differently given the same nutritional deficiency.

One of the earliest studies with humans to demonstrate the substantive effect of maternal diet on the health of the infant was that of Ebbs, Tisdall, and Scott (1942). These investigators studied a group of women all of whom were originally poorly nourished. Nearly half of the original group was given a diet that increased their intake of protein, calcium, iron, and calories to a desirable level. The women on the supplemented diet and their infants did better on all criteria than the subjects who remained on their usual diet. The poor diet was significantly associated with poor prenatal status, prolonged labor and convalescence, and a three- to four-fold greater incidence in illness of the infants during the first six months of life. Nearly 12 percent of the poor-diet infants were lost through miscarriage, stillbirth, or later death, while all of the supplemented-diet infants survived. Studies of women living under wartime conditions with very strict rationing of food have shown that about half of them stopped having menstrual periods, and the other half experienced irregular menstrual periods. For the women who did conceive, the rate of premature births, stillbirths, and congenital malformations of the infants was increased considerably (Smith, 1947). While such studies are subject to the confounding influence of nutritional deficiency and other wartime conditions, these confounded variables continued to exert detrimental influences in the form of lowered birth weights and higher frequencies of malformations during the immediate postwar years (Montagu, 1962, p. 85).

Since dietary history has a considerable influence on development and physical size, it is interesting to note that taller mothers have lower rates of Caesarean births, forceps deliveries, and fetal mortality than do shorter women. Bernard (1952) found that one-third of women under five feet tall had a flattened pelvic brim, which is known to increase the chances of difficult labor. Thomson (1960), corroborating these results, found that difficult labor, Caesarean sections, and deaths attributable to perinatal trauma became increasingly more frequent as the mother's stature decreased.

Maternal nutrition has also been found to influence the intelligence of children. Harrell, Woodyard, and Gates (1955) conducted a study that examined the influence of vitamin supplementation of pregnant and lactating women's diet on the intelligence of their children. The study involved 2,400 women from Kentucky and Virginia. Four kinds of vitamin supplements and a placebo that contained no supplements were administered in such a way that no participant knew the contents of the tablets. When tested at four years of age, the children of the Virginia mothers who were given the supplements surpassed the placebo group by an average of 5.2 Stanford-Binet IQ points. The average for the B-complex groups exceeded that of the placebo group by 8.1 points. There were no significant differences among the Kentucky groups, a finding that was attributed to the Kentucky groups' regularly good diet.

Nutrition continues to be an important factor in determining physical and behavioral status throughout postnatal life. Severe nutritional deficiencies during infancy and later preschool years have been associated with detrimental alterations in brain development, which in turn retard physical growth and behavioral development (Winick, 1976, 1979).

maternal age and parity

Difficulties during pregnancy and birth, as well as the frequency of developmental abnormalities, have been shown to be highly correlated with the age of the mother. The available evidence indicates ages twenty-three to twenty-eight years as being optimal for pregnancy, since this age span is associated with the highest survival rates for mother and child and the lowest abortion, miscarriage, stillbirth, prematurity, and malformation rates. The higher incidence of problems at younger ages has been attributed in part to the immaturity of the reproductive system (American Academy of Pediatrics, 1979); the pelvic organs are not fully developed until at least ten years after the beginning of menstruation. In the Uniteds States it has been estimated that one-third of all girls between fifteen and twenty years of age have at least one unwanted pregnancy. A decreasing number of unwed teenage mothers are choosing to give up their babies for adoption primarily because of the lessened social taboo against unwed mothers. Young mothers have a high probability of being undereducated and tend to remain economically dependent on family or government resources.

After the age of twenty-eight years, a gradual increase in the rate of problems associated with pregnancy begins, and this rate accelerates after the age of 35 when the reproductive system begins to lose efficiency. Evidence for the loss of efficiency is apparent in the increased rate of two-egg twins (due to the release of two ova instead of the usual one) in the older mother. Statistically higher rates of mental retardation and other behavior disorders have also been found to be correlated with the increased age of the mother.

Parity refers to the number of previous pregnancies that a mother has had. Most studies dealing with parity have not separated the effects of the confounded variable, maternal age; i.e., in the individual case, the mother's age increases with each subsequent child. In general, first-born children and those born at the end of a series of pregnancies are less viable than those born in between; this finding holds regardless of maternal age. Birth weight is clearly related to parity in that the average birth weight increases with each subsequent child. It is believed that if a mother has children closely spaced, then both her and her child's health will suffer. Stillbirth rates, however, are highest for both the shortest and longest intervals between births. Once birth has been accomplished successfully, birth interval appears to have no relationship to longevity or growth.

viral and bacterial infections of the mother

At one time it was believed that the mother's diseases could not affect the fetus. As the number of investigations has increased, evidence has accumulated that both viruses and bacteria can be transmitted from mother to child. A number of these infections are capable of seriously affecting the development of the fetus. We have also learned that when the mother is immunized during pregnancy the fetus will receive maternal antibodies and will be immune for several months after birth.

Until about twenty-five years ago, the idea that viruses could affect the embryo or fetus was strongly resisted. This position was understandable in view of the fact that most of the common viral diseases, such as mumps, measles, and chicken pox, usually occur in childhood giving the potential mother immunity that lasts through the childbearing years. Relatively few pregnant women would then develop these diseases, thus hindering adequate statistical analyses of these effects on the fetus. One exception is rubella (German measles), which is likely to occur in young adulthood. A relatively mild communicable disease, rubella can be very damaging to the fetus during the first trimester of pregnancy. Gregg (1941) reported the occurrence of congenital cataracts in thirteen children whose mothers had had rubella. Since the publication of this paper, there have been numerous confirmations of a relationship between rubella and developmental abnormalities. The rubella virus is now considered to be capable of causing more than a dozen kinds of pathological eye conditions, deafness, dental defects, cleft palate, cardiac defects, mental retardation, and microcephaly.

The effects of viral diseases on the fetus have usually been discovered retrospectively. That is, the condition of the child is noted first, and the history of the mother during pregnancy obtained later. This method is likely to lead to an overestimate of the risk, since normal children of mothers having had the infection during pregnancy are not taken into consideration. Prospective studies begin with the identification of mothers experiencing an infection and then assess the effect of the infection on the child. Several prospective studies have indicated that the risk of a major defect is 50 percent if the mother is infected with rubella in the first month of pregnancy, 25 percent in the second month of pregnancy, 17 percent in the third month, 11 percent in the fourth, 6 percent in the fifth, and essentially no risk in later months. Bell (1959) in a study of 712 women who had rubella during the first half of pregnancy found that 62 percent of the children were deaf, 50 percent had congenital heart disease, and 35 percent had cataracts. Milder forms of defects also occur, but they are frequently not detected in the first few years of life.

Since the risk of defects is so high, most physicians advise terminating the pregnancy if the mother has rubella during the first four months of pregnancy. Prevention has been greatly emphasized by advising parents to immunize their children to rubella. Pregnant women should take special precautions to avoid being exposed, since it is possible for the fetus to be affected by the virus without the mother's showing any clinical symptoms. The live virus vaccine for rubella should not be given to pregnant women. Gamma globulin is considered to be effective in preventing the disease if it is administered within eight days of exposure to rubella.

A number of other formerly common childhood diseases, such as measles and mumps, can lead to spontaneous abortions and possibly congenital defects. The live vaccines for these diseases also cannot be given to pregnant women because they may harm the fetus. Prevention of these problems would be largely accomplished if all parents were careful about getting their children immunized early in life and maintaining the recommended immunization schedule.

Until fairly recently, influenza was associated only with a high rate of abortion. Coffey and Jessop (1959), taking advantage of a predicted flu epidemic in

Ireland, studied women for whom influenza virus A was isolated during pregnancy and a group of pregnant women who had not had flu, both groups being matched for age, parity, and blood groups. They found that 3.6 percent of the babies born to the flu mothers had malformations, while malformed infants accounted for only 1.5 percent of the children of the mothers who had not had influenza. The risk for malformation was highest for the first trimester of pregnancy. While the risk of defect is considerably lower than that for mothers with rubella, the numbers of children involved may be considerably greater because flu epidemics are fairly frequent and affect large numbers of people.

As a group, bacterial infections of the pregnant woman have not been associated with congenital deformities of the child, but many of these infections are transmitted to the child from the mother. In the case of tuberculosis, for example, the mother may not know that she has the disease and gives birth to a child with congenital tuberculosis who will very likely die without treatment. Treatment of tuberculosis became quite effective following the introduction of antibiotics.

Syphilis, a bacterial disease transmitted by sexual intercourse, can also be transmitted from the mother to the child. Congenital syphilis is not as common as it once was because infected mothers can be successfully treated with penicillin. If the mothers are untreated, up to 80 percent of fetuses will contract the disease, but when treatment is begun before the fifth month of pregnancy, the rate will be less than 2 percent. Congenital syphilis has been associated with fetal abortion, death, and extensive damage to many organs.

Toxoplasmosis is a protozoan disease that is essentially symptomless in the adult but has serious consequences for the child *in utero*. Congenital toxoplasmosis is related to hydrocephalus (large head associated with an excessive amount of fluid in the cranium), serious damage to the eye, convulsions, and calcification (hardening) of small areas of the brain. Hydrocephalus occurs in about 80 percent of the cases. Mental retardation is almost always present, varying from mild to profound. Many of the infants die soon after birth. Since toxoplasmosis is a relatively common disease, it is advisable for all women to be given a skin test prior to pregnancy and for those with negative reactions to be reexamined at intervals during pregnancy. Prevention programs include avoiding cats (who may transmit the disease through their stools) and eating only well-cooked meat.

maternal dysfunction

In this section we deal with those physical conditions of the mother, other than infections, that bear on the subsequent status of the child.

Obesity is associated with an increased mortality rate for both mother and child. In a group of women weighing more than 200 pounds, Matthews and der Brucke (1938) found that 75 percent developed one or more complications and that 12 percent of the infants died. For overweight women, the fertility rate is half that of women whose weight is normal. Obese women also have high risks for a variety of other physical problems. Because of these relationships, physicians have exerted considerable pressure on pregnant women to gain only moderate amounts of weight. There have been recent suggestions that physicians have been too conservative in their standards for weight gain, and that some mothers and infants have thereby been subjected to possible nutritional deficiencies. Obstetricians are currently advising the average pregnant woman that a weight gain of 25 pounds is optimal.

In some cases, weight gain per se may not be a cause of complications during pregnancy. That is, unusual patterns of weight gain during pregnancy may be the result of a metabolic disturbance that is also causing the complications (Erickson, 1971).

The toxemias of pregnancy, preeclampsia and eclampsia, whose causes are unknown, affect about 5 percent of pregnant women. The symptoms of preeclampsia include excessive weight gain because of fluid retention in the tissues, a rise in blood pressure, and the detection of albumin in the urine. Eclampsia includes the foregoing symptoms with the addition of maternal convulsions. Toxemia is the principal cause of maternal death, although the majority of cases can now be prevented. There is some evidence that the brain of the toxemic woman's child can be adversely affected.

Pregnant women who have high blood pressure, or hypertension, also have a high rate of fetal and maternal mortality, especially in those cases where the mother was also hypertensive in her nonpregnant condition. Hypertension often alters the development of the placenta such that a condition of oxygen deficiency occurs, which results in a slower growth rate of the fetus.

Sickle cell anemia is a genetically determined blood disorder primarily affecting black people. This condition, when present in the pregnant women, increases the rate of abortions, stillbirths, and abnormalities; there is also a tendency for the children to have a low birth weight. Those that survive will either be carriers of the trait or manifest the condition themselves.

Diabetes is characterized by deficiency in the supply of insulin which controls the metabolism of carbohydrates. The principle symptoms are excessive urination, sugar in the urine, high blood sugar, excessive thirst and hunger, weakness, and loss of weight. Diabetes is largely controllable by treatment with insulin. Diabetes during pregnancy may create significant risks for both mother and child. Probably because of the hyperactivity of its pancreas, the fetus grows at a greater than usual rate, reaching the weight of an average newborn several weeks before the end of gestation. If permitted to go to term, many will be damaged during the birth process. Early diagnosis and treatment have greatly improved the originally poor prognosis. Dietary treatment and early delivery of the child can save the lives of virtually all infants of diabetic mothers. Special precautions after birth must be maintained. Even though quite large, the newborn of the diabetic mother is very much like a premature infant and must be handled as such in the hospital after delivery.

Maternal hormonal disorders may have both transient and permanent effects on the child. Hyperthyroidism in the mother is related to an unusually high abortion and stillbirth rate. Some infants will manifest a hypothyroidism, which usually subsides within a few weeks after birth. There are several types of hypothyroidism that are related to cretinism in the child which, if untreated, result in mental retardation.

Blood group incompatibilities present still another problem to the developing child, the most well known of which is the Rh factor. Second- and subsequent-born children of an Rh negative mother and an Rh positive father have an increased risk of dying *in utero* or soon after birth from a blood disorder called *erythroblastosis*. The baby suffers from anemia caused by the destruction of the blood cells by maternal Rh antibodies that are stimulated by fetal antigens passing through the placenta into the mother's blood. Infants born with this condition have a high probability of being brain damaged by a substance called *bilirubin*.

Infants who present high bilirubin levels are given exchange transfusions. Rh negative blood is used in the exchange transfusion because the mother's antibodies would continue to destroy Rh positive blood. The baby's damaged blood is removed at the same time it is given the transfusion of intact red blood cells. Prevention of this problem is now possible by the administration of a vaccine, Rh immune globulin, within seventy-two hours after the mother's first birth, abortion, or miscarriage.

medications and addictive substances

The thalidomide tragedy during the 1960s increased our awareness of the effects of medication on the developing fetus. Thalidomide was prescribed as a mild tranquilizer in Europe, primarily in Germany. When taken early in pregnancy, it caused the absence or shortening of the infant's limbs. Thousands of physically handicapped children were born before thalidomide was identified as the cause and taken off the market.

Medication and drugs are being manufactured and consumed in great quantities. For example, many of the foods we eat contain additives and preservatives. Although there are laws that govern the testing of drugs and other substances consumed by humans, much of this testing research has not been adequate. While it is true that medications that are to be administered to adults must be tested on adults, these drugs may not be tested for their effects on the unborn child. There is ample evidence that the adult's reaction to a particular drug in no way adequately predicts its effect on the fetus. Drugs taken by a pregnant mother may affect the fetus, but this effect depends on the particular drug, the period of pregnancy, the amount taken, and the genetic constitutions of mother and child.

The adverse effects may not become apparent for a number of years after the pregnant woman has been given the medication. In the early 1970s, it was discovered that the synthetic estrogen DES, used for threatened miscarriage during the 1950s and 1960s, increased the rate of vaginal cancer beginning in the early adulthood of the female offspring. This group of women may also have a higher risk of spontaneous abortions and lowered fertility rates, which are probably due to uterine structural abnormalities (Berger and Goldstein, 1980).

Studies with animals have also shown that mammals do not develop the biochemical mechanisms needed to inactivate many drugs prior to the first week of life (Jondorf, Maickel, and Brodie, 1958). These biochemical mechanisms are the enzyme systems in the liver; apparently, the uterine environment is not conducive to the formation of liver enzymes in the mammalian fetus.

There are a number of case studies in the medical literature linking the ingestion of particular medications to fetal abnormalities. Because most medications have not yet been evaluated with respect to their risk of causing developmental abnormalities, physicians are being extremely cautious in their prescribing of medication to pregnant women and are advising them against taking any drugs, even aspirin, without consultation. The role of the father in birth defects has largely been ignored, but evidence is beginning to show that a variety of substances ingested by the male affect his reproductive system and thus contribute to birth defects in the child.

Although much of the recent attention has been given to the relationship between drugs ingested during pregnancy (particularly the first trimester) and *physical* defects in the child, concern is developing about possible relationships between drugs and *behavioral* defects in the child, such as lower intelligence, shorter attention span, or higher activity levels. Animal studies (for example, Vorhees, Brunner, and Butcher, 1979; Kellogg, Tervo, Ison, Parisi, and Miller, 1980) have found that drugs given to pregnant females can affect the subsequent behavior of their offspring.

It has become common practice to administer drugs and anesthesia during delivery. Used primarily for the comfort of the mother and the convenience of the physician, drugs given during labor and delivery do present hazards to the infant. The fetus and newborn infant can survive for considerably long periods under conditions of oxygen deprivation in comparison to the adult, but the administration of drugs and certain complications of delivery can reduce the oxygen available to the infant to levels low enough to cause brain damage and death. Obstetrical medication has been found to have long-term behavioral effects on the infant and child (Bowes, Brackbill, Conway, and Steinschneider, 1970). These effects included slower motor, cognitive, and language development. Most anesthetics, analgesics, and sedatives produce depressed physiological functioning of the mother and, as a result, may alter the oxygen supply to the fetus. Fetal anoxia is capable of damaging all organs and tissues of the body. Premature infants are especially vulnerable to the adverse effects of anesthetics.

A woman who is addicted to narcotics during pregnancy will produce a child who is physiologically a drug addict. The baby appears normal at birth but within a day or two begins to show marked agitation, sleeplessness, tremors, convulsions, breathing difficulties, and feeding problems. The severity of the symptoms is directly related to the drug dosage taken by the mother. If the mother is deprived of drugs during pregnancy, the fetus manifests the withdrawal symptoms by excessive kicking. It is current practice now not to have the mother go through withdrawal therapy during pregnancy because of the risk of harming the baby *in utero*. Narcotics-addicted pregnant women have a high rate of complications, and their infants have high mortality and prematurity rates. The infant's drug addiction is relatively easy to cure. The mother who is a drug addict can also transmit narcotics to her infant through her breast milk.

Evidence has been accumulating that lysergic acid diethylamide (LSD) taken by the mother during pregnancy may be a hazard to the child. For example, Cohen, Hirshhorn, Verbo, Frosch, and Groeschel (1968) reported that the children of LSD users had a high rate of chromosome breakage. More recent analyses (Dishotsky, Loughman, Mogar, and Lipscomb, 1971) of the relationship between LSD and genetic damage, however, have suggested that chromosome breakage is significantly increased only in cases in which both illicit (in contrast to pure or laboratory controlled) LSD and other drugs have been ingested. In a study of 148 pregnancies in which one or both parents were LSD users, Jacobson and Berlin (1972) found a high abortion rate. Of the children born alive, nearly 10 percent had major congenital defects; the normal incidence of such defects is below 1 percent. Again, a definitive relationship between LSD and reproductive risk could not be established in this study because many of the women had infectious diseases and probably nutritional deficiencies during pregnancy that may have contributed to the increased rates.

A link between marijuana use and birth defects has not yet been established. A recent animal study (Dalterio and Bartke, 1979) has indicated, however, that the male offspring of mothers given cannabinoids orally during late pregnancy and early lactation later exhibited inferior copulating behavior.

Virtually all gases can pass through the placenta to the fetus. Carbon monixide poisoning, less than fatal to the mother, can cause multiple congenital abnormalities in the fetus as well as brain damage. In addition, excessive amounts of oxygen administered to premature infants have been found to be related to subsequent blindness in the infant.

Until recently, the intake of alcoholic beverages was not believed to have direct deleterious effects on the fetus. The higher mortality rate for the children of alcoholic women had been attributed to their poorer nutritional status. A study by Jones, Smith, Ulleland, and Streissguth (1973), however, has described a pattern of physical defects and behavioral problems found in children of chronic alcoholic mothers. This pattern, called "fetal alcohol syndrome," includes physical growth deficiency, abnormal development of the heart, defects of the joints, and facial abnormalities, especially the eyes. The children of chronically alcoholic women have a high death rate during infancy, and close to half of the survivors may be retarded, even if they are raised in good foster homes. Moderate amounts of alcohol ingestion may result in an increased risk of the infants showing one or more of the fetal alcohol syndrome characteristics. Animal research suggests that the skeletal abnormalities are due, at least in part, to a direct action of ethanol which causes a reduction in the number of cells (Brown, Goulding, and Fabro, 1979).

The effects of maternal tobacco smoking on the fetus have also been examined. As early as 1935, Sontag and Wallace showed that smoking one cigarette resulted in heart rate changes of fetuses in the last few months of gestation. Usually the pregnant mother's smoking caused a transient fetal heart rate increase, while occasionally the smoking was followed by a fetal heart rate decrease. There is no evidence that heart rate changes of the magnitude reported by Sontag are in any way detrimental to the child.

Smoking mothers give birth to children who weigh less than the children of nonsmoking mothers. Experimental studies with animals have also shown that the offspring of rats and rabbits exposed to tobacco smoke during pregnancy weigh less at birth than do the offspring of control subjects. Simpson (1957) found that human smokers have twice as many premature babies when compared with nonsmokers. Furthermore, prematurity rates rise as a direct function of the number of cigarettes smoked per day (Butler, Goldstein, and Ross, 1972). Frazier, Davis, Goldstein, and Goldberg (1961) hypothesized three possible mechanisms that could account for the lower birth weights: (1) tendency to smoke and prematurity may both be influenced by some unknown third variable; (2) smoking may decrease the appetite and thus reduce the weight of both mother and baby; and (3) smoking may cause constriction of placental blood vessels, resulting in a decreased blood supply to the baby.

psychological factors

There have been considerable folklore and speculation about the impact of maternal emotions on the developing fetus. For some time, scientists rejected the possibility of the mother communicating her feelings to the child. It was also during this period that physicians believed in the existence of a placental barrier that prevented all detrimental substances from reaching the blood supply of the infant.

Thompson (1957) reported experimental research with rats that examined the impact of emotional trauma during pregnancy on the emotional characteristics of the offspring. The stress procedure involved exposing pregnant rats three times a day to a buzzer sound that had previously been associated with shock in an avoidance situation, but avoidance was now prevented. The results indicated that there were striking differences between the offspring of the mothers who were under stress during pregnancy and the offspring of mothers not under stress (control group). The control group was found to be more active in an open field test and left their cages more quickly to secure food at thirty to forty days of age. Several measures of emotionality still discriminated between the two groups at 130 to 140 days of age.

More recent animal studies have suggested that prenatal stress may produce a variety of more long-lasting effects. Herrenkohl (1979) found that female rats whose mothers were under stress during pregnancy subsequently experienced more spontaneous abortions, longer pregnancies, and fewer live-born young than rats not under stress; the offspring weighed less and were less likely to survive the neonatal period. It was hypothesized that prenatal stress influences the balance of hormones in the fetus and thereby produces reproductive dysfunction in adulthood.

At the human level, pregnant women's attitudes and feelings have been found to be correlated with the later incidence of complications of pregnancy, labor, and delivery in the prospective studies. Davids (1961) noted that anxiety was higher for a group of women who later gave birth to children with developmental problems than for a control group. Erickson (1965), in a study of middle-class patients, found that multigravidae (women having their second or subsequent children) who later experienced one or more complications expressed more fears for self and baby, irritability, and depression than did multigravidae who were to have no complications. The psychological variables did not discriminate between primigravidae (women having their first child) who were to have complications and those who were to have no complications. Erickson has postulated that anxiety symptoms may be determined by many causes. Although investigators have tended to emphasize anxiety as the result of psychological conflict, the possibility exists that anxiety may be an early indicator of biological stress in the organism.

The psychological aspects of human pregnancy are complex and not yet well understood. A pregnancy that has been planned has a different impact from one that has not been planned. An unplanned pregnancy can create considerable stress in a family that depends on the mother's continued employment, as it can for a woman in graduate school who is preparing for a career. Physicians and psychologists have tended to attribute all emotional changes and most symptoms associated with pregnancy to psychological factors, particularly unconscious rejection of the pregnancy. Not enough research effort has been expended on the reality aspects of pregnancy or the psychological aspects of hormonal changes that accompany pregnancy. Research has shown that psychological variables, such as anxiety and depression, are correlated closely with the hormonal changes that take place during the menstrual cycle. The psychological impact of the hormonal changes during pregnancy is very likely to be of equal importance, although little is currently known about these relationships.

Research findings on the psychological aspects of pregnancy have frequently been misinterpreted through incomplete analysis of the possible reasons for correlational relationships. For example, in one study the authors found a positive correlation between rejection of the pregnancy and nausea during the early prenatal period and interpreted the results as indicating that the rejection of the pregnancy was responsible for the nausea. Among the possible alternative explanations, a plausible one is that three months of nausea could create bad feelings toward the pregnant state. Another investigator could find no relationship between nausea and rejection of pregnancy but did find one between nausea and disturbed sexual functioning, both of which were interpreted as being due to unconscous rejection of the pregnancy. Again, an alternative hypothesis is that nausea itself could cause a disruption of sexual activity.

perinatal factors

The dividing line between prenatal and perinatal factors in the etiology of child-hood disorders is difficult to specify, since the child's condition at birth is a product of the total intrauterine period. The perinatal factors to be discussed in this section will thus be a combination of those variables that seem to be relevant during labor and delivery and other variables that begin to be relevant earlier in pregnancy but which manifest themselves primarily during and immediately after the birth process.

anoxia

Oxygen lack is most likely to occur immediately before, during, and immediately after the child is born. It is estimated that difficulty in the initiation and mainte-nance of respiration occurs in 5 percent to 10 percent of newborn infants. Anoxia can occur if the placenta detaches too soon (placenta previa), if the umbilical cord becomes knotted, or if the cord gets wrapped tightly around the baby's neck, as sometimes happens during the course of delivery.

Even though anoxia has received considerable research attention, its effects are not clearly understood. The primary reason for our inability to interpret the find-ings is the confounding of anoxia with other complications of pregnancy. Indeed, the possibility exists that some other physical malfunction prevents the infant from withstanding the effects of anoxia. Many of the early studies used different criteria for the definition of anoxia and did not use control groups. One of the best studies with human subjects found that anoxia at birth was associated with mild impairments of intelligence, neurological status, and personality functioning. Graham, Ernhart, Thurston, and Craft (1962) and Thurston, Graham, Ernhart, Eichman, and Craft (1960) in this research did not include in their anoxic group those children who had experienced other complications, and all examinations were conducted without the examiner's knowledge of the child's birth status.

No discussion of the effects of anoxia is complete without a reference to Win-dle's (1958) classic studies on monkeys. He deprived full-term infant monkeys of oxygen for specific periods of time after he had delivered them by Caesarean sec-tion. He found that anoxia at birth resulted in impaired motor functioning; longer periods of oxygen deprivation were associated with more profound motor prob-lems. In humans, anoxia is frequently a correlate of both very rapid labors (less than one or two hours) and very long labors (more than twenty-four hours).

Although the fetus and newborn infant are quite resistant to the adverse effects of oxygen deprivation, the brain is the first organ to be affected when the minimum oxygen needs are not met. The brain requires more oxygen and has a more active metabolism than any other organ of the body. Within the central nervous system, the different parts vary in their vulnerability to oxygen deprivation, with the higher levels, such as the cortex and cerebellum, being least resistant, and the spinal cord and sympathetic ganglia being most resistant to anoxia.

prematurity and postmaturity

An infant is designated as premature when its birth weight is five-and-a-half pounds (2,500 grams) or less. The average birth weight in the United States is about seven-and-a-half-pounds. About 5 percent to 10 percent of births are premature, and the neonatal mortality rate for the premature infant is eleven times that of the mature infant. Prematurity occurs more often under conditions of poor nutrition and inadequate medical care and is correlated with many of the complications of pregnancy, such as hypertension and toxemia. Prematurity is so confounded with other variables that there is no agreement among researchers on the effects of prematurity *per se* on the infant. A premature birth in a healthy woman without other complications is relatively infrequent.

Without the technology of modern medicine many more premature infants would succumb. Most infants weighing over three pounds at birth can now be expected to survive, as can many whose birth weight is less than three pounds. Wiener (1962) has concluded that infants weighing between three pounds and five-and-a-half pounds may have only a slightly increased risk for mental retardation, neurological deficits, or behavior problems. The premature infant whose gestational age is less than full term has a decreased risk for later problems in comparison to the infant who is born underweight at term, a condition suggesting chronic problems *in utero*. Drillien (1961) has reported on a longitudinal study of infants of very low birth weight (three pounds or less); at school age, one-half of her group could not attend regular schools because of physical or mental handicaps, or both. One-fourth of the group was enrolled in special education classes, and only the remaining one-fourth fell within the low average or better range of intellectual functioning. Highly improved technology and a greater concern for the quality of the child's life have no doubt increased the number of premature infants who subsequently show normal development.

There is some possibility that the hospital procedures designed to ensure the life of the child may be otherwise detrimental to later optimal functioning. Immediately after birth the premature infant is placed in an isolette crib in which oxygen supply and temperature are carefully controlled. The child is handled slightly and is often fed in the isolette and remains there until a sufficient amount of weight has been gained. In the isolette, sensory stimulation is quite different from that received when *in utero* or in the natural environment after birth. The basic question is whether the alterations of sensory stimulation during the hospital stay have any adverse effects on the premature infant. Several studies (for example, Neal, 1970) have increased the amount of tactile, vestibular, or visual stimulation provided to the premature infants in the hospital and have found increases in the rate of weight gain and better performance on tests of developmental status.

Postmaturity is the term used when infants are born several weeks or more beyond the expected date of delivery. As is the case with prematurity, designation of postmaturity on the basis of gestional age may involve considerable error. The expected date of delivery is usually based on the date of the last menstrual period, but menstrual periods in some women may continue for one or several months after conception. Other women do not keep records of their menstrual periods and cannot accurately remember the dates. Usually, when obstetricians have to make decisions regarding the date for induction of labor or Caesarean section, they use additional criteria for determining the age of the fetus, such as the date the mother first felt the fetus move (quickening). About 12 percent of births occur two or more weeks after the due date, while 4 percent are delayed by as much as three weeks after the due date, while 4 percent are delayed by as much as three weeks. The mortality rate of the postmature baby is about three times that of the term infant. The average postmature infant weighs a little more than the term baby, but a number of postwar babies weigh less, suggesting a bimodal distribution within this group. The small infants do less well than the heavy ones, presumably because the former have experienced placental dysfunction over a period of time. Most of the deaths of postmature infants occur during labor, being secondary to anoxia and cerebral hemorrhage.

birth injury

During the birth process the fetus must be moved through the pelvic opening and vaginal canal. The strong muscular contractions that occur during labor serve to effect this movement. Usually the mother's pelvic opening is of adequate size such that, given that the baby's head position is right, the delivery proceeds smoothly. Babies are usually born head first with face downward and tilted slightly to the left or right. The head is pliable and usually undergoes some change in shape (molding) in the process of delivery, but it readily assumes its normal shape within a day or two after birth. Normally, the placenta remains attached during the passage of the baby through the canal.

There are several situations that may cause a difficult delivery and thus increase the risk to the child. Sometimes the infant presents itself feet first or in some other position; such deliveries are much more difficult mechanically, and the risk of anoxia or injury is increased (Prechtl, 1961). If aware of the abnormal position of the baby early enough, the physician may try to change the baby's position manually. Once a significant portion of the baby has descended into the birth canal, such manipulations are not possible. If the physician is concerned about the baby's status, forceps (high, mid, or low) may be used to deliver the head more quickly. Mid and high forceps are used with caution because of the damage they might do to the head. The use of low forceps ranges widely; some hospitals report physicians using them for the majority of deliveries, while others report their use only infrequently.

Generally, obstetrical procedures are designed to prevent death and injury to mother and child. There are instances in which some obstetrical procedures are used solely for convenience, however, and it is imperative that research be done to determine whether or not subtle injuries are the by-products of such elective procedures.

For example, induction of labor through the use of pitocin has been used to correct an irregular labor when all indications suggest that the child and mother are physiologically ready for delivery. Pitocin has sometimes been used for convenience, however, and in certain of those cases may have resulted in a premature child or a child whose head is pushed against an unready cervix. Normally, the cervix gradually dilates as the birth contractions get stronger and more frequent. Pitocin, unless used very carefully, can create very strong contractions before the cervix is adequately dilated. Rupture of the membranes holding the amniotic fluid is also occasionally performed to hasten the delivery process, but the child has a high risk for infection if delivery is not completed within twenty-four hours after the membranes have been ruptured.

About 2 percent of children are delivered by Caesarean section. This procedure involves making an incision through the abdominal wall and uterus. Most sections are done because of pregnancy complications, such as an inadequate pelvic outlet, toxemia, or maternal bleeding. Although the operation is quite safe for the mother, the subsequent effects on the child are not known, primarily because of the difficulty in separating the effects of the Caesarean section from the complications that caused the section to be performed.

Conclusions

It is generally accepted that genetic factors and a wide range of physical factors occurring during the prenatal and perinatal periods greatly influence the risk of developing behavioral disorders during childhood. Our knowledge with respect to these factors is far from complete. For many children with severe behavior disorders, the etiology is unknown, suggesting that important factors remain to be discovered. Limitations in our knowledge of etiological factors are also created by the fact that most of the data on humans is based on correlational studies and that most of the known physical factors do not affect children's behavior in a uniform manner. It is highly probable that the risk of behavior disorders is governed by a combination of genetic factors, physical factors, and the timing (stage of prenatal or postnatal development) of the physical factors.

Recommended Readings

Annis, L. F., *The Child Before Birth*. Ithaca, N.Y.: Cornell University Press, 1978. A description of genetic and prenatal factors.

Environment, Heredity, and Intelligence. Cambridge, Mass.: Harvard Educational Review, 1969. A collection of papers discussing the roles of heredity and environment in the determination of intelligence.

Persaud, T. V. N., ed., *Teratogenic Mechanisms: Advances in the Study of Birth Defects*. Vol. 1. Baltimore, Md.: University Park Press, 1979.

etiology, demographic, postnatal physical, and social– psychological factors

5

This chapter continues the review of factors associated with the etiology of children's behavior problems. It should be recognized that many prenatal and postnatal factors may be interactive; that is, the effect of a post-natal event may be governed to a significant extent by the child's genetic constitution and prenatal events. Demographic variables are not, strictly speaking, causal factors but rather are useful ways of subdividing the population, They have, however, facilitated the investigation of etiological factors. Certain demographic factors, such as the sex of the child, are involved in the child's development beginning at conception and should, therefore, be recognized as factors that span the entire period of life. Physical factors, such as infectious disease and head injury, continue to exert their influence by increasing the probability of children's behavior disorders. Among the social-psychological factors, the greatest attention has been given to parents as causes of their children's behavior problems.

sex

The human male is more biologically vulnerable in general than the female, beginning at conception and continuing through old age. It is generally believed that at least 120 males are conceived for every 100 females (McMillan, 1979). At the time of birth, the ratio has decreased to 106 males for each 100 females. Reproductive wastage in the form of abortions and miscarriages affects males more often than females. Since such a large percentage of spontaneously aborted fetuses show chromosomal abnormalities, and since a large number of chromosomal abnormalities involve the sex chromosomes, it is possible to hypothesize that the male is more vulnerable on a genetic basis. This explanation is more plausible when it is remembered that males express recessive genes that are on the sex chromosomes because there is no opportunity for a counteracting gene on the other sex chromosome. The male dies more often during the neonatal period and through childhood until the sex ratio of live persons approaches 100 males to 100 females during adolescence. Males continue to succumb to a variety of illnesses more often than females throughout the life span, resulting in proportionally fewer males during middle and old age.

Anthony (1970) has summarized the sex differences in relation to childhood behavior disorders as follows:

> Up until puberty, it is extremely difficult to find a pathological condition in which the incidence among girls is greater than among boys, and some authors have spoken of the "handicap" of being male. The developmental rates are markedly different, judging from bone age, dental age, and the development of the reproductive system. At the age of 6, girls are already a developmental year ahead, and this becomes 18 months by age 9. . . . During the first grade, the boy is referred eleven times as often as a girl for social and emotional immaturity, a syndrome characterized by a high rate of absenteeism, fatigability, inability to attend and concentrate, shyness, poor motivation for work, underweight, inability to follow directions, slow learning, infantile speech patterns, and problems in the visual-motor and visual-perception areas. As a school child, he is referred to the school clinic for stuttering (four to one), reading difficulty (five to one), speech, hearing and eye problems (four to one), and eventually to the psychiatric clinic for personality disorders (2.6 to 1), behavior problems (4.4 to 1), school failure (2.6 to 1), and delinquency (4.5 to 1). (pp. 722-723)

Although many studies of children report sex differences in a variety of characteristics, very few of these characteristics demonstrate consistent sex differences (Maccoby and Jacklin, 1974). During childhood, consistent findings include girls showing greater verbal ability than boys and boys showing more aggression than girls. It is becoming apparent that many, if not most, of the behaviors considered to be typically masculine or feminine are learned rather than primarily biologically determined. Even sex differences that occur early in infancy may be confounded with environmental variables. Research data (Korner, 1974) suggest that mothers may interact with their male and female infants in different ways: for example, boys are more likely to receive proximal (holding) and girls distal (talking, looking) stimulation from their mothers. These maternal behaviors can, of course, be the result of initial behavioral differences in the infants, but they could also be due to the mother's expectations and thereby differential reactions to particular infant behaviors. In a study of parental discipline techniques used by the mothers of fifth graders, Zussman (1978) found that boys received more power assertion and love withdrawal and less reasoning than did girls.

age

The number and types of behavior problems reported for children vary with age. Many children with developmental and cognitive problems are not diagnosed until after they have started school. The peaks for referrals to clinics occur within a few years after school entry and again within a few years after the onset of adolescence (Rosen, Bahn, and Kramer 1964). A significant number of these problems are recognizable during the preschool years, but there has been a strong tendency to delay referral of the preschool child and hope that the child will "grow out of it." Some abnormal conditions, especially those associated with congenital physical abnormalities, can be recognized at birth, while others, whose principal symptoms involve forms of behavior that develop at an older age, can only be diagnosed later.

sibling order

After birth, firstborn children have the lowest mortality rates, and each subsequent increase in the birth order is correlated with a higher mortality rate. The reason for this relationship has been attributed to infectious diseases, with the later born children being exposed to more infection from older siblings.

While there has been a large amount of clinical and correlational evidence regarding the relationship between sibling order and "personality," the relationship between sibling order and the prevalence of behavior disorders is poorly understood. A large study of nineteen-year-old males in the Netherlands revealed that firstborn children had fewer school failures, higher intelligence, and fewer psychiatric problems than last-born children (Belmont, 1977). Firstborn children are also known to be overrepresented in groups of higher than average achievement (college students, the gifted, and professionals). In addition to the physical factors associated with older mothers, the higher rate of behavior problems in last-born children has been attributed to the parents' overindulgence ("spoiling") or inadequate supervision of the child's behavior, or both.

infectious disease

Several diseases are known to cause brain damage in children. *Meningitis* involves an inflammation of the meninges, the covering of the brain. It is usually a bacterial infection and can be treated with antibiotics, thereby offering the possibility of preventing the adverse sequalae, if the disease is diagnosed early enough. Usually the child who develops meningitis has had normal physical and mental development up to the time of the illness. The onset of the illness is indicated by a rise in temperature, vomiting, and signs of neurological involvement. Likely to be accompanying the high fever are stupor, coma, or restless delirium; headaches, paralysis, rigidity of the neck, and convulsions are also often present. Treatment with antibiotics later in the course of the disease keeps many children alive who, without treatment, could die; many of these children are significantly impaired (Nickerson and MacDermot, 1961). The acute illness, if untreated, lasts for two weeks or more followed by gradual recovery. In almost all such cases, complete recovery is never achieved. Intellectual functioning may be grossly impaired, and behavioral changes can be profound.

Encephalitis is usually a viral infection that involves inflammation of the brain itself. There is often no medical treatment available, and the risk of serious consequences is always present. Encephalitis is known to occur as a complication following the common childhood diseases, especially measles but also chicken-pox, scarlet fever, and whooping cough. Immunization programs for measles will significantly reduce the incidence of encephalitis in the future. The clinical signs of encephalitis are extremely varied; sometimes they are sudden and cause death, other times they are in such a mild form initially that they resemble the symptoms of the common cold. In the case of epidemic encephalitis, or sleeping sickness, about one-third of the patients die; of the two-thirds that recover, half become physically or mentally disabled.

head injury

Injury to the head is quite common in infancy and childhood, but little is known about the effects of these everyday occurrences. Physically, the skull does not offer as much protection to the brain during the first six months of life as it does later in the child's life. Accidents, especially those involving automobiles, and beatings are responsible for many cases of head injury. The use of seat belts and other improvements in the design of cars can reduce the incidence of injury due to accidents.

Child abuse, physical and psychological, has begun to receive both professional and public attention. In earlier times, children were considered the property of their parents, and parents were allowed to abuse and neglect them, but strong counterpressures were also present in the form of wanting healthy children who could contribute to the family's economic welfare. In modern times, children are not expected to contribute significantly to the family's income, and the consequences of child abuse and neglect are felt more by society in general rather than the specific family.

An increasing number of research studies are beginning to identify the factors associated with parents abusing their children. For example, in a study of mothers and young children, Egeland, Breitenbucher, and Rosenberg (1980) found that the relationship between changing life events (increasing psychological stress) and child abuse depended on the mother's anxiety level, personality characteristics, and competence as a parent, as well as the infant's overall developmental status and social responsivity. Kempe and Kempe (1978, p. 24) suggest that child abuse occurs in the presence of the following factors: (1) parental background includes emotional or physical deprivation; (2) the child is perceived as unlovable or disappointing; (3) a crisis is present; and (4) the parents have no effective way of securing aid during the crisis.

Many states now have laws permitting, and sometimes requiring, professionals and other persons to report suspected and known instances of child neglect and abuse to local social service authorities, who investigate the case to determine whether court action, therapy, or other services are needed by the family. Parents who have been involved in abusing their children have recently begun to form groups voluntarily to discuss the circumstances under which their children have been beaten and to help one another prevent those circumstances from arising in the future.

brain tumors

Brain tumors rarely occur in children, but when they do behavior is likely to be affected. The most common early symptoms are those associated with intracranial pressure, such as convulsions, headache, dizziness, and vomiting. Additional symptoms vary with the size and place of the tumor and are likely to be due to damage at the site of the growth, or the pressure on the adjacent areas. Tumors of the cerebellum, the part of the brain involved in motor behavior, occur twice as often in children as tumors of the cerebral cortex, the area that is primarily involved with cognitive behavior. The behavioral symptoms associated with tumors are often too diffuse to be useful in the localization of the tumors. Skull films, neurological tests, and brain scans are used in the diagnosis and location of brain tumors.

poisons

Children sometimes ingest substances that can be harmful. Lead and arsenic are capable of producing severe inflammation of the brain with resulting hemorrhage and lesions. Lead poisoning was much more common a few decades ago than it is at present. Children became ill by chewing on furniture covered with paint containing lead. Laws have been passed designating that articles used by children be covered with lead-free paint. Children, mostly in slum areas, still occasionally eat the toxic substance in peeling paint from walls and windowsills. Of children hospitalized with lead poisoning, more than one-fourth die, and an equal number become permanently brain damaged. Another factor that is involved in the accidental poisoning of children is the resemblance in the packaging of certain inedible and edible products.

social-psychological factors

Societies vary in their definitions of behavior disorders; a behavior that is condoned and reinforced in one culture may be disapproved of or punished in another. The well-adjusted person, then, may be conceptualized as one whose behaviors are compatible with the prevailing norms of the dominant culture in the society. Almost any country has a variety of subcultures within it (for example, tribes, religious sects), but the United States is unique in its collection of people whose ancestors came from all over the earth. Children may perhaps be expected to encounter greater problems when they are subjected to cultural demands that may differ markedly from those of their subculture.

Group rivalries and prejudice occur in all nations, but they have received particular attention in the United States, perhaps because the population is uniquely complex. As far as can be determined after the fact, rivalry among groups of immigrants began with the arrival of the Mayflower. High social status, for example, is still attributed to those who are descended from the earliest settlers. Early arrival seems to be the most relevant variable, since relatively few of the early settlers had high status in their countries of origin. Many were rejected in their own countries for religious or political reasons, and more than a few came as an alternative to prison.

As each succeeding wave of immigrants arrived, they were assigned to the lowest rung of the social ladder. Many individuals were eventually able to better their situation; in most cases, their success was correlated with their adoption of the dominant cultural standards. Being white, Anglo-Saxon, and Protestant has been a significant advantage throughout our history.

Success in our society is also correlated with (and defined by) certain behaviors. For adults, those behaviors include being achievement-oriented, intelligent, and nonemotional and having a job that is dependent on mental, rather than manual, activity. Children who are raised by parents displaying these behavioral characteristics have a higher probability of acquiring them than children whose parents are poor, uneducated, blue-collar workers. Equal opportunity for learning has only in the last few decades become a major goal for our educational instutitions.

Low socioeconomic status (SES) has been associated with a higher prevalence of behavior disorders. Low SES, however, is also related to other etiological factors. For example, low SES mothers are apt to have had poor nutrition during their own development; during pregnancy, they have a higher incidence of almost all complications, including nutritional deficiencies. Their children are more likely to be born prematurely and to experience problems during the perinatal period.

At one time, orphanages for young children were much more common than they are today. The primary reason for their demise was the increasing awareness that children who were placed into institutional settings at an early age had high mortality and behavior problem rates. Goldfarb (1944), Spitz (1945), and Bowlby (1952) have described the conditions in which many of the orphans lived. The basic needs of the children were quite adequate; that is, they were fed, kept clean, and protected against contagious diseases. In spite of these efforts, between 30 percent and 75 percent of the children were dying within two years of being placed in the institutions and were found to be extremely susceptible to diseases and other illnesses. Each child was typically placed in a cot whose sides were draped in sheets, thus effectively preventing the infants from seeing the other children and the rest of the room. Unless the infant could stand up in the crib, he or she was confined to a world almost totally lacking in visual stimulation. Social contact between caretakers and infants was extremely brief, and the children were usually not held, even for feeding.

The observers of these conditions interpreted the high mortality rate, poor development, and emotional apathy (depression) as being due to the child's having been separated from his or her mother. Bowlby (1952) proposed that normal mental health required a continuous relationship with a mother or mother substitute during infancy. Casler (1961) and Yarrow (1964), however, have suggested that the devastating effects of institutions on infants and young children are not caused by the infant's separation from the mother, per se, but by the deprivation of all the stimulation which she provides and mediates. Infants apparently need a minimal amount of stimulation in order to develop normally. Children who are adequately stimulated, whether it be by one or several caretakers, do not present the symptoms of institutionalization.

Many people have been convinced that any care, other than that given by the mother or a comparable caregiver, is detrimental to the children's emotional development. This belief might account for the inadequate development of day-care programs for children and the refusal of many people to recognize in a concrete way that a substantial portion of working people are women, many of whom are mothers of preschool and school-age children. Research evidence is beginning to demonstrate that group care for infants and young children can be designed to be as effective, and sometimes better, than that given by mothers. A recent review by Belsky and Steinberg (1978) has concluded that high quality day care does not affect IQ scores, is not disruptive to the emotional bond between mother and child, and increases both positive and negative peer interactions.

A number of other countries with high proportions of working mothers have developed day-care programs that American psychologists have begun to visit and study. These investigators have found highly developed and specialized programs for children beginning within a few months after birth. Studies of children raised in kibbutzim suggest that group care of children produces individuals who have a strong allegiance to the group and who do not differ in their developmental or cognitive skills when compared with Israeli children raised by their own parents (Irvine, 1966). Such studies do not indicate the presence of detrimental effects such as were observed in the institutional children.

It seems reasonable to conjecture at this point that children's early experiences might best be oriented toward those situations that will confront them later in life. Protecting and raising children solely in the home environment for the first five years of life may, in fact, hinder their adjustment to the complexities of the world outside their homes. It is possible that some behavior problems may be due to a restricted environmental history.

family constitution

Increased mobility has been a primary factor creating change in the constitution of families. A few generations ago, the average person was raised in a small town where most of the individual's relatives also resided. The person was trained to do a job that would in some way benefit the community, usually married a person from the community, and spent the rest of their lives there. In these small towns everyone knew everyone else, and parents were soon informed when their children's behavior did not measure up to the expectations of the community. In a sense, the whole community participated in child rearing. Many of the old neighborhoods in more congested areas also demonstrated community rearing of children. But now, the transient quality of contemporary living precludes such participation. On the other hand, mobility has created certain advantages that facilitate the development of individuality. Children no longer have to choose the occupation of their father or one that is useful in a restricted geographical area. Their education need not be determined by local facilities, nor must a son's status as head of the household be postponed until the death of his father. The price for individuality has not yet been deemed too high.

With the contemporary emphasis on the nuclear (mother, father, and children) family and the high incidence of one-parent families, the potential for being an inadequate parent is at least present. Kallam, Ensminger, and Turner (1977) have reported that a higher risk of problem behavior in children is associated with mother alone and mother/stepfather family structures; in their poor, urban, black sample, mother/grandmother family structures were nearly as effective as mother/father structures.

Older models of being parents seem, at least retrospectively, to have been correlated with fewer behavior problems in children. The extended (inclusion of other relatives) family, now relatively uncommon in our society, appears to have been a situation in which children were likely to receive more individual attention from adults, and parents were less likely to be overwhelmed by child-rearing responsibilities. That is, all adults in the family shared in the child-rearing activities. Multiple parents are fairly common in the so-called primitive societies, although forms may vary. Among the Murngin, for example, children call their paternal uncles "father," and their relationships with the uncles are no different than their relationships with their biological fathers (Volkart, 1957).

Contemporary clinicians have indicated that the family should optimally be composed of a mother, a father, and their children. Deviations from that pattern have been felt to be detrimental to all members of the family, especially the children. The emphasis on having both a mother and a father in the home has been related to the appropriate sex role development of the children. That is, children are assumed to need strong and continuous models of both sexes in order to become adequate men and women.

Evidence for the necessity of being raised by both a mother and a father is usually confounded by other variables, such as the reason for the parental absence. Most of the research in the area has been conducted on families with absent fathers, since fathers are more likely to be away from their families than are mothers. Men go to war and take jobs that keep them away from home for long periods. The absence of a father has been theoretically linked with female identification in boys, but evidence for feminine behavior in such boys has not been forthcoming. However, the research data to suggest that boys raised in homes broken by parental desertion have an increased rate of delinquency (Gibson, 1969). The relatively poor cognitive performance of father-absent children has been attributed to financial hardship, high anxiety, and low parent-child interaction (Shinn, 1978).

When a marital relationship is terminated, it has been customary for the mother to assume custody of the children with the father providing all or some of the financial support. Whether or not she has worked prior to the separation, the probability is high that she will have to be employed in addition to having the major responsibility for child rearing. Even if the father is required to contribute to the support of the family, the total amount of available income may still be considerably less than what the family had to live on before the separation. Mother's working may mean that preschool children will have inadequate caregivers and that school children will be unsupervised in the afternoon. When the mother arrives home from work, she may be confronted with all of the household duties. The point to be emphasized is that the remaining parent and children may be faced with considerable change in their circumstances, and it is this change which is likely to be the key factor in determining child behavior. The implications are that gross changes in the child's environment may increase the probability of behavior problems. After a review of the research literature, Rutter (1971) concluded that separation or divorce of the parents increased the possibility of short-term distress in the child but generally did not affect the long-term behavioral status of the child. Behavioral problems, previously associated with separation, were found to be due to the family discord that preceded and accompanied the separation.

The clinical literature has implied that almost any separation from the parents during infancy and the preschool years can have adverse effects. The research literature suggests that brief separations can have transient short-term effects that are greatly affected by the circumstances of the separation and the child's previous history of separation. For example, Stacey, Dearden, Pill, and Robinson (1970) found that children who were accustomed to brief separations of a happy kind were less likely to be distressed by unhappy separations, such as going to the hospital. Distress in response to separation is most likely in children between six months and four years and those separated from their whole family.

The children of working mothers have also been assumed to have a greater likelihood of developing behavior problems because the child is separated from the mother. The research, however, has not supported that assumption. A review (Wallston, 1973) of studies revealed few differences between children of working and nonworking mothers. The critical variables related to maternal employment were the mother's satisfaction with working and adequate child-care arrangements.

The number of children in the family has also been assumed to be a factor influencing the incidence of behavior problems. Both only children and children from large families have been considered to be at a disadvantage (Verville, 1967 pp. 17, 19). Although only children tend to be referred to clinics disproportionately, there is no evidence suggesting that presence of a sibling would have affected the referral. Many parents have decided to have a second child to prevent the "psychological problems" assumed to be associated with being an only child.

Some behavior problems have appeared to be more prevalent in families with a large number of children. The obvious explanation is that parents cannot adequately care for and train more than a few children, but the findings on large families reveal that there are important additional aspects to be considered. In many cases, large families are acquired "involuntarily" because the parents have not been educated about birth control. Many children have been born who were neither planned nor wanted, and a high proportion of these children are born to parents who do not have adequate resources for their support. In such instances, both the physical and psychological environments are likely to be less than optimal.

In some instances, the arrival of even one child creates a major psychological stress that may have long-term consequences. One example is that of the adolescent parent whose economic and psychological resources are likely to be less than ideal for the responsibility of parenthood. More specifically, adolescent mothers have an increased risk of physical complications of pregnancy and delivery and inadequate skills to be a mother that may have a negative impact on the developing child (Sugar, 1976).

Middle-class parents have tended to believe that they can have all the children they can afford. Ecologists counter this attitude by showing that individuals with a high standard of living consume considerably more of the world's resources than do people with a low standard of living. Recent concerns about population and ecological problems have been cited as some of the reasons for the desire for smaller families expressed by married couples. Evidence of this intention has been reflected in the decreased birth rates during the last decade.

parent-child interactions: two theoretical views

This section focuses on parent-child interactions in the context of two contemporary theories. The concepts of psychoanalytic theory and behavior theory that relate to the etiology of children's behavior problems are described.

Psychoanalytic theory. Sigmund Freud was a highly respected physician throughout his long career. Among his many referrals, there were a significant number of patients for whom he could find no organic abnormality. On the basis of interviews with these patients, Freud began to develop a theory to account for their symptoms. His theory was based on the assumption that these patients' problems were psychological and had their origin in childhood, particularly during the preschool years. The information derived from interviews convinced Freud (1953, originally 1905) that young children experienced sexual thoughts and feelings-an idea that was not well received by his contemporaries in Victorian society.

According to Freud, the mature human mind comprises three basic parts: the id, ego, and superego. The *id* was conceptualized as a basic energy source or a biologically determined sex drive. (Freud later incorporated an aggressive drive into his concept of the id.) This sex drive was hypothesized to produce energy, or *libido,* that is focused on different parts of the body during biological development.

Freud hypothesized that preschool children go through definite stages of psychosexual development that are designated by the part of the body that provides sexual pleasure: the oral, anal, and phallic stages. During the *oral* stage, lasting from birth to about two years of age, the child derives pleasure primarily from oral activities (stimulation of the lips and oral cavity). During the third and fourth years of life, pleasure is obtained from *anal* activities (stimulation associated with defecation). Beginning in the fifth year, the phallic stage is characterized by pleasure derived from stimulation of the genital area.

The id, or unsocialized part of the mind, strives for maximum pleasure, but external reality often prevents the desired gratification. The representation of external reality in the mind is the *ego.* That is, the ego begins to develop as a result of the conflict between the id and external reality and comprises the child's experiences with the external world—experiences that begin to accumulate very early in life.

As the child proceeds through the psychosexual stages, the id impulses increasingly come into conflict with external reality, and the child is required to learn behavior that is acceptable by society. The *superego* represents the part of the mind that contains the values and prohibitions of society that are derived primarily from the parents. Development of the superego begins as soon as parents begin to communicate their approval and disapproval of the child's behavior. The young child, who is biologically and psychologically dependent on the parents, fears the loss of parental love, if parental values and prohibitions are not maintained. External factors, such as social approval and punishment, initially control the child's behavior, but the child gradually begins to utilize internal representations of these factors to control his or her own behavior.

There are a number of potential situations during the preschool years in which the various parts of the child's mind can be placed in conflict, the most common of which include feeding, toilet training, and masturbation. One of the principal effects of intrapsychic conflict is *anxiety,* a central concept in psychoanalytic theory and the basis for the formation of psychological problems. Anxiety is considered to originate as an inborn response to excessive stimulation. That is, humans are biologically designed to react with fears or anxiety to particular events. Psychoanalytic theory (Freud, 1959, originally 1926) postulates that anxiety also results from mental representations of these events, such as thoughts of forbidden behaviors and memories of traumatic occurrences.

One event that has been considered particularly traumatic is the primal scene, the witnessing of parental intercourse. The primal scene has been hypothesized as the primary cause of a variety of problems, including neuroses, learning disturbances, and juvenile delinquency. Observation of parental intercourse is believed to cause excessive sexual excitement which, in turn, results in anxiety. Moreover, clinical case studies suggest that the child inevitably interprets intercourse as being sadistic. Esman (1973) has recently pointed out, however, that the traumatic aspects of the primal scene are likely determined by the behaviors of the parents during intercourse and their reaction to the child's presence. Situations in which the parents display aggression toward one another or severely punish the child are more likely to have an adverse effect than those in which the parents are affectionate and react to the child's presence calmly.

The developing child is viewed as being confronted with a series of "normal" crises or conflicts, such as weaning and separation from the mother. The parents' handling of these crises is considered to have profound effects on the child's later personality. Satisfaction of the child's early needs by the mother is viewed as not only facilitating the child's relationship with the mother but also developing the child's capacity for relating to other people in general. Anna Freud (1971) has also indicated that when early bodily needs are not met the involved organ systems remain vulnerable in the future.

Among the developmental crises is the Oedipus complex, which is most evident during the phallic stage. As little boys become increasingly aware that they will grow up to be men, they begin to fantasize about the role they will play as adult males. In the boy's wish to be an adult, he wants to do everything that his father does, including having all of the experiences that his father has with his mother. Some of these experiences he at least vaguely conceptualizes as being sexual in nature. In his wish to have the mother completely, he begins actively to perceive the father as a rival and wants to be rid of him; the child also becomes fearful that he will lose the father whom he also loves. He fears that discovery of his hostility will lead both to a loss of love and retaliation.

The fears of punishment (castration) by the father force the boy to repress his Oedipal wishes and thereby to resolve the conflict. Repression is viewed as a means of controlling the libidinal urges and channeling them into other activities. Identification with the father, the resolution of the Oedipus complex, facilitates learning and socialization during the latency stage that lasts from the age of five years to puberty.

Parents can alter the timing and progress of the psychosexual stages in various ways and thus determine the child's later personality characteristics. The child may be deprived of an adequate amount of stimulation, such as being prevented from sucking long enough, or the child may be severely punished for obtaining sexual pleasure. These situations are viewed as creating excessive anxiety and the development of defense mechanisms to avoid the experience of anxiety.

According to Freud's later (1926) writings about anxiety and psychological symptoms, both libidinal (id) impulses and stimuli previously associated with anxiety are capable of producing signal anxiety in the ego. The resulting discomfort causes the ego to develop defense mechanisms against the signal anxiety and the threat of the earlier experienced traumatic situations. Psychological symptoms were hypothesized to develop in the ego when the initial defense failed to control anxiety. Freud described four defense mechanisms: *repression,* forgetting feelings or memories associated with anxiety; *reaction formation,* having feelings that are opposite to those associated with anxiety; *isolation,* inserting a period of no thoughts or behavior to prevent increases in anxiety; *undoing,* reversing behaviors or situations that previously caused anxiety. Anna Freud (1936) subsequently expanded the list of defense mechanisms on the basis of her psychoanalytic work with children and her relatively greater emphasis on the development of the ego.

Among the people who studied with Sigmund Freud, several came to disagree with some of the basic tenets of psychoanalytic theory and developed alternative hypotheses. One of the fundamental aspects of the theory, the psychosexual stages of development, was greatly deemphasized by several followers who preferred to acknowledge a broader variety of etiological factors, namely environmental impediments to optimal personality development. Freud's ideas with respect to the origin of anxiety were similarly challenged.

Several theorist-clinicians conceptualized anxiety as a causative factor of the underlying psychic conflict rather than a symptom of that conflict. The conflict was believed to be determined by environmental factors. For example, Horney (1937) described the cause of "basic anxiety" as the absence of warmth in the child's environment, which in turn causes feelings of insecurity and hostility. The basic conflict between the wish for love and the hostile feelings is expressed in the "neurotic personality." Thus, Horney views "basic anxiety" as a consequence of interpersonal deprivation, frustration, and disapproval.

Adler (1927) proposed that the primary motivational factor is not libido but the fundamental helplessness of the infant and the resulting feelings of inferiority. Much behavior, then, could be viewed as a quest for power and perfection as compensation for feelings of inferiority. Neurotic behavior results from the reactions to actual or imagined threats in the individual's present situation. For Adler, neurosis always involves the child's striving for power to compensate for the feelings of inferiority generated by environmental events.

Rank (1952), on the other hand, postulated that the basic source of anxiety is separation from the mother at birth and that man unconsciously attempts to re-store the original intrauterine life. Any subsequent moves toward independence reinstate a threat of separation and thus produce anxiety. Neurosis, then, reflects the conflict between the desire to mature and the desire to regain the former in-trauterine existence.

Sullivan (1956) hypothesized that the infant empathically senses and experiences the mother's anxiety. This reaction is the prototype for all subsequent anxiety reactions. Through experience, the child learns to associate anxiety with disapproval, and each time the child experiences anxiety, the child's self-concept is damaged. A defensive system becomes established to signal anxiety that permits the child to use selective inattention or disassociation to remain unaware of his or her unacceptable wants. During infancy, children develop a self-concept system in which they grade themselves in the context of parental expectations.

Erik H. Erikson (1963) is prominent among the theorist-clinicians who gave greater emphasis to the role of the ego in the development of personality. He proposed that the person's resolutions of a sequence of developmentally deter-mined conflicts have specific implications for later personal-social behavior. Erik-son's developmental conflicts are clearly derived from Freud's psychosexual stages, but Erikson specifies in greater detail the role of the parents in the resolutions of the conflicts and the behaviors engendered by the resolutions.

The resolution of the first conflict, which he calls *basic trust versus mistrust,* lays the foundation for all later development. The development of trust is based on the infant's feeling comfortable physically and experiencing a minimum of fear or uncertainty. To the extent that these conditions are met, the infant will expect new experiences to produce positive outcomes. The quality of interpersonal con-tacts while the child's needs (primarily oral) are being satisfied becomes the prin-cipal determinant of early social development. Children are considered to be capable of sensing both the conscious and unconscious thoughts of their parents. The child's social perception is based more on the feelings of the parents than on their specific caretaking skills. The infant who develops mistrust tends to be-come a demanding person preoccupied with physical needs.

The second conflict, called *autonomy versus doubt and shame,* coincides with Freud's anal stage. The child's greater ability in motor skills stimulates a strong interest to explore the environment and to accomplish new tasks. At the same time, the child experiences doubt about abandoning the previously enjoyed dependency. This conflict is most apparent during toilet training but is involved in all aspects of the child's behavior. Erickson specifies that the parents allowing the child freedom in some areas while maintaining firm limits in others facilitates the development of autonomy. Doubt is likely to be the result of parents' lack of control. Excessive punishment from the parents or failure to meet unusually high parental standards produce shame in the child.

The third conflict, called *initiative versus guilt,* coincides with Freud's phallic stage and the period of the Oedipus complex. Initiative results from the child's being challenged by the social environment to be active and to master new skills.

Again, the parents' role is primarily that of support and control. If the child's initiative either receives no limits from the parents or is excessively punished, then a feeling of guilt is likely to result. It is during this period that the child begins to identify with the parent of the same sex and that parental values become incorporated.

Erikson's fourth conflict, which is called *industry versus inferiority,* coincides with Freud's latency stage. During this period, the child's principal tasks are to learn the basic skills necessary for progressing toward the adult role. Peers become increasingly significant, and the child continuously compares his or her accomplishments with those of his or her peers. Failure to develop the culturally proscribed skills can lead to lasting feelings of inferiority.

The fifth conflict, *identity versus role confusion,* denotes the end of childhood and the beginning of adolescence. The feeling of identity represents a mastery of the earlier conflicts and a readiness to meet the problems of the adult world as well as the successful integration of psychosexual drives. During this period, the parent-child relationship is represented primarily by its common history; that is, the adolescent relies more on relationships outside of the family.

Erikson also described three conflicts that occur during adulthood: *intimacy versus isolation, generativity versus stagnation,* and *ego integrity versus despair.* The resolutions of these adult conflicts are hypothesized to be influenced by the results of the earlier childhood and adolescent conflicts. Erikson's view of the developing person may be characterized as a continuous process of balancing internal needs and the requirements of the social environment. Parents are expected to transmit the values of society to their children while remaining sensitive to the needs, abilities, and limitations of the growing child. Lack of adequate support and unrealistic expections, as well as excessive punishment of the child, can lead to less than optimal resolutions of the childhood conflicts.

Psychoanalytic theory and its variations, greatly emphasizing the impact of experiences during the preschool years, easily lent itself to the extrapolation that parents are primarily responsible for the development of behavior problems. A substantial body of correlational research has demonstrated a number of relationships between parental characteristics and children's behavior. For example, Sears, Maccoby, and Levin (1957), using a psychoanalytic frame of reference, conducted a retrospective study of the child-rearing antecedents of five-year-old children's personality characteristics. The data were secured from interviews with the mothers, who were asked to recall their interactions with their children from birth. Their results indicated that, while maternal warmth was not related to the child's current dependency, maternal rejection was to a slight degree positively related to dependency. Aggression in the child was found to be somewhat negatively correlated with warmth of the mother. That is, there was a mild tendency for high aggression in children to be associated with low warmth of the mother.

In examining the relationship between parent psychological status and child behavior disorders, two subject selection procedures have been utilized by investigators. One procedure involves examining the children of parents who have been clinically diagnosed as abnormal. Anthony (1959), for example, found that mothers whose depressions or obsessions overlay murderous feelings or impulses toward their children were likely to have negative influences on the children. In his study, the children were found to be withdrawn, passive and fearful, infantile, ill, or manifesting some other type of behavior disorder. Lewis (1954) also found that neurotic and psychopathic parents commonly had children with neurotic reactions.

The second procedure involves examining the psychological status of the parents whose children are clinically diagnosed as abnormal. Huschka (1941), for example, using clinical records of children with behavior disorders, found that forty-two percent of the mothers had neurotic symptoms, depression, suicidal impulses, or paranoid tendencies; he concluded that the mother's psychological status greatly affected children at all stages of development. A number of studies using objective personality tests for assessing the adjustment of parents of children with behavior problems have also been conducted. Wolking, Quast, and Lawton (1966) administered the Minnesota Multiphasic Personality Inventory (MMPI) to parents of six diagnostic groupings of children. They found elevations of several MMPI clinical scales for all groups of parents with behavior-problem children in comparison to control parents, but no relationship between parental profile types and specific child disorders could be determined.

These correlational studies have typically been interpreted as reflecting that the parental characteristics cause the children's behavior problems and have rarely been interpreted as suggesting the possibility that behavior problems in children can adversely affect the parents or that some other variable could be responsible for both the parent and child findings.

Particularly during the last decade, investigators have begun to turn their attention toward the individual differences among children and the impact of child characteristics on parents (for example, Lewis and Rosenburg, 1974). Thomas, Chess, and Birch (1968) and Thomas and Chess (1977) have delineated temperamental styles in infants that increase the probability of referral later in childhood. Genetic factors have been implicated in the etiology of temperamental traits, such as sociability, emotionality, and activity (Plomin and Rowe, 1977), suggesting the parent-child interactions do not create children's temperamental styles; however, negative changes in temperament have been associated with parental intolerance, inconsistency, and conflict (Cameron, 1977).

Behavior theory. In general, behaviorists have not concerned themselves greatly with the origins of behavior problems in children, and thus their interest in historical events has been considerably less than that of psychoanalytically oriented clinicians. Behaviorists' interest in etiology is usually confined to a search for the environmental stimuli that are currently maintaining the problem behavior. This search is based on the assumption that behavior is continuous in time; that is, regardless of its origin, behavior that is occurring is largely controlled by contemporary environmental stimuli rather than events that are remote in time. In some situations, the behavioral clinician does not even search for these controlling stimuli because other environmental stimuli can be used to change the behavior.

The basic assumptions of the behavioral theorists are that most behavior is learned and that both normal and abnormal behaviors are learned on the basis of the same principles. Only during the past few decades have these principles of learning been used to account for the behavioral problems of adults and children. The application of these principles is based on some fifty years of research with animals and humans. Much of the evidence supporting a behavioral account of etiology, however, comes to us indirectly through assessment and treatment programs, rather than through retrospective or longitudinal studies.

While behavioral clinicians recognize the important role of parents in the development of their children, a wide variety of other persons, including peers, have been credited with having a primary role in the etiology of behavior problems. Similarly, a wide range of nonhuman stimulus events have been suggested as having significant etiological functions. Thus, the behavioral clinician considers the child's total environment (Wahler, House and Stembaugh, 1976) rather than a narrow spectrum, to have the potential for increasing the probability of behavior problems. As mentioned in the Chapter 3 on behavioral approaches to assessment, the hypothesis with respect to the stimuli controlling the behavior problems are derived from both interviews and direct behavioral observations.

Several types of learning have been described in the psychological literature: operant conditioning, modeling, and respondent conditioning. These types of learning are distinguished on the basis of relationships between stimuli and responses. Responses include any activity, such as smiling, complaining, or crying, that can be counted or otherwise measured. Stimuli include all situations, objects, or events that have an effect on behavior. Stimuli may control responses in a variety of ways.

Operant conditioning refers to an increase in the occurrence of a response when it is followed by a reinforcing stimulus. The responses that are likely to be operantly conditioned are what we would call *voluntary* behaviors. It is assumed that humans are biologically designed to emit a certain spectrum of behaviors, but that the future occurrence of these behaviors depends greatly on the consequences of these behaviors.

Operant conditioning appears to have a significant role in the development of children's behavior problems. That is, a number of studies have shown that behavior problems were being maintained by certain reinforcers. This control was demonstrated when the reinforcers were omitted, and the behavior decreased. For example, in an early study Williams (1959) described a case study in which a twenty-one-month-old boy presented severe temper tantrums, particularly at bedtime. A parent was spending one to two hours per night in the child's bedroom; if the parent tried to leave the room before he was asleep, temper tantrums occurred. That is, temper tantrums were consistently followed by the parent remaining in the room. The intervention procedure consisted of the parents putting the child to bed and then leaving the bedroom. On the first night the child screamed for forty-five minutes. During the following nights, however, the tantrums were markedly reduced, and they were absent by the seventh bedtime. This study strongly suggests that the child's temper tantrums were being maintained by the parents remaining in the room.

While it can be assumed that many behavior problems are being maintained by reinforcement, it is not always possible to identify the reinforcers in the available time. In some of these cases, an intervention program in which all possible sources of reinforcement are controlled through a brief period of social isolation each time the behavior occurs may be successful. In these instances, one cannot determine whether the behavioral change is due to the omission of reinforcement or other factors.

The baseline data from many studies suggest that adults in the child's environment may be responsible for supplying the reinforcement that maintains the problem behavior. In the majority of cases, the adults do not realize that they are maintaining the behavior; in fact, they are usually the ones who are complaining about the behavior and are trying to "help" the child. In other words, it is often appropriate to conclude that these adults are inadvertently reinforcing the behavior. Most adults are not aware that giving social attention to inappropriate behavior may have the effect of strengthening that behavior.

Some behavior problems may best be described as deficits in the behavioral repertoire. In many of these cases, the child will not have had the opportunity to learn the necessary behaviors, while in others, effective reinforcers have not been employed. Few parents or teachers have been adequately trained to develop children's behavioral repertoires to their best levels.

Behavioral deficits could also be the result of negative consequences or punishment. That is, low rates of behavior could be due to the behavior having been followed by an aversive stimulus (for example, scolding, spanking) or the withdrawal of a positive reinforcer (for example, TV privileges). The behavioral research literature does not, however, contain adequate evidence of these factors having been involved in the maintenance of deficits in appropriate behavior.

Although we often do not know the factors that are responsible for the origin of a behavior problem, it can be demonstrated that many new responses are added to the child's behavioral repertoire through *observational learning,* or *modeling.* Observational learning is demonstrated when the child imitates a behavior after having observed it in another person. That is, simply observing another person engaging in a behavior may increase the probability of a child producing that behavior. One of the early demonstrations of modeling in children was reported in a study by Bandura, Ross, and Ross (1961). In this study, preschool children observed either aggressive adult models, nonaggressive adult models, or no models. When tested in a similar situation in the absence of the model, the children exposed to the aggressive model engaged in more aggressive behaviors than did the children in the other groups. These results were subsequently replicated in studies in which the modeled behaviors were presented on film rather than live (Bandura, Ross, and Ross, 1963a, 1963b). An interesting finding was that children who imitated the aggressive behaviors often spoke disapprovingly of the behaviors.

It may be hypothesized that persons in the child's environment serve as models for children and that children acquire many behaviors by imitating others. During the preschool years, parents are the most available models, while at older ages, teachers, peers, and others provide behaviors which the child may imitate. While modeling may affect the initial occurrences of these behaviors, subsequent consequences also affect their continuation.

Another type of learning that may be involved in the etiology of children's behavior problems is *respondent,* or *classical conditioning.* Respondent conditioning involves one stimulus taking on the function of another stimulus in eliciting a particular response, through a pairing of the two stimuli. Respondent conditioning is best demonstrated with involuntary behavior, such as eyelid closure to a puff of air. If another stimulus (one that initially does not cause eyelid closure) is paired with the puff of air several times, this stimulus may then become capable of eliciting eye closure when it is later presented without the puff of air.

A very early study (Watson and Rayner, 1920) demonstrated that fear of a white rat was learned through respondent conditioning by a young child who was previously not afraid of the rat. The investigators paired the presentation of the white rat with a very loud sound and found that the child later continued to express fear when the rat was presented without the accompanying loud sound. Respondent conditioning has been invoked as the process by which behavior problems associated with anxiety are learned. Certain environmental stimuli (for example, loud, sudden sounds) cause involuntary fear or anxiety responses; these stimulus-response relationships are biologically determined. On occasion, these stimuli are "accidentally" paired with other ("neutral") stimuli that may then elicit the anxiety responses. These fears are often maintained for long periods because the feared stimulus tends to be avoided, and the child is thereby prevented from learning that the feared stimulus poses no real threat. That is, according to the principles of respondent conditioning, repeated presentations of the feared stimulus, in the absence of the stimulus with which it was originally paired, should lead to a decrease in the conditioned response; avoidance of the feared stimulus therefore tends to maintain the anxiety response.

Accidental pairings may well account for a number of behavior problems, and more than a few of them are mediated, probably inadvertently, by people in the child's environment. For example, the goal of the teacher who suddenly yells at a child is usually to stop an inappropriate behavior, but one of the by-products of the teacher's yelling may be that the child learns to be fearful in the classroom.

Without knowing the principles of learning, parents and teachers may inadvertently foster the development of children's behavior problems. They may reinforce the very behaviors they consider to be inappropriate, or they may ignore appropriate behaviors that should be strengthened through reinforcement. Without knowledge of the effects of modeling, they may model behavior that, when imitated by the child, will be considered a behavior problem. Likewise, parents and teachers sometimes expose children to situations that foster the development of fears and anxiety. In these instances, the adults are not intending to create a behavior problem but are unaware of the relationship between their behavior and that of the child.

Conclusion

Demographic studies suggest that male children have an increased probability of developing behavior problems. Postnatal physical factors, such as disease, head injury, and the ingestion of poisons, cause brain damage which results in a variety of behavioral abnormalities. Certain environmental conditions, particularly those related to stimulus deprivation, can have a detrimental effect on both physical and psychological development. Psychoanalytic theory suggests that psychological disturbances, particularly neurotic problems, are caused by faulty parent-child relationships during the preschool years. Behavior theory, on the other hand, either focuses on the identification of stimuli currently maintaining the behavior problem or omits consideration of etiological factors. The available evidence suggests that significant persons (including parents) in the children's environment may inadvertently strengthen and maintain problem behavior.

Recommended Readings

Anthony, E. J., and Koupernik, C., eds., *The Child in His Family*. 4 vols. New York: John Wiley, 1970-1978.

Maccoby, E. E., and Jacklin, C. H., *The Psychology of Sex Differences*. Stanford, Calif.: Stanford University Press, 1974. A critical review of behavioral research on sex differences.

Wolman, B. B., ed., *Manual of Child Psychopathology*. New York: McGraw-Hill, 1972. Chapter 5, "Etiology of Mental Disorders: Sociocultural Aspects" and Chapter 6, "Some Basic Aspects of Family Pathology."

Kempe, R. S., and Kempe, C. H., *Child Abuse*. Cambridge, Mass.: Harvard University Press, 1978.

treatment: the psychotherapies and pharmacotherapy

6

The traditional approaches to the treatment of children's behavior problems include a variety of therapies that are either based directly on psychodynamic theory or represent a variation of psychodynamic theory. These therapies may be described as adhering to a medical model of mental illness in that the symptoms, or behavior, are not believed to be the "real" problem but rather reflect underlying defects in personality. Therefore, traditional treatment consists of a search for the underlying defects, the motives behind the behavior problem that are largely unconscious and not readily available to the client.

background

Virtually none of the treatment procedures currently being used to alleviate the children's behavior problems existed before this century. In fact, the need for treatment (outside of institutional settings) of children's behavior problems did not become formalized in this country until the 1920s. Through the ensuing years, psychodynamic theory came to dominate the treatment programs conducted by psychiatrists, psychologists, and social workers, and considerable effort has gone into the development of theoretical systems, professional training programs, and facilities for the provision of services. Until relatively recently, the research literature has consisted primarily of a collection of treatment technique descriptions and a large number of case studies that purport to demonstrate the effectiveness of these techniques.

Some evaluation of therapeutic effectiveness through the use of well-designed research studies has been done since the 1970s, but the early returns have tended to be disappointing. Evaluative research has failed to show that traditional psychotherapy with children is effective (Levitt, 1971, p. 474). In a review of child psychotherapy research, Barrett, Hampe, and Miller (1978) made the following conclusions: (1) child psychotherapists have not assumed an appropriate responsibility for evaluating therapeutic effectiveness; (2) child psychotherapy research has not provided adequate attention to important variables such as the developmental stage and diagnostic category; and (3) child psychotherapy research has lacked a model that takes into account the larger context (for example, family, school) in which psychotherapy occurs. Many clinicians continue to use the traditional treatment methods because they personally believe them to be effective in their own clinical work.

In recent years, training programs for psychologists and psychiatrists have begun to include in-depth exposure to a broader spectrum of theoretical orientations and treatment methods. This change in training programs is producing more professionals who adhere to an eclectic approach to the treatment of children and reflects the increasing recognition that no one approach to treatment is likely to be effective for all children.

psychoanalysis

It is generally recognized that Freud carried out the first systematic treatment of a child, although Freud himself did not conduct the treatment but rather advised the child's father who conducted the treatment program in the home. Freud had been particularly interested in the development of infantile sexuality and emotional conflict and had been collecting observations of young children from several sources. The child's father was supplying Freud with observations of his son's behavior for two years prior to the onset of the problem. When nearly five years old, the boy, called Little Hans, developed a fear, or phobia, that a horse would bite him.

The record of observations indicated that Little Hans had a lively curiosity about sexual matters and frequently verbalized his interest. Freud's treatment of the phobia was based on his knowledge of the child's history from the father's observations, the father's descriptions of Little Hans's current behavior, and Freud's own hypotheses regarding the source of the child's conflicts. Freud initially instructed the father to tell Little Hans about the anatomical differences between the males and females in the boy's household and that his fears of horses had come from his preoccupation with interest in their penises. After some discussion about his fears, Little Hans quickly improved in that he became able to go out for walks, and, his fear of horses appeared to be changed into a compulsion to look at them. Soon thereafter, Little Hans became ill with influenza and had to remain in bed for several weeks. This illness was followed by a recurrence of the phobia.

The father then arranged a personal interview with Freud, Little Hans, and himself. During this interview Freud interpreted the boy's fear of horses as representing his fear of his father with whom he was in competition for his mother's favors. Freud did not expect to cure the boy's phobia during this one interview, but he did expect that the information given to him would offer the possibility of further uncovering of unconscious material (Freud, 1955, p. 43). The boy's analysis by his father under Freud's direction continued for three months during which time the phobia was cured.

Although Freud published his famous case study of Little Hans in 1909, it was not until 1926 that the next significant event in the history of child psychotherapy occurred. During that year Anna Freud, Sigmund Freud's daughter, presented a series of lectures to the Vienna Institute of Psychoanalysis entitled "Introduction to the Technique of the Psycho-Analysis of Children." The publication of these lectures aroused great interest, and a group of psychoanalysts began to hold regular meetings with Anna Freud in Vienna to discuss the technique of analysis with children and to report on their case material. Both a wide age range (two years old through adolescence) and a broad spectrum of behavior problems were characteristic of the children whose cases were presented at these meetings.

The principal impediment to the use of psychoanalysis with children was their lack of skill in free association, one of the most important techniques of psychoanalysis with adults. The early analysts therefore needed a substitute for free association and finally settled on children's play as their choice. As early as 1919, Hug-Hellmuth proposed that children's play be utilized as a way of understanding their unconscious processes during therapy. Melanie Klein elaborated the idea, hypothesizing that children's play is equivalent to adults' free associations, and began to interpret the unconscious meaning of her clients' play during therapy in 1919.

One of the major differences between the Freudian and Kleinian approaches to child psychoanalysis centers on the role of interpretation of play during therapy. Kleinian interpretation included direct symbolic translation, such as elongated objects representing the penis, round objects the breasts, and cars running into one another the primal scene. Anna Freud, on the other hand, emphasized the interpretation of the emotional content of the child's play and a gradual approach to the interpretation of underlying conflict and impulses.

The writings of Anna Freud (1946a, 1946b, 1965) have been primary sources of information regarding psychoanalysis with children (Scharfman, 1978). She has described the motivational differences between adult and child patients—the child's tendency to externalize and to act when anxiety is experienced, thus presenting a problem to others in the environment, in contrast to adults who present themselves for analysis to alleviate internal suffering. The child is greatly dependent on his or her parents, and the therapist must determine to what extent the parents are protecting the child from experiencing anxiety and to what extent they are obtaining secondary gain from bringing the child for analytic therapy.

In child psychoanalysis the patient is seen by the therapist three, four, or five times a week, thus encouraging an intense patient-analyst relationship and a continuity of therapeutic activity. The frequent visits aid the child to tolerate anxiety engendered by the treatment, because the therapist is more available for support. As is the case for adults, psychoanalysis with children is a lengthy treatment procedure, usually lasting several years or more. The expense involved, more often than not, precludes its use for other than well-to-do families.

Although treatment is clearly focused on the child, the therapist will find it necessary to relate to one or both parents during the course of the child's analysis. The parents are the primary source of information about the child's development, symptomology, and personal interrelationships. When the child is younger than ten years old, the analyst must rely on the parents to obtain information about the child's status outside of the therapeutic sessions because young children tend not to be accurate reporters of past events. During the early phase of analysis many therapists see the parents once every week or two weeks to obtain information about events in the child's life. As the child becomes a better reporter, sessions with the parents are gradually reduced and finally terminated.

The primary goal of psychoanalysis is to help the child to achieve insight—to recognize his or her feelings and his or her defenses and to deal with them in a direct manner. The analyst hopes "to undo the various repressions, distortions, displacements, condensations, etc., which had been brought about by the neurotic defense mechanisms, until, with the active help of the child, the unconscious content of the material is laid bare" (A. Freud, 1946a, p. 49). Child analysis involves the investigation and examination of past emotional experiences by the analyst and the child, particularly those emotional experiences of which the child is only dimly aware or not at all aware (unconscious). The means for expressing the conflict, motivation, and impulses are fantasy, emotion, and behavior (Lesser, 1972). The course of the child's development is assumed to have been inhibited or retarded through the by-products of past emotional trauma, and the analyst attempts to show the child relationships between present and past feelings. The designation of such relationships is an aspect of the psychoanalytic technique called *interpretation,* which also includes delineating for the child relationships between defenses and feelings and between fantasies and feelings (Kessler, 1966, pp. 379–80).

For the neo-Freudian analyst, the relationship with the patient during the course of treatment is of paramount importance. The patient must develop a trust that the analysis will be of benefit. To that end the therapist provides a setting that is free of threat and communicates concern and interest. The therapeutic atmosphere must contribute to the attenuation of anxiety that will facilitate the patient's learning about himself and his interactions with others.

The major assumption by the analyst is that the child experiences a normal progression of growth and development unless the environment interferes. The analyst is interested in the present in an attempt to determine the present purposiveness of the neurosis. The analyst and child work together to examine the child's behavior and the context in which it occurs with the goal of redressing the imbalances uncovered. To that end, the analysts must learn the child's language, rather than impose their own, provide warmth and support, and communicate a commitment to the analysis. The child may then become free to progress toward individuation and independence. Implicit in this theoretical context is that the environment (that is, parents) is inhibiting the child's natural, and perhaps optimal, development and causes the child to fear or distrust close relationships.

Contemporary psychoanalysts no longer give a great amount of attention to the individual theoretical variations that were initiated by the followers of Freud. At one time, analysts strongly identified with particular schools of analytic thought, such as Freudian, Jungian, or Adlerian; individual analysts now tend to choose aspects of various theories and evolve their own pattern or techniques while remaining faithful to psychoanalysis as the best treatment choice. Many of the concepts introduced by the post-Freudians have become interwoven into the fabric of psychoanalysis, such that separate identification of individual theorists has been attenuated.

psychotherapy

While psychoanalysis was becoming the treatment of choice for clinicians who had access to Freud's teaching and writings, changes were taking place in society that would pave the way for the provision of treatment for children's behavior problems. Before the twentieth century, children and their problems received little public or professional attention. One of the reasons for this neglect might have been the high death rates for infants and preschool children from diseases such as diphtheria and smallpox—diseases which have been essentially eradicated through mass immunization. Parents had to have a large number of children in order to have several who would live long enought to make an economic contribution to the household. Children, then, were seen as economic assets rather than as persons in their own right. Indeed, they were put to work as soon as possible, often as young as six or seven years of age, originally on family farms and later in the factories. Abuse of children in the factories led to the enactment of child labor laws that put limits on children's work in the factories. Later, of course, compulsory public education kept young children out of the factories altogether.

The development of children's rights has taken an interesting course. As long as children were raised and worked within the context of the family, few rights accrued to them. As society moved toward urbanization and children were employed outside of the family, concern about their status gradually began to develop. Remnants of the compromise made between the early rural family model and society's recognition of children's needs for education may be seen in the nine-month school year. Children were needed to work on the farms during the summer months, and the school year was designed to accommodate the needs of the rural community.

Compulsory education began to have the positive by-product of alerting others to the problems of children—a function that it continues to have today. With larger numbers of children coming together in groups, similarities and differences among children began to become more dramatically apparent, and children whose behavior differed markedly from that of their peers were viewed as needing help. Of course, some of the problems identified in school settings were no doubt created in that environment. In fact, the first clinic for children, developed by Witmer in 1896 at the University of Pennsylvania, focused on the adjustment of children to the school environment.

The first few decades of this century saw the development of a number of clinics for children that were affiliated with mental hospitals, schools, colleges, and social agencies. At the same time there was a growing interest in all aspects of children's behavior that culminated in the founding of a series of child development institutes at universities. The period of the 1920s and 1930s saw a tremendous increase in the amount of research activity directed toward an understanding of children's growth and development.

Beginning in the 1920s a movement was also initiated to provide help for disturbed children and their families. This movement grew out of an increasing recognition that many of the emotional problems of adulthood originated during the years of childhood. The establishment of child guidance clinics, begun in 1922 by the National Committee for Mental Hygiene and the Commonwealth Fund, was a major milestone in the development of services for children with behavior disorders. These clinics were unique in their emphasis on a multidisciplinary team approach to the diagnosis and treatment of children's problems. The team usually included a psychologist who administered and interpreted the diagnostic tests, a social worker who counseled the families, and a psychiatrist who treated the child. Given the growing demands for treatment services, several changes in the original team format evolved over time. One change included psychologists and social workers becoming directly involved in the treatment of children. Other changes included the development of a number of treatment approaches that were more suitable for the broader range of children's problems being brought to practitioners and clinics. That is, although psychiatrists were being trained primarily in psychoanalytic theory, psychoanalysis was neither suited to many of the problems presented at the clinics nor feasible in terms of professional and financial resources. These practical considerations were to be responsible for a number of the treatment techniques that later evolved.

psychoanalytically oriented psychotherapy

Perhaps most of the therapy now being conducted with children in clinics and in private practice would be labeled by its practitioners as "psychoanalytically oriented psychotherapy" because the training received by a great majority of psychiatrists, psychologists, and social workers practicing today has been heavily imbued with psychoanalytic theory. Although relatively few practitioners have had training in psychoanalysis per se, they do attempt to use the theoretical system evolved by Freud and his followers and the techniques that are feasible within their professional settings. During the 1940s and 1950s the theoretical emphases in the training programs for the three disciplines most strongly involved in the treatment of children's behavior problems were very similar. Gradually, other theoretical orientations and treatment techniques have been introduced into some of the training programs such that substantial changes both within and among the disciplines are taking place. Among the younger members of the professions there is already a strong tendency toward eclectic approaches in which a treatment technique is chosen in order to fit the problem, rather than toward a strict adherence to a unitary theoretical model.

Psychoanalytically oriented psychotherapy usually has as its goal the relief of those symptoms that precipitated the child's having been brought to the therapist or clinic. That is, the therapist concentrates primarily on the behavioral manifestations of the underlying problem. On a practical level this concentration means that the therapist more actively guides the activities during therapy and is more selective about responses to the child's behavior. The therapist tends to be more active in identifying the child's feelings and defenses but at the same time does so only when the feelings and defenses appear to be related to the manifested problem. In psychoanalytically oriented psychotherapy, children are seen only once or twice a week over a period of months, although some problems require a year or more of treatment. Treatment of the child is almost always accompanied by the treatment of one or both parents by another therapist. The parent is usually seen once a week throughout the course of the child's treatment. The two therapists communicate at regular intervals regarding the progress of their patients.

relationship therapy

Relationship therapy evolved from Rank's view that the benefits resulting from therapy were best when the therapist understood and utilized the patient's reactions to the therapy situation. This idea was later expanded and had a substantial influence on the therapeutic procedures used by social workers and other child guidance professionals. In writing the first two books on psychotherapy of children published in the United States, Taft (1933) and Allen (1942) emphasized the importance of the patient's active participation in the therapeutic process. The patient's past history and unconscious are deemphasized in favor of attention being given to the present situation. The relationship between the patient and the therapist is viewed as a unique experience rather than a recapitulation of parent-child relationships. The technique of interpretation is not used, but the therapist does reflect what the child seems to be feeling. Some of the early proponents of relationship therapy advocated the setting of a time limit for therapy, an arbitrary date agreed upon by both patients and therapist. The reason behind the setting of the time limit is apparently its role in helping the patient to accept reality.

Although not all of the original aspects of relationship therapy are strongly supported now, several of the components have greatly influenced contemporary therapists who have seen the need to develop actively a positive relationship with their patients in order to establish themselves as significant persons in the interaction. This active participation on the part of the therapist may take a number of forms, ranging from warm acceptance of the child's verbalizations and activities to providing sweets during the therapy session. Relationship therapy does not imply indiscriminate acceptance of the child's behavior but rather a human reponse that is appropriate to the situation.

nondirective therapy

Axline's nondirective therapy (1947) bears some resemblance to relationship therapy. She too considered that the relationship between the therapist and the child determined the success or failure of therapy. First and foremost, the therapist must develop a warm relationship with the child. The child's behavior is completely accepted by the therapist; no effort is made to communicate to the child that he or she has a problem. Nondirective therapists believe that behavior problems are caused by adults' criticism and domination of children. Therefore, the therapist attempts to impart a feeling of permissiveness within the relationship.

The goal of nondirective therapy is to permit the child to reveal his or her true self, the self that has been hampered in its development by environmental forces. Paramount to nondirective therapy is the therapist's assumption that the child can solve his or her own problems. The therapist's role is to recognize feelings and reflect them back to the child to facilitate the child's insight into his or her own behavior. In this way, the child takes the lead by behaving, and the therapist follows by reflecting. Axline proposed that the child's play serve as the vehicle for establishing the therapist-child relationship.

release therapy

The therapeutic effect of release therapy is based on the child's acting out or talking about a traumatic event that is the source of the child's disturbance. David Levy (1938) described the use of release therapy with young children through the medium of play that he viewed as a substitute for language. He recommended it for children whose symptoms are clearly precipitated by a specific traumatic event, such as a car accident, rather than for children who have chronic behavior problems. Through play, the therapist arranges for children to repeat the traumatic event at their own rate, expressing the feelings and fantasies that were not expressed in the original experience. The assumption is that children's experiencing the appropriate emotions will serve to relieve their symptoms. While theoretically useful, therapists do not have many opportunities to use release therapy because very few children brought to clinics have symptoms that can be traced to a single traumatic event.

group therapy

Group therapy involves the assembly of a number of patients and one or several therapists and is conducted by therapists with a wide variety of theoretical orientations, particularly those who emphasize the importance of interpersonal and social factors in the facilitation of the treatment process. The composition of the group is considered to be an important determinant of success; ideally, the group should consist of children with various types of problems rather than children with the same type of problem.

The term *group psychotherapy* can be traced back to Moreno (1946) who developed psychodrama, a technique whereby patients act out their problems to one another. Group therapy aims at reducing the symptomology and improving interpersonal relations through controlled group experiences. On a practical level, group therapy is economical in that the members of the group share the cost of the therapist's time. While group therapy is not usually recommended as the sole therapy for the most serious disorders, it does seem to have a distinctive advantage over individual psychotherapy for persons with problems related to social functioning.

Slavson and Schiffer (1975) describe three basic types of group therapy for children: activity group therapy, activity-interview psychotherapy, and play group therapy. Activity group therapy is used for groups of up to eight elementary-school age children and consists of providing materials for arts and crafts and a setting for free acting out. The two basic criteria for including children in activity group therapy are: (1) a capacity to relate to others (the child's history should reveal at least one moderately positive relationship with a person in his or her family, a peer, or a teacher) and (2) the capacity to change attitudes and conduct through corrective experiences. The behavior problems considered to be optimal for activity group therapy are conduct disorders, habit disorders (bed-wetting and thumb-sucking, for example), defective sexual identifications, mild neuroses, and situational anxiety. Children with severe disorders, such as psychoses, mental retardation, and excessive generalized aggressiveness, and those with physical handicaps and deformities are not considered to benefit from activity group therapy.

The group members are carefully selected to achieve a balance between aggressive, active children and socially withdrawn children. The therapeutic effect is derived from the group activity that serves to attenuate the aggression of some children and increase the social responsiveness of the previously withdrawn children. A two-hour session is scheduled weekly with the average child becoming ready for termination of therapy at the end of two years. The therapist is totally accepting of the children, remains relatively passive, and gives no attention to the children's hostility and aggression. The therapist occasionally gives words of praise and, in general, serves as a model of self-control for the children.

Activity-interview group psychotherapy is a combination of activity group psychotherapy and individual psychotherapy. The children meet in activity groups in which they are free to act as they choose, and the therapist interprets their behavior and encourages them to communicate their problems and anxieties to one another and to the therapist. The goal of activity-interview group psychotherapy is to provide the children with insight into the reasons for their behavior and to help them develop more appropriate social responses.

Play group therapy is a form of group therapy for children between the ages of four and six years. Using play materials that encourage activities symbolizing psychological conflicts (for example, dolls representing adults and children), the therapist interprets the children's behavior at play in a manner that is appropriate for this age group. Five children, not more than one year apart in age, are considered to be the best number for a play group.

Relatively few adequately controlled research studies examining the effectiveness of group therapy with children have been published. One survey (Abramowitz, 1976) of the research literature revealed that one-third of the studies reported positive results, one-third showed mixed outcomes, and the remaining one-third found no improvement for children in group therapy.

family therapy

Clinicians have long believed that the family is the primary influence on the development or maintenance, or both aspects, of most childhood behavior problems. It is somewhat surprising, then, to find that psychotherapy with families has had such a brief history. A few therapists began to interview families together during the 1940s, but it was not until the 1950s and 1960s that the theoretical formulations and clinical presentations began to have a significant impact on clinical practice.

Family therapy seems to have evolved from investigations of severely disturbed (schizophrenic) adults and their families, the hypothesis having been that schizophrenia was caused by communication failure among family members. Ackerman (1958) presented a flexible model of family therapy that included various combinations of family members in individual and group psychotherapy; he is usually given credit for providing the impetus for family intervention in instances of childhood behavior disorders.

Like therapists who utilize group therapy, practitioners of family therapy are guided by a variety of theories. Some family therapists are psychoanalytically oriented and believe that treatment should include the uncovering of parents' unresolved conflicts that are reflected in the child's behavior problem. Therapists with this orientation tend to focus on providing an atmosphere that encourages open and free communication. Their assumption is that the family's interactions in the therapy setting will reflect their relationships in the home, thereby permitting the therapist to determine the ways in which the family system may be supporting the child's problem. The therapist carefully observes which members of the family dominate the conversation and which ones are submissive or silent and notes the relative frequency with which various members of the family speak and to whom their communication is directed. The therapist also attempts to ascertain the degree of marital conflict and the child's role in this conflict.

Satir (1964), a leader in the family therapy field, emphasizes the teaching of communication skills to family members and relies very little on the uncovering of unconscious conflicts. Marital therapy is a large component of Satir's family therapy in that she views children's problems as being a by-product of marital conflict. Usually the parents are seen together for a few sessions before children are included in the family group. Satir's therapy may be characterized as active, direct, and authoritarian in the sense that the therapist generally talks more than any family member during the session. The family members are taught to acknowledge and accept individual differences, to realize that disagreements and differences should not be viewed with alarm, and to communicate their perceptions and feelings clearly (Satir and others, 1975).

The systems-intervention approach (Minuchin, 1974) deemphasizes the typical focus on the referred client by considering the family as a biosocial system. This approach assumes that the child's problem serves as an important factor in maintaining the family's homeostasis. According to this theory, if the child's problem were to disappear, then new symptoms within the family would appear or the family unit would disintegrate. Systems-intervention family therapy attempts to change the family structure so that the child's problem is no longer "needed."

Family therapy is often recommended for children's problems that arise from failure of performance by parents and in crisis situations as well as from adolescent reactions. Much of the family therapy in clinics tends to be relatively brief and focuses on reality factors in child rearing, such as discipline, toilet training, and specific fears. This brevity of treatment is not necessarily a characteristic of the therapy itself but rather a consequence of the selection of patients and the practical problems associated with both parents attending the sessions, which are usually held once a week.

A review of research studies on the effectiveness of family therapy (DeWitt, 1978) indicated that there is some evidence that family therapy is superior to no treatment. Gurman and Kniskern's (1978) review concluded that "family therapy appears to be at least as effective and possibly more effective than individual therapy for a wide variety of problems" (p. 883).

settings for child therapy

Settings for psychotherapy have traditionally been designated as either outpatient or inpatient. Outpatient settings are those that the client visits for specific therapeutic sessions while living at home. Child guidance clinics and the offices of professionals in private practice are examples of outpatient facilities. An inpatient facility is one in which the child resides most of the time and one that is presumed to be a more therapeutic environment than the child's home. Institutions and hospitals are inpatient settings. Most psychotherapy with children is conducted in outpatient facilities with psychiatrists, psychologists, and social workers who are in private practice or employed by community or university-affiliated clinics. There is a growing trend, however, for these professionals to leave their offices and provide therapeutic intervention for children indirectly through consultation with other persons in the child's environment. For example, a psychologist employed by a mental health clinic might go to a school and consult with a teacher who is having a problem with a child in the classroom. School systems are increasingly hiring psychologists to provide both direct and indirect services to children.

Sometimes, the severity of a child's problem or the condition of the home environment, or both, leads to a recommendation that the child be placed in another setting. One such option is the residential treatment center that attempts to provide an optimal therapeutic environment to facilitate the child's recovery. Residential treatment centers may be public or private, and the quality of their programs varies greatly. Financial resources determine, in large measure, the number of professional and nonprofessional staff employed, but the centers with the highest per capita costs are not necessarily the most effective. Some centers, however, are so poorly supported that they have become nothing more than warehouses for children. Fortunately, legal suits declaring a patient's right to be treated are being won, and thus an end may be in sight for the warehousing of patients in institutions.

Communities sometimes have alternatives that appear to be less severe than residential care or institutionalization for a child who has to be removed from home. These alternatives are foster homes and group homes, both of which are frequently supported by public agencies. Foster homes provide a family environment for children who would otherwise be institutionalized or receive no help at all. Foster homes are provided: for children who are awaiting adoption; for handicapped children who are presumed to be "unadoptable"; for children whose parents are temporarily unable to care for them (if, for example, both parents are badly injured in an accident); for children whose parents are judged to be abusive or neglectful, or both, as well as for children whose parents decide that they cannot cope with their behavior at home.

Foster homes are licensed by the states and have to meet certain specifications for safety. Foster parents tend to be older couples whose children have grown up and left home or younger couples who have no or few children. They are examined and approved by the social service agencies that control the assignment of children to foster homes. The number of foster children cared for by one family is usually limited to about five children, although the family can choose to have only one or two children at a time. A monthly stipend for each child is paid to the foster parents for living expenses, and the agency also pays for other necessary expenses, such as medical and dental treatment. Some agencies provide financial support for psychotherapy when it is indicated.

Group homes are a relatively new development in services to children. A group home is usually supported by a public agency or other community groups that employs a married couple to be house parents and counselors. The counselors have usually received formal training that prepares them for their therapeutic role. These homes are used in various ways in different communities. Sometimes, they are a community holding facility for children awaiting court proceedings or used in lieu of sending delinquent children to training schools. They are also used as halfway homes for persons who have recently been discharged from mental hospitals or institutions for the retarded. In recent years, there has been an effort to decentralize the large state institutions in favor of keeping patients in their own community. One alternative to the large regional institutions has been the development of community-based group homes. The group home offers much potential for the improvement of treatment and rehabilitation of children with problems—a potential that is only slowly being realized.

pharmacotherapy

The relationship between physical status and behavior is not well understood. Behavior problems, including altered emotional states, have been related to a variety of chronic physical problems, such as malnutrition and abnormal hormonal levels. Because of the possibility that a behavior problem may be directly caused by a current physical malfunction, which may be best treated medically, therapists often request that the child receive a physical examination including tests of sensory functioning, prior to diagnostic examination. Sometimes, during the psychological examination the clinician observes certain behavior such as involuntary movements, or developmental abnormalities such as retarded physical growth, that are closely tied to physical malfunctioning and refers the child to a medical specialist prior to psychological intervention. In a few instances, medical treatment will eliminate the need for psychological intervention; however, psychological help is often required as an adjunct to medical intervention.

Physicians, particularly pediatricians and psychiatrists, have used a variety of physical methods to treat children's behavior problems. For example, electroconvulsive shock and chemical agents that induce convulsions, as well as prefrontal lobotomies, have been used with severely disturbed children. Bender (1955) has conducted much of the pioneer research with these methods that had earlier been found to be effective in alleviating adult psychological problems. Bender has maintained that the severe behavior problems (psychoses) of children are the result of organic pathology and would, therefore, be treated best with physical methods. Although Bender has claimed some of them to be effective, these methods have not been generally adopted by physicians. The physical treatment methods now in use consist almost exclusively of interventions with medication.

The use of psychoactive drugs with children has become increasingly more common since the 1950s when research began to demonstrate their usefulness with adult clients. Research on the effectiveness of drug therapy with children, however, has been greatly hampered by the inadequate criteria for diagnostic classifications of children's behavior problems (Conners, 1972, p. 316), as well as faulty research designs. The traditional diagnostic categories include children with widely heterogeneous behaviors, and this behavioral variability has probably contributed to the lack of findings in some studies. More recent drug studies are attempting to group children on the basis of more specific behavioral characteristics.

Studies using group designs must take several precautions to ensure the reliability and validity of the research findings: (1) subjects must be randomly assigned to groups or carefully matched across groups on the basis of relevant pretest measures, (2) a placebo control group should usually be included to control for nonspecific factors, such as increased attention to the child, and, (3) the study should have a double-blind research design in which group assignment is not known by the child, significant adults in the child's environment, or the person arranging the drug therapy with the family. These precautions must be taken because reports of improved behavior are frequently given when the client and other persons in the environment believe that treatment is taking place (even when sugar pills or placebos are given instead of medication).

Evaluation of drug therapy can also be done within the context of a single subject design. In a single subject design, periods of medication would be alternated with placebo periods. Ideally, no one in regular contact with the child should know whether the child is taking the medication or a placebo, particularly the person evaluating the child's behavior each day. Use of the single subject design also lends itself to establishing the optimal dosage of medication because dosage levels may be varied among the medication periods.

The average physician is likely to be conservative about prescribing drugs for children with behavior problems (Conners, 1978, p. 86). Many of the older physicians do not use the newer medications because they do not have the time to keep up with the research literature, or because they are satisfied with their previous practices. Physicians vary in their methods of placing children on medication. Some will start with the mean dosage level recommended by the manufacturer, while others will begin with a lower dosage level and systematically increase it, depending on its effects. Psychoactive drugs prescribed for children, however, are often inadequately evaluated, and many children are either prematurely taken off medication that would be effective at another dosage level or left on medication that is ineffective. Psychologists, with their special training in behavior observation and research design, could work more effectively with physicians to reduce this problem.

The medications currently being used for children presenting behavior problems may be classified into three principal categories: psychomotor stimulants, antidepressants, and neuroleptics (Campbell and Small, 1978, p. 16). In the remainder of this section each category is described in terms of the drugs' effects on behavior.

psychomotor stimulants

Several drugs, which have been found to stimulate the adult's central nervous system, have been found to be helpful in controlling hyperactivity, inattentiveness, and short attention span in children. Until recently, it was believed that these drugs had "paradoxical" effects on hyperactive behavior in that they apparently reduced the activity levels. The current view is that psychomotor stimulants affect attentional processes and that the improved behavior is secondary to the child's being able to concentrate and focus attention appropriately.

The most commonly used stimulants have been dextroamphetamine (Dexedrine)[1] and methylphenidate (Ritalin); both have been found to be equally effective in well-controlled studies. Magnesium pemoline (Cylert) and deanol (Deaner), more recently studied stimulants, are also considered to be effective (Gittelman-Klein, 1978). As in the case with virtually all drugs, psychomotor stimulants produce a variety of side effects that may vary among children. About one-third of children taking moderately high doses of dextroamphetamine or methylphenidate have a loss or reduction of appetite and difficulty falling asleep. A small percentage of children show an increase of a sad mood. These side effects are most pronounced when treatment begins and usually subside within several weeks. There are some data suggesting that dextroamphetamine may have an inhibiting effect on physical growth (Safer and Allen, 1973) when it is taken for long periods of time, such as several years. It is generally recommended that a growth chart be kept for children treated with stimulants to alert the physician to possible growth problems. Most physicians also suggest that drug "holidays" be scheduled both to counteract growth inhibition and to provide an opportunity for monitoring the drug's effectiveness.

The principal differences between magnesium pemoline and the other stimulants are that it requires two to three weeks to become effective and each dose is longer acting. Magnesium pemoline can be administered only once a day, while the other stimulants must be given two or more times each day.

antidepressants

Although research on childhood depression has yet to determine whether depression during childhood mirrors that found in adults (see Chapter 13), children with a variety of symptoms have been given the antidepressants found to be effective for adults, the tricyclic antidepressants and monoamine oxidase (MAO) inhibitors. The current view is that these drugs must be considered experimental in that research studies demonstrating adequate effectiveness have not yet been completed.

neuroleptics

Neuroleptics, or antipsychotic drugs, have been very successful in the treatment of adult schizophrenic and paranoid psychosis. More specifically, these drugs have

[1]Drugs are labeled by their generic name with the trade name in parenthesis.

been found to be effective in reducing adults' thought disorders, hallucinations, delusions, combativeness, anxiety, tension, restlessness, and social withdrawal. Although chemically unrelated to previously known sedatives, many of these drugs cause sedation possibly contributing to the therapeutic effect in some cases.

other drugs

In addition to those described above, a variety of other drugs are commonly prescribed by physicians for children with behavioral or emotional disorders. They will be described in the later chapters that focus on particular types of psychological problems.

A number of noncontrolled clinical studies suggested that children with a variety of symptoms could benefit from these drugs, and some children have received these drugs for long periods of time. Increasing evidence is accumulating that the side effects of neuroleptics may, however, be greater for children than adults. For example, there is clear evidence that the phenothiazines, a type of neuroleptic, are capable of impairing cognitive function. More specifically, the sedative type of neuroleptics such as chlorpromazine (Thorazine) and thioridazine (Mellaril) lower overall functioning and thereby interfere with learning and performance. Thus, the phenothiazines are recommended only in severe cases when other less debilitating drugs are not effective.

Conclusions

Since the 1940s psychotherapeutic methods for children's behavior problems have been dominated by psychoanalytic theory and variations thereof. The most frequently used model has involved a therapist conducting one or two treatment sessions with the child each week and a second therapist treating the parents during one session each week. Treatment lasts from several months to several years. Both the demands for psychotherapeutic services and the development of theoretical variations have created an increased emphasis on current environmental intervention in individual, group, and family therapies. Research has not yet demonstrated that the psychotherapies for children are effective, but relatively little research has been conducted on the results of the therapy. The lack of positive findings in the available research may have been due, at least in part, to diagnostic groupings that included a wide variety of behavior problems. The questionable effectiveness of psychotherapy and an increasing awareness of organic factors as being implicated in the etiology of children's behavior problems are likely to have contributed to an increasing use of psychoactive drugs with children.

Recommended Readings

Kaplan, C., "Pediatric Pharmacology," in *The Practitioner's Guide to Psychoactive Drugs,* edited by E. L. Bassuk, and S. C. Schoonover. New York: Plenum, 1977.

Garfield, S. L., and Bergin, S. L., eds., *Handbook of Psychotherapy and Behavior Change: An Empirical Analysis* (2nd ed.), Chapter 11, New York: John Wiley, 1978. A review of research on the results of psychotherapy with children.

Reisman, J. M., *Principles of Psychotherapy with Children.* New York: John Wiley, 1973. Describes the practice of psychotherapy with children and their parents.

Satir, V., Stachowiak, J., Taschman, H. A., Tiffany, D. W., Cohen, J. I., Robinson, A. M., and Ogburn, K. C., *Helping Families to Change.* New York: Jason Aronson, 1975.

Wolman, B. B., Egan, J., and Ross, A. O., eds., *Handbook of Treatment of Mental Disorders in Childhood and Adolescence,* Chapters 1, 2, 4, 5, 6. Englewood Cliffs, N. J.: Prentice-Hall, 1978. Chapters describing various treatment approaches.

treatment:
behavioral approaches

7

Behavior therapy with children is a recent development in the history of behavior therapy. The research that has substantiated the principles of learning has a history dating back to the early part of this century. Behavior therapy is the application of these principles to behaviors that are inappropriate, inadequate, or stressful to the person doing them or to significant people in that person's environment.

background

The emphasis on behavior, rather than on mental processes, has been an important aspect of psychological theory since its proposal by John B. Watson in the first decade of this century. Advocates of behaviorism, focusing on observable behavior, emphasized learned rather than unlearned behavior and proceeded to investigate those variables that affected learning. Through carefully controlled laboratory research with both animals and humans, experimental psychologists attempted to discover the conditions under which learning takes place. They then formulated principles concerning the prediction and control of behavior, and these principles of learning are the foundation upon which behavior therapy is based.

learning principles

Watson and Rayner (1920) were the first to demonstrate that an infant could learn a fear. At about nine months of age, Albert was tested and showed no fear to a number of live animals, such as a rat, a rabbit, and a dog, and to various inanimate objects, such as cotton and human masks. He did show fear, however, when a steel bar was unexpectedly struck with a hammer just behind him. Two months later, this loud sound was presented when Albert touched a white rat placed before him; seven pairings of the rat and the loud sound occurred in two sessions one week apart. Albert subsequently reacted with crying and avoidance when the rat was presented without the loud sound. Five days later, Albert reacted in fear not only to the rat but also to a rabbit, a dog, and a sealskin coat; he showed a moderately fearful response to a bearded Santa Claus mask and Watson's hair; and he had a mild response to a package of white cotton. Albert's negative responses to stimuli other than the rat were interpreted as evidence that a learned fear could be transferred to other objects.

Jones (1924), a student of Watson's, showed that a young child could both learn and unlearn a fear response. On this occasion fear to a white rabbit was learned in a manner similar to that in the Watson and Rayner study. To bring about the unlearning of the fear response, Jones arranged for the child to observe other children playing with the rabbit. She gradually brought the rabbit closer and closer to the child and simultaneously gave the child food each time he made approach movements toward the rabbit.

Although Watson became famous for his books on child rearing, a careful study of these books indicates that at the time they were written psychological theory was not yet well developed enough for application. These early studies, although important in retrospect, did not appear to have an impact on the clinical practitioners of the time. Moreover, the early learning psychologists were concerned about the development of psychology as a science and were not yet ready to develop practical applications. These factors may have encouraged the early clinical psychologists to adopt the psychoanalytic approach to treatment being used by their psychiatrist colleagues.

In 1949 Fuller reported the first study of operant conditioning in a clinical setting. He worked with a young man considered by physicians to be a "vegetative idiot" and incapable of learning. Fuller used a warm sugar-milk solution as a reinforcer for successively greater movements of the young man's right arm, thereby demonstrating in four sessions that he was capable of learning.

Another significant step taken in the application of learning principles is represented in a series of studies conducted by Lindsley and Skinner at Metropolitan

State Hospital in Massachusetts during the 1950s. In one study with patients who averaged seventeen years of hospitalization, they compared the effects of two schedules of intermittent reinforcement for lever pulling and found that the patients' lever-pulling behavior was stable and predictable, mirroring the results found earlier with lower organisms. Lindsley (1960) reported the interesting finding that the hospitalized patients had very slow rates of response in comparison to normal adults.

The early 1960s saw the beginning of applied behavioral research with children's problems by Donald Baer and Sidney Bijou at the University of Washington. Working with them were Ivar Lovaas, Robert Orlando, Jay Birnbrauer, Robert Wahler, Montrose Wolf, Todd Risley, James Sherman, staff members and graduate students who have subsequently contributed significantly to the applied research literature.

behavioral vs. traditional models

The behavior therapy approach has come to be contrasted with the traditional models of psychotherapy in several important ways. The traditional approaches emphasize a medical model of disease, namely, that behavior disorders are manifestations or symptoms of an underlying pathology. The goals of traditional psychotherapy are to extirpate the underlying pathology and thereby remove the symptoms. Behavior therapy, on the other hand, conceptualizes symptoms as abnormal behavior that has been learned in the same way that other behaviors are learned. Traditional psychotherapists believe that removal of the symptom alone will result in symptom substitution and would, therefore, be of very little therapeutic benefit. Behavior therapists view the removal of the symptom as the primary goal of therapy and cite follow-up studies that have found no evidence of symptom substitution for persons who have had behavior therapy. The behavior therapist emphasizes the importance of the current environment in maintaining the abnormal behavior, while the traditional psychotherapist views the abnormal behavior as a direct result of an historical antecedent.

From a behavioral point of view, therapy consists of establishing, increasing, and maintaining appropriate or desirable responses and decreasing or eliminating inappropriate or undesirable responses. Each child who is referred is recognized as having a unique pattern of responses and environmental stimuli, and therapy programs are individually designed for each client. Because the principles of learning are relatively easily understood, many people are under the impression that behavior therapy is easy to learn and simple to perform. Most behavior therapists, however, realize that knowledge of learning principles alone is not adequate for the treatment of children. The principles describe the lawful relationships between stimulus events and responses, but they do not tell the therapist what stimulus events are controlling the behavior of a particular child. The therapist must determine that information, and the success of the therapeutic program depends upon the therapist's obtaining the correct information. Securing this information requires considerable knowledge about children's environments in general and the client's environment in particular.

The behavior therapist must also be knowledgeable about the developmental sequences and norms for behavior. Therapists who are naive about normal child development and learning might expend much wasted energy working on types of behavior that have no precursors in the child's repertoire. Behavior therapists should know the research literature, both the basic research that serves as the foundation for behavior therapy and the applied research that describes the applications of learning principles with a variety of children's problems in a variety of environmental situations.

Behavior therapy, being a relatively new approach to clinical problems, has brought together a group of professionals with a broad range of backgrounds. Some child behavior therapists were trained in traditional clinical programs in psychology and later became advocates of the behavioral approach. Some of the most productive researchers in behavior therapy with children were originally trained in experimental child or developmental psychology. In recent years, clinical psychology training programs have begun to add behavior therapists to their faculties, thus increasing the number of graduate students who are being trained in behavioral theory and techniques. Concerns are now being raised about the qualifications of persons who provide behavior therapy services, and it is likely that standards for training and experience will soon be developed for the protection of the public and the professions, as they have been for the traditional clinicians.

treatment design and evaluation

One of the main characteristics of behavior therapy is the continuous collection of data throughout the course of treatment—data that will be used to evaluate the effectiveness of the intervention plan. The data obtained during the baseline phase (period before treatment has begun) is later compared with data obtained during the treatment phase. Since the goal of behavior therapy is to effect changes in behavior, either increases of appropriate behavior or decreases of inappropriate behavior, a comparison of the behavior's frequency during the baseline and treatment phases is conducted. Effectiveness is measured by the amount of increase or decrease in appropriate or inappropriate behaviors, respectively.

the AB design

The simplest type of treatment design is a baseline phase (A) followed by a treatment phase (B). A comparison of the behavior rates during the two phases may reflect a change, but this design does not allow us to say with certainty that the treatment program was responsible for the behavior change. That is, other occurrences in the child's environment, unrelated to the treatment program *per se*, may have taken place and may have been responsible for the observed behavior change. Behavior therapists are interested in more than a change in behavior; they want to know whether the program is responsible for that change.

ABAB design and variations

Several treatment designs have been developed to show that the therapy program, rather than other events, changed the behavior (Kazdin, 1973). One of these designs is the *reversal*, or ABAB design. In the reversal design, the treatment phase (B^1) is followed by a reversal to the baseline condition (A^2), which in turn is followed by the treatment phase (B^2). Changes from one phase to another are made when the behavior becomes stable or is different from the preceding phase.

Figure 7-1 presents an example of an ABAB design. During the initial baseline phase, the rate of appropriate behavior was at a low level, averaging about four each session. Following the initiation of treatment, the rate of appropriate behavior increased to a high of twelve each session. Reversal from the treatment phase to the baseline condition resulted in a decrease in the behavior; reinstatement of the

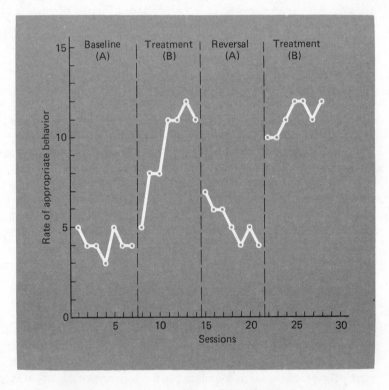

Figure 7-1. An example of an ABAB design.

treatment condition, however, was followed by a rapid increase of the appropriate behavior. That the behavior was observed to change as a function of the change of the phase gives us more confidence that the treatment program was indeed responsible for the increase in appropriate behavior.

Several variations of the ABAB design have been developed. Occasionally, it is necessary to begin treatment immediately; in these cases, a BAB or BABAB design might be used. In other cases, it is not possible to reinstate the baseline conditions, and the reversal phase will consist of a procedure that is different from the treatment condition. For example, if the treatment condition involves reinforcing on-task behavior in the classroom, a reversal condition could involve reinforcing other behaviors except on-task behaviors. This procedure is called *differential reinforcement of other behavior* (DRO).

There are situations in which a reversal might not be expected to lead to behavior change because the improved behavior comes under the control of consequences by others in the child's environment. An example might be that of a previously withdrawn child whose new social behaviors begin to be reinforced by peers. Removal of the treatment program, social reinforcement by the teacher in this case, would probably not result in a decrease in the child's social behaviors because they have come under the control of peer reinforcement. In other situations, reversal may be contraindicated when the problem behavior is severe or physically harmful to the child or others.

multiple baseline designs

Fortunately, other treatment designs are available when reversal is undesirable or not expected. The most popular of these are the multiple-baseline designs that demonstrate the effect of the treatment program by showing that the change in behavior is related to the introduction of the program at different points in time. There are basically three types of multiple-baseline designs that depend on the collection of data across behaviors, individuals, or situations.

In a design involving the collection of data across behaviors, baseline data are collected simultaneously on two or more behavior problems. After stability has been achieved, the treatment program is begun for only one of the behaviors. When stability is again achieved, the treatment program is applied to the second behavior, and so on. Treatment is considered to be effective when changes in the problem behaviors take place after, not before, the introduction of the program, and no systematic changes occur in the untreated behaviors.

In multiple-baseline designs across individuals, baseline data are collected on the same behavior problem for two or more persons at the same times. After the baselines for each individual become stable, the treatment program is begun for one person. After stability is again achieved, the treatment program is extended to a second person and maintained for the first person. The treatment program is considered to be effective if changes in the behaviors of each person follow the introduction of treatment for that person.

In multiple-baseline designs across situations, baseline data are collected on the same behavior of an individual in two or more situations (for example, home and school). After the baselines in the situations become stable, the treatment program is begun in one situation. When stability is again achieved, the treatment program is extended to the second situation while being maintained in the first situation. This procedure is continued until the treatment program is being used in all of the situations. The treatment program is considered to be effective if the behavior changes in each situation follow the initiation of treatment in that situation.

changing criterion design

In this type of design (Axelrod, Hall, Weis, and Rohrer, 1974), after the baseline period, the treatment program is initially focused on a relatively easy goal. After the easy goal is achieved, a change in the criterion for success is introduced. The treatment plan involves a series of progressive steps in the behavior goal so that, as the behavior is progressively changing from its baseline rate, the client is consistently rewarded for small improvements. The treatment plan is considered to be effective when the changes in behavior follow the changes in the behavioral goal or criterion.

methods for increasing behaviors

Many children are referred for therapy because one or more of their behaviors are occurring too infrequently. That is, the adults in the child's environment are concerned about behavioral deficiencies in the child's repertoire. Various methods have been developed based on learning principles to increase or establish behaviors that are considered to be necessary or desirable. In this section we describe the principal methods for increasing appropriate behaviors: contingent presentation of positive reinforcement, self-control, prompting, shaping, and contingent removal of negative reinforcement.

contingent presentation of positive reinforcement

The most frequently used method for increasing the rate of an appropriate behavior is to present a positive reinforcer immediately after the appropriate behavior occurs. This method is appropriate for children who have the behavior in their repertoire, but its rate is lower than what is considered optimal.

One example of an undesirably low rate of behavior might be that of a child who only rarely interacts with people at nursery school. The label of "socially withdrawn" would be used by some clinicians to describe that child, but the behavior therapist describes such a child as having a low rate of social responses. In this example, the behavior therapist's first step might be to delineate the behavior with the help of the child's teacher and to observe its occurrence in the school setting. The therapist would probably at the same time record what occurred both when the child was being social and when the child was not being social (the baseline phase). Therapy begins with the presentation of a stimulus, which the therapist has judged to have high potential for reinforcer effectiveness, following each occurrence of a social response.

Reinforcers. Choosing the reinforcer is an important component of operant conditioning procedures. The therapist looks for a reinforcer that is likely to be effective with the child and easily available in the setting in which the behavior occurs. One such reinforcer in the nursery school might be teacher attention. If teacher attention is the therapist's choice, the therapist would ask the teacher to go over to the child and make positive statements, such as "I'm really glad to see that you and David are having a good time together," each time that the teacher observes the child to be interacting with a peer. It should be stressed that the teacher's attention should coincide with the occurrence of the desired behavior.

There are several ways of determining which stimuli have a high probability of being reinforcers for a particular child. During the assessment procedure the therapist could ask the child, parents, or teacher, or all of them, about which things the child likes to have or which activities the child particularly enjoys, or the therapist could ask the child to complete one of several reinforcement survey schedules (see, for example, Keat 1974). Still another way is to observe the child in the setting in which therapy will occur and apply the *Premack Principle* (Premack, 1965), which states that a high frequency activity can be used as a reinforcer for a low frequency behavior. The general idea is to determine how the child prefers to spend time when free to choose activities. This principle is particularly useful for identifying potential reinforcers in the preschool and home environments.

In choosing a reinforcer, the therapist must take into account the child's motivational status with respect to the stimulus. Reinforcers that are freely available or that the child receives frequently may not be effective. Stimuli, such as food, are usually effective after a period of deprivation, but they are relatively ineffective immediately after the child has had a meal. The effectiveness of social stimuli, too, might be increased with deprivation and decreased under conditions of satiation. Thus, a teacher's *very* frequent use of positive statements could decrease the effectiveness of that kind of attention as a reinforcer. It is unusual, however, to find teachers who use a great amount of social reinforcement.

Although behavior therapists have become associated with the use of using M&M candies as reinforcers, sweets and other foods are not used or even preferred in most settings. Food sometimes has to be used because no other reinforcers can be found for particular clients. In addition, researchers in laboratory settings have often used food as a matter of convenience. In most natural settings, however, behavior therapists tend to avoid the use of candy and other snack foods for dietary and dental reasons, unless, of course, no other reinforcers are available.

Some adults express concern when a behavior therapist suggests the use of a tangible reinforcer, such as candy, trinkets, or money, in an intervention program.

One of these concerns is that the therapist is "bribing" the child. Two statements can be made in response to this concern. One is that the correct use of the word "bribe" refers to payment for an illegal activity, while the therapist's goals is to increase *appropriate* behavior. The second statement is that adults receive tangible reinforcers for much of their life's work: how many adults would continue working at their jobs if their salaries were cut off? In other words, there are situations in which tangible reinforcers are necessary to develop and maintain behavior.

The use of tangible reinforcers does present some problems to the therapist, however. The long-range goal of therapy is to increase the appropriate behavior and to have "natural" contingencies take over its maintenance. A natural contingency is a response-reinforcer relationship that exists in the child's environment prior to intervention by a behavior therapist. An example of natural contingency is the observation that a teacher will occasionally praise a child for good work. If the teacher's praise is not effective as a reinforcer for the child, however, the therapist might design a program that temporarily uses tangible reinforcement.

The therapist in this situation would introduce tangible reinforcers to be given by the teacher each time the behavior occurs. The teacher would also be instructed to praise the child at the same time the tangible reinforcer is given. The therapist's aim is that with a large number of such pairings stimulus substitution will occur through classical conditioning; that is, the teacher's praise will acquire reinforcing properties. After the desired rate of appropriate behavior is achieved, then a program is initiated in which the tangible reinforcer is carefully faded out while teacher praise is maintained. Teacher praise will later be gradually decreased until it approximates the natural contingencies available to all children in the classroom.

Evaluation of treatment effectiveness. Simultaneous with the initiation of reinforcement of the target behavior, the therapist arranges that observation records of the behavior's occurrence be collected at regular intervals, usually by the same person who collected the baseline data. During each therapy session comparison of the behavior with the baseline data will quickly reveal the effect of the intervention program designed by the therapist. Most behaviors begin to change rather rapidly, and it would be unusual for a therapist to continue a program that has not produced change within a few days or weeks.

If the behavior remains at a low rate, then the therapist would assume that there is something wrong with the program and would take steps to correct it. The therapist first has to determine whether the plan has been implemented correctly. Sometimes instructions are misunderstood, and the mediator may omit a crucial component of the program or add some factor to the situation that would decrease the program's effectiveness. If the therapist is satisfied that the program has been carried out as intended, then the fault may reside in the choice of the stimulus to serve as the reinforcer. In this event, the therapist would seek a more effective reinforcer. For example, teacher's praise is not a reinforcer for some children, but the same children will work very hard for points that will give them a free choice of activities later in the day.

When a particular stimulus does not have the intended effect on the behavior, it is incorrect to say that reinforcement does not work. The definition of reinforcement stipulates that a stimulus is properly called a reinforcer only after it has been demonstrated to affect behavior with its contingent use. Reinforcement always works, but therapists and other adults are not always accurate in their choice of stimuli to serve as reinforcers for particular children.

Schedules of reinforcement. A continuous schedule of reinforcement, that is, reinforcing every instance of the target response, has been demonstrated to be the most efficient technique for obtaining rapid increases in behavior. Once the desired behavior rate is achieved, however, reinforcement may be *gradually* decreased without a concomitant change in the behavior. Reinforcement following less than 100 percent of the responses is called an *intermittent* schedule of reinforcement. During therapy when responses are carefully monitored, it is possible to plan schedules of reinforcement that are most effective for maintaining an optimal rate of the appropriate behavior. Since large changes in the reinforcement schedule tend to disrupt behavior, the therapist might begin the process of reducing reinforcement by reinforcing every other response. When the behavior is stable, reinforcement might follow every third response and so on. Schedules that involve the presentation of reinforcement after a specific number of responses are called *fixed-ratio* schedules. At some point in the procedure the therapist will change to a variable-ratio schedule that involves reinforcing a response that follows an average number rather than a fixed number of responses. For example, a variable ratio five schedule indicates that reinforcement, on the average, follows every fifth response, but sometimes it might occur after the second response and other times after the third, fourth, fifth, sixth, or seventh responses. Variable ratio schedules of reinforcement are very effective in maintaining the behavior and thereby preventing the response from extinguishing.

Time-based schedules of reinforcement are also used for increasing and maintaining behavior. In a *fixed interval* schedule the first response that occurs after a specific period of time (for example, one minute) is reinforced. Initially, shorter periods of time are used to increase the rate of behavior. Later, these periods are lengthened, followed by the introduction of a *variable-interval* schedule in which the period of time varies around a specified average. A variable interval five-minute schedule, for example, might involve reinforcing the responses after three-, four-, five-, six-, or seven-minute periods. Interval schedules are particularly convenient in situations in which the passage of time may be easier to monitor than the counting of every response.

The token economy. In settings such as institutions and group homes, the token economy has been demonstrated to be an effective means for increasing appropriate behaviors. The token economy is a system by which children earn tokens for performing certain behaviors and exchange the tokens later for a variety of items, such as special clothing, trips, and records.

In designing a token economy, the behavior therapist must identify those behaviors that will earn tokens; such behaviors might include self-care and household work as well as academic accomplishments. Then, each behavior must be assigned a value in tokens, and finally a set of rules must be developed to effect the exchange of tokens and the token values of the desired items.

Token economies have been most effective in increasing a wide variety of appropriate behaviors of children who had not responded to other forms of therapeutic intervention before, but, several of the problems related to the token economy have not yet been solved. For example, since the token economy is very different from the contingencies in the natural environment, the behavior therapeutic intervention before, but several of the problems related to the token child is removed from the token economy setting. Researchers are currently working on procedures, one of which is similar to that described for fading tangible reinforcers, to ensure a successful transition from the token economy setting to the natural environment.

Contingency contact. A contingency contract may be one aspect of a token program or may be used as a treatment plan by itself. A written contract is drawn up stating what behaviors are expected from the child and what reinforcement the child will receive for performing the desired behavior. The contents of the contract are agreed upon in one or several joint meetings with the child, the therapist, and the parents. Daily records are kept on a chart at home and brought to the therapist periodically for evaluation. If the contract is not being kept by either party, the therapist in a joint meeting with parents and child attempts to determine the source of the failure, setting the stage for renegotiation of the contract. Parents can easily be taught the principles behind the use of the contingency contract and often continue to devise successful contracts without the help of the therapist.

Self-control. In this procedure the client effects his own behavior change with guidance from the behavior therapist through self-instructions, self-monitoring of behavior, or self-reinforcement, or through a combination of these methods. In a sense, all of these techniques involve self-control in that the client is free to behave or not behave, but other persons are arranging the contingencies. Society greatly values the learning of self-control because less effort then has to be expended to arrange externally determined contingencies. Until recently, children had seldom been the subjects of studies on self-control, although a substantial amount of research had been conducted with adults. The primary reason for this lack may have been an assumption that children were not capable of implementing self-control procedures.

However, the research literature suggests that the teaching of self-control to children holds considerable promise for increasing appropriate behaviors. Broden, Hall, and Mitts (1971) found that an eighth grade girl's method of studying was improved simply by asking her to record her own study behavior. Other children have been successfully taught to control their own behaviors by making statements to themselves covertly and prompting themselves to behave appropriately.

Prompting. Prompting includes several procedures that have been found to facilitate increases in the qualitative aspects of behaviors. These procedures essentially make it easier for the client to perform the response and thereby obtain reinforcement. After the behavior reaches a desirable level, the prompts can be removed (faded). Prompting procedures include instructions, modeling, and physical guidance.

Instructions. A large number of behaviors may be generated by someone describing the behaviors and requesting that they be performed. Being able to follow instructions, of course, requires having learned the words used in the instruction and the behaviors represented by the words. To be most productive, then, instructions must be compatible with the level of the child's verbal competence.

Modeling. Modeling refers to instances of behavior change after observing that behavior performed by another person. Modeling or observational learning is probably responsible for the initial occurrence of most of the responses in our repertoire. The development of language, for example, is highly dependent on the models heard during childhood.

Bandura (1969) has been a major investigator of modeling in children and the application of modeling to children's problems. Bandura and others have engaged in theoretical arguments about whether reinforcement is a necessary condition for modeling. Bandura does not view reinforcement as being necessary for the initial acquisition of modeled behavior but recognizes that reinforcement can increase the rate of the modeled response after its initial acquisition. Baer and Sherman (1964), on the other hand, view modeling as an instance of generalized imitation. They demonstrated that children will imitate new responses that are never reinforced after they have had experience getting reinforced for imitating other responses.

Theoretical differences such as these do not alter the fact that modeling is a powerful method for creating new responses. Various studies have shown, for example, that after the behaviors were modeled, children previously afraid of dogs increased their approach responses to dogs and that children who observed aggressive behavior on film emitted larger numbers of aggressive responses. Modeling has been demonstrated to occur in young children following the observation of both live and filmed models. One topic that has been receiving nationwide attention is the effect of televised aggression on children. From what we know about modeling, the effect would, at least in part, depend on what happens to the models. Children who observed others receiving punishment for aggressive behavior were less likely to model it than were children who observed the aggressive behavior followed either by reward or by no consequences (Bandura, 1965).

We may soon see the development of films of modeled behavior for use with children who exhibit certain behavioral deficiencies. Research studies would first have to determine which scenes and sequences of scenes would have maximum modeling effects for particular behavior problems. Such films could also be designed for the prevention of some of the more common problems of children, such as fears of going to the doctor or dentist.

Physical Guidance. When instructions and modeling are not effective, the behavior may be facilitated by the therapist's physically guiding the child through the behavior. For example, the learning of certain speech sounds presents considerable difficulty for some children, and physical guidance has been used to help them to produce these sounds. The physical guidance consists of holding the lips in a particular position while the child voices sound. Teaching children to respond to instructions or a model may also be helped through physical guidance. A child, unresponsive to the request, "stand up," for example, may be gently lifted to the standing position immediately after the request and then reinforced. After a succession of trials the therapist may gradually reduce the amount of physical guidance proportional to the child's participation in the response until the response is finally made to the verbal instruction alone.

In treatment programs, therapists may use instructions, modeling, or physical guidance or varying combinations of these methods. Even though the child may require considerable assistance with prompts, each response can be reinforced on a continuous schedule until it is reliably performed. Only after the behavior has reached a level that is qualitatively and quantitatively acceptable is reinforcement gradually shifted to an intermittent schedule.

Shaping. Shaping is a technique that is frequently implemented when the desired behavior is not in the client's repertoire. It consists of reinforcing successive approximations of the desired behavior. Because it is often a very difficult and time-consuming procedure, shaping would be used only if the response could not be obtained through instructions, modeling, or physical guidance.

The behavior therapist first determines what the final response should be and then on the basis of observation chooses the response that is most similar to the final response for reinforcement. The therapist continues to reinforce that approximation to the final response until another response, which more closely approximates the final response, appears. Then, that response gets reinforced and thereby strengthened. As responses closer to the final response become strengthened, the therapist gradually stops reinforcing those responses strengthened earlier. This process continues until the final response is obtained and strengthened. A study by Lovaas, Berberich, Perloff, and Schaeffer (1966) on teaching speech to severely disturbed children vividly demonstrated the application of shaping procedures for children who formerly had no functional language.

Contingent removal of an aversive stimulus. Responses can also be increased by the contingent removal of an aversive stimulus. For a number of reasons, very few examples of the use of this method have appeared in the applied research literature. One is that the method requires at least the initial use of aversive stimuli, and behavior therapists prefer not to use such stimuli when other methods can accomplish the same behavioral results. In addition, except under well-controlled laboratory conditions, the method is prone to generate negative side effects. For example, the onset of the aversive stimulus might coincide with an appropriate behavior, although not *the* appropriate behavior that the therapist plans to increase. This coincidence would serve to decrease the appropriate behavior (one of the methods to be described later), a result that is not particularly desirable. The importance of the behavior that is increased by the termination of the aversive stimulus may, however, outweigh the loss of the appropriate behavior.

It is apparent that much human behavior is controlled by this method outside of therapy situations. Few children have not had the experience of mother continuously nagging at them until the desired chore was accomplished. This method is even built into our seatbelts that produce a noxious sound until they are fastened.

methods for decreasing behaviors

More often than not, a child referred for therapy has behaviors that the adults in his environment consider to be excessive, inappropriate, or even harmful. The therapeutic goal in these situations is to decrease or eliminate such behaviors. Several methods, based on the principles of learning, have been devised to decrease or eliminate inappropriate behaviors. In this section we will describe the methods that have been used with children: extinction, punishment (timeout, response cost, application of aversive consequences), self-control, desensitization, and multimodal therapy.

extinction: contingent omission of positive reinforcement

When the therapist is able to identify and control the reinforcer that has been maintaining the high rate of an inappropriate response, extinction is likely to be an effective method for decreasing that response. Extinction refers to a procedure whereby a reinforcer, responsible for the maintenance of a response, is omitted, thus resulting in a decrease in the rate of that response.

The rapidity with which a response is extinguished after the initiation of the reinforcement omission depends considerably on the schedule of a reinforcement during maintenance. If the behavior has been reinforced on a continuous schedule, extinction takes place quite rapidly. Since most behaviors in natural environments appear to be maintained on intermittent schedules of reinforcement, they may be expected to extinguish more slowly.

Before coming to a therapist, parents frequently try different ways of changing the behavior themselves. Their approaches to the problem sometimes include the omission of reinforcement. When the therapist describes the procedure for extinction, parents may have occasion to remark that they have already tried that method, and that it only made the behavior worse. Psychologists have known for a long time that omission of reinforcement after a history of reinforcement for a particular response results initially in a temporary increase of the behavior followed by the more permanent decrease phase. Thus, because parents are not aware of these relationships, their efforts toward "extinguishing" a behavior are usually prematurely terminated. The behavior therapist is thus particularly careful to describe expected changes in behavior to prevent mediators from giving up. With extinction it is also extremely important that the withholding of reinforcement be consistent, because a few "accidental" reinforcers may well result in the reinstatement of a high rate of response.

Use of extinction procedures for decreasing inappropriate behaviors in children has often been reported in the applied research literature. Extinction is useful when the behavior problem can be allowed to occur without consequences; this qualification depends very much on the setting and the characteristics of the behavior itself. In some group settings, for example, a behavior may be disruptive to the point at which extinction or ignoring the behavior could not be tolerated. Similarly, extinction may not be the method of choice if the behavior involves self-injury or injury to others.

Extinction, or the omission of reinforcement, may be accompanied by emotional responses by the child, such as anger, frustration, and aggression. Although these reactions have not been studied extensively, they appear to be transient and diminish as the response being extinguished decreases. It is likely that they would decrease more rapidly if, during extinction, reinforcement is given for an alternate, appropriate response. In this manner, the level of reinforcement for the client would be maintained but would be provided contingently for an appropriate behavior. When using extinction to decrease an inappropriate behavior, behavioral clinicians often include a program for reinforcing an incompatible behavior (for example, extinguish social withdrawal while reinforcing social contact).

punishment

"Punishment" has had varied meanings in its everyday usage; therefore, psychologists have attempted to define it to facilitate communication among themselves. For the purpose of this section, Azrin and Holz's (1966) definition will be employed; they describe punishment as any procedure using "any consequence of behavior that reduces the future probability of that behavior" (p. 381). Three procedures that fit within this definition will be described: timeout, response cost, and the application of aversive consequences.

The term, *punishment,* also evokes a wide range of emotions and attitudes, among both professionals and nonprofessionals. Some people feel that punishment, particularly corporal punishment, is necessary to control children's behavior, while others believe that any form of punishment is not at all necessary and, in fact, may be harmful. As you will learn, punishment procedures themselves are varied in terms of their effectiveness in reducing inappropriate behavior, their intrusiveness, and their potential for unwanted effects.

Timeout. Timeout is a procedure that involves a child's being removed from all sources of reinforcement for a brief period immediately upon the occurrence of an inappropriate response. It is a brief period without the availability of reinforcers and should not be construed as a method to frighten children. For example, in a home the child might be taken to a room without television or toys, and in school, the child might be seated in the corridor. Timeout is a useful procedure when the reinforcers maintaining the behavior problem cannot be identified or controlled. Short timeout periods such as two to five minutes are usually effective.

The timeout method is not easy to implement in many natural environments because positive reinforcers, such as social attention from peers in the corridor, are too readily available. Portable timeout booths have been designed for such settings, and a few of the newer schools contain timeout rooms. The place for timeout is always fully lighted; all the children in the setting have had the opportunity to examine it and have been told which inappropriate behaviors will be followed by timeout.

Timeout is not the same as isolation, a method that is sometimes used in institutions and other settings. Isolation usually involves longer time periods, such as twenty-four hours, and is not necessarily initiated immediately after the inappropriate behavior. The effectiveness of isolation in reducing future occurrences of the behavior has not been demonstrated. On the other hand, isolation may be reinforcing for the staff in that the necessity for coping with the problem behavior is eliminated for the duration of the isolation period.

Response cost. Another method for decreasing the rate of a response involves removing a positive reinforcer immediately after the occurrence of the inappropriate behavior. An example might be removing a favorite toy for a period of time after fighting occurs.

Behavior therapists use contingent removal of positive reinforcement to decrease responses in situations in which the reinforcer for the inappropriate behavior cannot be identified or in situations that call for a more rapid decrease than would be obtained using extinction. One of the problems posed by this method is that the therapist may encounter difficulty in finding a positive reinforcer that can be taken away. Potential reinforcers for middle-class children, for example, might include a wide variety of privileges, such as going bowling or to a movie, riding a bicycle, and swimming. Lower-class children tend to have fewer privileges that may be controlled by parents.

Finding positive reinforcers that can be taken away is also difficult in many school settings. Certain activities that might be considered as privileges, such as recess, are felt to be necessary for the child's well-being and not to be used as positive reinforcers. In general, environments that provide either no reinforcers or primarily free (noncontingent) reinforcers present great difficulties to the behavior therapist. Several creative researchers, however, have found that there are substantial behavior improvements in school settings permitting the introduction of positive reinforcers that could be used both to increase appropriate behaviors by their contingent presentation and to decrease inappropriate behaviors by their contingent withdrawal.

Token economies provide an excellent example of using withdrawal of reinforcement to decrease behaviors. As described earlier, token economies are designed to provide positive reinforcement for appropriate behaviors. Since inappropriate behaviors have a high probability of occuring in the populations selected for the token economy programs, methods for decreasing inappropriate behaviors must be included. One effective method is to withdraw a certain number of tokens from the child for each occurrence of particular inappropriate behaviors. Before the program is initiated, the response cost (that is, the number of tokens withdrawn) is determined for each unacceptable behavior and is communicated to the client.

Application of aversive consequences. Presenting an aversive stimulus immediately after the occurrence of an inappropriate response also has the effect of decreasing the rate of that response. In comparison to other methods, it tends to decrease behavior faster and sometimes more effectively. The rapidity and relative strength of its effect usually depends on the strength of the aversive stimulus—the stronger the stimulus, the longer the decrease in responding will last. The stronger aversive stimuli tend to be those associated with pain and other physical discomforts; reprimands by parents and teachers, however, also serve as aversive stimuli for many children.

This method of decreasing behavior has presented the most controversy among both professionals and nonprofessionals and has been used more infrequently than other methods by behavior therapists. The use of aversive stimuli is itself aversive to therapists and tends to create ethical issues that are not easily resolved. For example, some children, usually in institutions, would engage in self-injurious behaviors to the point of seriously harming themselves if their arms and legs were not tied to the bed. Several investigators have found that a few administrations of electric shock to the skin contingent on self-injurious behavior may be effective in eliminating these behaviors, thus making it possible for such children to acquire repertoires of appropriate behavior. Ethical issues, however, have been raised regarding the use of electric shock for such therapeutic procedures, and strong attempts have been made (with some success) to prevent the use of such techniques in institutional settings. This issue may be posed as a question of whether it is more ethical to leave a child tied to his bed indefinitely than to administer electric shock to eliminate the self-injurious behavior.

Use of contingent aversive stimuli has also been avoided by behavior therapists because earlier research with animals (with painful stimuli) suggested that there may be certain negative by-products, such as emotional behavior, associated with the method. When an aversive stimulus is presented, the decrease in the inappropriate behavior may also be accompanied by a strong emotional response, characterized by fear or anger. The problem for the therapist is that the client may learn to associate one or more aspects of the environmental stimuli, including the therapist or mediator, with the emotional behaviors elicited by the aversive stimulus. That is, the client may learn through respondent conditioning to become fearful in the presence of the therapist or mediator, or the child could become fearful of the place in which the punishment is administered.

A problem that has only recently gained attention is the long-range effect of the modeling of punishment on children's behavior. Recent research has suggested that parents who have been found to abuse their children were themselves subjected to considerable physical or corporal punishment. The question, then, is whether the administration of punishment to a child unduly affects the child's use of punishment in the future.

self-control

Self-control procedures, utilizing self-instructions, self-recording, and self-reinforcement or self-punishment, have been increasingly explored as methods for decreasing children's inappropriate behaviors. The research suggests that self-control procedures produce effects that are comparable to external-control procedures and may be superior for maintaining therapeutic gains (O'Leary and Dubey, 1979). Meichenbaum and Goodman's (1971) initial work with impulsive children has stimulated the development of a variety of self-instruction programs. In training children to instruct themselves (by saying, for example, "take your time"), the therapist models the verbal statements and then asks the child to repeat the statements first aloud, then in a whisper, and finally covertly. The children are also taught to reinforce themselves for completing the task. Finch and his colleagues (1975; Kendall & Finch, 1978) have developed effective treatment programs for impulsive, emotionally disturbed children using psychoeducational materials. Self-control methods appear to be particularly effective for children who are hyperactive, disruptive in class, and aggressive.

desensitization

Desensitization refers to the complex of techniques that has proved to be effective in reducing anxiety responses in adults. The goal of desensitization is to substitute a relaxed or nonanxious state for the anxiety responses to a particular stimulus situation. The learning model is generally believed to be that of respondent conditioning but has components of operant conditioning as well. The procedures of desensitization with adults include the teaching of muscle relaxation, the construction of a fear hierarchy, and the gradual movement through the steps of the hierarchy while in a relaxed state. Each step of the hierarchy represents an actual situation that evokes a certain amount of fear as assessed by the client. The desensitization process itself begins by having the client either experience or imagine the scene, previously given the lowest fear rating, while in a relaxed state. Each scene is successively experienced by a client who attempts to maintain the relaxed state. If the client experiences anxiety, the therapist returns to the previous scene.

The procedure designed for adults, which uses a hierarchy of imagined scenes, only occasionally lends itself to therapy with children because the techniques for teaching children to relax systematically, to construct a fear hierarchy, and to imagine specific scenes are in an early stage of development. Emotive imagery has been used to counteract anxiety in children (Lazarus and Abramovitz, 1962). In emotive imagery the client is asked to imagine a specific pleasant scene into which the therapist gradually introduces anxiety-arousing stimuli. Other variations have also been used. For example, Lazarus, Davison, and Polefka (1965) successfully treated a child with school phobia by gradually exposing the child to the school environment (*in vivo* desensitization) and using positive reinforcement to strengthen going-to-school behaviors.

multimodal therapy

Lazarus (1976), recognizing that adult clients rarely present a single problem for treatment, designed a multimodal system for ensuring that all aspects of the client's psychological life are examined and treated, where necessary. Keat (1979) subsequently adapted Lazarus's system for use with children. The acronym, *BASIC ID,* is used to help the therapist to remember the seven interactive modalities: *B*ehavior, *A*ffect (feelings, emotions), *S*ensation, *I*magery, *C*ognition, *I*nterpersonal relations, and *D*rugs (physical factors). For children, a school modality is added to the sensation modality, and the interpersonal relations modality is expanded to include significant adults in the child's life. A treatment plan is designed by the clinician for each of the problems. While Keat's therapy model is primarily behavioral, his repertoire of treatments is extensive and reflects what he refers to as "pragmatic technical eclecticism."

Conclusions

Beginning in the early 1960s, an increasing number of studies have demonstrated that the learning principles derived from the earlier experimental research with animals and humans can be successfully used to increase appropriate and decrease inappropriate behaviors in children. The phase of simply demonstrating the application of learning principles to children's behavior problems is now giving way to a period of critical examination of the strengths and weaknesses of behavior therapy for specific behavior problems and in specific environmental situations. One of the salient features of behavior therapy is the continuous monitoring of behavior that permits constant evaluation of the therapy's effectiveness. To a large extent this close monitoring of behavior has facilitated the discovery of the weaknesses and methodological problems associated with the behavioral approach to treatment. Studies comparing the relative effectiveness of traditional and behavioral approaches to treatment have only begun to emerge in the research literature.

Recommended Readings

Gelfand, D. M., and **Hartmann, D. P.**, *Child Behavior Analysis and Therapy,* Chapters 4, 5, 6, 8 (Part 2), 9, 10. Elmsford, N.Y.: Pergamon Press, 1975. A step-by-step description of treatment methods based on operant conditioning principles.

Lahey, B. B., and **Kazdin, A. E.**, eds., *Advances in Clinical Child Psychiatry.* Vol. 2. New York: Plenum, 1979. Chapters 1, 2, and 6 contain reviews of self-control, generalization processes, and comparisons of clinical and community intervention strategies, respectively.

Marholin, D., ed., *Child Behavior Therapy.* New York: Gardner Press, 1978. Covers a broad range of children's behavior problems treated with behavior therapy.

O'Leary, K. D., and **Wilson, C. T.**, *Behavior Therapy: Application and Outcome.* Englewood Cliffs, N. J.: Prentice-Hall, 1975. Describes the behavioral approaches to the clinical treatment of children and adults.

Ross, A. O. *Child Behavior Therapy.* New York: Wiley, 1981. A review of the principles, procedures, and empirical basis for child behavior therapy.

mental retardation

8

Jamie, a five-year-old girl, was referred by her pre-school teacher because she appeared to lack many of the skills achieved by her peers. Her interactions with her classmates have tended to decrease over the past several months, her closest companion being the youngest child in the group of four- and five-year-old children.

Jamie was the first child of eighteen-year-old parents and was conceived out of wedlock. Her mother attempted to abort herself with an unknown substance early in the pregnancy. The mother experienced intermittent bleeding during the first half of pregnancy before she was under a doctor's care. Both parents dropped out of high school and married when the mother was five-months pregnant. Although Jamie was born at term, she weighed only five pounds. The doctor had difficulty initiating breathing at birth, and Jamie had several episodes of respiratory distress while in the hospital nursery. She was discharged from the hospital at three weeks of age.

Jamie's infancy was unremarkable except for two illnesses of unknown origin accompanied by very high fevers. The parents were not
particularly concerned about Jamie's development, although they remembered that she did not walk alone or say her first word until two
years of age. Neither parent had had experience with young children
before Jamie, but their observation of the children in the preschool
and their discussions with Jamie's teacher have led them to wonder
whether Jamie is "slow."

In comparison with the other types of behavior disorders described in this book,
perhaps the greatest amount of information has been acquired about mental retardation. There is at present a general consensus on the assessment procedures and
the criteria for classification. A wide variety of etiological factors have been investigated, and a great amount of research effort has been devoted to treatment and
development of remedial programs for retarded persons.

Our greater understanding of mental retardation is no doubt due to a long history of theoretical speculation and empirical attempts to investigate the nature of
intelligence and its individual variations. The beginning of the modern concep-
tualizations of intelligence may be placed at the turn of the twentieth century with
the work of Binet and Simon in 1905. Although many definitions of intelligence
have been proposed and strongly debated (Cronbach, 1975), most of the earlier
definitions were global and included as common elements the ability to learn, the
amount of acquired knowledge, and the ability to adapt to the environment. Other
definitions emphasized the possibility that intelligence is made up of several
independent components. For example, Spearman (1904) proposed a two-factor
theory in which one factor (the general or g factor) was reflected in all cognitive
functions and a second factor (the specific or s factor) comprised a variety of
elements reflecting different abilities. Using factor analysis on many different
specific test items, Thurstone (1938) later identified a series of factors, some of
which were labeled general reasoning, verbal comprehension, associative memory,
numerical reasoning, and word fluency.

The most complex and comprehensive view of intelligence has been presented by
Guilford (1959) who proposed a three-dimensional model consisting of contents,
operations, and products. Contents refer to four types of information to be proc-
essed: figural, symbolic, semantic, and behavioral. Operations represent the principal kind of processes for handling information; five types are described: evaluation, convergent thinking, divergent thinking, memory, and cognitive. Products
refer to the types of products that result from the processing of information;
six types of products are described. This three-dimensional model produces 120
hypothesized primary intellectual abilities; Guilford and his coworkers have identified or developed tests for about 100 of these abilities.

Contemporary intelligence tests reflect some of the diversity of thought about
the nature of intelligence. Some of them are global measures of intelligence, others
evaluate specific aspects of intellectual functioning, and still others combine the

two approaches in a single test. Practical considerations (such as time limitations), however, have precluded the use of tests or combinations of tests that measure greater than a dozen or so different aspects of intelligence in clinical settings.

assessment

referral

Referral for assessment may occur at any age beginning in earliest infancy. Even at birth, some physical abnormalities that are highly correlated with mental retardation may be observed. Children suspected of being mentally retarded early in infancy tend to be those who are more severely affected (moderate, severe, and profound retardation) and who show abnormalities on physical examination. Most retarded children, however, are not referred for diagnosis until the late preschool or early school years. Later referrals are associated with fewer physical abnormalities and less severe mental retardation. In the case of the children, it is the adult in the child's natural environment (home or school) who first suspects a problem. This suspicion is usually based on the behavior of the child who is typically described as being slow in development or learning. Parents often have a difficult time persuading their family physician to refer their child for testing because in many instances the physician has not had an opportunity to observe a sample of the child's behavior that is adequate for making a judement. Relatively few physicians include in their permanent files the ages at which their child patients achieve the important developmental milestones, and still fewer incorporate developmental screening tests into their routine practice. Records kept by the parents, teachers, and physicians as well as the information obtained during interviews mat greatly assist the clinician in the choice of additional assessment techniques.

definition and assessment methods

Definitions of mental retardation have been numerous and have tended to be influenced by the predominant conceptualization of intelligence at the time. Over the years, definitions that have relied on vague terminology, etiological factors, and prognosis have given way to definitions that describe current behavior or behavioral deficits relative to other persons in the population of the same chronological age. That is, mental retardation is defined as a slower rate of learning or as a collection of behavior deficits in relation to the rates of learning and behavioral repertoires of the average child of the same age.

The most widely accepted definition of mental retardation is found in the *Manual on Terminology and Classification in Mental Retardation* (Grossman, 1977), published by the American Association on Mental Deficiency (AAMD):

Mental Retardation refers to significantly subaverage general intellectual functioning existing concurrently with deficits in adaptive behavior, and manifested during the developmental period.

Mental retardation as defined denotes a level of behavioral performance without reference to etiology. Thus, it does not distinguish between retardation associated with psychosocial or polygenic influences and retardation associated with biological deficit. Mental retardation is descriptive of current behavior and does not necessarily imply prognosis. Prognosis is related more to such factors as associated conditions, motivation, treatment, and training opportunities than to mental retardation itself (p. 11).

Intellectual functioning is assessed by one or more of the standardized tests developed for that purpose; significantly subaverage refers to performance which is more than two standard deviations from the mean or average of the tests. On the two most frequently used tests of intelligence, the Stanford-Binet and the Wechsler, the IQ scores are 67 and 69, respectively. The upper age limit of the developmental period is placed at eighteen years and serves to distinguish mental retardation from other disorders.

Adaptive behavior is defined as the effectiveness or degree with which the individual meets the standards of personal independence and social responsibility expected of the individual's age and cultural group. Since these expectations vary for different age groups, deficits in adaptive behavior vary with different ages.

The AAMD definition defines mental retardation on the basis of scores on standardized intelligence tests, evaluation of adaptive behavior, and the age at which the problem was manifested. Although a large number of intelligence tests have been devised, the Stanford-Binet and the Wechsler scales are by far the most frequently used when a child is referred with a question of mental retardation. Group intelligence tests and shorter versions of individual intelligence tests, such as the Slosson Intelligence Test, may be used for screening purposes, but they are not considered adequate for making a diagnosis.

Until relatively recently, infant tests, such as the Cattell and Bayley, were not considered to be useful for diagnosing mental retardation because they were not good predictors of later intelligence scores for samples of normal children. However, several studies (see, for example, Erickson, 1968b; Werner, Honzik, and Smith, 1968) have presented evidence that children who obtain scores in the retarded range on infant tests during the first few years of life have a high probability of receiving scores in the retarded range at later ages. Although *all* children diagnosed as retarded should be retested at reasonable intervals, such as yearly, to check on the reliability of the original test results, follow-up testing is extremely important in the case of infants whose test performance is considerably more unreliable than that of older children.

classification

A diagnosis of mental retardation on the basis of a standardized intelligence test is made when the score is greater than two standard deviations below the average IQ score (100). Within the group of mentally retarded persons, four levels of classification are recognized. These levels and their corresponding IQ score ranges are as follows:

levels	IQ score	
	Stanford-Binet and Cattell SD=16	Wechsler SD=15
Mild	67–52	69–55
Moderate	51–36	54–40
Severe	35–20	39–25 (Extrapolated)
Profound	19 and below	24 and below (Extrapolated)

It may be seen that each successively lower level is one standard deviation below the level above it. Thus, children who obtain scores in the profoundly retarded range of intellectual functioning have scores that are more than five standard deviations below the mean.

When comparisons are made between the actual prevalence of mental retardation in the U.S. population and the number expected on the basis of a normal distribution curve (the bell-shaped curve), it has been found that there are nearly two thousand times as many profoundly retarded persons and a little over twice as many moderately and severely retarded persons than would be expected if the distribution of IQ scores were normal. The prevalence of mildly retarded persons closely approximates the expected frequency. Including all levels of mental retardation, approximately 3 percent of the population would be classified as mentally retarded on the basis of IQ scores.

assessment of adaptive behavior

The measurement of adaptive behavior presents greater problems to the clinician because few objective tests have been developed for this purpose. Before the publication of the AAMD Adaptive Behavior Scale (described below), clinicians had to rely primarily on information derived from interviews with significant adults and observation of the child in the clinic setting or on tests, such as the Vineland Social Maturity Scale, which evaluated relatively narrow ranges of the child's behavioral repertoire.

The revision of the AAMD Adaptive Behavior Scale (Nihara, Foster, Shellhaas, and Leland, 1975) is a comprehensive approach to the evaluation of adaptive behavior and uses the interview approach for data collection. Because the items on the scale are based on observed behavior, and the scale can be administered by persons without special training in psychological testing, information should be obtained from the person who spends the greatest amount of time with the child.

The scale consists of two parts. The first part includes ten behavior areas and twenty-one subareas:

  I.   Independent Functioning
       A. Eating
       B. Toilet Use
       C. Cleanliness
       D. Appearance
       E. Care of Clothing
       F. Dressing and Undressing
       G. Travel
       H. General Independent Functioning
 II.   Physical Development
       A. Sensory Development
       B. Motor Development
III.   Economic Activity
       A. Money Handling and Budgeting
       B. Shopping Skills
 IV.   Language Development
       A. Expression
       B. Comprehension
       C. Social Language Development
  V.   Numbers and Time
 VI.   Domestic Activity
       A. Cleaning
       B. Kitchen Duties
       C. Other Domestic Activities
VII.   Vocational Activity
VIII. Self-Direction
       A. Initiative
       B. Perseverance
       C. Leisure Time
 IX.   Responsibility
  X.   Socialization

Within each area or subarea items are arranged developmentally, that is, in the order that the behaviors tend to occur in the average person. Each item is scored on the basis of the client's most advanced performance.

The second part of the scale consists of thirteen areas of maladaptive behavior and one variable evaluating the use of medications:

   I.   Violent and Destructive Behavior
  II.   Antisocial Behavior
 III.   Rebellious Behavior
  IV.   Untrustworthy Behavior
   V.   Withdrawal
  VI.   Stereotyped Behavior and Odd Mannerisms
 VII.   Inappropriate Interpersonal Manners
VIII.   Unacceptable Vocal Habits
  IX.   Unacceptable or Eccentric Habits

    X. Self-Abusive Behavior
   XI. Hyperactive Tendencies
  XII. Sexually Aberrant Behavior
 XIII. Psychological Disturbances
 XIV. Use of Medications

Within each of these fourteen areas are varying numbers of subareas and specific behaviors that are scored on the basis of whether they never occur (0), occur occasionally (1), or occur frequently (2). Scores for the specific behaviors are combined to give subarea scores that are, in turn, combined to give one score for each of the maladaptive behavior areas with higher scores reflecting greater amounts of maladaptive behavior.

One major problem with the scale is that norms for a representative sample of normal children have not been reported (except for a School Form of the Scale by Lambert, Windmiller, Cole, and Figuerva, 1975). Rather, data for a group of institutionalized retarded children and adults (on the basis of IQ scores) are presented in the scale manual as a standard against which to compare individuals. While the retarded norm group may be useful for comparing the profiles of individual children from similar settings, it is not adequate for assessing the adaptive behavior of children from home settings referred for possible mental retardation.

One of the better standardized scales for evaluating adaptive behavior is the Alpern-Boll Developmental Profile (Alpern and Boll, 1972) whose norms are based on data from three thousand nonselected children from birth to twelve years of age. It includes 217 items that assess 5 behavioral areas: physical development, social development, self-help skills, preacademic and academic skills and communication skills.

In general, there is a correlation between level of intellectual functioning and level of adaptive behavior. Such a relationship should be expected in view of the fact that intelligence is involved in the acquisition of most behaviors. The AAMD standards specify, however, that individuals whose adaptive behaviors are within normal limits are *not* to be diagnosed as mentally retarded even when their IQ scores are within the retarded range. That is, there is recognition that some children and adults with subaverage IQ scores cope adequately with environmental demands and do not require special services; labeling such persons as mentally retarded would serve no useful function. Although labels have generally been assumed to have detrimental effects on children, very little research evidence has been presented to support that assumption (MacMillan, Jones, and Aloia, 1974).

medical classification

The AAMD *Manual* also contains a medical classification system in which known or suspected etiological factors and associated physical or environmental conditions may be coded and added to the diagnosed level of mental retardation. The major medical headings are:

1. Infections and intoxications
2. Trauma or physical agent
3. Metabolism or nutrition
4. Gross brain disease (postnatal)
5. Unknown prenatal influence
6. Chromosomal abnormality
7. Gestational disorders
8. Following psychiatric disorder
9. Environmental influences
10. Other conditions

These major medical headings include up to nine subheadings that vary from spec-cific medical syndromes to general types of disorders. Some of these medical conditions are described in the chapters on etiology. The medical classification system presented in the AAMD *Manual* closely follows those in the *International Classification of Diseases* and the *Diagnostic and Statistical Manual of Mental Disorders.*

behavioral assessment

Behavioral clinicians have worked extensively with retarded children, but their involvement has typically begun after the diagnosis has been made. From a behavioral point of view, "a retarded individual is one who has a limited repertory of behavior shaped by events that constitute his history" (Bijou, 1966, p. 2). This view, in general, rejects notions of defective intelligence and of mental retardation being a symptom of underlying pathology. Rather, the behaviorist focuses on the child's current behavior as being a product of past antecedent and consequent stimuli. Although retarded children engage in inappropriate forms of behavior, by far the greater problem resides in their behavioral deficits. Behavioral assessment typically includes an inventory of the child's behavioral repertoire through the use of rating scales or a behavior checklist and direct observation of the child in the natural environment. In addition, one or more interviews are conducted with the child's principal caretakers to determine the methods currently being used to manage the child's behavior and to evaluate the environment's potential for identifying, reinforcing, and shaping appropriate behavior.

characteristics of retarded children

It is sometimes believed that retarded children tend to resemble one another more closely than do nonretarded children. In actuality, the individual differences in behavioral characteristics among retarded children are substantial, even within groups having the same mental age or level of retardation, just as they are for normal children. For most developmental characteristics and learned behaviors, retarded children greatly resemble normal children of the same mental age. Retarded children have more behavior problems than their same-aged nonretarded peers, however (Gully and Hosch, 1979).

Perhaps more variability may be demonstrated for physical characteristics. Children with IQ scores below 50 have a higher probability (which increases with the severity of retardation) of a physical abnormality that is apparent to the casual observer. These physical abnormalities range from relatively mild defects to severe distortions of the body, such as an unusually large or small head or crippled limbs.

etiology

Many factors have been identified as increasing the risk of mental retardation. In some instances, the presence of a particular factor makes it a virtual certainty that the child will be retarded, while in many more instances, factors are associated with small increases in the probability that the child will be retarded. Even though a large number of etiological factors have been identified, specification of etiology for individual retarded children is not possible for about two-thirds of the diagnosed cases. Such identification is rare either because none of the known etiological factors has been found in the child's history or because more than one factor has been reported in the history, and there is no way of determining which single factor or combination of factors caused the mental retardation. In addition, there are likely to be a number of etiological factors that are yet to be identified.

genetic factors

An increasing number of chromosomal abnormalities are being identified in mentally retarded persons (Lubs and Walknowska, 1977). Among the various conditions involving abnormal numbers of chromosomes is Down syndrome which accounts for about 10 percent of moderately to severely retarded persons. Because individuals with this condition share a number of physical features, they have been identified and studied since the middle of the last century, but it was only in 1959 that Lejuene, Gautier, and Turpin discovered that Down syndrome involved an extra chromosome 21; that is, instead of the usual two chromosome 21's (one from the father and one from the mother) three are present, bringing the total number of chromosomes in each cell to forty-seven.

As more research has been conducted, three types of Down's syndrome have been described. The first type, called *nondisjunction,* accounts for 95 percent of Down syndrome cases and involves either an error during the egg or sperm development, in which the mother or father contributes two instead of one chromosome 21, or an error during the first cell division after fertilization. The probability of nondisjunction increases greatly with the age of the mother ranging from one in 1,500 for mothers under thirty years of age to one in sixty-five for mother forty-five years of age and older (Mikkelsen and Stene, 1970).

The second type of chromosomal abnormality resulting in Down syndrome is mosaicism, which accounts for less than 5 percent of the cases. In this type, the complement of chromosomes is normal when the egg is fertilized. During the second or subsequent cell division, an error produces one cell with forty-seven chromosomes (three chromosome 21's) and one cell with forty-five chromosomes (one chromosome 21). The cell with forty-five chromosomes dies, and the cell with forty-seven chromosomes continues to reproduce itself as do the remaining normal cells with forty-six chromosomes. The result is an individual whose body contains a mixture of normal and abnormal cells. The physical signs and the mental retardation are less severe in persons with mosaicism and probably depend on which organs of the body are affected by the abnormal cells.

Both nondisjunction and mosaicism involve errors in cell division and are *not* hereditary in the sense that the parents have the condition or are carriers and pass the condition to their children. A third type of Down syndrome, *translocation,* may, however, be traced directly to abnormal chromosomes in one of the parents in about one-third of the cases (the remaining two-thirds being due to an error in the development of the egg or sperm or in the first cell division). In these cases, the parent is normal physically and mentally and has the genetic material of forty-six chromosomes. Two of the chromosomes (usually chromosomes 14 and 21) are attached to one another, however, giving the parent forty-five chromosomes (forty-four normal chromosomes and one translocation chromosome). When these chromosomes divide to form the egg or sperm, an extra chromosome 21 may result, giving the fetus forty-six chromosomes (forty-five normal chromosomes and one translocation chromosome) but the genetic material for forty-seven chromosomes with chromosome 21 represented in triplicate. Individuals with the translocation type of Down syndrome are similar in characteristics to those with the nondisjunction type.

Having an extra chromosome 21 (trisomy 21) affects many aspects of development, the most salient of which is a decreased rate of intellectual development. Physical abnormalities, such as heart and intestinal defects, cause an increased mortality rate (20 percent to 30 percent) during the first few years of life, and about 1 percent of children with Down syndrome develop leukemia. Among the other physical abnormalities associated with Down syndrome are a small skull, a small nose with a flattened nasal bridge, eyes that tend to slant upward, small ears, small mouth with a normal-sized tongue which often protrudes, a short, broad neck, small hands with short fingers and abnormalities of the palm and fingerprints, and short stature. Sexual development is usually delayed or incomplete, although a few women have reproduced. In general, Down syndrome individuals seem to age at a more rapid rate. Mental retardation is almost always present in affected persons, although the level varies widely from profound to mild retardation.

Syndromes involving trisomies of other chromosomes have been reported, but most of them are associated with early death. Trisomy 18, for example, has an incidence of one per three thousand newborn infants, but only 10 percent survive the first year. The survivors are severely mentally retarded (Weber, 1967) and have a number of physical abnormalities such as an abnormally shaped head, a weak cry, low birth weight, and heart defects. Trisomy 13 occurs once in five thousand births, and 18 percent survive the first year. The survivors are severely retarded and have seizures. Physical abnormalities include defects of the eyes, nose, lips, and heart and extra fingers and poor growth.

Absence of genetic material seems to have more serious consequences than the presence of extra genetic material. Absence of only a portion of a chromosome is either incompatible with life or results in severely handicapped individuals. A partial absence of the short arm of chromosome 5, for example, results in severe mental retardation, poor growth, and a number of physical abnormalities, one of which causes the characteristic high-pitched catlike cry during infancy. A partial absence of the long arm of chromosome 18 has been found to be associated with moderate and severe mental retardation, a small skull, visual and hearing defects, and a variety of other physical abnormalities.

In comparison with the autosomal chromosomes, abnormalities in the sex chromosomes appear to be more compatible with life. That is, a greater proportion of individuals with abnormal sex chromosomes survive, and relatively fewer of them are mentally retarded. In Turner syndrome, the female has one, instead of two, X chromosomes, giving a total of forty-five chromosomes. Turner syndrome results in higher rates (about 20 percent) of mild retardation and is strongly associated with substantial space-form perceptual deficiencies. In one study with eighteen Turner syndrome adults the mean Verbal IQ on the Wechsler Adult Intelligence Scale (WAIS) was 118, while the Performance IQ on the WAIS was 88 (Alexander, Ehrhardt, and Money, 1966). Many individuals with Turner syndrome are not diagnosed until adolescence, when sexual development fails to occur and short stature is noted. Others are diagnosed at birth when certain physical abnormalities, such as webbing of the neck, are present. Although women with Turner syndrome are sterile because they lack functional ovaries, development of the secondary sexual characteristics is possible with the administration of female hormones.

Klinefelter syndrome is a genetic abnormality in which the male has more than one X chromosome in addition to the Y chromosome. Individuals with up to four extra chromosomes have been identified. Klinefelter syndrome occurs at the rate of 1 per 450 male births (Jacobs and Strong, 1959). Mental retardation occurs in 25 percent to 50 percent of cases but is usually mild with no outstanding deficits. In addition to their decreased rate of growth and sexual development Klinefelter individuals have been described as socially unskilled and likely to drop out of school (Nielsen, 1969).

Conditions associated with mental retardation that are inherited on the basis of a specific dominant gene are relatively infrequent in comparison to those inherited on the basis of recessive genes. A dominant genetic condition is usually one in which a parent has the condition. In some instances, the presence of the condition in the child is indicative of a new mutation and has not been inherited. Dominant gene syndromes associated with mental retardation in children are probably relatively infrequent because retarded individuals procreate at greatly reduced rates and therefore do not pass on the defective gene.

Neurofibromatosis affects one out of three thousand persons, but mental retardation and epilepsy occur in only 10 percent of the cases. *Tuberous sclerosis* may not be diagnosed until adulthood when vital organs may be affected by tumors. In some cases, mental retardation, due to the development of tumors in the brain, is the first abnormality to be noted and will later be followed by the development of seizures and the characteristic facial skin lesions.

Many disorders due to specific recessive genes have been identified. Carrier parents can be identified through biochemical tests in some instances, but testing of adults is usually confined to high-risk persons or groups because the incidence of any particular recessive condition in the population is quite low. Since most of the recessive conditions do not begin to manifest their adverse effects until after birth, considerable effort has gone into the development and implementation of mass screening programs for newborn infants for those conditions amenable to a treatment program.

Phenylketonuria (PKU) is a recessive condition occurring once in approximately every seventeen thousand births and is related to a high incidence of mental retardation that is a by-product of an inactive liver enzyme. PKU individuals also manifest a high rate of behavior problems such as hyperactivity, anxiety, and temper tantrums. Inexpensive screening methods for PKU have been developed; some states have mandatory screening programs for newborn infants, while others rely on voluntary screening programs. An effective dietary treatment program has been developed and will be discussed in the treatment section of this chapter.

Another recessive condition, although more rare than PKU, is *galactosemia*, which is a disorder involving the metabolism of galactose that is derived from foods containing lactose. This disorder results in malnutrition, cataracts, and mental retardation, but it may be effectively treated. *Microcephaly* (small head) may also be inherited as a recessive condition and usually results in severe mental retardation.

prenatal, perinatal, and postnatal physical factors

Most of the prenatal, perinatal, and postnatal factors described in the earlier chapters on etiology have been implicated as causes of mental retardation. Again, most of the research studies are correlational and retrospective, and some of the findings must, therefore, be considered tentative, requiring further research for their corroboration. In addition, the etiological factors for some syndromes related to mental retardation have yet to be identified.

Experimental studies with animals have clearly demonstrated that severe malnutrition of the mother during pregnancy adversely affects the growth and development of the offspring. Protein restriction in pregnant rats, for example, has been shown to reduce the number of brain cells in their offspring (Winick and Rosso, 1973). In humans, it is generally accepted that severe malnutrition reduces the infant's birth weight and the number of cells in the placenta and increases the rate of abortions and premature births. Research suggests, however, that malnutrition of the mother only during pregnancy does not lead to an increased rate of mental retardation (Stein, Susser, Saenger, and Marolla, 1972). It may well be that the fetus is able to draw from the mother whatever resources are necessary for brain development.

Postnatal malnutrition, especially during the first few years after birth, does appear to retard intellectual development, but, unfortunately, the research with humans is almost always confounded by socioeconomic factors, pre- and perinatal obstetrical complications, and postnatal infections. In addition to the obvious physical effects, hunger very likely also reduces the child's attention to the environment and thereby the opportunity to learn (Birch and Gussow, 1970).

A number of chronic viral and bacterial infections in pregnant women are known to increase the risk of mental retardation in the offspring. Of the infants who survive a prenatal case of toxoplasmosis, 85 percent will be mentally retarded and manifest various severe physical abnormalities, such as hardened areas of the brain, microcephaly, and seizures. Untreated maternal syphilis greatly increases the rate of death, mental retardation, blindness, and deafness in the child. Other viruses, such as a certain type of herpes virus and one that causes cytomegal inclusion disease, have mild or no effects on the mother but may adversely affect the developing brain of the fetus or newborn infant.

Among the acute maternal infections that increase the abortion and stillbirth rate (Sever, 1970), rubella has the most profound effects in terms of congenital defects and mental retardation. Chess, Korn, and Fernandez (1971) reported that one-fourth of a group of children who contracted rubella prenatally were found to be mildly to profoundly retarded.

Of the maternal dysfunctions known to increase the mortality rates of infants, knowledge is still inadequate to determine their effect on the rate of mental retardation. In the case of maternal diabetes, however, it has been found that children are more likely to have intellectual deficits when the diabetes is not well controlled. Medicine has clearly decreased the risk to the diabetic mother and her child, but not all cases of diabetes are easily controlled. Since hypertensive disorders affect between 5 percent and 10 percent of pregnant women and are implicated in a sizable percentage of maternal and fetal deaths, research on the surviving infants is greatly needed to assess the possibility of their being at high risk for mental retardation.

Deficits in intellectual functioning may also be the result of maternal sensitization, such as Rh incompatibility. Brain damage is caused by substances that cannot be metabolized by the fetal liver thus reaching the brain in toxic concentrations. Although ABO incompatibility is twice as common as Rh incompatibility, the risk of mental retardation is quite low.

Our understanding of the effects of drugs and addictive substances on later physical and cognitive functioning is only beginning to develop. Although more than six hundred drugs are known to produce physical defects in animals, only about twenty of them are known to produce defects in the human fetus; the effects of most of the remaining drugs on the unborn child are unknown. In a few instances, widely used drugs have been demonstrated to have adverse effects when ingested by the mother early in pregnancy. For example, Milkovich and Van den Berg (1974) found that anxious women who took meprobamate or librium during pregnancy had more children with physical defects and mental retardation than did an equally anxious group of women who did not receive either of these two drugs. The absolute number of cases, however, was quite small.

The administration of sedatives and anesthesia during labor and delivery is highly variable among physicians. General anesthetics are usually avoided because it has long been known that they may depress the newborn's respiratory functioning. The long-term consequences of various drugs and drug dosages on the cognitive development of children remains to be explored. The recent research on the effect of maternal alcoholism during pregnancy has revealed a significant incidence of mental and physical retardation in addition to a syndrome of congenital physical defects (Jones, Smith, Ulleland, and Streissguth, 1973). Future research may be expected to delineate the effects of the amount of alcohol and the period during pregnancy when it was ingested.

Although a relationship between maternal anxiety and complications during pregnancy and delivery has been demonstrated in several studies, very little follow-up research on the children of anxious and nonanxious mothers has been conducted. One such study (Stott, 1973) has shown that long-term, chronic stresses, such as severe marital problems, are related to higher incidences of physical and intellectual disabilities.

Prematurity, or low birth weight, has been linked with higher rates of mental retardation. Niswander and Gordon (1972) found that premature children were three times as likely to show neurological abnormalities at the age of one year as nonpremature children. A study of six- and seven-year-old children reported higher incidences of intellectual deficiencies for those with low birth weights, even after children with IQ scores below 60 and those with obvious physical or emotional handicaps were excluded from the study (Wiener, Rider, Oppel, Fischer, and Harper, 1965). In a study with nine pairs of identical twins in which one twin's birth weight was significantly less than that of the other, the twin of lower birth weight had the lower rate of physical growth and intellectual development into adulthood (Babson and Phillips, 1973). At one time, a number of premature infants were given high concentrations of oxygen as part of their postnatal care in the hospital. It has subsequently been discovered that premature infants may become blind (retrolental fibroplasia) and sometimes become mentally retarded when they are subjected to high concentrations of oxygen. Use of hexachlorophene soap in bathing newborn infants has been discontinued since it was found to cause brain damage in premature infants and sometimes led to death that appeared to be due to oxygen deprivation. Thus, it appears that the premature infant may be especially vulnerable to certain environmental conditions.

Anoxia may also produce long-lasting cognitive deficits, although the problems are not severe in most cases. One of the most thorough examinations of anoxia effects involved over three hundred preschool children who were divided into groups, those who had normal full-term births, those who were full term but anoxic at birth, and those who had other complications at the time of birth (Graham, Ernhart, Craft, and Berman, 1963). The children judged to be oxygen-deprived at birth were found to have lower scores on a variety of cognitive measures and a greater number of neurological abnormalities than the children who had normal births.

In comparison with anoxia, the occurrence of perinatal head injury is considerably less frequent. Head injury is usually the result of head compression during birth. Head compression may be caused by a number of factors, such as size of the pelvic opening, head position during birth, and length of labor. A few studies with large numbers of children have examined some of the relevant variables; the findings typically reveal small differences in IQ scores in favor of the group with normal delivery.

Postnatal head injury appears to be occurring with a high frequency due to car accidents and child abuse, as well as the usual accidental falls, and the resulting brain damage can permanently impair the child's intellectual functioning. Several studies of retarded persons have indicated that postnatal head injury has occurred in about 1 percent of the cases.

Animal research has led us to believe that injury to the brain of the young organism has less severe consequences than the same injury to the older organism. Teuber (1970) has suggested, however, that the situation with humans might be different in that early injury may lead to even greater deficits in particular behavioral functioning—probably the more complex, higher-level behaviors—not usually tested in animal studies, while the lower-level behaviors may be relatively more often "spared" for younger human organisms, as they are for younger infrahuman animals.

Among the diseases of childhood, encephalitis probably carries one of the highest risks for mental retardation. The viruses that cause encephalitis are often those involved in common childhood diseases, such as measles and chicken pox. Of the children who survive, half are severely mentally or physically impaired. Lead and mercury poisoning, now more commonly caused by air, water, and food pollution, are capable of causing brain damage that may manifest itself in mental retardation. There are, no doubt, other physical factors, most of them probably artificial, that increase the risk of mental retardation. Our efforts to identify these factors have only begun.

demographic factors

Age of the mother is related to the risk of having a retarded child with teenage mothers and women over thirty-five having the higher risks. Older mothers are more likely to have children with chromosomal abnormalities as well as multiple births (for example, twins). Young mothers tend to have unfavorable backgrounds involving nutrition, medical care, and psychological history. In addition to their increased risks for complications during pregnancy, labor, and delivery, both young and older mothers may provide postnatal environments for their children that are different from those of other children.

Socioeconomic status also affects the child's risk for mental retardation with children from the lower socioeconomic groups having the higher risk. This factor is, of course, related to many of the physical factors mentioned earlier in that lower socioeconomic groups tend to have poorer nutrition, medical care, and general physical status. Moreover, socioeconomic status continues to affect the child through both postnatal physical and environmental-psychological factors, which are discussed in the next section.

Sex of the child is related to the risk of mental retardation; most studies have found a higher proportion of males than females, usually a ratio of two or three males to one female (Mumpower, 1970). Genetic factors no doubt contribute to these differences in view of the more numerous chromosomal abnormalities affecting males, but consideration must also be given to the possible effects of differential societal expectations for the two sexes. Perhaps more males have been referred, and therefore diagnosed, because parents have been more concerned about the implications of slow development for males than for females. In addition, males may manifest other behavioral characteristics that may increase the probability of their being referred.

environmental and psychological factors

Theoretically, a child with optimal genetic material and physical background who is deprived of environmental stimulation postnatally would become mentally retarded. Occasional case studies of children who have been confined to one room or an attic have reported severe behavioral consequences of extreme reduction in environmental stimuli, although, in these instances, we cannot determine the child's initial status. Similarly, studies conducted in certain institutional settings in which infants were greatly deprived of environmental stimulation also demonstrated that mental retardation was a frequent occurrence. It appears, then, that children require a certain amount of interaction with the environment to develop a behavioral repertoire that is within normal limits. The only problem remaining is to describe the necessary quantity and quality of environmental stimulation. On the basis of animal studies and research with infants, there is a strong indication that the infant's sensory capacities are well developed at birth and that early sensory stimulation is necessary for development. Although speculative, it is reasonable to assume that virtually all home environments have the potential for providing the minimal stimulation required for development of the infant. Even the poorest of homes can provide a wide variety of visual, auditory, and tactile experiences.

Mental retardation in infants, however, may also be found for children whose environments are chaotic or extremely variable. Case studies of children who have been abandoned and who have had a succession of caregivers (for example, multiple foster homes) suggest that there are limits to the infants' capacities to adjust to changes in environmental stimulation. When these limits have been exceeded, the child fails to develop at a normal rate.

The demonstrated importance of environmental factors to the developing child has led to their implication in the etiology of mild mental retardation, which accounts for over 70 percent of the retarded population. In examining the relationship between level of retardation and five socioeconomic groups, Birch and his colleagues (1970) found that retarded children with IQ scores below 60 were equally represented among the socioeconomic groups, while children with IQs of 60 or higher were greatly overrepresented in the lower socioeconomic groups, suggesting that the etiological factors were different for the higher- and lower-IQ children. Organic conditions were present for most of the low-IQ children, while two-thirds of the higher-IQ children presented no evidence of organic conditions relating to etiology. Compared with nonretarded children from the same lower socioeconomic groups, the retarded children were more likely to come from large families and live in poorer housing (more people in each room). Half of the siblings of these retarded children had IQ scores below 75. Other investigators have found similar familial and environmental factors for large percentages of mildly retarded children and have coined the term, *cultural-familial,* to describe the etiological factors.

At various times, greater or lesser emphases have been given to specific aspects of the obviously confounded variables involved in the etiology of cultural-familial retardation. Many researchers have proposed the view that mild mental retardation simply represents the lower end of the normal IQ distribution and is not reflective of pathological conditions; they support this view by pointing out that mildly retarded persons are not overrepresented in the population. On the other hand, there is reason to believe that mildly retarded children are primarily the products of less-than-optimal environmental and psychological conditions, such as the lack of opportunity to learn (inadequate models and antecedent stimuli) and the lack of reinforcement for learning cognitive skills. Evidence for this belief comes from intervention studies that are discussed in the next section.

In general, research permits us to conclude that mild mental retardation, like other levels of intellectual functioning, is a product of both genetic and environmental influences. The correlation between children and natural parents' IQ scores remains essentially the same whether or not the children are raised by the natural parents (Achenbach 1974, pp. 241–242). The absolute IQ score, however, tends to be determined by environmental factors. Mildly retarded children have received particular attention in recent years because it has become increasingly apparent that they have problems adapting to contemporary society. This attention also raises the issue of the extent to which all children, retarded and nonretarded, might benefit from improved environmental and psychological conditions.

Certain behavioral patterns formerly attributed to mental retardation per se have been shown to be determined by environmental conditions. Zigler (1973), for example, concluded that perseveration (that is, repetition of a task) was more likely to be due to the effects of social reinforcement (after a history of social deprivation in an institutional setting) than to mental retardation. In a similar vein, retarded children's history of experiencing failures has been invoked as the basis for the research results showing that, in comparison with normals of the same mental age, the retarded set low goals for themselves and are content with minimal success on tasks on which they could do better.

treatment

Physicians, educators, and psychologists have long been involved in the treatment of the retarded. At the beginning of the nineteenth century, Itard, a physician, spent five years attempting to train a boy who had been captured in the forest of Aveyron, France. Although Itard was far from successful in "curing" the boy, his program, with its emphasis on sensory training, contained much that is still used in contemporary education. Seguin, a student of Itard, who arrived in the United States in the middle of the nineteenth century and became the superintendent of the Pennsylvania Training School for Idiots, designed programs that involved both sensory and motor training and emphasized the necessity of individualized teaching as well as a good relationship between child and teacher. Montessori, a student of Seguin and working in Rome, was successful in teaching a number of retarded children to read and write. Although she used Seguin's methods, her successes were also due to her unique contributions, namely an emphasis on early education, practical life experiences, and self-teaching, a method whereby the child chooses materials from an array. Montessori's innovations have subsequently become popular in preschool programs for middle-class children.

Although institutions for the retarded have a long history, the training of teachers and the establishment of programs for the retarded did not begin until after the turn of the twentieth century. The slow increase in the number of college training programs for teachers and special classes in public schools between 1915 and 1930 was suddenly terminated probably due to a combination of the financial problems associated with the depression and changes in educational philosophy. After World War II, public support of special classes for the retarded was reinstated and was substantially influenced by pressures from the parents of retarded children, most of whom had previously received no special services in school or had been excluded from school altogether.

Historically, treatment of the mentally retarded has not generally had a high priority among mental health professionals. Before the 1950s and 1960s very few clinical psychologists and psychiatrists had used psychotherapy with retarded persons, the principal reasons for this neglect being that mental retardation was not curable and that the characteristics of the retarded (such as, poor verbal ability and low motivation) precluded the successful use of psychotherapy. During the last few decades, beginning with the Kennedy presidential term, the availability of financial resources for professional training programs, research, and direct services to the retarded has encouraged the exploration of both traditional and newer forms of therapy.

The 1960s to the early 1980s have been a time of considerable gains for the retarded. In addition to the increases in funds for education and treatment, a number of changes in the law have benefited retarded persons. Public Law 94-142, the Education for All Handicapped Children Act, requires the schools to provide education for retarded children between the ages of three and eighteen years and in the later 1980s will provide for retarded children beginning at birth. In addition, Public Law 95-602, the Rehabilitation Comprehensive Services and Developmental Disabilities Amendment of 1978, specifies the right of the retarded person to services in the least restrictive environment. In effect, these laws guarantee all retarded children the right to education. In addition, community groups are beginning to take more responsibility for the retarded persons in their neighborhoods who are now less likely to be institutionalized at some distance from their homes.

It has gradually become acknowledged that parents are rarely able to understand and accept a diagnosis of mental retardation when it is first presented. Initial reactions frequently include denial and a search for another professional opinion. In some cases, treatment programs may be postponed or ineffective treatment programs initiated on the basis of the parents' denial of mental retardation. Under the best of circumstances, most parents need a continuing interpretation of the child's problem, concrete suggestions for child rearing, and psychological support (Magrab and Johnson, 1980).

One of the more difficult decisions that some parents have to make is whether or not to institutionalize the child. Such a decision is based on many factors. In the past, for example, physicians strongly urged parents to institutionalize children with Down syndrome at an early age because the burden of their care was considered to be excessive and parental rewards minimal. Institutionalization during infancy and the preschool period is relatively uncommon now and is determined more by the family circumstances and the behavioral characteristics of the child. Farber (1959, 1960) has reported that the presence of a severely retarded child may often be detrimental to marital adjustment and to normal female siblings who are expected to provide more of the care and help with housework than male siblings. Both the sex of the retarded child and the amount of disruption perceived by the parents are significant factors in the decision to institutionalize retarded children; males and disruptive retarded children are more likely to be institutionalized than females and nondisruptive children who are equally retarded (Wolf and Whitehead, 1975).

In general, the decision to institutionalize depends greatly on the family's ability to cope with the practical problems presented by the retarded child, such as day-to-day care, increased cost of medical care and treatment, and limitations on social activities. These practical problems significantly affect the psychological lives of the family members both within the family structure and in relationship to persons outside the family. Mothers having to spend a disproportionate amount of their time with the retarded child necessarily spend less time with their spouses and normal children as well as less time outside the home.

In spite of the many problems posed by the retarded child in the home, relatively few retarded children (approximately 4 percent) are institutionalized. Most parents choose to keep their retarded child at home. Unfortunately, community services for the retarded preschool child are still not easily available, although considerable progress has been made in the availability of preschool educational programs; the Head Start programs, for example, are now required to include children with physical and behavioral problems (La Vor & Harvey, 1976). Physicians and community clinics also offer supportive services and advice to parents. The National Association for Retarded Citizens (NARC), consisting primarily of local parents' groups, has been an important source of psychological support for many families and has been responsible for the development of many programs that provide services for retarded children.

To the extent that families can be helped with their overwhelming problems, the necessity for institutionalization will be decreased. Improvements in community services might also facilitate the release of children and adults for whom institutionalization was deemed necessary. For example, the development of foster home placement and group homes offers considerable promise for an early release from institutions as well as an alternative to initial institutionalization. Even the most severely handicapped retarded child might be benefited more by an inpatient facility that is located in the home community than a regional institution located at some distance from the family's residence, since the family might be more likely to visit the child and take an active interest in the child's care and treatment program.

educational programs

Special education programs have traditionally involved the assignment of retarded children to separate classrooms or schools. Most public school systems divide retarded children into two groups on the basis of IQ scores: educable mentally retarded (EMR) and trainable mentally retarded (TMR). Although there is some variability with respect to the exact IQ score limits, EMR children usually have IQ scores within the mildly retarded range and TMR children within the moderate to severely retarded range. Special classes are typically smaller than regular classes to allow for greater individual attention from the teacher, but they contain children with a wider age range.

The EMR elementary primary class is for children between the ages of six and ten years. The focus of this class is on readiness skills that are compatible with their mental ages of three to six years. In the EMR elementary intermediate class for children from nine to thirteen with mental ages of six to nine years, emphasis is placed on the learning of basic school subjects, reading, writing, and arithmetic.

The EMR secondary class for children of junior and senior high school ages continues to emphasize basic school subjects with a significant addition of practical skills and occupational training.

In recent years, there has been a strong movement away from self-contained classes for EMR children. The impetus for change comes from several sources or assumptions with some of them having meager or no research support. Research comparing the achievement of retarded children in special education and regular classrooms has presented equivocal results. This failure to establish the academic effectiveness of special education has also led to the idea that EMR children might enjoy greater social adjustment in regular classrooms. Research suggests, however, that retarded children in regular classes are more often rejected by peers and have poorer adjustment than their retarded peers in special education classes (Goldstein, Moss, and Jordan, 1965).

Current educational programs tend to fall between the regular class and self-contained special education class in structure. EMR children are assigned to regular classrooms with similar-age peers and participate in many of the regular activities. For specific academic subjects, however, they leave the classroom and receive special training in small groups from resource teachers. Evaluation of this newer model has not yet been conducted, and there may well be serious roadblocks, such as less-than-enthusiastic teachers, to its success (MacMillan, Jones, and Meyers, 1976).

Although there has been considerable discussion and development of curricula and materials for EMR pupils, many teachers continue to use a conventional curriculum and modify it to meet the needs of their pupils. Modification may involve little more than slowing the pace at which new material is presented. Another approach to curriculum design involves the selection and teaching of skills that are necessary to function in everyday adult life (Kolstoe, 1970). Although the retarded child's rate of learning is slower than average, delineation of the most utilitarian behavioral goals would allow the retarded person to function optimally in contemporary society.

While it is reasonable to assume that most special education teachers are conscientious and competent, there tend to be few incentives for excellence. School systems have been more lax about evaluating the progress of retarded children and, in the past, were prone to assign the less-qualified (in training and experience) teachers to special education classes. Unfortunately, negative attitudes about the retarded and poor expectations for their future still prevail in our society and adversely affect the quality of education and social experiences. The development of special training programs, particularly at the master's degree level, for teachers of the retarded has no doubt had a positive influence on the quality of education; the goal now is that this improvement in the quality of education will lead to changes in the expectations for the retarded.

Because of their relatively small numbers and greater diversity of physical problems, education of *trainable* mentally retarded children poses greater challenges. In urban settings, it has been feasible to provide special education classes. Most professionals are in agreement that TMR children should not be placed in regular classes because it has been assumed that they are not generally capable of achieving useful academic skills. The goals of special education for TMR children have been self-care and social adjustment; these goals are generally compatible with those for normal preschool and early elementary school-age children. Alternatives to public school education include home-bound programs and institutionalization.

Special education programs are offered within institutional settings for the mentally retarded. Although children at all levels of mental retardation may be found in institutions, proportionately more severely and profoundly retarded persons are admitted. Institutions would seem to offer more potential for the training and education of the severely handicapped because the facilities, trained personnel, and clients are relatively easily brought together. Research, however, suggests that institutionalization is more often followed by slower rates of progress. Decreases in the rate of progress found for institutionalized retarded children have been attributed to a lack of opportunity to learn; that, in turn, has presumably been caused by a shortage of personnel. Institutions, like schools, have been lax in the evaluation of their programs and in the qualifications of persons who have daily contact with the retarded residents. Recent and pending legal decisions are expected to upgrade the quality of programs for children residing in institutions.

Educational programs for the preschool retarded child have been receiving increased research attention during the past ten to fifteen years. Most of this attention has been focused on disadvantaged children who are at high risk for mild mental retardation. The earlier studies in this area concentrated on relatively brief programs with older preschool children and were able to demonstrate small amounts of gain that were subsequently lost. The more recent studies have concentrated on training programs with children in the first or second year of life. One of the most intensive studies (Heber and Garber, 1975) selected children from a poverty population in which the mothers had IQ scores below 75. The program was begun when the children were between three and six months of age and continued through the preschool years. The full-day stimulation program emphasized language skills, a structured environment, and maternal training. Differences between the experimental and control groups were apparent at eighteen months of age; at seventy-two months of age the average Stanford-Binet IQ score of the experimental group was 121 and that of the control group 87. Subsequent comparisons revealed some declines for both groups after the intervention ceased and the children entered regular schools. There has, however, been a consistent 20 or more IQ (WISC) point difference between the groups through age nine (Garber and Heber, 1977). A review of seven infant and preschool programs for low-income children conducted in the 1960s revealed that they were successful in helping the children to meet regular school requirements and in preventing special education placement and grade retention (Darlington, Royce, Snipper, Murray, and Lazar, 1980). While IQ scores showed some increases for several years after preschool, these increases, were not maintained; these results replicate those found in other studies. Zigler and Trickett (1978) have recommended that evaluations of early childhood intervention programs include multiple measures of social competence, such as physical health status, school achievement, motivational and emotional variables, school attendance, and incidence of juvenile delinquency, rather than be based only on IQ scores that are, at best, indirect measures of school performance.

Early intervention programs seem to offer some hope for attenuating mental retardation, particularly in children who are reared in disadvantaged or impoverished environments. The available research does indicate that successful programs must be intensive and, therefore, costly. Cost-effectiveness analysis may, however, reveal that the price represents a bargain when it is compared with the price of nonintervention.

behavior therapy

Although the application of behavior principles with retarded children has had a relatively short history, the results have been impressive. Behavioral clinicians have effected changes in a wide variety of behaviors in both institutional and school settings. Much of the pioneering research has been conducted with institutionalized severely and profoundly retarded children who were considered incapable of learning and who lived under custodial care conditions.

Self-feeding. Correct self-feeding is a behavior that many institutionalized retarded children lack. Applied researchers (see, for example, Azrin and Armstrong, 1973) have found that a combination of *backward chaining* and physical guidance is an effective method for teaching self-feeding. In this procedure, the child's hand is physically guided through the sequence of picking up the spoon, putting food on the spoon, and bringing food to the mouth; the hand is released immediately before the spoon enters the mouth, thus allowing the child to complete the behavioral chain that is followed by reinforcement. This physical guidance is gradually decreased to allow the child to complete greater portions of the behavioral chain, with the last step of physical guidance involving picking up the spoon. Training in correct self-feeding, however, does not automatically eliminate the quicker method of eating with the hands or food stealing. These inappropriate behaviors have been successfully decreased by short-term (for example, fifteen seconds) removal of the plate for inappropriate feeding behaviors and removal from the dining hall for stealing (Barton, Guess, Garcia, and Baer, 1970).

Toilet-training. Toilet-training of institutionalized retardates has also received considerable research attention because, like self-feeding, successful use of the toilet decreases the aversive chores of attendants, probably contributes to better social interactions between attendants and residents, and provides time for attendants to teach other constructive behaviors. Improved use of the toilet has been reported with the use of methods commonly used by parents of normal children: placing the child on the toilet at intervals when the child is likely to urinate or defecate, rewarding the child for successes, and either ignoring or punishing "accidents." These methods typically lead to gradual decreases in accidents over a period of weeks or months. Azrin and Foxx (1971), however, devised a method whereby accidents were reduced by 80 percent after one to fourteen days of intensive training. Their training procedure was carried out for eight hours each day during which placement on the toilet was scheduled every thirty minutes, lasting for twenty minutes or until urination occurred, and fluids were given every thirty minutes. Special toilets were designed to signal urination or defecation immediately, as were moisture-sensitive pants that signaled accidents. Both social and edible reinforcers were given every five minutes if the resident was dry and after toilet successes. Azrin and Foxx's "package" also includes the procedures for establishing and maintaining self-initiated use of the toilet.

Another approach to toilet-training has been proposed by Van Wagenen, Meyerson, Kerr, and Mahoney (1969). The child wears moisture-sensitive pants, and when the tone sounds, the trainer shouts "no," which has the effect of stopping urination briefly but long enough to get the child to the toilet where it can be resumed. Success at the toilet is then reinforced. All eight profoundly retarded children in the training program for three to four hours each day responded to the tone by going to the toilet and voiding, within forty-five hours or fifteen days of training. Some problems that were independent of the tone did arise, however, in developing and maintaining urination. These examples represent only a few research approaches to toilet-training of institutionalized retarded children—approaches that opened up the possibility of toilet training to a large proportion of children previously believed to be untrainable.

Motor and verbal skills. Combinations of reinforcement and modeling have been useful in the teaching of both motor and verbal skills. Modeling and reinforcement of friendly behavior were effective in increasing appropriate, friendly behaviors of retarded adolescents who formerly displayed frequent aggressive behaviors toward other residents (Fechter, 1971). This combination has also aided retardates in the learning of basic communication responses (Talkington, Hall, and Altman, 1973) and concept acquisition (Yoder and Forehand, 1974).

Perhaps the most significant behavioral research has been in the area of language. Operant conditioning procedures have been successfully employed to establish imitative verbal behavior and to teach functional and spontaneous speech in children who have never talked or who have exhibited minimal vocalizations (Garcia & De Haven, 1974). These procedures are described in Chapter 9 on childhood psychosis.

Aggressive and destructive behavior. Researchers have also evaluated procedures for decreasing or eliminating a variety of severe behavior problems in institutionalized retarded children. Instances of aggressive and destructive behavior have been decreased when they were followed by periods of timeout, brief administrations of electric shock, and "restitution" (Foxx and Azrin, 1972), which involves a period of time during which the resident performs work tasks.

In comparison with the procedures of extinction and differential reinforcement of other behavior, brief, contingent electric shock has been found to decrease self-injurious behaviors most rapidly. These behaviors are unusually difficult to control and require long-term maintenance programs. Several investigators have reported an absence of negative side-effects and even the presence of positive "side-effects" in their use of contingent shock for severe and frequently occurring behavior problems.

Classroom behavior. Behavior principles have also been utilized to improve both academic and nonacademic behaviors in classroom settings. Birnbrauer, Wolf, Kidder, and Tague (1965) designed a token economy in conjunction with social reinforcement for appropriate behavior and timeout for inappropriate behaviors for two programmed classes for retarded children and found that most of the children performed better when the token system was in effect. The behaviors observed in the classroom studies have typically been attending behaviors and specific inappropriate behaviors. Reinforcers such as tokens and free time have been shown to increase attending behaviors, while response cost (loss of tokens or free time) and timeout have been effective in decreasing inappropriate behaviors. Unfortunately, increases in attending behavior and decreases in inappropriate behaviors do not necessarily lead to gains in the learning of academic material; such gains are optimally demonstrated when specific contingencies are arranged for correct strategies or answers, or both.

One of the most impressive behavioral projects to date is a curriculum for EMR children from five to ten years of age (Ross and Ross 1974) that is based on a series of experimental studies. The experimentally based training areas included in the curriculum are: (1) basic academic skills (reading, vocabulary, verbal expression, and arithmetic), (2) general learning skills (listening and following directions, planning, and problem solving), (3) social behavior, (4) gross and fine motor skills (physical education and fine motor skills), and (5) fine arts (painting and music). In their studies, Ross and Ross used a combination of modeling the correct behavior, requiring the children to respond, and reinforcing the correctly modeled behavior with tokens that could be exchanged for prizes. The unique aspect of these studies is their successful attempt to teach retarded children cognitive strategies that transfer to new situations.

A number of problem areas in applied behavioral research with retarded children still remain. While positive reinforcement and punishment have been quite effective in changing behavior, the improvements tend not to be maintained when the specific contingencies are removed and are rarely transferred to other behaviors or settings. Generalization and maintenance of behavioral gains is, therefore, an important problem area for future research. In addition, more attention needs to be focused on the selection and training of behaviors with long-term positive consequences, such as social behaviors required in everyday interactions and asking of questions (Bondy and Erickson, 1976).

psychotherapy

The indications for psychotherapy with retarded children are essentially the same as those for the nonretarded, namely, maladaptive behaviors. Several types of psychotherapy have been utilized with the retarded. Play therapy has perhaps been used most frequently with younger retarded children because of their less-well-developed verbal skills. Newcomer and Morrison (1974) reported a study in which five- to twenty-year-old mildly and moderately retarded institutionalized children were given either individual play therapy, group play therapy, or no therapy. The results indicated that, while the no-therapy group showed no progress, both play therapy groups improved on the Gross Motor, Fine Motor, Language, and Personal-Social scales of the Denver Developmental Screening Test (Frankenburg and Dodds, 1970) over thirty sessions (eighteen weeks) of therapy. The therapy techniques used in this study were based on the earlier writings of Axline (1947) and Leland and Smith (1965). In a second study Morrison and Newcomer, (1975) found no differences in improvement for retarded children given directive play therapy and those given nondirective play therapy.

Group psychotherapy has been reported most often with older retarded children, particularly adolescents, and is usually conducted in institutional settings in which groups may be easily formed. Group therapy is viewed as having particular advantages for the retarded: increasing the residents' awareness of the problems of others, reducing social withdrawal, and orienting the resident toward the immediate environment (Gunzburg, 1975, p. 716).

Very few well-designed studies on the effectiveness of psychotherapy with older retarded children are available; of these studies, several report increases in IQ scores and improvement of behavioral problems, while the remaining ones report no differences between treatment and no-treatment groups. These results, however, are similar to those of studies with nonretarded children.

physical treatment

Various types of medication have been used in the treatment of the retarded. They are employed primarily to control seizures and to aid in behavior management. In the treatment of seizures, phenobarbital is probably the most commonly used drug because it has been effective for the broad range of seizure disorders. Dilantin may also be used to control certain types of seizures, particularly grand mal seizures that are characterized by total loss of consciousness and repetitive motor movements. For purposes of optimal seizure control and the counteraction of various drug side-effects, combinations of medications may be employed. Seizures in a significant number of retarded children cannot, however, be eliminated with our current medications. Concern has also been raised about inappropriate use of anti-convulsant medication for institutionalized retarded persons (Kaufman and Katz-Garris, 1979).

Use of psychoactive drugs with the retarded is widespread, especially in institutional settings. There have been complaints that these drugs are used excessively as substitutes for behavioral training programs. A study by Lipman (1970), for example, surveyed over one hundred institutions with nearly 150,000 retarded residents and found that 37 percent were being administered major tranquilizers, 8 percent minor tranquilizers, and 4 percent antidepressants. Unless carefully monitored, one could expect to find large percentages of residents being given these medications because the resulting changes in behavior are very likely to reduce the amount of work required by attendants who, in many instances, are responsible for twenty or more residents. Thus, the shortage of personnel and the unavailability of programs for behavior management have the combined effects of making drugs an attractive alternative.

One of the most dramatic breakthroughs in the treatment of the retarded has been the development of special diets for children with some of the hereditary disorders. In the case of galactosemia, for example, the omission of milk and other foods containing lactose from the child's diet prevents most of the mental retardation. When the diet is initiated soon after birth, the effect on intelligence test scores is best (Kalakar, Konoshita, and Donnell, 1973); however, some improvement occurs even when the diet is begun later in the infancy period. The diet is usually continued through the preschool years, although deprivation of milk and milk products may continue for longer periods. A number of the treated children do seem to have learning problems in school and visual-motor difficulties. Two of the problems associated with the evaluation of dietary treatment programs are that: (1) the child may obtain and ingest the forbidden foods without the parents' knowledge and (2) the deprivation of these foods may have negative effects on other areas of functioning.

Perhaps the most well-known diet is that used for children with phenylketonuria (PKU). This diet restricts the intake of foods containing phenylalanine, the substance that cannot be metabolized and is responsible for the ensuing brain damage. Most of the children placed on the diet very early in life do not become mentally retarded, but as a group they do not achieve the intellectual level of non-affected family members (Berman and Ford, 1970). Later initiation of the diet, while ineffective in reversing the brain damage already present, has been found to improve behavior problems and to facilitate the effectiveness of drugs for seizure control. The diet is difficult to administer in that extreme restriction of phenylalanine leads to protein loss in the body and growth retardation. New advances in dietary control offer the promise of complete prevention of mental retardation in children with PKU. Commercial preparation of milk substitutes are available. Most children are taken off the diet between the ages of six and nine years. Women with PKU have a very high probability of having children who are retarded. It is possible that strict adherence to the diet immediately before and during pregnancy could prevent the mental retardation of their offspring (Goldstein, Auerbach, and Grover, 1973).

cerebral palsy and mental retardation

Cerebral palsy refers to a collection of disorders that primarily affect motor behavior. The earliest symptoms may be a delay in motor development and abnormal reflexes on the neurological examination. As the child grows older, other problems become apparent. The majority of children with cerebral palsy develop spasticity in one or more limbs. Spasticity refers to an inability to move the limb voluntarily because the muscles are contracted. Spasticity usually involves the two limbs on one side of the body (hemiplegia), the two lower limbs (paraplegia), or all four limbs (quadriplegia). Other children with cerebral palsy have abnormal movements of the limbs (dyskinesia) that may be rapid or slow. The smallest group of children with cerebral palsy develop ataxia, an inability to coordinate the muscles for maintaining posture or for walking. The motor disabilities often prevent the child from speaking or communicating in other ways.

The severe motor disabilities of children with cerebral palsy for a long time prevented valid assessment of their cognitive functioning. In fact, it was generally assumed that all persons with these severe motor handicaps were also mentally retarded, and many were institutionalized under that assumption. It now appears that probably only one-half of the children with cerebral palsy are mentally retarded. This finding, however, does not negate the fact that many of the intellectually normal children are severely hampered in their use of that intelligence by their physical handicaps, but it has probably contributed toward a greater effort in the treatment of these physical handicaps.

It has been recognized since the last century that cerebral palsy is correlated with physical complications of pregnancy, labor, and delivery. Oxygen deprivation during the birth process has been implicated as the principal etiological factor in many cases of cerebral palsy, although other factors, such as prematurity, head injury, and infections, have also been acknowledged as having a causal role.

Treatment of the motor handicaps associated with cerebral palsy is moderately successful with some types of disorders, particularly when it is begun early in life. Köng (1969) reported that treatment begun in the first year of life is the most effective. Treatment of the motor problems is conducted primarily by physical therapists in clinic and hospital settings. Since treatment must be conducted daily, physical therapists design home therapy programs for the parents and work with the child at less frequent intervals.

Some communities provide special schools or other facilities for children with cerebral palsy. Many of these children would otherwise not receive an adequate education because their physical handicaps prevent their attending most public schools. The law now requires public buildings to provide access routes and facilities (for example, bathrooms) for persons who need wheelchairs, braces, or crutches to ambulate. This law has greatly facilitated the effort to provide normal environments for physically handicapped persons.

Much of the treatment of the motor disabilities in cerebral palsy is an attempt to prevent further handicaps. When the muscles of the body are not used, they are highly susceptible to atrophy, a wasting or decrease in the tissues, and physical therapy can help to prevent this atrophy and related problems. If cerebral palsy is not diagnosed early enough, certain abnormalities of the muscles, and thereby the limbs, may not be corrected by physical therapy alone. In some of these instances, orthopedic surgery, which often involves the severing or rearranging of muscle tissue, or both methods, can alleviate otherwise intractable physical handi-caps.

Conclusions

Mental retardation refers to a subaverage rate in the development of cognitive and adaptive behaviors detectable before the age of eighteen. The criteria for diagnosis have been established by the American Association on Mental Deficiency and are generally accepted by clinicians and researchers. The causes of mental retardation include genetic, pre-, peri-, and postnatal physical factors as well as environmental and psychological factors. The cause or causes of mental retardation in *individual* children cannot, however, be specified in the majority of cases.

Although "cures" of mentally retarded children are rare, several approaches to treatment have been successful in preventing mental retardation in high-risk chil-dren—namely, special diets for children with certain genetic abnormalities and stimulation or education programs, or both, for disadvantaged children. Behavioral approaches to the treatment of retarded children have been successful in the teaching of a variety of self-care and cognitive skills. Additional research on etio-logical factors and treatment effectiveness is especially needed.

Recommended Readings

Birnbrauer, J., "Mental Retardation," in *Handbook of Behavior Modification and Behavior Therapy.* Edited by H. Leitenberg. Englewood Cliffs, N. J.: Prentice-Hall, 1976. A review of applied behavioral research with the retarded.

Farber, B., "Effects of a Severely Mentally Retarded Child on Family Integration," *Monographs of the Society for Research in Child Development,* 24, Whole No. 71 (1959). Family Organization and Crisis: Maintenance of Integration in Families with a Severely Mentally Retarded Child." *Monographs of the Society for Research in Child Development,* 25 (1. Serial No. 75), (1960). Classic papers on the impact of retarded children on their families.

Haywood, H. C., Filler, J. W., and **Shipman, N. A.**, "Behavioral Assessment in Mental Retardation." Edited by P. McReynolds. *Advances in Psychological Assessment.* Volume 3. San Francisco: Jossey-Bass, 1975. Presents two alternatives to traditional assessment of the retarded: assessment of learning potential and direct behavioral assessment throught a functional analysis of behavior.

Mittler, P., ed., *Research to Practice in Mental Retardation.* 3 Vols. Baltimore, Md.: University Park Press, 1977. A selection of papers presented at the Fourth Congress of the International Association for the Scientific Study of Mental Deficiency in 1976.

Robinson N., and **Robinson, H.,** *The Mentally Retarded Child* (2nd ed.). New York: McGraw-Hill, 1976. An excellent general textbook on the retarded child.

childhood psychosis/ pervasive developmental disorders

9

Tim, a three-year-old boy, was referred by his family physician because he exhibited unusual behaviors and lacked a number of behaviors, particularly social and verbal skills. The physician had seen Tim only a few times, and only when he was physically ill, during the past two years.

Tim was the second son of a young couple in their 20s. He was conceived four months after the birth of their first child when the mother believed that she could not get pregnant while breast-feeding the first child. She went to her physician complaining that she had not yet had a period, and he gave her a shot which was supposed to bring on her period. The mother reported that she became extremely ill after the shot; she experienced severe nausea, vomiting, and dizziness for a week and had to remain in bed.

The pregnancy was later confirmed and proceeded uneventfully. The birth was normal with

Tim weighing a little over eight pounds. The mother reported that there were some difficulties caring for two infants, but that Tim was a very good baby and gave her no trouble at all. In fact, he seemed happier when left alone. The mother recalled that Tim didn't smile and didn't seem to recognize her as a young infant. He learned to walk early, at nine months, and from the beginning was especially adept at motor skills, never falling or hurting himself.

The parents first became concerned about Tim's development during his second year when he did not begin to talk. They were advised that he was probably a "late bloomer" and perhaps did not need to talk because his needs were being anticipated by his parents. Their concern increased, however, as they gradually realized that Tim was not responding to their speech, and they insisted on a hearing test, the results of which indicated no hearing loss. The continued lack of speech and responsiveness to people and an increase in unusual behaviors, such as turning the wheels of his toy cars and rocking his body for long periods, finally led to his referral.

Childhood psychosis is perhaps the most severe form of behavior disorder in that many aspects of the child's behavioral repertoire are affected. Although it occurs rarely in comparison with other types of behavior disorders, childhood psychosis has received a great amount of attention from psychiatrists and psychologists. This attention has been reflected in the substantial body of clinical research on assessment, etiology, and treatment.

The incidence of childhood psychosis is not precisely known because various criteria for diagnosis have been used. There is general agreement, however, that psychosis affects more boys than girls with the sex ratio being approximately three boys to one girl during childhood (Rosen, Bahn, and Kramer, 1964). This ratio tends to decrease when the onset of psychosis occurs during adolescence. The incidence of psychosis in the child population has been estimated as varying between .008 percent and .06 percent (Werry, 1972, p. 187). Childhood psychosis accounts for between 3 percent and 9 percent of clinic referrals. The onset of psychosis may occur at any age from birth on, but diagnosis is often delayed until several years after onset. The most severe forms of childhood psychoses have their onset during the early preschool years.

assessment

As is the case of children with other severe disorders, the family physician is usually the first professional from whom the family seeks assistance. If psychosis is suspected, the physician will probably refer the family to a psychiatrist, since psychiatrists have historically contributed most of the available information about the diagnosis and treatment of the psychoses. Often, however, the child's behaviors may suggest other possible problems, and referral to a psychiatrist may be delayed for months or even years. Diagnosis by the psychiatrist is based primarily on the interview with the parents and observation of the child in the office. The psychiatrist frequently requests psychological testing and sometimes a complete physical examination, including a neurological examination, to aid in the diagnosis.

A proliferation of labels referring to the psychoses of childhood have appeared in the research literature. Unfortunately, even the same label does not always have the same meaning for different investigators. The reader should be aware that some clinicians and researchers use the terms "childhood schizophrenia," "atypical child," and "autism" interchangeably with "childhood psychosis." Some investigators include all psychotic children under one label, while others recognize different types of psychoses. There has been increasing support for recognizing two types of childhood psychoses: autism and schizophrenia.

The Diagnostic and Statistical Manual of Mental Disorders (DSM-III) has deleted the term *psychosis* from the categories related to child diagnosis on the grounds that "these disorders apparently bear little relationship to the psychotic disorders of adult life" (p. 86); the term *Pervasive Developmental Disorder* was substituted and defined as follows: "The disorders in this subclass are characterized by *distortions* in the development of multiple basic psychological functions that are involved in the development of social skills and language, such as attention, perception, reality testing, and motor movement" (p. 86). In this definition, distortion refers to the disorders being qualitative abnormalities, not normal at any step of development. The major subdivisions of pervasive developmental disorders are *Infantile Autism* and *Childhood Onset Pervasive Developmental Disorders.* Because *childhood schizophrenia* has been the term used in the research literature to date, it is retained in this chapter.

autism

In 1943, Leo Kanner made the first attempt to describe a particular type of childhood psychosis when he published a paper entitled "Autistic Disturbances of Affective Contact." His original description of early infantile autism included the following features that were considered to be characteristic of the condition: (1) severe withdrawal of contact with other people, (2) an intense need to preserve sameness, (3) an inability to deal with people, (4) particular skills in motor functioning, (5) apparently good intellectual potential as reflected by average or better performance on some tasks and by an intelligent facial expression, and (6) severe disturbance of language functioning.

During his career Kanner examined several thousand psychotic children referred by other clinicians; he diagnosed fewer than two hundred of them as having early infantile autism. Kanner's criterion that the child have at least one area of normal functioning was probably the basis for separating children with early infantile autism from the many other children who also manifested other autistic behaviors. In other words, there were perhaps a substantial number of children referred to Kanner who showed most of the features of autism, but only a relatively small percentage who gave evidence of having a particular ability that was age-appropriate or above. This evidence for normal functioning in at least one area of development has been inferred by many clinicians to reflect the child's potential in all areas, potential that was somehow being masked by the psychosis. If no evidence of normality was present, the child was probably considered to be mentally retarded. The incidence of Kanner-type autistic children has been estimated at 5 per 100,000 (Rimland, 1964, p. 139).

The relationship between mental retardation and autism has been a subject of controversy among clinicians. For theoretical reasons that will be discussed later the earlier clinicians did not consider the mental retardation that was observed in the majority of autistic children to be severe or irreversible. It was viewed more as an artifact of the test situation and the child's inability to relate to others (including the tester). The assumption was that the autistic child was in fact quite intelligent but "chose" not to demonstrate intelligence.

In the past, it seemed particularly important to decide whether a child was autistic or retarded, probably because retardation implied a more permanent condition, and autism was inferred to be a problem that could receive remedial aid. More contemporary clinicians are deemphasizing this aspect of differential diagnosis and are increasingly recognizing that the retardation observed in autistic children represents true deficits in their learning.

Kanner's papers on early infantile autism greatly influenced research and clinical work in the area of childhood psychosis. His original descriptions of the characteristics of autistic children continue to be widely used in the diagnosis of this condition.

To delineate the various characteristics of autism more clearly, Rimland (1964) devised a checklist to be completed by the child's parents. Scoring the checklist consists of subtracting the number of responses that are not considered to be typical of autism from the number of responses that are characteristic of autism as originally described by Kanner. An analysis of over two thousand checklists for psychotic children who had been diagnosed as autistic by clinicians from a number of countries revealed that only about 10 percent of the children met the criteria for autism (a score of 20 or more).

DSM-III describes the following diagnostic criteria for infantile autism:

1. Onset before thirty months of age.
2. Pervasive lack of responsiveness to other people.
3. Gross deficits in language development.
4. If speech is present, peculiar speech patterns such as immediate or delayed echolalia, metaphorical language, pronomial reversal.
5. Bizarre responses to various aspects of the environment, for example, resistance to change, peculiar interest in or attachments to animate or inanimate objects.
6. Absence of delusions, hallucinations, loosening of associations, and incoherence.

Infantile autism typically originates very early in the child's life with some behavioral manifestations being present during the first year, although very few autistic children are recognized as such prior to their second year. Parents frequently report that their autistic children did not make anticipatory postural adjustments (for example, tensing the body) to being picked up and were not responsive in social situations. During this period the parents often become concerned about possible deafness because the infant's responses to sound seem to be erratic. Hearing tests usually reveal that the child's ability to hear is normal. Parents also report that the infant seems happiest when left alone. Excessive repetitive body movements, such as rocking and head banging, are very common.

During the second year, the child's lack of social responsiveness becomes more apparent. In contrast to younger normal children, autistic children do not make eye contact (look at another person's eyes) and only infrequently turn toward the sound of a person's voice. The absence or severe delay in speech begins to be recognized during this period when most children are beginning to acquire labels for common objects. Some parents have reported the use of a few words, which were later "lost."

Many clinicians believe that the autistic features are most pronounced around the age of three or four years, an age when many autistic children are referred and diagnosed. Eye contact and speech development continue to be absent or minimal. If speech has begun to develop, certain abnormalities are likely to be present. The voice quality may be unusual and intonation exaggerated. Echolalia, a repetition of a speaker's words, is often a characteristic of autistic children with speech. For example, if asked "Do you want a cookie?" the echolalic child responds "Do you want a cookie?" Some echolalic children display remarkable memory for phrases and television commercials, which may be repeated long after they were originally heard. If they do learn functional speech, autistic children tend to use minimal speech; that is, one word may convey the meaning of several sentences. The meaning conveyed in their speech continues to be literal and concrete; abstract, subtle, or symbolic meanings are seldom utilized.

The motor development of autistic children may be normal, retarded, or superior, but it is often the child's most advanced area of functioning. Some autistic children show remarkable skills in visual-motor tasks, such as completing puzzles, and tasks involving visual discrimination (for example, rapid learning to discriminate among printed words). Both hyperactivity and hypoactivity are considered to be characteristic of autistic children. Peculiar repetitive movements, such as arm flapping, hand twisting, spinning, facial grimacing, and walking on tiptoe, are also frequently reported. Their play behavior with toy vehicles, for example, may consist solely of a repetitive spinning of the wheels.

Although relatively unresponsive to auditory stimuli, certain sounds appear to generate greater than normal responses in autistic children. Music, for example, may be particularly enjoyed; some autistic children learn to sing before learning to talk and can reproduce complex tunes. Some sounds, such as loud noises and speech, appear to be aversive in that the child will move away, cover his or her ears, or become distressed in their presence.

Reponses to other sensory experiences may also be unusual in the autistic child.

For example, some autistic children are described as being insensitive to pain in that they do not cry or complain when they are obviously physically hurt. Autistic children sometimes spend long periods of time feeling materials of certain textures and repeatedly scratching surfaces. Vigorous physical play, including tickling and swinging, is particularly enjoyed and often the only occasion when the child laughs or appears happy.

Although they are typically described as being remote, aloof, or distant, autistic children react with temper outbursts on occasion. The temper tantrums may be the result of a frustration, but they also seem to occur randomly. Laughing and giggling are also likely to occur and stop suddenly for no apparent reason. Autistic children seem to lack the normal fears of real dangers, but they often exhibit fear of harmless objects and events.

Infantile autism is considered to be a chronic disorder and is about three times more common in boys than girls. About 90 percent of autistic children have IQ scores in the mentally retarded range (DeMyer, and others, 1974). Most of them remain severely handicapped and are unable to function independently at maturity. Some autistic children with higher IQ scores and better language skills do eventually lead independent lives, but poor social skills frequently persist.

schizophrenia/childhood onset pervasive developmental disorder

DSM-III designates that where children or adolescents show symptoms that meet the criteria for the (adult) category, schizophrenia, that diagnosis is used. Acknowledgement is also given to the fact that the criteria for Childhood Onset Pervasive Developmental Disorder are those that have been used by clinicians to diagnose childhood schizophrenia. Apparently, the DSM-III Task Force decided to substitute the new category because it was not certain that the preadolescent and adult forms of schizophrenia are indeed a single condition. Both previous research and the DSM-III diagnostic criteria for schizophrenia and for Childhood Onset Pervasive Developmental Disorders suggest a strong similarity between the childhood and adult forms of schizophrenia.

Adult schizophrenia is a relatively common condition affecting approximately 1 percent of the population. Only a small percentage (approximately 4 percent) of adult schizophrenics became psychotic during childhood; for most of them the onset was during adolescence and young adulthood. The majority of schizophrenic children continue to be considered schizophrenic throughout adulthood, with the remaining individuals' being relabeled mentally retarded (Bennett and Klein, 1966).

The DSM-III criteria for the diagnosis of Childhood Onset Pervasive Developmental Disorder are as follows:

1. Gross and sustained impairment in social relationships, for example, lack of appropriate affective responsiveness, inappropriate clinging, asocial behavior, lack of empathy

2. At least three of the following:
   a. sudden excessive anxiety manifested by such symptoms as free-floating anxiety, catastrophic reactions to everyday occurrences, inability to be consoled when upset, unexplained panic attacks
   b. constricted or inappropriate affect, including lack of appropriate fear reactions, unexplained rage reactions, and extremely labile moods
   c. resistance to change in the environment or insistence on doing things in the same manner every time
   d. oddities of motor movement, such as peculiar posturing, peculiar hand or finger movements, or walking on tiptoe
   e. abnormalities of speech, such as question-like melody, monotonous voice
   f. hyper- or hyposensitivity to sensory stimuli
   g. self-mutilation, for example, biting or hitting self, head banging
3. Onset after thirty months of age and before twelve years of age
4. Absence of delusions, hallucinations, incoherence, or marked loosening of associations

With the exception of the fourth criterion, the DSM-III criteria are in substantial agreement with earlier diagnostic criteria for childhood schizophrenia. With "corrections" for differences in the developmental levels of the clients, these DSM-III criteria are remarkably similar to DSM-III's criteria for both infantile autism and (adult) schizophrenia. It is possible that the apparent differences could be accounted for primarily by the age of onset and the concomitant cognitive deficits. For example, absence of delusions in children with pervasive developmental disorder may mean no more than that the development of a delusional system requires a higher level of cognitive functioning. Mental retardation is not considered to be a cardinal feature of childhood schizophrenics, but between one-third and one-half of them have IQ scores in the mentally retarded range.

Psychotic children are difficult to assess with standardized tests. With autistic children, the examiner must frequently use infant tests in order to obtain a basal mental age for language items. Testing tends to be prolonged both because the autistic child's behavior is rarely under social control and because the range between the basal mental age and ceiling mental age is much wider than average.

Schizophrenic children's test behavior is likely to be very erratic; they may successfully complete complex tasks and then fail simpler ones. The persistent examiner usually finds the schizophrenic child's IQ score to be within normal limits and achievement scores to be low. Both autistic and schizophrenic children present severe educational problems and require special education programs.

For the present, behavioral assessment appears to offer the most relevant data for the purpose of planning remedial programs. While many of the psychotic child's behavioral excesses and deficits are obvious during the initial interview process, formal observations are usually scheduled in addition to the behavioral interview and standardized test administration.

Some of the pervasive diagnostic problems could be solved with further research. We need to learn more about the developmental norms of psychotic children, that is, to design longitudinal studies in which standard behavioral assessments are conducted at specific ages over a period of years. This behavioral assessment could ideally include all aspects of the children's behavioral repertoire rather than just the presence or absence of psychotic characteristics. Factor analysis could then be performed on the behavioral data collected at each age level to determine the extent to which behaviors are related. The number of factors obtained would provide some guideline about the possible types of psychoses and the behaviors associated with each type.

etiology–autism

The lack of common criteria for the diagnosis of the childhood psychoses has posed a substantial impediment to our understanding of etiological factors. Some of the investigators examining etiological factors in childhood psychosis have selected a specific type of psychosis, while others have used heterogenous groups of psychotic children. Unfortunately, adequated descriptive characteristics of individual children are not available in most of the research articles.

genetic factors

Chromosomal studies of autistic children have not revealed any consistent abnormality in the morphology of the chromosomes. Probably because autism is relatively rare, concordance rates for twins are based on collections of individual case studies. Judd and Mandell (1968) reported that concordance is close to one hundred percent in identical twins for which zygosity has been adequately established; their study however, was based on a very small number of twins. Folstein and Rutter (1977) studied twenty-one pairs of twins and found that none of the ten fraternal pairs was concordant for autism, but four of the eleven identical pairs were concordant. Rutter and Bartak (1971) have proposed the presence of some small, but significant, genetic contribution based on the finding that the rate of autism in siblings (approximately 2 percent) is considerably above the population rate of four or five per ten thousand. If reliable, the data reported on the heritability of autism can be interpreted as supporting a physical, rather than a genetic, basis for autism. The high concordance rates for identical twins could also be attributed to an interactive effect of physical insult occurring during the prenatal or perinatal period when identical twins are more equally vulnerable (are in comparable embryological stages of development) than are fraternal twins.

Rimland (1964) has proposed an interesting theory that includes both genetic and biological factors. Rimland hypothesized that autistic children inherit genes for high intelligence and that high intelligence requires a higher level of blood circulation in the brain. Thus, children with the genes for high intelligence would be more vulnerable to factors that affect the quality or quantity, or both, of blood circulation in the brain.

physical factors

In his original paper, Kanner (1943) clearly specified his assumption that autism was due to some biological defect, but the role of biological factors in the etiology of autism was not seriously examined until the later 1960s. A number of studies have found higher than normal rates of pre- and perinatal complications in autistic children, while other studies have found no differences. These apparent discrepancies in the results appear to be due to the criteria for diagnosis: children who meet Kanner's criteria appear to have less evidence of neurological damage than do autistic children who do not meet Kanner's criteria or who are institutionalized (Achenbach, 1974, p. 443). Chess (1971; 1977) has reported an increased incidence of autism (Kanner criteria) in children infected with rubella during the prenatal period, suggesting a possible role of prenatal physical factors.

High rates of neurological abnormalities have also been reported for autistic children. Rutter, Bartak, and Newman (1971) found that 29 percent of the autistic children they followed over a twelve- to twenty-four-year period developed epileptic seizures during adolescence or adulthood. High rates of abnormal electro-encephalograms (EEG's) have also been found, but the patterns have not been consistent or indicative of a particular type of dysfunction.

The results of biochemical studies have been equivocal (Guthrie and Wyatt, 1975), but they have provided some excellent leads for future research. Preliminary findings are suggestive of a defect in the immunilogical system of autistic children (possibly manifested only when there is exposure to particular viruses).

psychological factors

Until fairly recently, the dominant view among clinicians has been that childhood psychosis is a functional disorder, that is, caused by adverse psychological conditions. These adverse conditions have been described primarily in terms of parent-child interactions by proponents of both psychoanalytic and behavior theory. Most of what has been learned about the parents of psychotic children has been derived from the clinical assessment of parents during or after diagnosis and interpretation of the child's condition. In this context, a number of studies have reported that the parents of psychotic children are themselves clinically deviant. Virtually all of these studies, which are basically correlational in design, assumed that the parents' problems originated before the child's problem and that the parents' psychological problems in some way caused the child's psychosis.

Attention to the parental role was initiated by Kanner's (1954) description of the parental characteristics of his first one hundred autistic children. As a group, these parents were highly intelligent, and the majority of fathers were employed as professionals. Although Kanner noted that there was very little mental illness in the families of the autistic children, the parents were described as very obsessive, unemotional, and lacking in warmth ("refrigerator parents"). Bettelheim (1967) took a more extreme position arguing that autism was the child's defense against the hostility of parents who had emotionally rejected the child.

Ferster (1961) used behavior principles to account for the development of autistic behavior and thereby implicated parent-child relationships in the etiology of autism. He suggested that the behavior of autistic children is quantitatively, but not qualitatively, different from that of normal children, that is, characterized by very low response rates. Ferster hypothesized that these very low response rates may be the result of the parents' failure to provide adequate reinforcement for the development of a normal response repertoire. Yates (1970, p. 257) has pointed out the similarity between Ferster's description of the parental role and Kanner's "refrigerator parent" concept.

After a long period of assuming that parents had a strong role in causing their children's autism, clinicians have begun to acknowledge that indeed there are no data to support that assumption. A number of studies have shown that, although the parents of autistic children show more evidence of psychological problems than the parents of normal children, they show no more evidence of these problems than do the parents of children with other types of handicaps, such as mental retardation, brain damage, and dysphasia (Erickson, 1968a; Cantwell, Baker, and Rutter, 1979; DeMyer and others, 1972). These studies suggest that the parents' psychological problems are due to the stress of having a handicapped child.

etiology-childhood schizophrenia

genetic factors

No chromosomal abnormalties have been found consistently in schizophrenic children (Böok, Nichtern, and Gurenberg, 1963). Our knowledge of genetic factors in childhood schizophrenia has come primarily from twin and family studies. In addition, a much larger body of twin and family research indicates that heredity is a significant etiological factor in adult schizophrenia (Gottesman, 1978); the major twin studies have found higher concordance rates in identical than fraternal twins, and family studies have indicated that the risk for schizophrenia increases proportionally with the closeness of blood relationship to a family member with schizophrenia.

Only one twin study (Kallman and Roth, 1956) has focused on the role of heredity in childhood schizophrenia. In a sample of fifty-two preadolescent twin pairs, the concordance rates for identical and fraternal twins were found to be quite similar to those found for adult schizophrenics, supporting a significant role for heritability in childhood schizophrenia and the idea that child and adult forms of schizophrenia may be the same condition.

Several studies have examined the risk of schizophrenia for children born to schizophrenic mothers but reared by foster or adoptive parents. Heston (1966) located forty-seven adults who had been born to schizophrenic women in mental institutions and raised by foster parents. Control subjects who were from the same foundling homes were matched to the experimental subjects on the basis of sex, length of time in child-care institutions, and type of foster home placement. Evaluations of the subjects were made without knowledge of experimental or control group placement. The data collected were based on personal interviews by psychiatrists, IQ and personality tests, and agency records. The results of this study showed significantly greater amounts of psychopathology in the group born of schizophrenic mothers. Five of the subjects in the experimental groups were diagnosed as schizophrenic and four as retarded, while none of the control group members received either diagnosis. Of the experimental group, 23.4 percent had spent more than one year in psychiatric or penal institutions compared with 4 percent of the control group. A subsequent study by Heston and Denney (1968) compared experimental and control subjects raised either in foster homes or primarily in child-care institutions. The experimental subjects with both foster home and institutional histories had higher rates of psychopathology than the control subjects. No differences were found between foster home and institution-reared subjects, however, suggesting that these environments did not have differential effects on the incidence of schizophrenia and other psychological problems. Several adoption studies (Rosenthal, 1972; Rosenthal, Wender, Kety, Welner, and Schulsinger, 1971) have demonstrated higher rates of schizophrenia in persons whose biological ancestors were schizophrenic whether or not schizophrenia was present in the adoptive families.

physical factors

With the exception of Bender who has been studying the neurological and physical correlates of childhood schizophrenia since the 1930s, serious interest in biological factors as etiological agents did not appear until the early 1960s. Bender has continuously maintained that schizophrenia is the result of a faulty nervous system that is genetically vulnerable, that is, subject to both organic and psychological stresses that may precipitate the onset of schizophrenia.

Goldfarb (1961) conducted an intensive study of twenty-six psychotic (a mixture of schizophrenic and autistic types) children and found that seventeen of them showed evidence of neurological abnormalities. Goldfarb hypothesized that childhood psychoses could be the result of either organic or psychological stresses, that is, that there are two types of childhood psychosis: organic and nonorganic. On nearly all of the neurological and psychological test measures in his study the organics performed more poorly than the nonorganics who, in turn, performed more poorly than the normal control group matched for age and sex. For example, the average IQ for the organics was 62 as compared with 92 for the nonorganics. His measure of family adequacy, however, based on a three-hour observation session in the home, revealed the families of organics to be more adequate than the families of nonorganics.

Creak (1963) reported that about one-half of her one hundred schizophrenic children had selective or overall retardation in developmental milestones. Several studies have found higher rates of EEG abnormality in schizophrenic children.

Prenatal and perinatal complications have been examined in a number of studies. After reviewing the literature, Pollack and Woerner (1966) concluded that these complications occurred more frequently in the histories of psychotic children. This higher rate of incidence is comparable to those for mentally retarded and nonpsychotic behaviorally disturbed children (Fish, Shapiro, Campbell, and Wile, 1968).

The role of prenatal, perinatal, and postnatal physical factors has been amplified in a study of eleven sets of adolescent and adult identical twins who were *discordant* for schizophrenia (Pollin, Stabenau, Mosher, and Tupin, 1966). In all cases, the schizophrenic twin weighed less at birth than the nonschizophrenic twin. In addition, the schizophrenic twins had more physical illness and injuries and showed more signs of subtle neurological dysfunction. A subsequent biochemical study (Pollin, 1971) revealed that both members of the pairs had higher levels of neurotransmitters active in brain metabolism (Dopamine, norepinephrine, epinephrine) than a normal control group but that the schizophrenic twins had significantly higher levels of 17-hydroxysteroids than either the nonschizophrenic twins or the normal control group. Other biochemical studies have resulted either in negative findings or isolated findings that required replication.

psychological factors

As early as 1938 Despert reported that the mothers of nineteen out of twenty-nine schizophrenic children were "aggressive, over-anxious, and over-solicitous," while the fathers displayed a "subdued role." During the 1940s and 1950s theoreticians writing in the clinical literature tended to blame childhood psychosis on mothers who were characterized as narcissistic and incapable of mature emotional relationships. The term, *schizophrenogenic mother,* was coined during this period and frequently used as an explanatory concept with respect to the etiology of childhood psychosis. Variations on the theme of schizophrenogenic mother have included mothers who reject their children emotionally and whose responses to their children reflect hostile feelings in the husband-wife relationship. A more recent study by Ricks and Berry (1970), however, suggests that this maternal characteristic may not have had a causal role. They examined the child guidance clinic records of individuals who later developed schizophrenia or other psychiatric disorders, or who were evaluated as adequately adjusted. "Schizophrenogenic mothers" were found in all three groups but *least* often in the group that subsequently became schizophrenic.

In his depiction of organic and nonorganic types of childhood schizophrenia, Goldfarb implicated faulty parent-child interactions as a primary etiologic factor in nonorganic childhood schizophrenia. His conclusions were based on observational studies of mothers and their schizophrenic children and the assumption that the observed interactions were characteristic of interactions throughout the child's life. Meyers and Goldfarb (1961) described mothers of schizophrenic children as reacting to their children with greater uncertainty and indecisiveness, with less spontaneity and empathy, and with a lack of control and authority. In comparison with the mothers of normal children, the mothers of schizophrenic children gave less evidence of guiding, instructing, reinforcing, and inhibiting their children. Goldfarb (1970) has summarized maternal communication deficiencies as follows: "(1) failure to stimulate the child's interest in active communication; (2) failure to maintain the continuous flow of communication with the child; (3) failure to re-inforce normal and acceptable speech and communication in the children; (4) active confounding of the child in regard to his construction of reality; (5) missing or not responding to the child's cues; (6) failure to cope with the child's unusual deviancies in communication" (p. 812).

Goldfarb (1961) also found behavioral and familial variables that discriminated between organic and nonorganic schizophrenic children. The nonorganic children had higher IQ scores and were also superior in the areas of perception, body orientation, and psychomotor functioning. In contrast, the families of nonorganic schizophrenic children were lower in interactional adequacy; schizophrenia had been diagnosed in 44 percent of the mothers of nonorganic schizophrenic children in comparison with 21 percent of the mothers of organic schizophrenic children. These data were interpreted as supporting a psychological etiology for schizophrenia in the nonorganic children.

Goldfarb's data on the families of the two groups could be interpreted in an alternative way, particularly if findings from other research studies are taken into consideration. The nonorganic group, for example, might have consisted of children who became schizophrenic primarily on the basis of heredity and secondarily on the basis of the psychological stress of living with a schizophrenic mother. The organic group, on the other hand, might have included children at a lesser genetic risk, whose schizophrenia and retardation were substantially determined by physical insults during the prenatal and perinatal periods. The differences between the two groups of parents may have been due primarily to the higher incidence of schizophrenia in the parents of the nonorganic children.

The distinction between organic and nonorganic schizophrenic children may present problems of validity. In Goldfarb's study the distinction was based on findings from the neurological examination and an implicit assumption, namely, that abnormal brain function is always detectable by neurological examination. There is ample evidence that the neurological test does not provide an exact determination of an organic problem but rather is capable of detecting only some types of brain dysfunction. For example, although the rate of abnormal neurological findings increases with the severity of mental retardation, many severely retarded children do not manifest neurological abnormalities other than developmental delays. Thus, in the case of psychosis, it is possible that all schizophrenic children may have an organic impairment that is not detectable by the neurological examination and that the neurological abnormalities detected for some schizophrenic children are either secondary etiological factors or represent by-products of the original cause of the schizophrenia.

This alternative explanation of Goldfarb's study is made in the context of subsequent research and is not intended to diminish the study's historical importance. Following two decades of clinicians' being convinced that childhood psychosis was determined primarily by pathological parent-child relationships, Goldfarb's study made a strong impact on subsequent research by presenting an intermediate view, namely, that psychoses might have either an organic or a nonorganic basis, and thus prepared the way for further research on biological factors which had previously not been investigated.

This section may be summarized by stating that there is no evidence that faulty child rearing is the basis of childhood schizophrenia. Although psychological studies have found that the parents of schizophrenic children show more psychological disturbance than do the parents of normal children, they do not differ from parents of children with other psychiatric labels (Klebanoff, 1959; Wolking, Quast, and Lawton, 1966). It can probably be assumed that schizophrenic parents were not participants in the studies requiring completion of questionnaires and objective personality tests. As suggested in the section on autism, the parental problems found in these objective studies may be due to the stress of coping with a handicapped child.

treatment

Clinicians' theoretical orientations with regard to the etiology of childhood psychosis have greatly affected their approaches to treatment. The types of therapies that have been used with psychotic children have represented a broad spectrum, including psychoanalytic, behavioral, and physical treatments. In general, clinicians who have considered childhood psychoses to be caused by faulty parent-child relationships have tended to use psychotherapies with a psychoanalytic orientation, while those with strong persuasions toward an organic etiology have focused on physical treatments. There has been no consistent and uniform match between hypothesized etiology and treatment, however; in addition, a number of clinicians, particularly those espousing a behavioral approach to treatment, have developed therapy programs relatively independently of etiological considerations.

psychotherapy

Until the 1970s psychoanalytic psychotherapy was the primary form of treatment for psychotic children. One of the intial goals of psychoanalytic psychotherapy with psychotic children is to engender a close relationship with a permissive and loving mother figure—a relationship that the child's own mother failed to provide. This relationship, which may take years to develop in therapy, is believed to be the foundation from which all other progress in treatment will be made. Rank (1955) has described two phases of psychotherapy with psychotic children. During the first phase, the therapist provides the maximum amount of support possible, offering gratification in large amounts and avoiding frustration of the child. The therapist attempts to be more understanding and emotionally consistent than the real parents are assumed to have been. The second phase focuses on the development of socialization skills, including the postponement of gratification.

Most of the psychotherapeutic programs for children described in the clinical research literature have taken place in inpatient settings. Inpatient facilities have been viewed as offering the potential for constructing an emotionally healthy environment for the child. The term *milieu therapy* refers to programs in inpatient settings that emphasize full-time socialization of the child by the encouragment and teaching of interpersonal and educational skills. Milieu therapy also frequently includes varying amounts of psychotherapy. Several studies have evaluated the effectiveness of milieu therapy with psychotic children. Goldfarb, Goldfarb, and Pollack (1966) compared the effects of full-time milieu therapy and a similar day-treatment program in which children spent the remaining time at home. These findings indicated that the most severely psychotic children did not benefit from either program. No differences in improvement for the "organic" schizophrenic children in the two programs were found; the "nonorganic" schizophrenic children in the full-time program showed greater improvement than did those in the day-treatment group, however, suggesting to these researchers that the residential program may have been serving the function of protecting the "nonorganic" children from emotionally unhealthy home environments.

Apparently different results were obtained in a study that compared the effectiveness of full-time treatment and day treatment for autistic children (Wenar, Ruttenberg, Dratman, and Wolf, 1967). At the end of one year, improvement was greater for children in the day-treatment program than for those in either of two full-time residential facilities. Children were not randomly assigned to the various programs, however, and the full-time programs had a greater staff turnover, poorer staff-to-child ratios, and older children, who would probably have been more difficult to treat.

Perhaps, from a psychoanalytic point of view, the epitome of a program that includes both milieu therapy and psychotherapy is Bettelheim's Orthogenic School in Chicago. Because his program is privately supported and requires at least several years of treatment, most of the psychotic children referred to it have parents who are highly educated and wealthy. Bettelheim's program is based on the assumption that the primary cause of psychosis is emotional rejection of the child by the parents; during the course of treatment parent visitation and home visits are restricted. In the earlier phases of treatment, the staff provides a totally accepting environment for the child regardless of the individual's behavior. The psychotic child is encouraged to regress (become more infantile) in order to relive earlier experiences in the more optimal emotional environment. Emphasis is put on the child's need to derive pleasure from bodily functions (for example, eating and defecating) in an atmosphere of warm acceptance to replace the earlier experiences of faulty care by the mother. It would not be unusual, for example, to observe an older child being held on the lap of a caretaker and being fed from a bottle as one would feed an infant. By experiencing adults (caretakers and thera-pists) as positive agents, the children are expected to be able to begin interacting with people in human, rather than mechanical, ways.

Bettelheim has written several books describing the treatment of individual psychotic children treated in his program. In one of them (Betttelheim, 1967, p. 414) he reviewed the outcome of forty children discharged from the Ortho-genic School and he described 17 or 42 percent as "good" or "cured," 15 or 38 percent as "fair," and 8 or 20 percent as "poor." Bettelheim indicated that the treatment outcome for his children was greatly superior because it was based on intensive institutional treatment carried out over a period of years. It should be noted that these improvement figures have not been independently confirmed or replicated by other investigators.

Several studies have suggested that psychoanalytic psychotherapy may not be effective for psychotic children. Brown (1960) compared twenty children who made the most progress with twenty children who made the least progress during several years of outpatient treatment. No differences between the groups were found for length of treatment, number of therapists, or experience of the thera-pists. Brown found that children who initially presented the most severe symptoms had the worst outcome. A later study by Brown (1963) comparing children who had either individual, small group, or no treatment also failed to find significant differences due to treatment. A study by other investigators (Kaufman, Frank, Friend, Heims, and Weiss, 1962) found that length of treatment was inversely related to improvement, suggesting that longer treatment periods were associated with poorer outcomes.

Although many psychotic children have received and probably continue to receive psychotherapy either on an inpatient or outpatient basis, demonstration of its effectiveness has not been forthcoming. In fact, there has been very little out-come research during the last decade, but case histories continue to be reported (Kestenbaum, 1978). A few experimental studies comparing psychotherapy with behavior therapy (Ney, Palvesky, and Markely, 1971) and with structured special education (Rutter and Bartak, 1973) have found either no improvement or signifi-cantly less improvement for psychotic children given psychotherapy.

physical treatment

Bender has been the principal advocate for the physical treatment of psychotic children and has conducted a significant portion of the pioneer research on physical treatments. She has been a particularly strong proponent of electroshock therapy. Her follow-up study (Bender, 1960) of children receiving electroshock therapy during the 1940s and 1950s revealed that over 50 percent of the children improved socially. Moreover, no adverse effects, such as impaired cognitive functioning, were discovered leading Bender to conclude that shock therapy was more effective with children than adults. Unfortunately, Bender's research design did not include control group conditions. Electroshock therapy is rarely used today in the treatment of psychotic children.

Use of drugs for treating psychotic children greatly increased during the 1960s, probably as a result of successes in treating psychotic adults with medication. Most clinicians consider drugs as an adjunct to therapy rather than as a primary form of treatment.

The neuroleptics are the most widely used drugs with psychotic children. Their effectiveness appears to be related to the child's age and level of functioning. Chlorpromazine may be useful for older psychotic children (Fish, 1976). Side effects have been reported for psychotic children and adolescents treated with the neuroleptics, thus necessitating careful monitoring to ensure that the minimally effective dosage is being given. Psychomotor stimulants appear either to have no effect or make the behaviors of psychotic children worse.

behavior therapy

During the 1960s, investigators began to apply learning principles in treatment programs for psychotic children. Most of the earlier studies focused on the reduction of a specific behavior problem, such as temper tantrums or self-injurious behavior, through the use of extinction, timeout, punishment, and reinforcement of incompatible responses. Punishment in the form of contingent presentation of an aversive stimulus has been used infrequently and essentially only for problems that were severe and not efficiently treated through the use of other behavior principles. For example, some psychotic children engage in high rates of forms of behavior that can result in serious physical damage to themselves, such as head banging and biting their own bodies. To prevent these self-injurious actions, such children are often tied down to their beds in institutional settings. Several studies (see, for example, Risley, 1968) have demonstrated rapid decreases in self-injurious behavior through the use of brief contingent electric shock. Moreover, no negative effects of this procedure were observed; in fact, the elimination of these behaviors appeared to increase the occurrence of appropriate behaviors and facilitated the further development of appropriate behaviors during treatment.

The initial therapeutic attention to abnormal or inappropriate behaviors has seemed to be necessary because the rate of such behaviors for psychotic children is very high and greatly hampers programs for increasing appropriate behaviors. Subsequent research has increasingly focused on the development of behaviors not previously present in the psychotic child's repertoire and comprehensive therapeutic programs that dealt with multiple aspects of the child's behavioral repertoire. For example, considerable effort on the part of behavioral researchers has been invested in programs to develop speech and language skills in psychotic children who lacked verbal repertoires or whose speech was echolalic. Early in these programs it was discovered that autistic children had either deficient or absent imitative skills and, furthermore, did not attend to stimulus patterns that would facilitate imitation and the learning of other behaviors. Therefore, several research studies were directed toward the development of imitative skills and their relevant attending behaviors. This research has shown that the application of behavior principles has been successful in establishing eye contact, social interactions with adults, imitative repertoires, and expressive and receptive speech. Identifying reinforcers for psychotic children often presents problems for the researcher and clinician; therefore, many of the behavioral programs rely on food, at least initially, and may pair social stimuli with the presentation of food reinforcement in an effort to increase the effectiveness of social stimuli as reinforcers.

The work of Lovaas and his colleagues at the University of California at Los Angeles has epitomized the behavioral approach to the treatment of psychotic children (Stevens-Long and Lovaas, 1974; Lovaas, Koegel, Simmons, and Stevens-Long, 1973). In the initial study, a total of twenty children, labeled as autistic by at least one other agency not associated with the research project, were treated intensively for about one year. Two groups of children were treated as inpatients eight hours each day, six to seven days a week, for about one year. The parents of the first group were not involved in treatment, but the parents of the second group were taught the treatment procedures. The remaining children were outpatients and essentially treated by the parents, while the project staff provided training and consultation to the parents about two to three hours per week.

From this project has come a series of studies indicating that behavior principles may be effectively applied to modify psychotic children's behavior. Therapy typically begins with training the child to respond appropriately to simple commands, such as "sit down" and "look." At the same time, inappropriate behaviors, such as tantrums and those forms of behavior that are aggressive, self-injurious, and repetitive are put on extinction or punished.

Although a significant amount of effort went into the reduction of the inappropriate behaviors, by far the greatest amount of attention was devoted to the development of imitative and language skills. The imitative language program consisted of four phases: (1) increasing the rate of all vocalizations, (2) teaching the child to vocalize immediately after the adult vocalized, (3) increasing the similarity of the child's vocalization to the adult's vocalization, and (4) teaching the child to discriminate between new and less recently learned imitative sounds. This training program included the use of contingent reinforcement and shaping, prompting, and fading. Subsequent language programs focused on the development of receptive speech (for example, pointing to the object labeled), verbal labels for common objects and activities, and language abstractions (such as, pronouns, prepositions, and words for temporal relationships). (Research is currently examining the feasibility of teaching sign language to children who remain mute after repeated attempts to teach spoken language.)

The major findings of the project were that all of the children in the intensive program improved; that is, inappropriate behaviors were decreased, and appropriate behaviors increased. Characteristic of the various program results was the very substantial variability in the rate of progress among the children. Given the same programs and comparable amounts of professional time, dramatic improvements were achieved for some children, while other children made relatively little progress. Follow-up studies indicated that the initial four children who were institutionalized after their treatment in the project failed to make additional gains, while children who remained at home with parents, trained by the project staff, continued to show improvement. Although the majority of children could not be tested at the beginning of treatment, all of them could be tested at the end of the treatment period, with most of the children functioning in the mild to moderate range of mental retardation. The average social quotients on the Vineland Social Maturity Scale was 48 before treatment and 71 after treatment.

Lovaas and others (1973, p. 159) have indicated that the parents must bear the major responsibility for treatment and that the success of parental treatment seems to depend on the following: (1) a willingness to use strong consequences, such as spankings and food, and to display both positive and negative emotions, (2) a willingness to give the child responsibility and to deny that the child has a psychological "need" to be sick, and (3) a willingness to devote a major portion of their lives to the treatment program that involves the continuous arrangement of contingencies throughout the day.

Because improvement seems to be greatly dependent on a treatment program conducted in the child's natural environment, the role of parents as therapists for their own children has received increased attention. In their more recent work with younger autistic children, Lovaas and his staff train the parent, usually the mother, to become the child's primary therapist. Most of the training is done in the home environment with assistance from undergraduate students (ten to twenty hours a week), siblings, and neighbors (Lovaas, Young, and Newsom, 1978). After about six to eight months of treatment, placement in a normal preschool is carefully staged; the child is slowly faded into the group, and the teacher is given both training and aides.

The next frontier in the treatment of psychotic children appears to be special education. Public Law 94-142 includes autistic children in its mandate that the public schools provide educational services for preschool developmentally disabled children beginning at two years of age. Although a number of classroom programs using applied behavior principles have been established (see, for example, Koegel and Rincover, 1976), their effectiveness in comparison with other forms of treatment has been evaluated in only a few instances (see p. 182).

Conclusions

Childhood psychosis is a severe behavior disorder for which prognosis has been very poor. While no single cause of psychosis has been identified, research data strongly suggest that the primary etiological factors are physical in nature. Genetic factors and physical insults during the pre-, peri-, and postnatal periods have been associated with both infantile autism and childhood schizophrenia. A variety of treatment approaches have been used with psychotic children, but most of the studies are inadequate for evaluating the effectiveness of these therapies, primarily because they lack control conditions or groups. Behavioral studies have perhaps offered the most convincing evidence of therapeutic effectiveness, but even the most comprehensive treatment programs have not produced "cures" or normal children. It appears that comprehensive programs begun very early in life result in greater effectiveness.

Recommended Readings

Lovaas, O. I., Young, D. B., and Newsom, C. D. "Child Psychosis: Behavioral Treatment," in *Handbook of Treatment of Mental Disorders in Childhood and Adolescence*, pp. 385–420. Edited by B. Wolman, J. Egan, and A. O. Ross. Englewood Cliffs, N.J.: Prentice-Hall, 1978.

Ritvo, E. R., ed., *Autism: Diagnosis, Current Research and Management*. New York: Halsted Press, 1976.

Rutter, M., and Schopler, E., eds., *Autism: A Reappraisal of Concepts and Treatment*. New York: Plenum, 1978.

Schopler, E., and Reichler, R. J., eds., *Child Development, Deviations, and Treatment*. New York: Plenum, 1976.

Wing, L., ed., *Early Childhood Autism* (2nd ed.) Elmsford, N.Y.: Pergamon Press, 1976.

specific learning
disabilities

10

Jeff, a nine-year-old boy, was referred by his third-grade teacher because of poor achievement in reading and spelling. His teacher reported that he was in her lowest reading group and seemed to lack even the most basic word-attack skills. Jeff's first- and second-grade teachers had emphasized a phonics approach to reading. Jeff was beginning to act sullen and refuse to participate in his reading group and had torn up his spelling papers several times. His teacher felt that his intelligence was at least above average based on his participation in class discussions.

Jeff's mother was eager to have an evaluation to find out what could be done about his problem. She was an avid reader and attended college for two years, dropping out to get married. She was considering returning to college when her youngest child entered first grade but was somewhat ambivalent because of its possible effect on her husband who had not attended college. Jeff's father was less concerned about his son's problem. He reported that he and several members of his family had reading problems in school. He disliked school and remained in school only to please his mother. His job as an auto mechanic was not particularly fulfilling, but he was proud of his ability to support his family in reasonable comfort. He didn't think that reading was "as important as people say it is."

Jeff was the first of two sons born after three pregnancies had ended in two spontaneous abortions and a stillbirth. The pregnancy with Jeff was normal except for a very long labor and a difficult delivery. His development during the preschool period was normal. Jeff's reading problem was not brought to the parents' attention until he was in the third grade.

Learning disabilities refer to deficits in specific skills in relation to expected levels of performance. The deficient skill areas involve basic academic subjects taught in elementary school, such as reading, arithmetic, and writing, as well as expressive and receptive oral language. DSM-III (1980) uses the term "specific developmental disorders" to describe the same constellation of deficits.

Specific learning disabilities were originally described by physicians who emphasized the organic etiologic factors, an emphasis which has continued into the present. From the earlier literature, there evolved a series of medical diagnostic labels, such as dyslexia, dyscalculia, and dysgraphia, which had fairly precise clinical definitions. For example, dyslexia orginally referred to a person's inability to derive meaning from the written word. The medical labels have subsequently lost much of their precision of meaning. Contemporary use of the term *dyslexia* tends to make it equivalent to almost any problem related to reading. The writings of professionals currently working in the area of learning disabilities also reflect frequent interchanging of the terms *learning disability* and *minimal brain dysfunction*. A brief view of historical factors may serve to clarify this situation.

During the 1930s, Werner and Strauss initiated a series of studies with retarded children to determine whether there were behavioral differences between children with and without brain damage. A child was classified as *exogenous* if the retardation was considered due to neurological abnormalities; this label was given when there was no evidence of mental retardation in the child's immediate family and when the child's history included a prenatal, perinatal, or postnatal insult capable of brain damage. Children with retarded relatives and no history of complications were classified as *endogenous*.

The behavioral studies conducted by Strauss, Werner, and their colleagues suggest that there are substantial behavioral differences between exogenous and endogenous retarded children. For example, exogenous children showed visual-motor impairment manifested in disorganized reproductions of designs. An accumulation of research findings indicate a general impairment of the perceptual aspects of all the sensory modalities of exogenous children. Exogenous children also could not concentrate their attention on specific tasks and seemed not to be able to screen out irrelevant stimuli. In addition, data from a behavioral rating scale indicated that exogenous children were more impulsive, disinhibited, uncoordinated, and socially unacceptable than endogenous children (Strauss and Kephart, 1940). These studies resulted in recommendations for improving the educational programs of endogenous retarded children (Strauss and Lehtinen, 1947).

During the 1950s and 1960s, Cruickshank and his colleagues extended the research of Strauss to include nonretarded children. They discovered that brain-damaged, nonretarded children exhibited behavioral characteristics that were similar to those of the exogenous, retarded children. Although evidence of brain damage could not always be produced, children with behavioral characteristics similar to those of children with substantiated brain damage came to be considered minimally brain injured. In recent years professionals have tended to replace the brain damaged label with the term *learning disabled,* but diagnosis is based primarily on the behavioral constellation of perceptual and coordination deficits, hyperactivity, labile emotions, short attention span, and impulsiveness in addition to poor achievement in academic subjects. A substantial group of researchers and clinicians infers from the label *learning disability* that the etiology in these cases is brain damage.

Increasing criticism has been focused on the use of labels referring to brain damage for children for whom the primary assessment and treatment techniques are behavioral or educational. Such labels may be detrimental to the child, particularly if the average teacher or parent perceives the child's condition as being untreatable; these labels are poorly defined and sometimes used when there is minimal or no direct evidence of brain damage; and, finally, the labels are not useful in assessing the child's educational needs. Proponents of the medical labels have expressed concerns about decreasing interest in etiology and said there is a risk that children with learning disabilities may receive inadequate medical attention.

Although important work in the area of learning disabilities has been continuing since at least the 1930s, the clinical descriptions and research findings were not incorporated into either medical or educational training programs until relatively recently; the average physician, teacher, and psychologist has thus not been trained to diagnose or provide remedial care for learning disabilities. In the 1970s and 1980s clinical and educational training programs have been adding courses and lectures in this area at an accelerated rate, and during this time perhaps the greatest attention to learning disabilities has been given in schools of education.

As has been true in the area of mental retardation, parents' groups have been greatly responsible for the acceleration in services for children with learning disabilities. During the 1960s parents' associations, such as the California Association for Neurologically Handicapped Children, have been formed and have mobilized the passage of legislation to support special programs for educationally handicapped children. Professionals have similarly begun to respond to the needs of children with learning disabilities by adding to our knowledge of etiology, diagnosis, and treatment. The initiation of the *Journal of Learning Disabilities* in 1968 was a major indication that professional interest in the area had begun to grow.

Meanwhile, most children with learning disabilities who also exhibited behavior problems were diagnosed as emotionally disturbed, and the "emotional disturbance" was designated as the cause of the learning problems in school. Those children without significant behavior problems were often assumed to be mentally retarded by their teachers.

specific disabilities related to basic school subjects

This section focuses on specific reading disability (RD) because it accounts for the great majority of the learning problems related to school subjects. In addition, very little research has been focused on specific disabilities in arithmetic, writing, and spelling.

assessment

The primary difficulty in describing reading disabilities is that our knowledge has derived from the clinical experiences and research of professionals representing variety of disciplines, and this knowledge has not been well integrated.

In the past, clinicians tended to agree with Eisenberg's (1966) definition of specific reading disability: "Operationally, specific reading disability may be defined as the failure to learn to read with normal proficiency despite conventional instruction, a culturally adequate home, proper motivation, intact senses, normal intelligence, and freedom from gross neurological defect" (p. 14). It is immediately apparent that this definition is more a description of what a reading disability is not than of what it is. While we do have adequate operational definitions of "intact senses," "normal intelligence," "proper nutrition," and, perhaps, "gross neurological defect," specification of "normal proficiency," "culturally adequate home," and "conventional instruction" has not been forthcoming. Currently, clinicians focus particularly on chronological age, grade placement, and mental age as predictors of expected reading achievement and compare the expected achievement with measures of actual achievement to determine whether a child has a specific reading disability.

Referral. Many RD children have probably never been referred for diagnosis because most schools do not have screening programs that are adequate for purposes of initial identification. Although classroom teachers are usually the most well-informed persons in the child's environment with regard to the child's status in reading, they often do not have the background knowledge or access to information that is necessary to identify the RD child. The RD child with a behavior problem is probably more likely to be referred for a diagnostic examination than an RD child who presents no behavior problem to the teacher. Thus, many children may be referred primarily for behavior problems and are later discovered to have specific learning disabilities.

Preliminary information. When a child is having learning problems in school, it is particularly important to determine whether physical factors are involved. For this reason, many clinicians suggest that the child receive a general physical examination as well as tests for vision and hearing prior to undergoing psychological and educational testing procedures. Most schools have periodic screening programs for vision and hearing, and the results of these tests may be used if they have been obtained within six months to a year of the referral. The clinician also requests a copy of the child's school grades and standardized group test scores for background information.

Interview. When the child is referred to a clinic, an interview is usually conducted with the parents and sometimes with the child. During the interview with the parents, the clinician obtains a history of both learning and behavior problems in school in an attempt to determine whether the problems have been evident throughout the child's school years or whether they have developed in the recent past.

While the behavioral clinician focuses on the child's present and recent past academic problems, the traditional clinician is more likely to inquire at some length about the parents' own school experiences, the assumption being that parents who have had adverse school experiences can unconsciously transmit their attitudes to the child. The traditional clinician may be particularly interested in determining whether the affected academic subject has a special symbolic meaning for the child or the parent-child unit. Doing poorly in reading may, for example, represent the avoidance of seeing or reading about forbidden (sexual) material.

Parents are often not well informed about the child's actual progress in school and report that the child's grades did not reflect a problem in the early years. In some cases, parents have received no oral or written indication of learning problems before the recommendation that they arrange for a diagnostic evaluation. The lack of psychological preparation in such cases often contributes to greater defensiveness and complaints about the school during the interview.

The interview with the child attempts to secure the child's perception of the school problems. The clinician inquires about the child's favorite and disliked school subjects as well as the quality of interactions with teachers. Occasionally, a strong antagonism has developed between the child and a particular teacher, and the teacher may or may not be aware of such feelings. Children vary considerably in their responsiveness during interviews; they range from extreme withdrawal to complete candor about the problem. At least some of their variability is due to what has previously been told to them about their referral for diagnostic evaluation. In spite of these difficulties, the child's contributions are generally believed to be a meaningful component of the diagnostic process.

Another important source of information is the child's teacher. If the clinician is employed by the school system, an interview with the teacher is frequently arranged. Because of the time and expense, clinicians outside of the school system are seldom able to conduct a personal interview with the teacher, although a telephone interview or written comments by the teacher, or both, are becoming increasingly common.

The teacher interview focuses on the child's behavior and learning in the classroom. The teacher is asked to describe the child's behavior under various conditions, such as during different instructional periods. Is the child having difficulty only with reading and reading-related school subjects, or are there problems in several areas? The teacher is asked about the methods used to try to help the child and the relative successes of these approaches.

Standardized tests. The use of standardized tests with children suspected of RD may be viewed as a two-phase process: the identification phase and the diagnostic phase. Since RD children cannot be identified on the basis of grades or criteria other than tests, screening tests must be administered to identify the children who require the more extensive diagnostic testing. The initial phase may include mass testing of large numbers of children, such as whole grades or schools. After a child has been identified as RD, a battery of tests will be administered to determine the pattern of strengths and weaknesses for each identified child.

Identification. The minimum testing requirements for identifying an RD child are an individually administered intelligence test and a reading achievement test. Since initial identification requires only an IQ score (an estimate of rate of intellectual development), the Slosson Intelligence Test is an appropriate choice in terms of expenditure of time and money when large numbers of children are to be screened.

For purposes of gross screening and initial identification, several of the available achievement tests are suitable, for example, the Wide Range Achievement Test (Jastak and Jastak, 1976) and the Peabody Individual Achievement Test (Dunn and Markwardt, 1970). The child's responses on these tests are recorded verbatim because they may contain useful diagnostic information.

Group intelligence and reading test scores are readily available from most schools; it is particularly unfortunate that they have not been demonstrated to be valid with respect to the identification of RD children. Because most group tests are highly dependent on reading skills, they tend to penalize children with specific reading disabilities. Thus, an RD child is very likely to obtain a considerably lower IQ score on a group test than on an individual test. This possibility precludes the use of group intelligence and achievement tests for identifying RD children.

There are three basic approaches to the identification of RD children by educators and psychologists: the Years Below Grade Level Method, the Discrepancy Method, and the Regression Method. These approaches have usually involved the elimination of children with IQ scores below 90, although a case can be made that a child at any IQ level can manifest a specific reading disability. In addition, most clinicians agree that a diagnosis of RD should not be made until the child has been in school one year.

The Years Below Grade Level Method designates a child as RD if the child's reading score is significantly below the actual grade placement. The difference between the grade placement necessary to be "significant" is somewhat arbitrary, although general guidelines are followed. For example, a child in the second grade who is more than six months behind grade placement and a child in the fifth grade who is more than one year behind grade placement would both be considered to have significant reading disabilities. The difference required becomes larger as the child's school grade increases.

The Discrepancy Method involves computing an expected reading level on the basis of the child's IQ score and subtracting from it the child's actual reading level. Children with reading levels that are significantly lower than expected on the basis of their IQ score are considered to be RD. The formula most often used to compute the expected reading level is (years in school $\times$ IQ) + 1.0 (Bond and Tinker, 1967, p. 92). Again, the absolute difference between the two levels required for diagnosis has not been generally agreed upon, but a difference of 1½ years at the fifth or sixth grade level, for example, would usually be considered adequate for diagnosis of RD.

The Discrepancy Method seems to have considerable advantage over the Years Below Method for identifying children with specific reading disabilities. It has long been known that the IQ score is the best available predictor of reading achievement. That relationship is logical in view of the fact that both scores are measures of rate of learning. Thus, rate of learning to read could be expected to approximate the rate of learning a wide variety of cognitive skills. The Years Below Method would identify the poorest readers in a group of children without regard to IQ score. The resulting sample of RD children identified by the Years Below Method would consist primarily of the children with the lowest IQ scores in the group. Children with high IQ scores who are reading only at grade level would not be identified.

The Discrepancy Method has been criticized for not taking into account the "regression effect" (Thorndike, 1963), which would result in an overestimation of reading disability in highly intelligent children and an underestimation in less intelligent children (McLeod, 1979). The regression effect refers to the tendency of extreme scores to regress toward the population mean when the same tests are readministered; this phenomenon also occurs for different tests that are highly correlated with one another. To correct this problem, the Regression Method formula utilizes the reliability correlations of the IQ and achievement test scores and the intercorrelation of the two tests obtained during their standardizations or subsequent research.

After a child has been identified as RD, the clinician begins to focus on identifying those psychological processes that might be responsible for the learning deficit. Hypotheses regarding deficient areas are derived from the child's responses on a variety of individual diagnostic tests.

Diagnostic tests. The list of testing instruments that may be used in the diagnosing of learning disabilities is particularly extensive. A typical test battery may include the Wechsler Intelligence Test for Children — Revised (WISC-R), The Frostig Developmental Test of Visual Perception, the Developmental Test of Visual-Motor Integration, the Lincoln-Oseretsky Motor Test, and the Wepman Test of Auditory Discrimination, as well as diagnostic reading tests. Such batteries require an extensive commitment of professional time for administration and interpretation. Several of these more widely used tests will be described.

The WISC-R subtests are not considered reliable enough to permit strong diagnostic inferences to be drawn from them. Many clinicians do examine the profile of WISC-R subtest strengths and weaknesses closely, however, for hypotheses regarding the nature of the child's problem. In addition, a system has been devised to determine those instances in which two subtest scores are statistically different from one another (Newland and Smith, 1967). Differences of three to five points between subtest scaled scores are necessary before they can be considered statistically different.

The Marianne Frostig Developmental Test of Visual Perception (Frostig, Lefever, Whittlesey, 1964) was the product of many years of observation and trials. Frostig had early observed a relationship of learning disabilities to visual perception problems and set out to devise a scale that would assess visual and visual-motor abilities. The purpose of the test is to identify kindergarten and early elementary school children with visual perception problems who might profit from an early intervention program in perceptual training. The test is composed of five subtests that measure the following abilities: (1) eye-motor coordination, (2) visual figure-ground discrimination, (3) form constancy, (4) position in space, and (5) spatial relations. The eye-motor coordination subtest requires a series of drawing tasks with a pencil in which the child draws a continuous line between two boundaries that vary in width and direction. In the figure-ground subtest the child outlines with a pencil a specific figure that is imbedded in a complex line drawing. The form constancy subtest requires the child to discriminate among geometric shapes. In the space subtest the child must choose a particular figure from among a series of figures that vary in rotated positions. The spatial relationships subtest assesses the child's ability to detect the positions of objects in relation to himself or herself and other objects.

The results of the test are presented in terms of scaled scores, age equivalents, and perceptual quotients. The reliability of the total scores has been reported as being high, but the reliability of the individual subtests is low enough to cause serious reservations about their use in diagnosing specific visual perception problems. Other criticisms of the test include an inadequate standardization sample and a possible lack of subtest independence. Moreover, validity studies suggest a decreasing relationship of visual perception skills and reading achievement with increasing grade levels.

When strictly evaluated, the Frostig Test should be considered a screening test for visual perception problems. It must be recognized, however, that Frostig's test represents a substantial departure from that of most test constructors who were almost wholly involved with the concept of intelligence; Frostig's work has strongly supported the notion that abilities other than intelligence may serve a major role in the learning of academic subjects.

The Developmental Test of Visual-Motor Integration (VMI) (Beery, 1967) consists of twenty-four geometric forms that are copied with pencil and paper. The forms are arranged in order of difficulty and can be administered to children between the ages of two and fifteen years. The VMI was designed to assess the degree to which visual perception and motor behavior are integrated. The VMI is highly correlated with both mental age and reading achievement in school-age children. The test is frequently included in the initial assessment battery for children referred for possible learning disabilities.

The manual contains scoring criteria and examples of passes and failures for each geometric form. The child's score is presented as an age equivalent that is determined from the raw score or number of forms correctly reproduced. Age norms are also provided for each geometric form.

A diagnostic battery for the assessment of learning disabilities frequently includes a test of auditory perception. The one that is most often used is the Wepman Test of Auditory Discrimination (Wepman, 1958). The Wepman consists of a series of word pairs that are presented orally to the child who then indicates whether they are the same or different. The test-retest reliability of the Wepman is reported to be high.

Since children with learning disabilities sometimes present motor development problems, a test of motor development may be included in the test battery. The most frequently used motor test is the Lincoln-Oseretsky Motor Development Scale (Sloan, 1955), which has been through several revisions since the original test was published in the Soviet Union in 1923. The Lincoln-Oseretsky has high reliability and is particularly useful for children six to fourteen years of age. Administration time is usually about one hour.

administration phase of the diagnostic process. Rather than simply designating whether a response to a test item is correct or incorrect, the clinician records the response itself. The types of errors seen on a test protocol give valuable information with respect to the deficiencies in reading behavior. Types of errors may include, for example, lack of letter discrimination within words, lack of discrimination of similar words, omissions of letters or words within sentences, and mispronunciation of words.

Although clinicians have utilized the informal reports of classroom performance by teachers for some time, behavioral clinicians have been responsible for introducing the use of systematic observations to the classroom. Whenever a child has been referred for a problem in school, the behavioral clinician will attempt to arrange observation sessions in the school setting. Much of the behavioral research in classroom settings has been directed toward disruptive children, but academic behaviors are beginning to receive increased study.

In some situations, the teacher will be asked to observe the child's behavior, but research is beginning to suggest that using teachers as observers may present methodological problems that could obscure assessment findings. It has been proposed that teachers' observation of behavior may lead to change in both teachers' and pupils' behaviors before the initiation of an intervention program. The mechanisms for these changes are not yet fully understood, but teachers themselves report that their perception of the child changes as a result of recording the frequency of specific behavior. It is interesting to note that their subjective reports tend to reflect an increasingly favorable attitude toward the child.

The forms of behavior, the observer, and the classroom schedule determine the timing of the behavioral observations and the recording methods. If the child is having problems in reading, for example, behavioral observations are conducted during the class's reading period. A teacher observing the child's behavior would likely be observing only one or two types of behavior that could be easily counted while the class was being conducted. An observer other than the teacher would probably be able to monitor a greater number of behaviors using a time sampling technique. In the case of children with specific learning disabilities, it is particularly important to monitor both academic and nonacademic types of behavior because the probability of problems in both areas appears to be high and tends to increase with children's age.

Medical assessment. Those professionals who link a diagnosis of learning disability to minimal brain dysfunction recommend the most comprehensive multidisciplinary evaluation. These evaluations differ from the usual psychoeducational approach primarily in the addition of formal medical assessment. The physical and neurological examinations are conducted as part of the current evaluation of the child; medical examinations obtained at an earlier time for other purposes, such as a routine annual check-up, are not considered adequate.

The general physical examination is conducted to determine whether abnormal physical or organic factors are present and contributing to the child's problem. In the neurological examination, the physician also includes an asssessment of the developmental aspects of neurologic integration. Children with learning disabilities tend to present abnormalities of integrated motor behaviors rather than abnormal reflexes. The medical examination also includes an evaluation of visual acuity and auditory discrimination as well as the physical aspects of the visual and auditory systems. Routine blood and urine laboratory tests are usually included. The special laboratory tests, such as the EEG, X-rays, and biochemical analyses, are conducted only when indicated by findings from other portions of the medical examination.

A history of the child is obtained through one or more interviews before the medical examination is given, The medical history includes information related to the pre-, peri-, and postnatal periods. The physician obtains descriptions of the child's illnesses with particular attention given to their severity, the age of the child, and the symptoms. Often included in the history is the parents' description of the child's motor and language development and information regarding the family constellation as well as events that might be related to psychological stress.

The diagnostic report. After all of the assessment procedures have been completed, the clinician writes a report in which the behavioral characteristics of the child are described. The most important aspect of the test report is that it describes the child's strengths and weaknesses in the various areas such that a treatment program can be derived from the information. It is also important to remember that assessment does not terminate with the diagnostic report but should be a continuing process that is interwoven with the treatment program. In this manner, the child's status relative to the behavioral goals of treatment is continuously available.

General description of learning disabled children. The typical learning-disabled child is in an early elementary grade when referred. The child's IQ score is within the average or above average range, but the performance on the IQ test and tests of special function is more variable than average; that is, some abilities are adequate or excellent, while others are extremely poor. Achievement in some subjects is average, while achievement in others is well below what would be expected on the basis of grade level and IQ score. For many learning-disabled children teachers and parents are likely to report present and past behavior problems, such as short attention span, impulsiveness, hyperactivity, and disruptive classroom behavior. Learning-disabled children tend to have poor self-images, often referring to themselves as stupid.

etiology

Because reading disabilities have been diagnosed on the basis of many different criteria in the past, our knowledge with regard to etiological factors remains somewhat ambiguous. Very few studies have been conducted in which RD children were selected from large populations on the basis of objective criteria and then compared with appropriate control groups on variables related to possible etiological factors. The available studies typically include RD children referred by teachers or diagnosed in clinic settings, or both. It is, of course, unknown to what extent these RD children are representative of RD children in the population. The children in these studies may have been referred primarily because they presented behavior problems in addition to their academic problems, while RD children without behavior problems may not have been referred for diagnosis. Brain dysfunction has been strongly implicated as the primary etiological factor because a substantial number of RD children exhibit behaviors that are similar to those of persons known to have experienced brain damage. These behaviors include hyperactivity, short attention span, impulsiveness, and distractibility (see Chapter 11, "Conduct Disorders"). In addition, perceptual and short-term memory problems are frequently present and manifested, for example, by left-right confusion and inability to remember recently learned auditory information (Cohen and Netley, 1978).

The evidence that implicates genetic factors in the etiology of RD has been derived primarily from family studies. In 1950 Hallgren reported that reading disabilities were found among the relatives of 103 out of 116 RD cases. A more recent study (Finucci, Guthrie, Childs, Abbey, and Childs, 1976) found that 45 percent of the first-degree relatives of twenty reading-disabled children had reading disabilities. Because family analysis confounds genetic and environmental factors, no conclusions can be derived from these studies. They do suggest, however, the possibility that hereditary factors may be involved in some cases of RD. One study, cited by Owen (1978), found that eleven monozygotic sets of twins were 100 percent concordant and twenty-seven dizygotic sets of twins were 33 percent concordant for reading disabilities.

Additional indirect evidence supporting a genetic basis is the consistently higher proportion of males identified as RD. Reports of ratios ranging from two males for each female to ten males for each female have been made. Variability among the ratios appears to be due to differences in diagnostic criteria across studies.

Prenatal, perinatal, and postnatal physical factors. Most of the physical factors that have been implicated in the etiology of severe learning problems, such as mental retardation, have also been suggested as causes of learning disabilities. Again, the available studies are few in number and also tend to be inconclusive because the criteria for RD are not adequately specified. Kawi and Pasamanick (1959) recorded data from the obstetrical records of retarded readers with IQ scores above 84 and found a greater frequency of pregnancy complications and premature infants in their RD group in comparison to the control group. Jayasekara and Street (1978) found that older mothers and fathers had a higher risk of having a dyslexic boy, while parity had no effect on risk.

Considerably more research is needed before we can begin to identify the prenatal and perinatal physical factors that may be related to learning disabilities. Although retrospective studies are not optimal approaches, clearer hypotheses may be derived with respect to etiology if more precise diagnostic criteria were used. Much information could also be obtained, if comparisons of the incidence of physical factors were made for groups of RD children identified on the basis of different criteria (for example, Years Below vs. Discrepancy approaches).

Hallahan and Cruickshank (1973, p. 40) and numerous other investigators have suggested a strong relationship between nutritional deficiencies and learning problems. Studies conducted primarily in underdeveloped countries demonstrate that children malnourished early in life score more poorly on tests of intellectual functioning. Evidence linking nutritional deficiencies and specific learning disabilities, however, has not yet been presented.

Rourke (1978) has recently reviewed the research on the neuropsychological aspects of reading problems. He concluded that the evidence suggests a "significant, positive correlation between severity of reading retardation and severity of impairment on a large number of brain-related variables" (p. 170). He stated further that finding a single deficit or even a set of deficits responsible for reading retardation is highly improbable, given the data describing deficiencies in the left hemisphere, right hemisphere, and both cerebral hemispheres.

Kinsbourne and Caplan (1979) have proposed that the underlying bases of learning disabilities are either cognitive power disorders or cognitive style disorders. Cognitive power disorders refer to selective developmental lags, namely, immaturity of certain brain functions. Cognitive style disorders are of two types: (1) the overfocused or compulsive and (2) the underfocused or impulsive-distractable. Overfocused children tend to maintain their attention on one thing too long, while underfocused children shift their attention from one thing to another too quickly. Underfocused children are also the children considered to be hyperactive. Cognitive power disorders tend to affect specific learning tasks, while cognitive style disorders have more generalized effects on school performance and social relationships. Cognitive style disorders are discussed at greater length in the next chapter.

Psychological factors. Psychological factors have been considered primary by many traditional clinicians because they have observed a high incidence of behavior problems in children with learning disabilities who have been referred to clinics. For those children whose behavior problems are viewed as the cause of learning problems, one of the traditional forms of psychotherapy is usually recommended.

Kessler (1966, p. 201) suggested that poor school performance may be viewed as a neurotic solution to an underlying conflict. Learning requires psychic energy; if much of the psychic energy is being utilized by intense feelings and motivations, then learning will be impaired. Among the etiological factors that have been related to learning disabilities within a psychodynamic framework are poor parent-child relationships, inadequate self-concept, excessive failure, and inadequate early stimulation.

Perhaps the greatest attention has been given to the role of parents in the genesis of children's learning problems. The parents have been the child's teacher prior to school entry and thereby determine much of the child's behavior in the school environment. If the child resents the authority of the parent at home, then that child is likely to resent the authority of the teacher at school. Interactions between parent and child around developmental tasks during the early years are believed to influence the quality of the teacher-child interaction, and, therefore, learning. For example, if the parent plays a prominent role in encouraging and rewarding the child during toilet training, this positive experience predisposes the child to react favorably to learning later academic skills. Repression of curiosity about sexual matters in the home is also felt by many clinicians to contribute to the child's lack of involvement in learning. Sperry, Ulrich, and Staver (1958) presented a series of case studies in which passivity, based on the denial of hostile feelings learned in the home, appeared to be the basis for severe learning problems in school.

In the case of specific learning disabilities, the traditional clinician tries to determine why that particular school subject was "chosen" for failure. That is, on the basis of information derived from the assessment procedure, the clinician attempts to derive the psychological reasons for the child's failure to learn to read when success has been achieved in other school subjects. This search for the underlying cause continues through the course of treatment.

treatment

Children with specific reading disabilities have received a wide variety of treatments ranging from drug therapy through educational remediation to psychotherapy. Often several types of treatment are conducted simultaneously. The treatment program designed for a particular child depends on many factors, such as the theoretical orientation of the diagnostician, the services available in the school and community, and the socioeconomic status of the family. Most professionals are beginning to agree that educational remediation should be the primary form of treatment, although other types of treatment are frequently indicated and recommended.

Educational remediation. Some children with reading disabilities, particularly those in the early elementary school years, present no outstanding behavioral problems and thus would benefit optimally from an educational remediation program. Children with behavior problems, on the other hand, sometimes require other forms of treatment before they can be helped by an educational program. In this section, we describe the basic principles of educational remediation and several types of programs that have been designed to help children with specific reading disabilities. Intervention programs for the behavior problems frequently associated with learning disabilities (hyperactivity, impulsiveness, and disruptive behavior) are discussed in Chapter 11.

Educational remediation is usually conducted by a teacher who has been trained in a special education program, although teachers without the formal credentials do serve in the same capacity, and many provide excellent remediation programs. Most teachers in these programs are employed by school systems and work with children in schools; teachers with special training are being added to the professional staffs of clinics, however, and some teachers provide tutorial services on a private basis.

Children with reading disabilities differ from one another to such a great extent that remedial instruction must be highly individualized. This suggestion is particularly applicable to children referred to clinics on an individual basis. In large school systems, which screen children for reading disabilities, it might be possible to form small groups of three to five children who would benefit from the same program, however.

Information obtained from the diagnostic procedures forms the basis for designing each child's remedial program. The most important information is related to the child's level of functioning in the various aspects of the reading process: word recognition, comprehension, and word-attack skills or phonics. The program is designed on the basis of the child's strengths and weaknesses in reading performance, and reading materials are chosen to be compatible with the child's levels of functioning. That is, the materials chosen initially for the remediation program should ensure a high level of success to develop optimal motivation on the part of the child.

The best remedial programs are those that specify behavioral goals and the steps that will be taken to achieve those goals. The use of learning principles has also been included in many remedial programs. For example, various forms of reinforcement are used to accelerate the learning process. Some programmed instruction materials that incorporate learning principles are useful and appropriate for children with learning disabilities. Recent research suggests that programmed instruction is at least as effective as much teacher-presented instruction. Children with a history of reading problems in school, however, may work more efficiently when praise from the teacher and personal instructions in the teaching process are components of the program.

In summary, the basic principles of educational remediation are essentially those of any sound educational program: know the child's level of performance, individualize instruction, and use antecedent and consequent stimuli appropriately in order to effectuate the best possible learning and performance.

The oldest remediation program still in use today is that outlined by Orton in 1925. More recent contributions to the program by Gillingham have resulted in the program's being designated as the Orton-Gillingham approach (J. Orton, 1966).

Orton viewed reading as one aspect of the child's total language development that was controlled by one of the two brain hemispheres and thought that problems in learning to read might reflect an impairment of the natural development of the nervous system. From his clinical practice and research with reading-disabled children he observed the high frequency with which they gave evidence of instability in recognizing and recalling the orientation of letters as well as the order of letters in words. Such difficulties suggested to Orton that perhaps both, instead of one, of the hemispheres were being called upon to process the information and that the messages to the two hemispheres were mirror images of each other, thus causing considerable difficulty for the child attempting to learn the appropriate orientation. Orton also observed that many reading-disabled children also presented motor patterns that reflected mixed left and right laterability (that is, lack of cerebral dominance).

While his neurological theories have not received research confirmation, Orton is recognized as introducing the first remedial program dealing directly with learning to read. Orton presented two principles for his remedial programs: (1) train the child for simultaneous association of visual, auditory, and kinesthetic stimuli by having the child look at, sound, and follow the letters with the fingers simultaneously (Orton, 1928), and (2) find the basic reading level from which the child can learn and direct the training toward a fusion of these stimuli (Orton, 1937.) Thus, children with reading disabilities are first taught the basic language units, individual letters and phonemes, with special attention given to the clarification of the visual and auditory patterns that are being linked together through association with the motor elements of speech and writing. The synthesizing of these basic units is conducted in a specified order. In 1946 Gillingham, a teacher and an associate of Orton's for several years, published a manual (Gillingham and Stillman, 1960, 6th ed.) that provided teachers with the necessary instructions for conducting a program of remedial help according to Orton's principles. The manual specifies that the remedial program should be conducted daily for forty-five to sixty minutes for a minimum of two years. During this period, the child is not allowed to read, write, or spell in the classroom or at home. To enable the child to keep up with the content of the school subjects, the parents are advised to read the material aloud to the child.

Marianne Frostig's program (Frostig and Horne, 1964) for children with learning disabilities emphasizes the development of visual perception skills. This program was devised to train the abilities evaluated by the Frostig Developmental Test of Visual Perception: figure-ground perception, form and size constancy, perception of position in space, perception of special relationships, and eye-hand coordination. Work sheets, workbooks, and teachers' guides contain exercises that represent various levels of competence for all five visual perception areas. Frostig's program was intended to be used with preschool children to prevent learning problems as well as with school-age children who require remedial attention. While visual perception skills are emphasized in the program, recognition is given to other sense modalities, motor activities, and their integration into the program. The emphasis on visual perception in the Frostig program is based on research findings that indicate a strong correlational relationship between visual perception and reading for beginning readers. Evaluations of the Frostig program have revealed disappointing results in that reading achievement seems not to be significantly improved. Current research suggests that more progress may be accomplished by teaching the reading skills directly than by trying to correct the so-called underlying defects, such as perceptual-motor problems (Vellutino, Steger, Meyer, Harding, and Niles, 1979).

A more fundamental approach to the teaching of reading has been reflected in the introduction of the Initial Teaching Alphabet (i/t/a). Because the English language has many spelling inconsistencies (that is, irregularities between sound and symbol), the task of learning to read it is especially difficult. The i/t/a is a reading system in which the child learns to associate forty-four symbols with their sounds (see Fig. 10-1) rather than the twenty-six letters of the alphabet with their labels. It is considered a temporary medium, a way to facilitate the transition from non-reading to reading. After the child has mastered the basic associations, sounds are combined and blended into larger units, and eventually, into words. When the child has achieved the fundamental word-analysis skills (after about a year of instruction), the transition to the traditional twenty-six symbols is begun. The transition is facilitated by the planned similarities between the two types of orthography. Although the system was designed to facilitate normal children's learning to read, the i/t/a has been described as particularly useful for children with learning disabilities because of the reduced number of sound-symbol associations and the higher probability of initial successes. Formal evaluation of the i/t/a with reading-disabled children, however, has not yet been completed.

Woolman's Progressive Choice Reading Method (1962) is also an approach that seeks to facilitate the learning of sound-symbol relationships. It provides a system of reading instruction that combines all the necessary components of reading. Instruction begins with the selection of a target word, a word that is in the child's oral vocabulary and has letters that present regular sound-symbol relationships. The first step involves a discussion of the meaning, use, and pronounciation of the word. In the second step, the child learns to discriminate the various letters of the word from other letters that are similar. Subsequent steps in the first cycle add the verbal labeling of the printed word, the written word in response to the oral presentation of the word, and the compounding of previously learned components. Two additional cycles emphasize the systematic expansion of decoding skills and the learning of the irregular sound-symbol relationships. Other aspects of Woolman's program worthy of mention are the use of upper-case letters and the avoid-

Figure 10–1 Pitman's initial teaching alphabet with its 44 symbols and words illustrating the sounds these symbols represent. Printed with permission of Pitman Publishing Corp., Belmont, Calif.

ance of naming letters during the first cycle; both techniques have been designed to minimize confusion and errors. Special materials have been developed for older children with reading disabilities.

These remedial reading approaches represent only a few of the available methods, but most of the methods have many elements in common. There has been a distinct movement in recent years away from the teaching of general, presumably underlying, skills toward the teaching of skills involved in reading *per se*. A number of psychologists and educators have been engaged in the analysis of reading as an example of operant behavior. This research has called into question the idea that children have to be a certain age to learn to read because demonstrations of successful reading programs have been achieved with children well below school age (Staats 1968, p. 285) as well as with retarded children.

It appears, then, that a remedial approach that utilizes behavioral principles with careful attention to the antecedent stimuli (materials) and consequent stimuli (reinforcers) would have the highest degree of success. Because many children with reading problems have not adequately learned the most fundamental behaviors required for progress in reading, behavioral analysis of the child's repertoire is a necessary first step. Following this assessment, the teacher should designate behavioral goals and choose from the large selection of materials those that are appropriate for the behavioral goals. Reinforcers should also be carefully chosen for each child. Children with histories of poor academic achievement have very likely experienced considerable negative feedback for their attempts or, at best, have been ignored in the classroom; as a result, their motivation is, no doubt, extremely low. A great deal of reinforcement may be necessary to get these children to respond at normal levels to academic materials.

Learning theory has made a substantial contribution to our understanding of children's academic progress. Behavioral clinicans have generally not given research attention to the unique problems that may be encountered by children with specific learning disabilities, but a number of studies have examined the effect of certain stimulus variables on the behavior of children with deficiences in specific academic subjects. From learning theory, the idea of individualized instruction has been developed and is manifested in teaching machines and programmed texts. Programmed instruction may be described as a method of presenting academic material in small sequential steps. Each step presents information, and the child is required to respond to the information. Feedback is given to the child's response before the next step is taken. The principal advantage of programmed instruction is that each child can proceed at his or her own rate in contrast to traditional classroom teaching in which the slower child may be left behind and the brighter child may become bored. Being allowed to proceed at their own pace, children with learning problems may be spared much of the negative feedback that accompanies performance that is below average. Another advantage of programmed instruction is that it frees the teacher to provide assistance to children when they need it.

Many programmed-instruction materials have been developed and marketed.

While research has not yet substantiated the superiority of programmed instruction over regular classroom instruction, only a few disadvantages of the former have become apparent. Perhaps the greatest problem associated with programmed instruction is the lack of evaluative research both before and after publication of the programmed materials. That is, materials are often published before there is any evidence that they accomplish the goals they were intended to reach. Not having been trained to evaluate the quality of materials, teachers may be unduly swayed in their choices by possibly irrelevant factors, such as descriptions in advertising brochures. In addition, very few studies have directly compared the achievement levels of children taught with programmed materials and those taught by conventional methods. A second problem is that programmed instruction materials may be more expensive than comparable traditional textbooks; their extra cost cannot be justified if they are not demonstrably effective. A third problem is that some of the programmed workbooks are designed so that cheating is much too easy; such materials may require that the children be monitored so closely that the teacher will not be able to provide the necessary instructional assistance to individual children.

   Psychotherapy. Some children with specific learning disabilities have problems that may be helped with psychotherapy. These problems are basically "inner-directed" emotional disturbances that include feelings of anxiety, depression, and poor self-image. Many learning-disabled children have had an accumulation of negative experiences at home and school that could account for these disturbances. Such feelings are not easily overcome, but many clinicians believe that psychotherapy has been moderately successful in helping to alleviate them (Clarizio and McCoy, 1970, p. 174).

speech and language problems

Speech and language problems are among the more common of the childhood behavior disorders. The acquisition of an expressive and receptive speech repertoire is an extremely complex learning task that may be disrupted by a variety of events throughout the life-span. Normal speech development requires an unimpaired auditory sensory and perceptual system, memory functions, intact expressive speech motor functions, and adequate speech and language stimulation. The receptive and expressive speech acquisition processes are so strongly intertwined that distinctions between expressive and receptive speech problems cannot always be made. To a large extent, expressive speech is dependent on receptive speech or language comprehension; if expressive speech is faulty, the problem may be due to a dysfunction of receptive speech or primarily to the expressive speech functions themselves.

   The professional most frequently involved with the diagnosis and treatment of speech and language problems is the speech pathologist who has been trained in a master's level graduate program. Doctoral level speech pathologists also provide services, but they usually spend most of their time teaching and doing research in college and university settings.

This section presents a brief review of preschool speech development followed by discussion of four types of speech and language problems: receptive and expressive developmental language disorders, speech delay, and disorders in articulation. Some of these problems may occur in conjunction with other behavior problems; speech delay, for example, is often associated with mental retardation.

normal language development

Speech and language skills develop in an orderly manner during the early years. That is, normative data allow us to determine whether a child's speech productions are within normal limits. It is from these norms that we may begin to understand the stages of speech development and the significance of the language development sequence.

Infants are born with the capacity to vocalize; during the first month of life crying is the dominant vocal response and seems to occur primarily when the baby is uncomfortable (for example, hungry, wet, or cold). Beginning in the second month, crying becomes differentiated in that different cries may signal different states of need. In addition, other vocalizations begin to emerge and are correlated with more positive states. During the second and third months of life a variety of vocal sounds, such as "oh," "uh," and "ooh," begin to emerge. Although infant responses to sound are apparent at birth, it is not until three or four months of age that the children consistently turn toward the source of a sound or interrupt their own vocalizations to search for the sound.

Between three and six months of age, most infants spend considerable amounts of time vocalizing. Toward the end of this period a number of consonant-vowel combinations are added to their repertoire. Some of the combinations appear in repetitive form (for example, "bah-bah," "ga-ga"), and the infant is described as babbling. The babbling stage is considered to be particularly important, since it is at this time that the vocalizations of deaf and hearing infants can be discriminated and that environmental contingencies have a significant influence on the quality and quantity of sound production.

At about eight or nine months of age, infants begin their attempts to imitate the speech sounds of others. This is the time when many infants learn to wave and say "bye-bye" in imitation. Their comprehension of language is also becoming more readily apparent in that they respond appropriately to specific words or phrases. For example, an infant may reach for or look at a ball when hearing the word *ball*.

Between twelve and eighteen months of age, most children begin to say their first words. While parents tend to count some of the earlier utterances, such as "mama" and "da-da," as words, they usually do not meet the criterion for true words. The criterion requires the child to produce the word spontaneously in the context of the appropriate stimulus (for example, the child says "ball" while reaching for a ball). During the second year the child acquires up to fifty single words, which designate common objects, familiar persons, and requests. Sometimes, the single-word utterances stand for more complex communications, for example, the child saying, "up" to indicate a desire to leave the playpen or crib. At about two years of age, children begin to combine words into two-word phrases or sentences. During the third year these phrases and sentences are expanded and modified to be compatible with the grammatical structure of the English language.

While children are acquiring single words, they also appear to be learning the language system. Soon after children begin to combine words, combinations of words that have never been presented or taught to them begin to appear in their verbal repertoire. That is, children at this stage of development begin to demonstrate some knowledge of syntax and word order. At the same time, they are intent on communicating with others and show frustration when adults do not respond or indicate that they do not understand what the child is saying.

Between the ages of two and three years, the rate of vocabulary growth is probably higher than at any other period in a child's life. In addition, average sentence length is expanded to three and four words, which include prepositions, conjunctions, and articles. By the age of three years the child is typically able to use the pronouns, "I," "me," and "you" correctly. The three-year-old can understand several thousand words and has an active vocabulary of about one thousand words. Between the ages of three and seven years a child's speech productions increasingly approximate those of adults. By about eight years of age, a child's use of syntax closely matches that of adults and lacks only the nuances of complex sentence productions.

speech delay

While the norms for the onset and development of speech provide a general outline of expected progress, variability among children is substantial. For many physicians it has been difficult to determine whether a particular child's delayed speech development is within normal limits or whether the delay is indicative of some abnormality. Because most physicians know at least one instance of severe speech delay in which a child later developed normal speech, they are often reluctant to refer children younger than two or three years of age who are using minimal or no speech. On the other hand, research has indicated a very close relationship between speech development and general intellectual functioning. Since early speech development is beginning to be recognized as crucial to a child's later intellectual status, many professionals are now emphasizing early identification and intervention for children whose speech is delayed.

Assessment. Until fairly recently, very few professionals from any discipline were trained to assess speech and language development in a child of less than three years. Typically, a psychologist would administer a developmental or intelligence test and clinically estimate a child's level of speech development from the relevant items on the test. More often than not, these estimates were valid, but they certainly did not reflect a child's total behavioral repertoire in the area of speech and language development.

With the increasing availability of norms and standardized tests for assessing speech and language in the preschool child (Lee, 1974), more speech pathologists are now being trained to assess a young child's speech behaviors. An interview is also conducted in which parents are asked to relate their child's history of speech development and to describe their current speech repertoire. During the evaluation session, the child's spontaneous speech productions and responses to the speech of others are recorded. The speech pathologist also presents to the child materials that are designed to evoke speech responses.

Assessment of speech development in the child under three years of age presents special problems for the evaluator. Young children typically react to strange environments by becoming nonverbal. Since pathologists need an optimal response from the child, they must arrange the situation to bring about the most revealing verbal behavior.

In addition to the formal and informal speech assessment, a child referred for a possible speech delay problem would usually receive a hearing test; a general physical examination and a psychological evaluation would also be recommended. Often, the hearing test is conducted by an audiologist who is a member of the speech clinic staff. Auditory testing includes evaluation of hearing sensitivity, speech discrimination, and middle ear functioning (Northern and Downs, 1978).

The evaluation of hearing sensitivity is described in terms of decibels and cycles per second; the decibel is a measure of sound intensity, while cycles per second designate the frequency of sound waves. In the hearing test children listen through earphones to tones of varying decibel levels and frequencies and signal those occasions when the sound is heard. Younger children, or those who do not have clear responses for "yes" and "no," are typically conditioned to respond to sound through a learned association between visual and auditory stimuli. The frequencies presented during the hearing test are 125, 250, 500, 1,000, 2,000, 4,000, and 8,000 cycles per second, although only the testing frequencies of 500, 1,000, 2,000, and 4,000 cycles per second are necessary for screening hearing capacity related to speech sounds. Decibel levels represent the level of energy required for the average person to hear a particular frequency. Figure 10-2 presents an audiogram for a child with a moderate hearing impairment.

Hearing loss is expressed in terms of the number of decibels for each frequency. Decibel levels of 0 and 10 are considered to be normal, while a decibel level of 75 is generally agreed upon to be the equivalent of deafness. Decibel levels between these two extremes reflect the continuum of hearing impairment. Both the amount of hearing loss and the range of frequencies affected determine the length of speech delay and the characteristics of the speech acquired.

Speech discrimination refers to the child's ability to discriminate among the various speech sounds. The sounds may be single syllables, words, or sentences, and

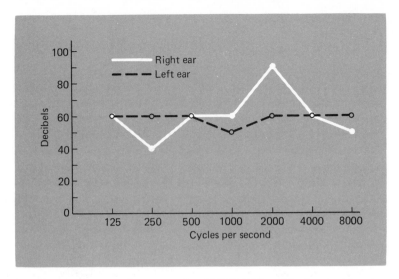

Figure 10-2. Audiogram of a Child With a Moderate Hearing Impairment.

they are presented with different backgrounds, such as quiet, noise, and competing language sounds. The assessment of the functioning of the middle ear focuses primarily on the responsiveness of the eardrum (tympanic membrane) to air pressure changes. Certain types of abnormalities are indicative of present or past ear infections and structural abnormalities.

Since speech delay can occur alone or in conjunction with other behavior disorders, differential diagnosis becomes particularly important. The assessment procedure should include an attempt to determine possible etiological factors, since such information may be useful in treatment.

Etiology. A delay in speech may occur as a result of several factors, some organic and others environmental. As is true with other behavior disorders, determining etiology for individual children is not always possible. Occasionally, the assessment procedure does not identify any possible etiological factors, but more often it identifies several possible causes of the problem.

Perhaps the single greatest cause of speech delay is hearing loss. The speech-delayed child may be deaf or have varying amounts of hearing loss, particularly in the speech range of frequencies. Recent research is also suggesting that temporary hearing losses during the first few years of life may also be correlated with slow speech development. Children with frequent or untreated ear infections, or both, during infancy are particularly prone to speech delays.

There are two principal types of hearing loss: conductive and sensorineural. A conductive hearing loss is due to a malfunction of the external canal or of the middle ear containing the eardrum and the very small bone transmitters, while a sensorineural loss indicates defects in the cochlea, the acoustic nerve, or the auditory centers of the brain. Particular speech problems tend to be associated with the two types of hearing loss.

In about half the cases of hearing loss the etiology is unknown. Heredity is believed to account for a little more than 10 percent, while prenatal and perinatal factors are causes in an additional 25 percent. German measles during the mother's first trimester of pregnancy is related to a high incidence of hearing loss among the children from these pregnancies and is probably the largest single cause of deafness in children. Prematurity is also a frequent correlate of hearing loss; the frequency of hearing impairment among low birth weight children is two to three times that for children in the general population. Postnatal insults, particularly meningitis, account for the remainder of the cases.

Speech delay is often associated with other behavior disorders, such as mental retardation and autism, problems whose causes appear to be largely organic. Most clinicians feel that it is important to label these disorders differently, although the children in the different groups may have some problems in common. Having a behavioral deficit in common, however, does not mean that they share the same etiologic factors or that optimal therapy will be identical.

Environmental causes of speech delay have also been proposed. Children whose language environments are grossly deficient can present speech delays and slow speech development of the magnitude observed in some children with organic impairment. Children need speech models in order to acquire speech themselves. While extreme cases in which children have been totally deprived of language stimulation are rare, instances in which the quality and quantity of language stimulation are minimal are frequently documented. Such instances are almost always correlated with other forms of deprivation making it difficult to ascertain the specific role of language deprivation. These other forms of deprivation may include malnutrition, poor medical care, and general parental neglect—conditions known to retard development.

Language delay is known to be more common in children from the lower socioeconomic classes. Some of this delay is no doubt accounted for by differences between middle-class standards and the models available to children who are members of the various subcultures (Baratz, 1969). Living conditions, such as crowding and noise, could, however, alter some of the contingencies usually available for the young child's vocalizations and speech attempts. For example, the busy mother with many children vying for her attention may ignore the vocalizations of her infant, or the noise level in the household could often be great enough to prevent others from hearing the infant's babbling and reinforcing it.

Even in families for which environmental deprivation is not a factor, otherwise normal children fail to develop appropriate speech. Many clinicians are convinced that speech delay can result from parents being overprotective and anticipating the child's needs. That is, some children don't talk because they have no need to talk; their every wish is fulfilled without the necessity for speaking. Many of these situations are initiated by an episode of illness during which the parents devote a great deal of attention to the child. The child, in effect, trains the parents to continue their high rate of attention even after the illness has subsided.

In the past, some speech pathologists viewed these etiological factors in psycho-analytic terms. Since the demands for speech production usually coincide with initiation of toilet-training, delayed speech may present an anal conflict; that is, the child who is resisting toilet-training also tends to resist other demands, such as parental pressures to speak. While we cannot be sure in what way toilet-training and learning to speak affect each other, clinicians tend to agree that most children go through a period, later in the second year of life, when they strongly resist requests and demands of all kinds.

Treatment. The treatment of speech delay depends greatly on the etiological factors known or hypothesized to have affected the child's speech development. If hearing is found to be impaired and correctable causes identified, medical or surgical treatment is indicated. Some types of hearing loss, not correctable by medical treatment, can be alleviated by fitting the child with one or two hearing aids. Correcting the hearing problem medically or with a hearing aid, however, does not often completely eliminate the need for speech therapy. Corrective therapy is indicated if the child has acquired speech patterns based on faulty hearing or if the child needs intensive experience with speech models to make speech acquisition possible.

Children who are deaf or severely hearing impaired present great therapeutic challenges. Residential and day schools for the deaf are increasing rapidly; this trend depicts the growing professional belief that intensive therapy is required for deaf children to acquire the necessary language skills. It is also being recommended that deaf and severely hearing-impaired children begin their language training as early as possible, ideally when they are two or three years of age.

Methods of training in the schools for the deaf vary; in most schools, speech is the sole means of communication, while in the others, hand signs and finger spelling are permitted in addition to speech. Although speech is more difficult to learn in comparison to the other forms of communication, most teachers of the deaf feel that the effort is worthwhile in terms of the greater positive side effects speech has in the natural environment.

Since almost all deaf children have some, albeit minimal, residual hearing, auditory training is included as part of the treatment program. Every effort is made to provide the child with information about the environment through the auditory channel. The first phase of the training involves teaching the child to listen to sounds by presenting amplified sounds and encouraging the child to play with noise makers. The child's surroundings are arranged such that amplified sounds occur frequently and regularly. After this period of sound exposure, the child is taught to discriminate between sounds. Initially, sounds that are greatly different from one another are used; gradually, speech sounds increasing in similarity are introduced.

Lip reading is another method whereby deaf children can receive verbal communication. Prior to formal instruction, the child is taught to watch the face of the speaker. Occasionally, children with impaired hearing have learned many of the lip-reading skills before their auditory problem is diagnosed. In some of these cases, their lip reading is so efficient that the parents do not suspect a hearing impairment to be the cause of their speech delay, but most deaf children have to be made aware of the potential information emanating from the mouth movements of speakers. In both auditory training and lip reading, there is a deliberate effort to emphasize pairing with other sensory stimuli. That is, when the word *apple,* for example, is said to a child learning lip reading, a real apple or a picture of an apple is paired with the mouth movement stimuli.

For the child whose lack of expressive speech is caused by deafness, the speech and language program is long and arduous. Since the child cannot use speech models against which to match his or her own sound productions, another procedure for learning speech must be devised. Perhaps the most successful approach is one similar to that used by Lovaas for autistic children—an approach that utilizes the learning principles of shaping, fading, and reinforcement. The child's initial vocalizations are increased and gradually shaped into words. Sounds that are not in the child's repertoire are initially produced by the therapist manually forming the appropriate lip positions for the child and modeling the proper tongue position, while the child is expelling air. The physical prompts are gradually faded as the child learns how to make the correct mouth and tongue movements.

Most speech pathologists agree that the initial goal of treatment is to get the child to attend to speech. Their programs, then, usually include methods for increasing the child's attention to speech stimuli. One method is to have the adults in the child's environment engage in self-talk, a kind of running commentary describing current behaviors interjected by brief requests to the child. The parents are advised to begin by using only key words, such as noun-verb combinations, in order to make the speech stimuli as simple and nonfrustrating as possible. Parents are also instructed to reinforce the child for behaviors indicating attention, such as looking at the face of the speaker.

Imitation training is a particularly good method for securing an increase in speech productions from children with less than total hearing impairment. The techniques used are similar to those that most parents employ when their infants are beginning to make babbling sounds and involve the reciprocal imitation of simple sounds between parent and child. Sound imitation is often coupled with motor imitation to make the experience more salient (for example, waving and saying "bye-bye").

When the child's speech delay is considered to be due to environmental deprivation (lack of appropriate models and inefficient contingencies), treatment is designed to overcome those deficiencies. Project Head Start and subsequent experimental preschool programs have provided important data on the early speech and language development in disadvantaged children, clearly substantiating deficits in those areas.

Several research projects conducted in the home and in preschool settings have also demonstrated that these language problems can be ameliorated by remedial training. One of the most successful of these projects was that conducted by Bereiter and Engelmann (1966). The Bereiter-Engelmann technique of teaching includes the following eighteen procedures (pp. 110–120):

1. Work at different levels of difficulty at different times.
2. Adhere to a rigid, repetitive presentation pattern.
3. Use unison responses whenever possible.
4. Never work with a child individually in a study group for more than about thirty seconds.
5. Phrase statements rhythmically.
6. Require children to speak in a loud, clear voice.
7. Do not hurry children or encourage them to talk fast.
8. Clap to accent basic language patterns and conventions.
9. Use questions liberally.
10. Use repetition.
11. Be aware of the cues the child is receiving.
12. Use short explanations.
13. Tailor the explanations and rules to what the child knows.
14. Use lots of examples.
15. Prevent incorrect responses whenever possible.
16. Be completely unambiguous in letting the child know when his response is correct and when it is incorrect.
17. Dramatize the use value of learning whenever possible.
18. Encourage thinking behavior.

Bereiter (1972) has reported that programs that teach a specific series of tasks (from the simple to the complex) and have specific behavioral goals facilitate achievement more than do traditional, child-centered, preschool programs.

If the child's speech delay is considered to be the result of parental overprotection or of parent-child conflict, then psychotherapy or behavior therapy for the parents may be recommended. The goal of therapy is to communicate the relationship of the child's speech delay to parental behavior and to suggest ways that changes in their behavior may facilitate the child's speech development. Either direct observation of the parent-child interaction or information derived from the interview provide the hypotheses regarding which parent and child behaviors should be changed.

Therapy with parents is not always successful. A few parents have difficulty accepting their role in the problem and deny the possibility of such a relationship. Other parents acknowledge the possibility but cannot change their own behavior in response to the child. Such cases challenge even the most experienced and talented clinicians.

expressive and receptive language disorders

Until recently, these disorders were labeled "developmental aphasias" (Eisenson, 1972, p. 61) because they resembled the language problems of adults who had experienced strokes and other cerebral insults. The label was perhaps not well chosen because: (1) most of the children given the diagnosis had not developed normal language and then lost it, and (2) the etiology was assumed to involve damage to the central nervous system and was not based on independent examinations for each child. Some clinicians refer to these disorders as "dysphasias (Wyke, 1978)," while the DSM-III (1980) refers to them as "developmental language disorders, expressive or receptive types."

Expressive and receptive language disorders are communication disorders related to the production and understanding of oral language. Successful communication requires that individuals be able to decode the oral productions of others and to encode their own messages with all the participants sharing the same linguistic system or set of rules. There are rules for combining speech sounds (phonology), for choosing symbols to express meaning (semantics), and for combining symbols to produce sentences (grammar). Language disorders may reflect a disuse or misuse of these rules. Diagnosis of a particular language disorder necessitates a comprehensive assessment of language functioning and related abilities.

Assessment. A diagnosis of an expressive or receptive language disorder requires the ruling out of certain other diagnoses and factors, particularly infantile autism, mental retardation, and general hearing loss. Formal assessment includes auditory, psychological, and language testing as well as interviews and medical evaluations.

Assessment of general intellectual functioning for children with language disorders poses special problems in that both expressive and receptive language are important components of cognitive functioning. Since the major intelligence tests, such as the Stanford-Binet and the Wechsler scales, rely heavily on both expressive and receptive language, children with these disorders would be penalized on these tests. If the child's handicap is not severe, that is, the child has some language skills, these tests might be administered and used for assessing strengths and weaknesses.

The clinician may also want to administer one of the intelligence tests that are not dependent on expressive or expressive and receptive language. The Peabody Picture Vocabulary Test (Dunn, 1965) uses verbal instructions, but the child is required only to point to one of four pictures; this test provides a measure of receptive language. The Arthur Adaptation of the Leiter International Performance Scale (Arthur, 1952) is administered without the clinician using spoken language and does not utilize the child's language for scoring. This scale has fifty-four items arranged in order of difficulty; each item requires the child to match a set of blocks with a picture.

An expressive, developmental language disorder is diagnosed when the child's vocal language is significantly delayed, but the delay is not associated with a hearing impairment, mental retardation, or the other features of infantile autism. Evidence of age-appropriate understanding of language must be present. Certain aspects of learning may be impaired, in particular, perceptual skills.

A receptive, developmental language disorder is diagnosed when a significant delay is apparent in both the understanding *and* expression of language, but these delays are not associated with a hearing impairment, mental retardation, or the other features of infantile autism. There may also be evidence of impairment in auditory, short-term memory, auditory discrimination, and reading and spelling skills.

Etiology. The families of children with developmental language disorders have a higher-than-average incidence of these and other specific developmental disorders, suggesting the possibility of some genetic contribution to etiology.

A comparison of language-disordered, articulation-disordered, and normal children revealed that the normal and articulation-disordered children had left-hemisphere dominance, while no cerebral dominance pattern emerged for the language-disordered children (Pettit and Helms, 1979). Such findings are difficult to interpret because an absence of left-hemisphere dominance could conceivably be either a precursor or a result of the poor language development.

About one-third to one-half of developmentally aphasic children present clear evidence of damage to the central nervous system. For example, Goldstein, Landau, and Kleffner (1958) found that 40 percent of their sample of aphasic children had abnormal EEG findings. Another third showed signs of minimal brain dysfunction or borderline neurological dysfunction.

Certain behavioral deviations are also accepted as evidence of brain dysfunction by some investigators. Clements (1966, pp. 6–7) has stated that visual-motor-perceptual irregularities and learning disabilities are in themselves valid indices of brain dysfunction. This position, unfortunately, carries the risk of erroneously classifying children as brain damaged, particularly in those instances in which the behavioral measures have not been validated against neurological criteria.

The behavioral findings that have been considered highly indicative of brain dysfunction in children with developmental language disorders are speech-sound imperception and memory defects. In the normal child, speech perception is correlated with pure-tone audiometric findings. For the aphasic child with a receptive developmental language disorder, this relationship does not pertain; that is, the aphasic child's ability to respond to pure tones does not mean the child has the ability to discriminate among speech sounds. Although the aphasic child can usually be taught to discriminate individual speech sounds, the child often has difficulty retaining these discriminations.

Treatment. The speech therapy program for the developmentally aphasic (especially the receptive type of language disorder) child is usually quite complex and extensive. Eisenson (1972) has described a program in which representational behavior is established through initially bypassing the auditory modality and focusing on the visual modality. Later, auditory stimuli are associated with visual stimuli, and, finally, the child is taught to process and produce speech.

The first level begins with a series of match-to-sample tasks in which the child selects from an array of objects an object that is identical to a target object. The objects are supposed to be familiar to the child and may include items such as toys, keys, dishes, and buttons. The child is then moved to a series of tasks in which the matching of objects is based on similar, rather than identical, features.

The second level consists of training in object categorization. That is, the child is taught to choose objects that represent a class or a concept. For example, the child may be asked to choose from an ear of corn, a pencil, and a ball the object that "goes with" a carrot and a potato. In level three, matching of objects is based on function. From an array of objects, such as a soup spoon, a crayon, and a comb, the child is asked to choose the one that goes with the target object, a bowl. At this level the child is encouraged to pantomine the function of the two objects (that is, eating soup).

After these levels are achieved through the use of three-dimensional objects, pictures of the objects are substituted, and training at the three levels is repeated. Matching of geometric forms may also be included in the training.

The therapy program up to this point has focused on visual perception. The next step involves the association of visual stimuli with auditory stimuli. Initially, the pathologist chooses representations of common objects that emit sounds (human speech is not included). Each object is presented visually and paired with its sound a number of times. Then the child is asked to choose from a small array the correct object on the basis of hearing its sound. In that way, the child is introduced to using sound to direct behavior.

The sounds that are used in the visual-auditory training procedure are carefully selected to ensure that the child will pay attention and to include those phonemes that are most easily reproduced. Sometimes, the child spontaneously begins to attempt imitations of sounds during the visual-auditory training procedures, and these attempts are reinforced. In other cases, sound imitation training might be initiated through the use of shaping and reinforcement procedures.

Aphasic children who have successfully completed the above program or who already have those behaviors in their repertoire are then provided with a therapeutic program aimed at establishing and developing speech. The specific program is usually determined by the level of expressive speech as assessed through formal testing and the language sample.

Since normative data have provided relationships between the average number of words per utterance and specific grammatical constructions, knowledge of a child's length of utterance enables the pathologist to design a speech program that is appropriate to the child's developmental level. Thus, for children whose average utterance is two words, the pathologist formulates two-word utterances that include verbal-noun, adjective-noun, noun-verbal, and noun-adverb combinations, since these are the combinations that tend to occur developmentally. The pathologist's formulations are also determined by the possibility of their being acted out visually or presented pictorially. For example, the pathologist might choose "eat cookie" because it represents a behavior that the pathologist could demonstrate or show in a picture. Therapy consists of pairing the pathologist's verbal presentation of the construction with a visual representation of the construction followed by asking the child to repeat the construction and perform the behavior. Through these pairings the child begins to acquire a speech repertoire for describing events in his or her environment. Similar procedures are used for the acquisition of longer speech utterances.

Developmental language disorders are sometimes very difficult to treat or do not improve with the usual forms of speech therapy. A follow-up study of children with disorders in articulation and language revealed that language problems continued through adulthood while problems with articulation did not (Hall and Tomblin, 1978). Programs similar to that of Lovaas' for autistic children and training that emphasizes nonvocal communication (signing) appear to offer some promise for the more severely affected children (Vanderheiden and Grilley, 1975).

speech articulation problems

Problems with articulation refer to errors in the production of speech sounds or phonemes (the smallest elements of a language). Phonemic errors are evaluated in the context of development norms; that is, the capacity to produce certain sounds varies as a function of both age and sex. During the early years, articulatory proficiency is quite variable. Girls, for example, tend to approximate adult-level proficiency by the age of six to seven years, while boys achieve this level of proficiency about one year later.

The articulatory errors that young children make are not a random sample of possible errors. The child's earliest words consist of sounds that can be produced with ease. These words almost always consist of nasal consonants, labial (lip) sounds, and vowels (for example, "ma-ma," "da-da"). The production of specific sounds tends to occur in a developmental sequence (for example, /d/ before /l/, /k/ before /t/, /m/ before /n/. This ordering may be due to several factors: the structure of the speech apparatus, ease of sound production, and relative difficulty of sound discriminability.

Assessment. Deficiencies in articulation are the most common type of speech disorder among children. Occasionally, preschool children are referred for articulation problems, but children with these problems are not usually identified until they enter school. Prior to evaluating speech and language, the speech pathologist usually requests the administration of an audiologic (hearing) test. An interview with the parents is also considered an essential part of the assessment procedure. The parental interview focuses on the child's developmental history with respect to responsiveness to sounds and words as well as verbal expression. The parents are also asked about the child's early eating behavior and whether there were problems with sucking, swallowing, or chewing.

The information provided by the parents and other professionals who have seen the child often facilitates the assessment procedure in that the focus of diagnostic testing may be sharpened. Generally, the speech pathologist's assessment includes an inspection of the interior of the mouth and an evaluation of tongue movement, since structural abnormalities of the mouth, lips, and teeth as well as limitation of tongue movement interfere with normal articulation.

The evaluation of speech itself is conducted both formally and informally. During informal assessment the pathologist attempts to engage the child in conversation about topics of interest to the child. The child's spontaneous speech is evaluated in terms of the standards for phoneme usage. A record is kept of the occurrence of sound substitutions, sound omissions, and sound distortions. Formal evaluation consists of the administration of standardized articulation tests (Darley, Fay, Newman, Rees, and Siegel, 1979). The goal of the speech pathologist is to determine whether there is evidence for either articulatory immaturity or articulatory dysmaturation. Articulatory immaturity refers to an articulatory speech pattern that is typical of children younger than the client. Such patterns frequently occur in children who are mentally retarded or of borderline intelligence. Articulatory dysmaturation refers to articulatory speech patterns that are not typical at any developmental stage. These patterns are usually associated with structural defects, motor problems and neurological abnormalities.

Etiology. Articulation problems have been associated with a variety of etiological factors. Articulation skills are highly correlated with mental age, suggesting that the factors associated with slow rates of intellectual development are also possible causes of problems with articulation. For example, a high rate of problems with communication has been associated with prematurity and neonatal respiratory distress (Ehrlich, Shapiro, Kimball, and Huttner, 1973). Hearing deficits may also account for deficits in articulation. Ear infections are relatively common in preschool years, and left untreated they may impair hearing for substantial periods of time during the critical period of speech acquisition. There may be hearing loss that is confined to certain frequencies. If the impairment is limited to the lower range of frequencies, speech patterns may be markedly affected; in such cases, parents would not necessarily suspect a hearing loss because the child responds to most environmental sounds that usually consist of a broad range of frequencies. Sometimes the child is described as stubborn or preoccupied by the parents because the child's responses to their directions are minimal. Children with hearing deficits rapidly become adept at learning to lip read and respond to gestural cues, thus, often causing a postponement of referral until the articulatory speech problem is severe.

Articulatory problems may also be the product of learning experiences. If a child has as a primary speech model a person who has deficits in articulation there may be an increased probability of the child's learning the same pattern through modeling. Likewise, if a child is strongly reinforced for immature speech patterns by adults frequently imitating the child's speech, then these speech patterns may become strengthened. Fortunately, most children are exposed to a wide variety of speech models through urban living arrangements and exposure to radio and television.

Treatment. Historically, several approaches have been taken to treat articulatory problems remedially. During the 1920s and 1930s, emphasis was given to the phonetic-placement method in which the child was taught the "correct" position of the tongue and mouth for production of specific sounds. Subsequent research, however, has shown that a specific sound may be achieved with a variety of positions in different persons.

Since hearing is the primary sensory system for the acquisition of speech during the preschool years, many pathologists have advocated the teaching of auditory discrimination as fundamental to the correction of articulatory problems. Although originally developed thirty-five years ago, the "stimulus method" of auditory training has gained increasingly wide acceptance through the years. This method also provides the child with a system of monitoring his or her own speech. Training auditory discrimination, including self-discrimination, makes probable the generalization outside of the speech therapy sessions.

Most contemporary speech pathologists do not restrict themselves to any single approach to therapy, although among the various options, auditory stimulation is still the principal component or foundation of most therapeutic programs. The process of correcting misarticulated speech sounds must focus on these related tasks: learning to identify the sounds and discriminate among them, learning to produce the sounds in a variety of phonetic contexts, and learning to generalize the correct sounds outside of the therapy setting (Powers, 1971, p. 894).

Auditory discrimination training takes up the larger proportion of the initial therapy sessions and is reduced as the sound production phase is undertaken. The pathologist introduces the sound in an interesting manner to ensure that the child will pay attention. The sound is given a name to establish its identity; for example, the /s/ sound may be called the "snake sound." To facilitate the child's learning to discriminate the stimulus sound from other sounds, the pathologist presents a series of sounds that includes the stimulus sound, and the child makes a particular response each time the stimulus sound occurs.

Initially, sounds that are easily confused with the stimulus sound are not included in the series; they are gradually included as the child becomes proficient in making the easier discriminations. After the child is able to discriminate the stimulus sound from all other speech sounds, the pathologist begins to introduce the sound as the initial sound in single words. This series of discriminations is followed by training the child to discriminate the stimulus sound when it appears in any position in the word. Training also includes the pathologist's presenting both the correct and incorrect versions of the sound and teaching the child to differentiate them. Throughout this phase of discrimination training, the pathologist may use other sense modalities to facilitate the learning process. With young school-age children, for example, visually presented letters and words may be presented in conjunction with the auditory stimuli.

Relatively little research has been done on the production phase of articulation training. Webb and Siegenthaler (1957), however, in a study comparing training methods, found that verbal instructions on how to make the sound and auditory presentation of the sound followed by evaluation of the child's sound production was the most effective combination. Training in sound production proceeds from the single sound through words, phrases, and sentences to spontaneous speech. Again, the child's motivation and attention are best used by the careful choice of stimuli including visual materials and by the reinforcement of successful productions.

Generalization outside of therapy is considered by the pathologist beginning in the earliest stages of treatment. That is, the pathologist chooses words to use in therapy that are commonly said in everyday verbal interactions. The pathologist's hope is that the correct production of a word in the therapy sessions will be learned well enough to be reproduced in other environments. To facilitate such carry-over the pathologist may ask the child to perform specific tasks at home or school, such as finding pictures of objects that contain a specific stimulus sound.

Speech therapy with children often involves the parents as well. Most pathologists agree that the parents should be well informed about their child's problem and the steps that will be taken to remediate it. In addition, parents are encouraged to be supportive and positive toward the child. Pathologists disagree, however, on the extent to which parents should be directly involved in the speech therapy itself. Some research studies suggest that trained parents can be effective therapists for their own children, while other studies suggest that parental involvement may be detrimental. Future research will likely begin to delineate those factors that will predict which parents will be more effective than others.

Conclusions

A specific learning disability refers to significantly poor progress in a particular area of functioning, such as basic academic skills (reading, spelling, arithmetic, and writing) and expressive and receptive language skills, relative to an expected level of achievement. The expected level of achievement is based primarily on the child's chronological age and IQ score.

The available research indicates that specific learning disabilities may be caused by prenatal, perinatal, and postnatal physical factors; hereditary factors may be implicated, but definitive research evidence is lacking. While psychological factors may exacerbate both learning and behavioral problems, there is no evidence that such factors are responsible for the initiation of specific learning disabilities.

The most successful treatment programs appear to be those that focus directly on developing the deficient skill area. Older learning-disabled children may benefit further from psychotherapy or behavior therapy to ameliorate either a poor self-image or classroom behavior problems, or both.

Recommended Readings

Benton, A. L., and **Pearl, D.**, eds., *Dyslexia: An Appraisal of Current Knowledge.* New York: Oxford University Press, 1978. An excellent review of current information on the diagnosis, etiology, and remediation of specific reading disabilities.

Farnham-Diggory, S., *Learning Disabilities: A Psychological Perspective.* Cambridge, Mass.: Harvard University Press, 1978.

Kinsbourne, M., and **Caplan, P. J.**, *Children's Learning and Attention Problems.* Boston: Little, Brown, 1979.

Morehead, D. M., and **Morehead, A. E.**, eds., *Normal and Deficient Child Language.* Baltimore, Md.: University Park Press, 1976.

Schiefelbusch, R. L., and **Lloyd, L. L.**, eds., *Language Perspectives: Acquisition, Retardation, and Intervention.* Baltimore, Md.: University Park Press, 1974.

conduct
disorders

11

Mo, a thirteen-year-old boy, was referred by juvenile court because he had been caught stealing a television set. His previous contacts with the court involved truancy from school.

Mo was the third of seven children. His father deserted the home when Mo was two years old and has not been seen since that time. The younger children were fathered by a man with whom his mother currently lives. Mo does not get along with this man who has physically abused him on several occasions while drunk. His older brothers are currently in a juvenile training school for car theft.

Mo's mother, who looked much older than her age, could not recall any problems during her pregnancy. She did not receive prenatal care, and Mo was delivered in a hospital emergency room because "he came so fast." The mother reported that Mo's problems were due to his "getting in with the wrong people."

The school reports indicated that Mo had

academic problems beginning in the early grades. Although his intelligence test scores were only slightly below average, his achievement in all school subjects was poor due to "motivational" problems. The attendance record indicated sharp increases in the number of absences during the past two years.

Mo freely admitted that he hates school and is looking forward to dropping out, getting a job, and moving away from his family. When asked what kind of a job he would get, he responded that he didn't know but that "something would turn up." Mo's enjoyment in life seemed to revolve around his friends, some of whom were older than he and had already dropped out of school. He and an older boy were assigned the job of stealing a television to furnish the group's club room. Mo would not identify the other boy, who had escaped, or other members of his group.

Certain behavior disorders tend to cluster together because they are what might be termed "acting out" behaviors. That is, the children who have these problems are doing something that violates the standards or norms set by adult society. The general label of "conduct disorders" was chosen to describe this group because factor analytic studies provide considerable evidence that these problem behaviors are intercorrelated (Quay, 1979). These disorders may vary in their impact both on the individual child and on the persons in the child's environment; that is, some are primarily harmful to other persons, while others have their greatest negative impact on the individual displaying the disorder. In this chapter, we discuss several classes of conduct disorders: the hyperactivity syndrome, delinquent behavior, and substance abuse.

hyperactivity, impulsivity, and attentional problems

In contrast to the socially withdrawn or anxious child whose disorder is characterized by deficiencies in the normal behavioral repertoire, the hyperactive, impulsive, or disruptive child may be characterized as having behavioral excesses. That is, some behaviors occur too often or quickly or are inappropriate in particular settings. As is true for some of the other behavior disorders, the criteria for referral and diagnosis are variable and depend largely on the standards of the adults in the child's environment and the other problems that the child may be having. Although a number of objective methods for assessing hyperactivity (for example, Routh and Schroeder, 1976), and impulsivity (Kagan, 1966) are available, their results do not strongly agree with other criteria; the objective methods tend to be used for research, while methods based on clinical observation and interview are used for diagnosis of referred children. The disorders described in this section are sometimes found in combination with other disorders, such as mental retardation, learning disabilities, and delinquency.

assessment

The hyperactive child syndrome (hyperactivity, impulsivity, and short attention span) has received considerable focus in the research literature during the past ten to fifteen years, although it was described in the professional literature as early as the turn of this century. It is likely to be one of the most common behavior disorders (Weiss and Hechtman, 1979). During its long history, the syndrome has received a variety of diagnostic labels; some labels, such as "hyperkinetic" are descriptive, while others, such as "minimal brain dysfunction" and "maturational lag" imply etiologies or prognosis, or both. While most diagnostic labels give primary status to the hyperactivity, the authors of DSM-III have chosen to give primary status to the attentional problems. The two subtypes of the disorder are (1) Attention Deficit Disorder with Hyperactivity and (2) Attention Deficit without Hyperactivity. DSM-III (pp. 43-44) specifies the following diagnostic criteria for children between the ages of eight and ten for Attention Deficit Disorder with Hyperactivity:

A. Inattention. At least three of the following:
    1. often fails to finish things he or she starts
    2. often doesn't seem to listen
    3. easily distracted
    4. has difficulty concentrating on schoolwork and other tasks requiring sustained attention
    5. has difficulty sticking to a play activity
B. Impulsivity. At least two of the following:
    1. often acts before thinking
    2. shifts excessively from one activity to another
    3. has difficulty organizing work (this not being due to cognitive impairment)
    4. needs a lot of supervision
    5. frequently calls out in class
    6. has difficulty awaiting turn in game or group situations
C. Hyperactivity. At least two of the following:
    1. runs about or climbs on things excessively
    2. has difficulty sitting still or fidgets excessively
    3. has difficulty staying seated
    4. moves about excessively during sleep
    5. is always "on the go" or acts as if "driven by a motor"
D. Onset before the age of seven
E. Duration of least six months
F. Not due to Schizophrenia, Affective Disorder, or Severe or Profound Mental Retardation.
    The diagnostic criteria for Attention Deficit Disorder without Hyperactivity are the same except that the child has never had signs of hyperactivity.

Recognition is given to the likelihood that younger children will have more symptoms and that the symptoms may decrease in one-to-one and new situations and increase in classroom situations. Teachers' reports are considered to be valid because they are more familiar with age-appropriate norms.

Although they also tend to vary with age, a number of other characteristics have been associated with this syndrome:

1. obstinacy
2. stubbornness
3. negativism
4. bossiness
5. bullying
6. increased mood lability
7. low frustration tolerance
8. temper outbursts
9. low self-esteem
10. lack of response to discipline

These characteristics may be by-products of the academic and social problems frequently encountered by children with attentional deficits or hyperactivity. In a significant number of instances, these children have specific learning disabilities and may experience a greater amount of negative responses from teachers and parents for poor school performance. Children with this disorder are also more likely to have conduct disorders at older ages. Retrospective research suggests that during infancy hyperactive children have a higher frequency of irregular and poor sleep patterns, colic, and feeding problems (Stewart, Pills, Craig, Dieruf, 1966). As toddlers, the hyperactive children are described as getting into everything and rapidly moving from one play object to another. They are more likely to have accidents and require more supervision. Preschool hyperactive children present an increasing number of problems to their parents. They require more individual attention because they tend not to get along with peers and are apt to be disruptive in the neighborhood and nursery school. Parents' admonitions are frequently described as not working, and other adults begin to reject the child.

Referral is most commonly made during the early elementary school years. Behavior that was tolerated by parents and some nursery school teachers becomes unacceptable in the classroom where activities are more sedentary and oriented toward larger groups. The child's attentional deficit may begin to manifest itself in poor classroom achievement as well. Poor peer relationships continue to be manifested. During adolescence, poor school performance and conduct disorders are likely to be the primary problems; although the lack of appropriate peer relationships takes on increasingly greater importance with age.

Weiss and Hechtman (1979) recommend a comprehensive assessment battery for hyperactive children that includes a careful history of the pregnancy and the child's development, cognitive educational assessment, behavioral assessment, neurological examination, and assessment of the child's intrapsychic processes and family interactions. This recommendation indicates a recognition of the psychological complexities that are likely to be involved in the child's problem. In general, the older the child at initial diagnosis, the greater is the likelihood that the disorder is affecting virtually all aspects of the child's life.

etiology

Hyperactivity, impulsivity, and attentional defects are diagnosed in boys at a greater frequency than in girls; ratios ranging from five to one to 10 to one have been reported. Estimates of the prevalence in the population vary widely, probably reflecting differing diagnostic criteria.

Most of the research conducted thus far has indicated that this syndrome is associated with genetic and physical etiological factors. Several family pedigree studies and adoptive studies (Cantwell, 1975) support the view that hereditary factors play a significant role in the etiology of hyperactivity. Hyperactive children have family histories of hyperactivity and learning problems. The histories of hyperactive children include a higher incidence of vaginal bleeding and preeclampsia during mothers' pregnancy, prematurity, and low birth weight. They have more minor congenital disorders (Waldrop, Bell, McLaughlin, and Halverson, 1978) and an increase in the incidence of seizures, encephalitis and brain injury in their backgrounds. Several biochemical studies have found differences between hyperactive and nonhyperactive children (for example, Shaywitz, Cohen, and Bowers, 1977), suggesting deficiencies or abnormalities of neurotransmitter substances or of enzymatic systems. The role of food additives in causing hyperactivity (Feingold, 1975) continues to be examined, but the results to date indicate either no effect or a possible effect for a small number of children. It also appears that lead poisoning may be a factor in a small number of cases (Baloh, Sturm, Green, and Gleser, 1975).

treatment

Medication has perhaps been the most common treatment for hyperactivity. The use of medication for behavioral control has aroused much controversy and suggestions that high percentages of school children are being subjected to "behavior modification" drugs. Surveys in the early 1970s indicated that between 2 and 3 percent of school children were receiving medication for hyperactivity.

During the 1960s and 1970s a large number of studies described positive effects on the behavior of hyperactive children through the use of the stimulant drugs methyphenidate (Ritalin) and dextroamphetamine. These short-term studies (three to six weeks) found decreases in aggression, purposeless activity, and impulsivity and increases in sustained attention, learning of rote material, and performance on fine motor tasks (Weiss and Hechtman, 1979). A nine-week study showed a peak enhancement of learning in hyperactive children after a dose of 0.3 milligram of Ritalin per kilogram of body weight, while social behavior showed the most improvement after a dose of 1.0 milligram per kilogram, suggesting that the effects of medication may vary depending on both the dosage and the behavior being evaluated (Sprague and Sleator, 1977).

Until recently, the responsiveness pattern of hyperactive children to stimulants was attributed to a "paradoxical effect," namely, that hyperactive children were being slowed down by drugs that serve as stimulants for nonhyperactive persons. A study by Rapaport and her colleagues (1978), however, indicated that normal pre-pubertal boys showed comparable cognitive and behavioral effects.

The negative effects of stimulant drugs are being increasingly investigated. Among the known side effects, reduced appetite and weight loss frequently occur when stimulant drug treatment is initiated; these effects are diminished when the medication is administered at mealtimes. In addition, some children experience stomach aches, headaches, irritability, or sad feelings. These side effects are some-times relieved by reducing the dosage. Long-term use of stimulants may result in a decreased rate of growth. A review of the literature by Roche and his colleagues (1979) concludes that "high-normal" doses moderately suppress weight increases and may cause mild suppression of growth in stature; these effects are only partially reduced when treatment is discontinued during the summer early in treatment.

Controversy has arisen over the long-term behavioral affects of stimulant medi-cation, although very few adequately designed studies have been conducted. There has been some suggestion that the beneficial effects tend to decrease over time. One outcome study (Weiss, Kruger, Danielson, and Elman, 1975) found no differ-ences during adolescence among groups of hyperactive children treated with Ritalin for 3 to 5 years or chlorpromazine for 1½ to 3 years and those receiving no medica-tion on the following measures: school performance, hyperactivity, emotional ad-justment, antisocial behavior, and mothers' views of overall improvement. It has been documented that hyperactive children continue to have a variety of problems through adolescence, particularly in school and do not "grow out" of their prob-lems as previously believed.

What can be concluded from the research on medication is that stimulant drugs appear to have a beneficial short-term effect but that they do not seem to affect the hyperactive persons's status later in a long-term treatment program or after the treatment has ceased. These conclusions suggest that stimulant drugs should no longer be considered a primary form of therapy for hyperactivity.

It appears that greater long-term success may be found in behavior therapy (O'Leary, Pelham, Rosenbaum, and Price, 1976) and educational programs with perhaps some assistance from medication for short periods of time. The research history on the effects of behavior therapy is much shorter than that for medication, but during the 1970s a large number of studies demonstrated significant changes in the behavior of hyperactive children (O'Leary and O'Leary, 1977 and Ayllon and Rosenbaum, 1977). Operant conditioning methods using a variety of rewards has been a popular approach, but long-term positive effects have not yet been demon-strated.

Several studies have utilized a combination of behavior therapy and medication in the treatment programs and found that medication facilitated the improvement of behavior initially but could be phased out (O'Leary and Pelham, 1978; Ayllon, Layman, and Kandel, 1975). In the Ayllon study reinforcement of academic per-formance suppressed hyperactivity; the academic gain produced by the behavioral program was considerably greater than that found during the medication phase.

It is perhaps premature to specify which type of treatment is the more effective. The effects of stimulants appear to be general, while the effects of behavior therapy tend to be more specific. It may be suggested that medication makes it easier for the hyperactive child to learn in the classroom if an individualized educational program is designed for that particular child; the child on medication alone may be less disruptive but may not be making adequate academic progress. The greater expense of the behavior therapy programs may be necessary to demonstrate long-term gains in behavior and school performance.

Another series of studies has evaluated the effectiveness of behavior therapy approaches for reducing impulsive behavior. In this context, impulsive behavior is viewed as behavior that is lacking in self-control and includes problems such as aggression, overactivity, and inadequate attention (Kendall and Finch, 1979). Many of these studies use Kagan's (1966) Matching Familiar Figures Test (MFFT) for identification of impulsive children and evaluation of the treatment program. Children who make an excessive number of errors and who respond to the items too quickly are designated as impulsive. The approaches that have been used to modify impulsivity include imposed delay, modeling, response contingencies, and self-instructional training.

Several studies examined the effect of an imposed delay period before the child was allowed to respond to the training task. The results generally indicated that an imposed delay increased the amount of time children took before responding to subsequent tasks but did not improve the error rate. Research findings of studies using modeling by nonimpulsive adults were similar, namely, increases in latency and no changes in errors. When peer models also verbalized their task strategy, however, both latency and errors improved (Cohen and Przybycien, 1974).

Studies using response contingencies have attempted to train impulsive children to be reflective (longer delays before making a response and fewer errors). The use of rewards alone (either verbal or nonverbal) was not optimally effective for modifying impulsiveness. Response-cost contingencies (initially giving the child a number of rewards, such as tokens, and then taking one away each time an inappropriate response is made), on the other hand, have proven effective. Research comparing the effectiveness of reward and response cost for impulsive and reflective children indicates that impulsive children perform better under response-cost conditions and reflective children perform better under reward conditions (Nelson, Finch, and Hooke, 1975).

Self-instructional training has perhaps received the most emphasis in attempts to modify impulsive behavior. Verbal self-instructions appear to have an important role in normal children's control of their own behavior. The assumption has been that impulsive children lack an adequate self-instructional repertoire and therefore have poor control of their own behavior. Meichenbaum and Goodman's (1971) procedures for training self-instruction have been the basis for most of the research with impulsive children. These procedures include modeling of self-instructions, overt and covert rehearsal, prompts, feedback, and social reinforcement.

Self-instructional procedures have been very successful in altering the inappropriate behaviors of impulsive, hyperactive, disruptive, and aggressive children (Meichenbaum, 1979).

delinquency and antisocial behavior

Juvenile delinquency refers to a wide range of behaviors that are considered to be legal offenses for persons who are younger than the statutory age limit (between sixteen and twenty years). These behaviors may or may not be illegal for adults and may vary somewhat from state to state. A specific behavior is judged to be delinquent on the basis of community and state law and the age of the person performing the behavior. Strictly speaking, the term "delinquent" refers to a child (in the eyes of the law) who has been convicted of a legal offense. In the gathering of statistics, investigators use a variety of labels and of operational definitions, such as *agency delinquents* (number of persons arrested), *alleged delinquents* (number of persons brought to court), and *adjusted delinquents* (number of persons convicted). In addition, several researchers interested in population statistics utilize the terms *legal delinquents* (number of persons committing a delinquent act) and *detected delinquents* (number of persons caught engaging in a delinquent act).

Since conviction of a crime is usually preceded by a number of events and correlated behaviors, researchers have tended to study delinquency in its broadest context, society, in contrast to focusing on the specific behaviors of specific individuals. Thus, sociologists have provided us with much of our knowledge with respect to etiology and assessment and have made significant recommendations in the

chiatrists focused primarily on the treatment of individual delinquents, but, more recently, behavioral clinicians have begun to design effective intervention programs for groups of delinquents.

assessment

It has been estimated that at least half of the teenage population has committed one or more delinquent acts. Only a small minority of these teenagers are brought to court and convicted. A number of factors determine whether or not a person will be caught, arrested, and convicted of a delinquent offense: the specific act (who or what it affects), background characteristics of the individual (for example, socioeconomic status, history of previous antisocial or delinquent acts), and presence or absence of adequate parental control.

Reports during the last ten to fifteen years indicate that criminal offenses in general have been increasing at a rate higher than that of population growth. The rate of delinquent acts has been increasing steadily since 1950 both in the United States and in many other industrialized countries. Current figures indicate that about 3 percent of children between the ages of ten and seventeen are referred to juvenile courts. Juvenile males are arrested far more often than females, and four times as many boys as girls reach juvenile court. The charges against boys tend to be related to property offenses, while those against girls include unmanageability, running away, and sexual misconduct. In recent years, however, the proportion of girls involved in the more serious crimes has been increasing.

Delinquency occurs at a higher rate in urban, or congested, areas than rural areas. One study of delinquency among ethnic groups in a large city indicated that the highest rates occurred for the children of the most recent immigrants to the city. Persons of lower socioeconomic status are arrested proportionately more often than their middle-class peers. About half of the juveniles appearing in court are being charged for the first time or for minor offenses. Juveniles crimes account for a greater proportion of thefts and a smaller proportion of violence against persons.

Until the last century, juveniles who committed crimes were treated in essentially the same way as adults. Around the beginning of the 1900s laws began to be changed to provide more protection for children. One of these laws provided for the establishment of the first juvenile court in Chicago. The purpose of this court was to provide help for children who were neglected or delinquent. The delinquent thus became viewed as a child without adequate family or financial support. The juvenile court adopted as its goal the diagnosis and treatment of children rather than punishment, and its proceedings were considerably less formal than those of the regular courts with judges being allowed considerably greater discretionary powers.

While there are now juvenile courts in all U.S. legal jurisdictions, the quality of these courts varies greatly. Few of the juvenile courts function ideally, however, because large numbers of cases are being handled by too few case workers, probation officers, and judges. Moreover, the courts generally do not have adequate psychological or psychiatric services and must either depend on other agencies for these services or process cases without these services. Studies have determined that juvenile court judges spend an average of ten to fifteen minutes on each case. Probation officers spend about half their time gathering data in preparation for court hearings; the other half of their time is given to the supervision of an average of seventy-five posthearing cases.

The process of becoming identified as a legal delinquent involves a series of decisions made by persons in the law enforcement and judicial systems. A police officer, who has been called to investigate a potential crime, is often the first decision maker. In many instances of juvenile offenses the police officer determines whether a crime has been committed and whether the juvenile is referred to juvenile court. Even in cases where the juvenile clearly engaged in the criminal behavior, the police officer may choose not to refer the juvenile to the court; such a decision usually rests on the severity of the behavior and the officer's estimate of the likelihood of future delinquent behavior. The estimate of recurrence is based on the child's home environment and the amount of parental control. It is not uncommon for the parents to report that they cannot control the juvenile's behavior.

Police officers are not the only source of referrals to juvenile court. Any adult, including the juvenile's parents, may file a petition and require a hearing in juvenile court. In cases involving arrest, the juvenile may be released to the parents or incarcerated while awaiting the hearing. Over 90 percent of juvenile court districts have only county jails for incarcerating juveniles who are awaiting hearings. A small, but increasing, percentage of juvenile court districts have juvenile detention homes in which arrested juveniles may be held.

The law requires that juveniles wait no longer than five days for a hearing by a judge. During this period a juvenile court counselor or a social worker gathers information regarding the juvenile's environmental (home, school, social) background. Although these court employees are called counselors and social workers, frequently they have had no formal training in these professional areas. The requirement for these positions is usually a bachelor's degree, but the academic field of study is not specified as a requirement in the job descriptions.

In recent years there has been some movement away from the informal court hearing in that the juvenile now must be represented by legal counsel. Present at a typical juvenile court hearing are the presiding judge, the juvenile and the parents, the arresting officer or petitioner or both, the prosecuting attorney, the defense attorney, and the court counselor. The judge hears the evidence and recommendations and makes a decision as soon as possible. More than one session of a hearing may occur in instances in which more information is requested by the judge.

In many contemporary juvenile courts, the specific charges are formulated in terms of either a delinquent act (a crime) or an undisciplined act (a behavior that is not a crime for adults). Relatively few juveniles are brought to court without strong evidence of their involvement in the alleged behavior. A proportionately greater number of juveniles who have engaged in illegal behaviors do not reach the courts, but there is reason to believe that those who receive court hearings are not a random sample of individuals who have engaged in the small illegal behaviors.

A number of investigators have attempted to classify delinquents and to determine the personality and behavioral characteristics of juveniles within each category. As in the cases of other behavior disorders, the classification labels themselves reflect a heterogeneity of descriptive and behavioral characteristics as well as known and inferred etiologic factors.

DSM-III describes four classifications that relate to delinquency: (1) undersocialized, aggressive, (2) undersocialized, nonaggressive, (3) socialized, aggressive, and (4) socialized, nonaggressive. The undersocialized types have not established normal patterns of affection and close relationships with other persons, including peers. While there may be superficial relationships, they are generally one sided; egocentricism is a primary feature, and others will be manipulated for advantages with no consideration for reciprocation. Concern for the feelings and well-being of others as well as feelings of guilt are usually absent. The age of onset for the undersocialized types is usually prepubertal. The socialized types have a history of close attachment to others but may be manipulative and guiltless toward people to whom they are not closely attached. The age of onset for the socialized types is usually during adolescence.

The aggressive types repetitively violate the rights of others through physical violence, such as assault or rape, or thefts outside the home that involve confrontation with a victim. The nonaggressive types are characterized by repeated violations of important rules, such as truancy and running away from home, persistent lying both in and out of the home, vandalism, fire setting, or stealing.

These disorders tend to be far more common among boys than girls, except perhaps for the undersocialized, nonaggressive type that may be as common among girls as boys. They are also associated with a variety of problems in the home, school, and community. Smoking, drinking, drug abuse, and sexual precocity are common. School achievement is typically below that expected on the basis of age and intelligence test scores. A history of hyperactivity, attentional problems, or specific learning disabilities, or a combination of these problems, is also likely to be present. The socialized types may be members of gangs that promote the antisocial behavior.

Another approach to the classification of problems related to juvenile delinquency and antisocial behaviors involves the application of factor analytic techniques to behavioral and personality characteristics. Data on these characteristics or test items are collected from a large number of delinquents. Correlations are then determined for all possible pairs of items, and factor analysis identifies groups of items that seem to be measuring the same characteristics. These groups of items are factors and represent types of delinquency. Each factor is given a name that the investigator determines is descriptive of the items relating to that factor.

Quay's (1964) factor analytic study of the behaviors (obtained from case history files) of institutionalized, delinquent boys identified three types of delinquencies labeled "socialized-subcultural delinquency, unsocialized-psychopathic delinquency, and disturbed-neurotic delinquency." Factor analysis of items completed by the delinquents themselves has also resulted in essentially the same types or dimensions of delinquency.

The socialized-subcultural delinquent typically lives in an environment that is supportive of delinquent behavior. This environment is characterized by slum neighborhoods, poverty, large families, ample models of criminal behavior, and inadequate parents. The delinquent child tends to have a lower-than-average IQ score and a history of poor school work.

The unsocialized-psychopathic delinquent appears to be very similar in characteristics to persons traditionally diagnosed as antisocial personality. These individuals seem to be incapable of developing and maintaining close relationships with other persons, and they tend to defy authority and actively seek trouble. Research studies indicate that a large percentage of children diagnosed as sociopathic continue to engage in antisocial behavior and are arrested for nontraffic offenses during adulthood. Socioeconomic status and family inadequacy are not as significant in unsocialized-psychopathic delinquency as they are in socialized-subcultural delinquency.

In contrast to the previous two groups, the delinquents labeled as "disturbed-neurotic" share very few common characteristics. There is a strong suggestion that delinquency in this group is accompanied by other behavior problems such as mental retardation, psychosis, and neurosis, and evidence of brain damage.

Most of the research on the classification of delinquency has focused on males because of the higher proportion of male delinquency, but recent trends suggest that the incidence of crimes by females is increasing at a greater rate than that of males. Both clinical descriptions and a small amount of research suggest that the types of delinquency described for males are also found for females. Hetherington, Stouwie, and Ridberg (1971) observed family interaction patterns for institutionalized female delinquents. Their results indicated that neurotic-disturbed delinquent girls were passive and inactive in contrast to the unsocialized-psychopathic and socialized-subcultural delinquent girls who were both assertive and disruptive. Other research (Butler, 1965) has identified two subtypes of the female unsocialized-psychopathic delinquency pattern: "immature-impulsive," characterized by overt manipulation, aggression, and impulsive behavior and "covert manipulation," characterized by an outward appearance of conformity and hostile reactions when the manipulation is discovered.

The use of behavioral descriptions and the application of factor analytic techniques in the area of juvenile delinquency have served to clarify some of the diagnostic and classification problems. The usefulness of these approaches will be determined on the basis of whether these types of delinquency can be associated with specific etiological factors and whether they respond differentially to various forms of treatment.

etiology

A number of etiological factors have been hypothesized to be involved in juvenile delinquency and antisocial behavior. Although the great majority of contemporary studies have focused on the psychological or environmental causes, the earliest theories emphasized constitutional and genetic causes. Earlier searches for a simple etiologic factor have largely given way to a general agreement that delinquent behaviors have multiple causes, and current research is being conducted on a broad spectrum of potential etiologic factors.

Genetic and physical factors. A recurring theoretical question has been whether man is by nature an aggressive animal or whether aggressive and antisocial behaviors are learned. Freud presented two views of aggression. He initially believed that aggression was simply a response to the frustration or prevention of id-related behaviors. Later, he revised his theory and elevated aggression (death instinct) to the level of a basic drive on a par with, and antagostic to, libido (life instinct). Freud's revised theoretical view has not been generally accepted by his followers.

In more recent years, renewed attention has been given to the possibility of instinctual aggression in humans by the research and writings of Konrad Lorenz (see, for example, 1966). Extensive observation of a wide range of animal species reveals recurrent patterns of aggressive behaviors. Lorenz points out that these patterns serve important functions in the evolutionary scheme, those of selecting the stronger members of a species for mating, ensuring a safer territory, and defending the young. It is interesting that aggressive episodes between members of the same species only rarely result in death. Lorenz builds a case for humans' having the same instinct as animals to act aggressively against their enemies, namely, "that he [the enemy] should be soundly thrashed." Only through the "mistake" of weapon invention have humans killed their enemies, since killing members of one's own species serves no evolutionary purpose. Lorenz recommends that humans' aggressive instincts be recognized and that more effective methods be designed to control or divert them in relatively harmless directions.

Animal research suggests that aggression may be an innate response to a variety of aversive stimuli. For example, aggressive behaviors have been produced in animals by electric shock, separation of the young from their mothers, extinction procedures, and crowding.

A series of studies with humans has supported the frustration-aggression hypothesis formulated by Dollard and others (1939) and based on Freud's earlier descriptions of the genesis of aggression. The hypothesis stated that frustration is always followed by aggression (in varied forms) and that aggression is produced solely by frustration. Frustration was defined as interference with a continuing goal-directed behavior. Laboratory studies with children (for example, Mallick and McCandless, 1966) have also revealed that experimentally manipulated frustration results in a greater number of aggressive responses. Other studies have suggested that the probability of aggressive behavior varies as a function of both the amount of frustration and the amount of anticipated punishment that would result from the aggression.

The frustration-aggression hypothesis has been used to account for the occurrence of antisocial and delinquent behaviors. The environments of a high proportion of delinquents are described as creating high frustration, for example, lack of money, poor job opportunities, and low social status. Moreover, punishment in the form of incarceration is not optimally effective as a deterrent because there is little to lose.

Although genetic factors have repeatedly been suggested as causes of delinquency, relatively few behavior genetic studies examining the role of heredity have been conducted. A review of the research (Christiansen, 1977b) on adult criminals provided no evidence that genetic factors were dominant in the etiology of criminality. Although the studies show higher corcordance rates for identical twins than for fraternal twins, the concordance rates for identical twins tends to be quite low (for example, 15 percent in the Christiansen 1977a study).

The discovery that men with XYY chromosomal configuration (an extra Y chromosome and a total of forty-seven chromosomes) are overrepresented in mental-penal institutions has renewed interest in the role of genetic factors in antisocial behavior. The data suggest that a man with XYY chromosomal configuration has an eighteen times greater chance of being incarcerated in a mental-penal institution than a man with a normal XY configuration. XYY men tend to have greater than average height and below average IQ scores. Height is apparently not a predisposing factor, since tall XY men are not overrepresented in penal institutions. It must be kept in mind that many questions remain unanswered. The great majority of XYY men do not become incarcerated, and we need to discover what factors determine whether or not an XYY individual engages in antisocial behavior. The crimes of XYY men tend to be against property rather than persons (Witkin, 1976), and the amount of crime that they account for is actually quite low. In an effort to learn more about why XYY individuals are more likely to be incarcerated, research studies have been initiated in which chromosome screening is used to identify the XYY boys at birth. The investigators plan to evaluate the children's behaviors at intervals through the developmental years.

Certain constitutional differences between delinquents and nondelinquents have also suggested at least an indirect role of genetic factors. Sheldon (1949) and others have found mesomorphism (muscular body build) to be overrepresented in a sample of delinquent boys.

Additional differences found between delinquents and nondelinquents could reflect the roles of either hereditary factors or early physical trauma (prenatal, perinatal, and postnatal). Several studies have reported a high incidence of abnormal EEG patterns for delinquents; these studies, however, have been criticized for lacking adequate control groups. A particular EEG abnormality, the 14-6 spike pattern, has been associated with delinquent behavior that is characterized by extreme rage and violence under conditions of minimal provocation, but only when it was present in combination with other EEG abnormalities. Neuropsychological test data also show that delinquents are more likely to demonstrate neurological dysfunctions (Berman and Siegal, 1976).

Adolescents and adults in penal institutions, who were diagnosed as psychopathic or antisocial, have been found to show less anxiety on a variety of measures in comparison with other criminals and normal controls. The antisocial criminals had significantly greater preferences for frightening or dangerous activities. In learning tasks involving the avoidance of shock, the antisocial criminals made more shocked errors and showed less physiological responsiveness to the buzzer signifying shock. More recent research has confirmed the earlier finding that sociopaths do not respond normally to painful stimuli. When incentives were offered for tolerance of increasing levels of shock, the sociopaths tolerated significantly higher levels than nonsociopathic prisoners.

Schmauk (1970) compared the efficiency of avoidance learning under these punishment conditions: physical punishment by shock for each incorrect response, loss of a quarter from a pile of forty quarters for each incorrect response, or the verbal statement "wrong" for each incorrect response. Sociopathic prisoners and normal controls were randomly assigned to the three experimental conditions. The sociopaths and controls showed the same amount of learning under the "loss of a quarter" condition, but sociopaths performed significantly more poorly than the controls under the shock and social punishment conditions. The results of this study indicate that physical punishment in the form of shock and verbal feedback for incorrect responses are not as effective in reducing incorrect responses for sociopaths as they are for normal controls. The reasons underlying these differential effects are not well understood but may involve both constitutional factors and past learning experience.

At one time it was believed that mental retardation was a major factor in juvenile delinquency. That is, earlier studies of groups of delinquents showed mean IQ scores to be lower than those of the general population. Subsequent group studies with improved methodology have revealed somewhat smaller differences between the IQ scores of delinquents and nondelinquents. Several hypotheses have been suggested to account for these differences. First, children with lower levels of general intellectual functioning are also slower to learn societal standards for behavior and are more likely to become involved in delinquent behavior. Second, children who are intellectually slower are more likely to be caught while engaging in delinquent behavior and, therefore, are more likely to be brought to court and incarcerated. Third, many lower-class persons (who tend to have lower IQ scores) lack familial and financial support systems that help to keep middle-class people from going to court or being incarcerated.

Brain damage has been suggested as a possible etiological factor on the basis of findings showing that the majority of delinquents have average or better IQ scores but marked deficiencies in academic achievement. That is, the incidence of specific learning disabilities appears to be substantially higher in delinquents than in the school population at large. Since learning disabilities have been associated with a variety of organic factors, the inference is that brain damage may be either directly or indirectly involved in delinquent behavior. Direct causes would include inability to attend to relevant environmental stimuli and consequences and impulsive decision making. Indirect causes would include the psychological effects of poor school achievement (such as decreased levels of social approval and increased levels of extinction and social punishment by teachers, parents, and some peers) that may magnify the reinforcing effects of other peers for delinquent or other antisocial behaviors.

Psychological and environmental factors. Environmental and psychological variables have been considered the primary etiological factors in juvenile delinquency by sociologists, psychiatrists, and clinical psychologists. At the broadest level of analysis are the sociological theories that are applicable to the development of socialized-subcultural delinquency. The anomie theory (Merton, 1957) proposes that lower-class people have the same values and goals as middle-class people, but they are frustrated in their attempts to achieve these goals by legitimate means and resort to illegal methods. This theory seems to be particularly relevant to American society in which nearly every household has a television set that continually propagandizes the advantages of material goods. The lower-class culture theory (Miller, 1958) proposes that lower class children learn values and behaviors that are different from those taught to middle-class children. Miller suggests that lower-class children are not rewarded for obeying rules, are not taught to delay gratification, and have less moral training.

The available research does not support either of these theories as the sole factor in socialized-subcultural delinquency. Ambitious studies by Glueck (1950, 1959, 1968, 1970) and Sheldon have begun to identify variables that discriminate between delinquent and nondelinquent samples of children from the same neighborhood. One study indicated that the following variables occurred more often for delinquents than nondelinquents: lower verbal than performance IQ scores, serious physical or psychological problems in the parents, poor financial management in the family and dependence on welfare, disorganized family life including broken homes, and inadequate supervision by the parents. Although it is generally agreed that these variables are involved in the etiology of juvenile delinquency, our present knowledge does not yet permit an adequate prediction of which children will, in fact, become delinquent. Many children with such adverse conditions in their background will not become delinquent, while others from presumably good home environments will commit crimes.

By far the greatest research attention has been given to the role of learning in the development of aggressive behavior. Although stimulus antecedents may be important determinants in the occurrence of aggression, most investigators have focused on the role of stimulus consequences. Observational studies of young children have suggested that aggressive behavior is often followed by reinforcing consequences, such as peer acquiescence and teacher attention. One might easily speculate that much of the antisocial and delinquent behavior observed in older children is likewise reinforced by peer social approval as well as tangible reinforcers, such as the money or objects stolen. Developmental studies suggest that parents may tend to reinforce certain aggressive behaviors in boys but not in girls. Most of the studies show that boys are more aggressive than girls (Feshbach, 1970). Longitudinal studies, however, reveal significant positive correlations between certain aggressive behaviors during the preschool period and later ages for boys but not for girls. Although other explanations are possible for the apparent sex differences in the continuity of aggressive behavior, it is generally held that parents are more permissive of aggressive behavior in boys. To decrease the incidence of aggression, Eron (1980) has recommended that parents be advised to socialize boys as they currently socialize girls.

Modeling and imitation have been invoked as important determinants of aggression. A number of studies (Bandura, 1965; Bandura, Ross, and Ross, 1963) have suggested that exposing children to either live or filmed aggressive models increases the probability of the children's engaging in aggressive behaviors. The modeling research, however, also shows that modeled aggression is affected by the child's perception of the social status of the model and the consequences to the model or to the child, suggesting that the child's previous learning history may predispose or discourage modeled aggression.

Family factors. One large-scale study of nearly one thousand third-grade children attempted to relate child aggression (measured by peer and teacher ratings) and family demographic and psychological variables (Eron, Walder, and Lefkowitz, 1971). Increased aggression was found for children whose parents used physical punishment and were themselves aggressive, but not all of the physically punished children were highly aggressive. Boys who had strong empathic feelings toward their fathers showed decreases in aggression with increases in their fathers' punishment for aggression, while boys who did not "identify" with their fathers showed increases in aggression with increases in their fathers' punishment for aggression. In this study, only a minority of the boys were judged as strongly identifying with their fathers.

Influence of television. A number of studies have shown a positive correlation between aggression in children and amount of time spent watching television programs with aggressive content (Rubinstein, 1978). A follow-up study of about half of the Eron, Walder, and Lefkowitz subjects revealed that preference for violent television shows in the third grade was significantly correlated with aggression at age nineteen, even after variance due to past and present aggression, parent characteristics, and amount of television watching was statistically partialled out (Eron, Huesmann, Lefkowitz, and Walder, 1972). Experimental studies also show that aggression in children who are exposed to violent television programs is especially marked when the children are already judged to be aggressive and rated as enjoying such programs.

School factors. The poor overall achievement in school in spite of average or better general intellectual functioning that has been reported for delinquents can indicate a generalized underachievement that is due primarily to poor motivation or lack of reinforcer effectiveness in the learning environment. Schools are generally oriented toward middle-class values in the materials used and available types of reinforcement. Large numbers of children cannot relate to the standard school materials because of wide discrepancies between their own experiences and those emphasized by the schools. In addition, many children in the schools are relatively unresponsive to their teachers as social reinforcers. A child's history of experience during the preschool years has a substantial impact on his subsequent school experiences. In the normal course of events most children learn to perceive adult social attention as reinforcement, at least partly because of a long history of adults' being mediators for, or making available, a wide range of other reinforcers. What if a child has had only minimal experience with adults' providing reinforcement, tangible or social? The answer is that the behavior of the child would be less likely to be controlled by teacher attention. Learning and academic achievement may be greatly hampered in some children because the reinforcers usually available in schools are not effective.

Since schools have traditionally been concerned about stimulus antecedents (materials) and their relationship to learning, there has in recent years been a movement toward developing materials that represent a broader spectrum of children's experiences. Much more effort, however, has to be devoted toward finding effective reinforcers for all children.

Public schools have been accused of being one of the causes of juvenile delinquency on the basis of sociological data suggesting a strong relationship between delinquent behavior and negative school experiences. Several authors (for example, Polk and Schafer, 1972) have proposed that the educational system is often inadvertently responsible for the occurrence of delinquent behavior because academic programs do not adequately serve the needs of children.

It is readily apparent that delinquent behavior may be learned in a variety of ways. The child's history of learning socially appropriate behavior most likely contributes to the relative probability of future behaviors. Parents are generally held responsible for the transmission of society's standards for appropriate behavior, but other people and institutions are also involved in the teaching of moral behavior, particularly after the preschool years.

During their early years, children frequently exhibit behaviors that are not appropriate by adult standards. Parental reactions to these behaviors are the beginning of moral training. To the extent that parental reactions confirm the general societal norms for behavior, so will the values and behavior of the child. Not all parents, however, conform to society's norms either in terms of their own behavior or in their expectations for their child's behavior. Certain inappropriate behaviors may be overtly modeled, thus increasing the probability of the child's imitating them. In many cases, the parents do not intend for the child to imitate these behaviors and are surprised when the child's behavior occurs. That is, some parents seem not to be aware of the impact of their behavior on their children. In other instances, parents, either deliberately or inadvertently, reinforce a behavior that, outside of the home setting, would not be acceptable. Sometimes, the behavior is viewed as "cute" because it is occurring in a young child. Lack of concern about generalization from the home setting may also produce a higher incidence of delinquent behaviors (for example, the child who is reinforced for taking money from his mother's purse may try to remove money from other women's purses).

Certain behaviors, such as stealing, provide their own reinforcers (the object stolen). Lack of adult supervision during childhood has the by-product of allowing the "natural" contingencies to be effective. Both family and societal circumstances, however, have tended to create large numbers of unsupervised children.

This lengthy section on etiological factors suggests that a large number of physical and psychological factors have been associated with antisocial behavior. What seems to be a necessary next step is the separation of delinquents into more homogeneous groups and the investigation of etiological factors in these groups. Studies of the undersocialized and aggressive types, for example, are beginning to reveal a larger role for the genetic and other physical factors when compared to the socialized and nonaggressive types. Such information would serve to make more likely the development of optimal treatment and intervention programs for individual delinquent children.

Probation. After a court decision that a juvenile has committed a crime, the judge has substantial latitude in deciding what the consequences of the act will be. One alternative is to place the child on probation for a certain period of time. Probation is essentially a situation in which the court continues to monitor the child's behavior after specifying acceptable and uncacceptable behaviors. The monitoring consists of periodic interviews with a probation officer. The specified behaviors may include a broad range of possibilities. The child is, of course, instructed not to engage in the criminal behavior, but judges frequently add other conditions, such as being at home by a certain hour, performing household chores, avoiding social contact with certain people, and attending school regularly. Many of the conditions set during probation are designed to help the child to avoid situations that might increase the probability of further criminal behavior. In some situations, judges have focused on the child's giving restitution to the injured party by working and paying for damages. Other innovations have also included having the child work a certain number of hours per week for volunteer agencies and public projects as a means of restitution. Close monitoring of the child's activities by the parents is also requested by the court.

Probation with and without restitution is used frequently by the courts. It is probably the most frequent decision for children who are appearing in court for the first time and whose crimes are not considered to be serious. Probation is also preferred when there is reason to believe that the parents are willing and able to monitor and report on the child's behavior.

Probation may also include the stipulation that the child receive psychological treatment. Such treatment may be obtained from private practitioners and public agencies. We will now examine the various forms of outpatient and community treatment that have been used with children who have engaged in delinquent or antisocial behaviors.

Probation has generally been considered as a form of treatment. That is, the probation officer's continuous contact with a child was viewed as a therapeutic intervention, but the current situation, namely that the majority of probation officers are without training in the psychological disciplines and spend an average of one hour each month on each child, does not permit much opportunity for treatment per se. Recidivism (committing another crime) tends to decrease when probation officers are adequately trained and can spend more time with their clients.

Psychotherapy. The traditional forms of psychotherapy have been used with delinquents both on probation and in institutions, and the results have been mixed, but mostly negative. In a review of the outcome research prior to 1960 on psychotherapy with children, Levitt (1971, p. 475) concluded that children with acting-out symptoms had the poorest improvement rate. Similarly, many clinicians have reported a lack of success in their attempts to apply traditional psychotherapeutic techniques. Several hypotheses have been presented to explain the negative results.

One is that the average delinquent tends to be quite different from the client who has typically benefited from psychotherapy and is considered to have a good prognosis. Such a client is usually described as intelligent, verbally facile, and highly motivated to secure help. Delinquents, on the other hand, have been viewed as average or below average in intelligence, poor in verbal skills, and minimally motivated for psychological intervention. Moreover, delinquents are often described as having character disorders, that is, a personality disturbance less amenable to change than neurotic problems. The failure of psychotherapy has also been related to the inflexibility of these techniques, their bypassing of social and environmental factors that exert much control over the behavior of delinquents, and the apparent strong preferences of therapists to select clients similar to themselves in cultural background and socioeconomic status. In recent years, more recognition has been given to the fact that a therapist's characteristics substantially influence the course of psychotherapy. There have, in addition, been suggestions that therapists from a broader spectrum of the population be trained to provide services for clients who are not responding to the psychological interventions of middle-class psychiatrists, psychologists, and social workers.

Truax has conducted a series of studies in which therapists' interpersonal skills have been related to psychotherapeutic outcome. His research with a wide variety of clients has indicated that therapist's nonpossessive warmth, genuineness, and accurate empathic understanding significantly affect the probability of improvement. Low levels of these interpersonal skills by therapists were found to be associated with significant deterioration in client status. The outcome of group psychotherapy with either outpatient or hospitalized delinquents was also found to depend on these therapist skills (Traux and Mitchell, 1971), suggesting that past psychotherapy failure with delinquents may have been primarily due to the inability of therapists to relate to their clients. The delineation of these skills now makes it possible to assess the extent to which they may be taught to those therapists with deficiencies.

Massimo and Shore (1963) and Shore and others (1966) designed an innovative intervention program for lower-class, delinquent adolescents in response to the general ineffectiveness of conventional psychotherapy for this group. The therapist in their program became extensively involved with his clients. He taught his clients a wide variety of skills that are helpful in everyday life, accompanying them on shopping trips and job interviews, and helping them to get a driver's license. After ten months of treatment, significant improvement was observed for the group. The follow-up study several years after the termination of the program revealed dramatic differences between the treatment group and a control group. Of the ten treated clients, nine were employed, five had continued their education in the interim, five had married, and none had had a felony arrest. Of the ten control clients, six were employed, and six had been convicted of felonies.

The success of this program reflects the validity of other research findings in which, when given a choice among a wide variety of treatment methods, delinquents expressed a preference for a directive, mature therapist who serves as a parent substitute and teaches them social and practical skills (Gottesfeld, 1965).

Institutional settings. If probation with or without psychotherapy is not considered to be adequate or appropriate punishment, the judge may recommend incarceration, removal from the home setting to another environment. Until recently, incarceration meant being sent to a correctional institution or a training school. The institutions for delinquents are physically less restrictive than prisons in that they are not usually surrounded by fences or walls with armed guards, but, in other respects, they tend to greatly resemble prisons. The training schools are usually large, impersonal, and custodial. That is, although some programs in the educational and vocational areas may exist, they are almost always inadequate for the needs of the inmates. Psychological treatment is available only infrequently.

Daily life in the training schools is highly regimented, and few decisions by the inmates are expected or allowed. As in the prisons, social power structures readily develop in the training schools where the more experienced delinquents further control the behaviors of the relatively weak or naive inmates. Socialization is geared toward conforming to the power structure and institutional requirements rather than toward societal standards outside of the institution. There is substantial evidence that delinquents learn a great deal more about criminal behavior and how to avoid getting caught in the training schools. Much of their spare time is spent discussing and boasting about their crimes and planning for future crimes for which they will not be caught. These factors are probably involved in the high recidivism rates found for delinquents who have been incarcerated in training schools. About 70 percent to 80 percent of boys released from training schools are rearrested within a few years (Gibbons, 1970).

Several research projects in training school settings have indicated that recidivism rates can be decreased by specialized programs. One of the best known of these projects was conducted at Highfields, a training school for first offenders. The specialized program emphasized nightly group therapy sessions, called "guided group interaction," in which the residents were encouraged to discuss their problems in a nonthreatening, supportive atmosphere. The average length of treatment at Highfields was approximately four months. The boys had considerably more freedom than is typical in training schools, and they had outside employment as well. Evaluation of the program based on 240 boys who had completed it indicated that recidivism had been cut in half during the first three years of follow-up (McCorkle, Elias, and Bixby, 1958).

In recent years, behavior therapists have begun to report research in which operant conditioning procedures have been used to change delinquent behaviors in institutional settings. Burchard (1967) designed a token program for twelve boys in an intensive training unit that included reinforcement of appropriate social behaviors. Token reinforcement was also administered for working behaviors in the workshop. Punishment consisted of timeout and the loss of tokens. These contingencies were demonstrated to improve the youths' behaviors.

Other behavioral studies with individual residents or small groups of residents in institutional settings have subsequently shown reductions in the rates of a variety of antisocial behaviors through the use of timeout and the reinforcement of incompatible behaviors. Increased attention is being given to the development of self-control, and academic, and vocational skills of institutionalized offenders. The emphasis on skill development is likely to have a considerable long-term benefit in that many delinquents lack the necessary prerequisites for alternative life-styles (Little and Kendall, 1979).

Several large-scale behavioral studies are providing data supporting the use of behavior principles in treating the problems of delinquents. The CASE-II-MODEL project at the National Training School (Cohen and Filipczak, 1971) consisted of a one-year comprehensive token economy program in which each token, or point, was worth one cent. The point system went into effect at the time of the resident's arrival where, during the initial battery of tests, he was paid one point for each correct answer. The main objective of the program was to develop academic skills and thereby increase the opportunity for jobs after release. The resident received points for correct responses in their academic work that was individualized with the use of programmed materials and teaching machines. The points could be traded for a wide variety of goods and privileges—a private bedroom and shower, better food, clothing, recreational activities, coed social events, and weekend passes. Progress in academic work thus resulted in reinforcement that allowed normalization of the youths' daily lives.

The results of the CASE-II-MODEL project included substantial increases in both average IQ scores (from 93 to 105) and achievement scores (several grade levels). Of the residents who had spent at least three months in the project prior to being released, the recidivism rate was 27 percent in the first year and 36 percent by the end of the second year. The previous recidivism rate for comparable youths in the same training school was 76 percent in the first year after release.

The Robert F. Kennedy Youth Center in Morgantown, West Virginia, has been built to replace the National Training School and is continuing to implement much of the CASE program. One of the interesting facets of the newer program is that the youths are initially classified on the basis of Quay's (1964) factor analytically derived dimensions (socialized-subcultural, psychopathic aggressive, neurotic-conflicted, and inadequate-immature) and assigned to treatment units on the basis of their subtype. The specifics of the token economy are worked out cooperatively by the treatment staff and the residents. As the goals are met, the resident is promoted to higher levels with increased pay and privileges. The outcome of this treatment program will further evaluate the utility of behavioral treatment in the rehabilitation of delinquents.

Group homes. A strong current trend is to avoid the incarceration of young offenders. A viable alternative has been developed through research in group homes that are staffed with trained husband-wife teams. The youths continue to be in their community and to attend public school.

One of the most carefully designed group home programs is the Achievement Place Model (Phillips, 1968). Young delinquents who have been suspended from school, who have been considered uncontrollable by their parents, and who have been in trouble in their communities are placed into a group home (about six to eight youths to a home) managed by trained foster parents. A token economy, in which the youths earn points for appropriate behaviors, such as cleaning their rooms and studying, has been designed to teach skills that are important in everyday life. The points are later traded for privileges, such as attendance at movies and sports events. The Achievement Place program is thus primarily educational in orientation.

Preliminary evaluation of the Achievement Place program has demonstrated its success (Kirigin, Wolf, and Phillips, 1979). The youths who participated in the program were much less likely to be institutionalized within two years after treatment and were more likely to continue school. Furthermore, the cost of operating the program was less than half of the comparable epxenses in the state institution for delinquents.

Changing the laws, schools, and parenting. Reserach has repeatedly demonstrated that the traditional court processing and punishment systems neither prevent delinquency nor rehabilitate young people. The juvenile court system has been described as supporting ambiguous definitions of delinquency and setting arbitrary penalties. In view of the findings from sociological research, Scheer (1973) has presented a proposal of "radical nonintervention" as a means for dealing with the problem of delinquency. Some of his recommendations are: (1) behaviors that are illegal only for children should be eliminated from the court's jurisdiction, (2) courts should focus on dispensing justice with respect to specific criminal behavior and not become involved in treating "the whole child," a disguised form of punishment; and (3) society should become more tolerant in its acceptance of behavioral diversity rather than expect all persons to adjust to one standard of behavior.

A number of recommendations have been made for changing those aspects of public school systems that appear to be fostering delinquent behavior patterns (for example, Schafer and Polk, 1972). The assumption behind these recommendations is that schools are sometimes responsible for both the academic and behavioral problems presented by delinquents. While few researchers would agree with a one-factor model for etiology, several of the proposed recommendations appear to be worthy of serious evaluation. One suggestion has focused on the training of teachers to recognize the educability of all pupils and to reward a broader spectrum of achievement behaviors. To that end, teachers and administrators must be convinced of the ultimate educational benefits of rewarding learning increments in individual children in contrast to rewarding performance superior to that of other class members or matching standards arbitrarily set by the teacher. Another suggestion has been to modify the educational structure and materials to eliminate the exclusion of large numbers of children from educational opportunities and advancement. For example, tracking systems are occasionally seen as detrimental to optimal achievement because decisions with regard to track placement are sometimes based on irrelevant data (for example, socioeconomic status, race) or made prematurely for many children.

The general idea behind most of the recommendations is to make all children more aware of and satisfied with their abilities and less aware of and frustrated by their disabilities. In order to effect these goals schools will have to develop greater emphasis on societal needs for a wide diversity of adult roles and functions. A reinforcement system based on a broader range of accomplishment may well prevent the delinquency problems that appear to be caused by the lack of reinforcement for all but traditional academic achievement.

Recognizing the link bwtween poor school performance and delinquent behaviors, attention is also being drawn to preschool and parental education as prevention strategies. Recent studies have suggested that performance during the school years is highly predicted by the child's abilities at the time of school entrance. This relationship leads to an hypothesis that preschool experiences may have a critical role in determining later school performance and thus, directly or indirectly, the probability of delinquent behaviors. It will be particularly interesting to discover in the follow-up studies of preschool intervention programs whether the incidence of delinquent behavior is reduced in proportion to the increases in learning skills. One study (Bachara and Laba, 1978) has shown a marked decrease in recidivism for delinquents provided with a remedial program in basic school subjects.

While education for parenthood has certainly been advocated and many books advising parents on child rearing written, experimental research on the effects of parent education programs on delinquent behavior has not been reported. Such research poses many practical as well as ethical problems, but it would seem to be a necessary requirement before parents are advised on how to rear their children.

substance use disorders

During the past several decades, increasing percentages of children and adolescents have been reported as using alcohol and nonmedicinal drugs. The criteria for abuse of these substances have not been very precise, but, in general, they reflect use in a manner that substantially differs from the accepted patterns within a given society (Millman, 1978). A society's concern about substance abuse no doubt depends on the perceived harm to the abuser and other persons in the abuser's environment. Almost all of the substances involve illegal activities when they are used by minors.

DSM-III distinguishes among substances that are associated with abuse and dependence (alcohol, barbiturates, opioids, amphetamines, and cannabis), abuse only (cocaine, phencyclidine (PCP), and hallucinogens); and dependence only (tobacco). Substance abuse is recognized on the basis of three criteria: (1) a pattern of excessive use, (2) impairment in social or occupational functioning caused by the pattern of excessive use, and (3) a duration of at least one month. Substance dependence requires evidence of physiological dependence as demonstrated by tolerance (an increased amount of the substance is needed to achieve the desired effect) and withdrawal (a substance-specific syndrome follows reduction or cessation of the substance).

alcohol

Reflecting their adult environment, children and adosescents use and abuse alcohol more than any other drug. Use of alcohol is usually begun with peers in social contexts, but more than a few children and adolescents are either introduced to or experiment with alcohol in their homes. Its relative accessibility and low cost permit repeated use, although very few youthful abusers ingest alcohol on a daily basis.

The psychoactive effects of small amounts of alcohol include reduced anxiety and greater ease in social situations. Moderate amounts impair visual-motor coordination, attention to stimuli, and judgment. Large amounts of alcohol lead to severe drowsiness, coma, and death. Level of intoxication is determined by blood-alcohol level tests.

The chronic abuse of alcohol is associated with a variety of medical disorders affecting the intestinal organs and nervous system. It is also a leading cause of accidents and a significant factor in violent crimes. Alcohol may be a factor in adolescent suicide as well.

Combining alcohol with other drugs can be dangerous. When taken together, alcohol and depressants, such as barbiturates and tranquilizers, produce effects that are greater than additive; this combination has proven to be lethal.

Alcohol abuse usually develops within the first five years after regular drinking is established. According to DSM-III, there are three principal patterns of alcohol abuse: (1) regular daily intake of large amounts, (2) regular, heavy drinking on weekends, and (3) "binges" or periods of sobriety interspersed with periods of daily heavy drinking lasting weeks or months.

Alcohol abuse and dependence is more common among family members; behavior genetic studies indicate a significant hereditary contribution to alcohol dependence (Rainer, 1979). Persons with other psychological problems (for example, anxiety disorders) and environmental stresses appear to be more likely to develop a pattern of alcohol abuse.

Although alcohol abuse has been and continues to be a serious social problem, appropriate treatment programs have been slow to develop. Alcoholism appears to require long-term intervention after the initial detoxification. For adults, short-term hospitalization followed by outpatient treatment has been moderately successful. Community groups, such as Alcoholics Anonymous, have been most helpful in preventing excessive drinking by their members. Such groups for children and adolescents have begun to be formed.

central nervous system depressants

CNS depressants include the barbiturates, tranquilizers, and hypnotics; these drugs are prescribed by physicians for relief of anxiety and tension or for sedation in cases of insomnia. Children and adolescents sometimes obtain these drugs from unknowing family members for whom the drugs have been prescribed. Otherwise, they are usually obtained through illegal channels. Depressants produce effects that are similar to those of alcohol. At low doses, there are feelings of relaxation and freedom. The risk of overdose increases with repeated use because larger amounts of the drugs become necessary for maintaining the same effects. The aftereffects of these drugs include impairment of performance and judgment, irritability, sleepiness, and depression. Overdoses of the depressants result in symptoms similar to those of alcohol intoxication: slurred speech, slowness of thinking and movement, and mood changes. The withdrawal signs are also similar to those of alcohol withdrawal. The withdrawal symptoms are more abrupt and severe for the barbiturates than the tranquilizers and may be life threatening.

Treatment of habitual users of depressants is considered to be more difficult than of those who abuse other drugs. Abusers of depressants tend to have more serious preexisting psychological problems and frequently relapse during the course of treatment. In some cases, long-term hospitalization or a therapeutic community may be necessary to prevent early relapses.

stimulants

The most commonly abused stimulants are the amphetamines and cocaine. The amphetamines are prescribed by physicians in the treatment of obesity, fatigue, and depression. These stimulants are sometimes used by students, athletes, and performers to achieve the best performance possible; such intermittent use does not produce dependence. Abuse tends to occur when stimulants are taken for their mood-elevating properties. In these cases, the drugs are often either injected or sniffed and produce a more powerful initial effect of well-being. The aftereffects of stimulants include depression and apathy. The usual pattern of amphetamine abuse is "runs" of daily use for ten to fourteen days at a time. For the chronic user, increasing dosages of amphetamines are needed to maintain the same effects. Concurrent abuse of stimulants and depressants (for sleep) sometimes occurs.

Stimulant abusers tend to have preexisting psychological problems that may be worsened by the abuse. Common adverse effects include paranoid thoughts and compulsive behaviors. Chronic use of the amphetamines has been associated with the development of psychosis that is similar to paranoid schizophrenia; the psychotic symptoms usually abate within several days or weeks after the last drug dose.

Many adolescents who use stimulants intermittently do not require formal treatment, but they should be informed about the dangers of chronic use and supported in their efforts to stop taking the drugs. In cases of chronic use, the individual may have to be hospitalized or confined in a supportive environment during the early phase of drug cessation. Depression and suicide have been associated with stimulant withdrawal.

hallucinogens

Hallucinogens include cannabis (marijuana and hashish) and the psychedelic drugs, such as mescaline, peyote, and certain synthetic chemicals. As is well known, cannabis has become the most commonly used illegal drug in the United States; up to 70 percent of adolescent samples have reported using it. Although many young people try it and then discontinue its use, a large number of others use it intermittently in social situations. A few adolescents use cannabis throughout the day on a daily basis; in those instances, cannabis may become the primary feature of their life-style. These adolescents tend to have had serious preexisting psychological problems.

Cannabis may be either smoked or ingested with food. The effects are highly variable and dependent on the individual's expectations and the setting. Users frequently report enhanced perception of stimuli, a feeling of relaxation, mood changes, drowsiness, and hilarity. The sense of time, motor activities, and reaction time are impaired. Adverse physical effects have been hypothesized but not demonstrated. No deaths have been attributed to the use of cannabis. The known adverse effects appear to be primarily psychological and include acute panic reactions, paranoid thinking, and depression that last several hours. Psychotic reactions have also been reported.

Other hallucinogens, such as LSD and mescaline, produce greater effects on perception, thought, feeling, and behavior. The use of hallucinogens peaked during the 1960s and has subsequently declined, probably due, in part, to fear of adverse reactions. LSD is usually manufactured in illegal laboratories and made available in the form of a liquid, in sugar cubes, tablets, and capsules. Use is normally intermittent and takes place in a group setting.

The effects of these drugs may be extreme, although they appear to be somewhat dependent on the expectations of the user, the setting, and the dose. Sensory perceptions may be extremely distorted sometimes to the point of the user's feeling overwhelmed. Body distortions are frequently perceived and time seems to pass slowly. Lability of mood is apparent and may range from euphoria to depression and panic. Most of the effects disappear within twelve hours.

The most common adverse reaction is an acute panic reaction ("bad trip") that includes both hysterical and paranoid features; the user may experience fears of physical harm, paralysis, and insanity. Occasionally, prolonged psychotic episodes are precipitated as are depressive reactions. Another adverse reaction is the "flashback" in which the person reexperiences a part of a previous "trip" when not taking the drug. Treatment of acute panic reactions and flashbacks relies primarily on a supportive environment in which the person is repeatedly assured that time will cure the symptoms.

opioids

Heroin is the most commonly abused opioid in the United States. It is converted from morphine (a 10 to 1 reduction of crude opium) in illegal laboratories and sold in powdered form; morphine is used in the medical treatment of severe pain. Children and adolescents are usually introduced to heroin by a friend or relative who uses the drug. Although usually informed about the dangers of the drug, few youngsters believe that they will be unable to control its use. The drug is first taken by "sniffing" or inhaling the powder. Because its euphoric effects require either increased doses or more direct introduction into the body, users begin to inject the drug under the skin and later directly into the veins. Tolerance continues to increase, and larger amounts of the drug must be used more often. Most young addicts have few legitimate financial resources to support their habit and must expend all of their energy attempting to secure the drug. Illegal behavior often becomes a by-product of opioid addiction.

Physical dependence on the drug sometimes develops after very few exposures. Within four to six hours after the last dose, the first withdrawal signs occur; they include craving for the drug, anxiety, and irritability. Withdrawal symptoms continue to increase and peak at two to three days, subsiding in seven to ten days. The symptoms are commonly experienced as life threatening and extremely painful. Drug craving usually returns after withdrawal, and most addicts resume their habit. The mortality rate for opioid abusers is about 1 percent to 2 percent a year; this high death rate is due primarily to dose errors, nonsterile conditions of the drugs and equipment, and the criminal life style.

Treatment is necessarily long term. A number of programs based on drug abstinence have been developed; these are generally inpatient therapeutic communities that provide a strong, supportive system. Methadone, a synthetic chemical, has been used in treatment programs; it can be administered orally in doses large enough to prevent withdrawal symptoms and drug carving. It is usually given daily over a period of time up to two years and then gradually decreased. Methadone programs have been conducted primarily on an outpatient basis that allows the addict an opportunity to develop normal life skills in the natural environment. DSM-III indicates that cessation of opioid dependence takes an average of nine years.

Conclusions

Conduct disorders account for a substantial number of referrals to clinicians and mental health agencies. Hyperactivity has been receiving considerable attention in recent years, and our knowledge of etiological factors associated with behavioral and learning problems and optimal treatment programs has improved significantly. Delinquency and substance abuse disorders continue to present a substantial challenge to society. Community-based programs that emphasize the teaching of academic, vocational, and social skills appear to offer the greatest promise for reducing the incidence of these disorders.

Recommended Readings

Lahey, B. B., ed., *Behavior Therapy with Hyperactive and Learning Disabled Children.* New York: Oxford University Press, 1979. A collection of recent studies focusing on the assessment and treatment of children with hyperactivity and learning problems.

Mednick, S. A., and **Christiansen, K. O.**, eds., *Biosocial Bases of Criminal Behavior.* New York: Gardner Press, 1977.

Millman, R. B., "Drug and Alcohol Abuse," in *Handbook of Treatment of Mental Disorders in Children and Adolescents,* pp. 238–267. Edited by B. B. Wolman, J. Egan, and A. O. Ross. Englewood Cliffs, N. J.: Prentice-Hall, 1978.

Ribes-Inesta, E. L., and **Bandura, A.**, eds., *Analysis of Delinquency and Aggression.* New York: Halsted Press, 1976.

Ross, D. M., and **Ross, S. A.**, *Hyperactivity: Research, Theory, and Action.* New York: John Wiley, 1976.

Stumphauzer, J. S., ed., *Progress in Behavior Therapy with Delinquents.* Springfield, Ill.: Charles C. Thomas, 1979.

anxiety and other emotional disorders

Maria was an attractive, dark-haired, ten-year-old girl whose parents referred her because she had developed a recurring fear that her father was going to die. She was also spending a considerable amount of time engaging in ritualistic behaviors, such as tapping objects a certain number of times and arranging her possessions in particular ways. Maria reported that she felt good only when she was completing her rituals. Although she was very intelligent and did superior work in school, Maria became upset if her performance was not the best in the class. She spoke at length about minor problems in school and perceived herself as an inadequate student.

Although her concerns about school had been present for several years, her fear of her father's death and the ritualistic behaviors at home had a sudden onset after the accidental death of one of her uncles whose funeral she attended.

Maria's mother described herself as a perfectionist and was proud of her accomplishments as

251

a manager of the household, but she had a long history of a lack of relationships with other people and was unable to discuss her feelings. She acknowledged that her marriage was not satisfactory and that her husband did not meet her expectations either at home or in his job.

Maria's father was considerably warmer and more friendly than his wife, but he reported episodes of depression that had been increasing in frequency during the last two years and felt that they were related to his dissatisfaction with his job and his marriage. The death of his brother had further increased his family responsibilities, responsibilities with which he felt unable to cope. Concern with his own problems seemed to prevent him from acknowledging Maria's problems. His withdrawal from her difficulties was characterized by his stating that "she is just like her mother."

Anxiety or fear is an appropriate response in a number of situations; for example, being afraid of a hot stove after being burned and, therefore, not touching it will prevent future burns. Thus, anxiety can be conceptualized as a signal of impending danger. However, some psychological problems of childhood and adolescence appear to be characterized by anxiety that does *not* seem to be related to physical danger; while the etiology of individual types of anxiety disorders is not always known, it is generally believed that they are learned in the same way that appropriate fears are learned.

Several factors appear to be involved in the development of anxiety disorders. Sometimes, the disorder can result from an "accidental," classical conditioning pairing, such as a pairing of thunder and swimming resulting in a fear of water. A few children seem to be especially sensitive, that is, constitutionally vulnerable to such situations. Some parents overestimate the child's ability to cope with potentially anxiety-producing situations and make the child more vulnerable by excessive exposure; they may also fail to teach their children ways of coping with new situations.

Several of the disorders described in this and the next chapter had been classified as neuroses prior to the publication of DSM-III (1980). The reason that the diagnostic class, neurosis, was deleted is that it incorporated a specific view of etiology. Namely, it meant that a neurosis was caused by unconscious conflict, and this conflict aroused anxiety and led to an excessive use of defense mechanisms that were reflected in the symptoms. Because there is no consensus among psychiatrists about their etiology and because the authors of DSM-III wanted to make a special effort to emphasize description of symptoms, these disorders have been grouped with other similar emotional disorders.

In general, this chapter follows the DSM-III terminology and classification system. The disorders have been rearranged to approximate a developmental sequence; that is, disorders are presented in an order that reflects the earliest age of onset. Oppositional disorder is described in Chapter 11 on conduct disorders. Schizoid disorder has been omitted because there is no compelling evidence that this or other personality disorders are representative of a useful diagnostic category during childhood and adolescence.

reactive attachment disorder

Pediatricians and other physicians have found that some infants fail to develop adequately even though they have no apparent physical problems and have labeled this condition "failure to thrive." All aspects of the infant's development appear to be affected — physical, social, and emotional. The poor physical development is manifested in low weight gain (although head circumference and usually length remain normal), immature feeding patterns, excessive sleep, and less movement than is usual. The child's social and emotional behaviors are characterized by a lack of appropriate social responsiveness, such as eye contact, smiling, and reaching for the caregiver. The onset of the problem is usually before eight months of age.

The DSM-III has called this condition, "reactive attachment disorder," because the etiology is believed to be a lack of adequate physical or emotional caregiving. While in some cases physical neglect may be a factor, lack of positive, social attention by the caregiver appears to be a dominant cause. Infants with this disorder are more likely to have caregivers who are depressed, isolated, or indifferent to the infant. The caretaker may have had an extremely deprived childhood or lack of education about how to be an adequate caregiver for an infant. In some cases, the infant may have been difficult to manage or initially more unresponsive than expected, suggesting that some infants may need or demand more than some caregivers can provide.

The disorder is considered to be reversible with appropriate treatment, namely affectionate caregiving, although hospitalization frequently leads to improvement. Some infants have died from the physical complications because diagnosis was not made soon enough. This disorder is essentially the same one observed by Spitz (1945) and others in infants who were in orphanages and other institutions that provided only physical care.

avoidant disorder of childhood or adolescence

normal social development

Social behavior in the child begins very early in life; the smile in response to a person's face occurs around two to three months of age. By six months of age the infant has a repertoire of facial expressions and vocalizations to use in getting the attention of and response of others. During the second half of the first year of life, many infants, particularly those whose social experiences have been restricted to the parents, go through a period in which they seem to withdraw from the attention of strangers. Some children react to the approach of a stranger by crying loudly, while others watch warily. During this period, however, infants are greatly interested in people, and, if allowed to approach strangers at their own rate, they rapidly become quite friendly.

During the second year of life, increased mobility and the development of verbal behavior greatly expand the quality and quantity of the child's social behaviors. During this period the child hears the word "no" quite frequently as she begins to explore the environment, and usually cooperates. Cooperation tends to be short-lived, however, and the child begins to challenge parental requests and routines. The height of uncooperativeness may be at the end of the second year when the child often strongly resists social pressures and may begin to respond to them with temper tantrums. It is during this period that the child may begin to associate with peers, and these early encounters reflect the same variability of behavior.

The child continues to be primarily self-centered through the third year of life. Communication skills and curiosity are rapidly developing; the child talks incessantly and formulates endless questions to which the parents must respond. The birth of a sibling during this time often produces a negative reaction in the forms of the child's trying to hurt the baby, telling the mother to return the baby, or engaging in regressive behaviors, such as drinking from the baby's bottle and wetting himself or herself.

During the remaining years of the preschool period, increasingly more time is spent with peers, and preference for playmates of the same sex is emerging. The later preschool years are accompanied by high levels of activity involving peers. Four- and five-year-olds engage in many behaviors for the entertainment and admiration of their friends. If allowed to proceed uncontrolled, these activities reach such a high level that children may be hurt or property damaged, or both. That is, the excitement of performance precludes efforts at self-control. Aggressive behavior, both verbal and physical, is very common in the four-year-old, and it may be directed toward the parents as well as peers. Nursery schools, kindergartens, and parents expend considerable effort toward socializing the child during this period.

Soon after the child enters school, teachers and peers begin to take on substantial importance in the child's social life, and social behaviors are evaluated in the context of many children of the same age. Sometimes, behaviors that were acceptable or tolerated in the home and neighborhood are quite unacceptable in the school. The parents themselves come under the scrutiny of outside "authorities" whose comments may be received with ambivalence. The parents, too, must deal with the challenge of their child's models being increasingly from outside the home. Indeed, during the school years peers become more and more effective social reinforcers of children's behaviors. Direct contact time with parents begins to decrease during the school years and is minimal during adolescence.

Social responsiveness to other persons varies greatly among children with some of the variability no doubt due to hereditary factors. Such variations are easily tolerated by some parents and reacted upon negatively by others. These reactions are often determined by the parents' own level of social responsiveness or history with regard to social interactions. Introverted parents, for example, might be less concerned about a shy child than parents who are highly social.

diagnosis and treatment

According to DSM-III the criteria for avoidant disorder of childhood or adolescence includes the avoidance of contact with strangers to the degree that social functioning with peers is impaired. This disorder is not diagnosed before the age of 2½ years, and the duration must be at least 6 months. Children with this disorder have normal, affectionate relationships with members of their families and other familiar persons.

In general, concern about the shy or withdrawn child is not manifested until the child enters nursery school or kindergarten. Preschool teachers tend to have more uniform standards upon which they evaluate children's social behaviors. The principal goal of the nursery school for many decades has been socialization of the child. Only recently has the nursery school been considered an important training ground for preacademic skills.

Some of the methods that nursery school teachers have typically used to increase social behaviors in children may not be very effective. These methods include the teacher's talking to the child and trying to persuade the child to interact with others. Several behavioral studies (for example, Allen, Hart, Buell, Harris, and Wolf, 1964) suggest that these methods may be inadvertently strengthening withdrawal. Giving social attention to the child who is approximating or actually engaging in social interactions has resulted in increases of these behaviors.

After the child enters elementary school, concern about relatively withdrawn children diminishes, primarily because they do not interfere with the school program. That is, teachers with their larger numbers of children tend to be more aware of active, inappropriate behavior than absences of appropriate behavior and are more likely to seek help for the former than the latter. Concern, particularly on the part of parents, may emerge during adolescence when this disorder may manifest itself in a low rate of the typical adolescent social activities.

elective mutism

The most common feature of elective mutism is the child's refusal to speak in virtually all social situations except the home. The problem is usually brought to the parents' attention by a preschool teacher. The child's language skills in the home are usually normal. In most cases, the problem lasts several weeks or months, but sometimes it may continue for years.

The backgrounds of children who develop elective mutism are likely to include maternal overprotection and behavior problems, such as social withdrawal, school refusal, negativism, and temper tantrums. Trauma, such as hospitalization and immigration, and mental retardation may also be related factors.

A recent review of the research on elective mutism (Kratochwill, Brody, and Piersel, 1979) revealed a substantial number of treatment studies using both traditional and behavioral approaches. The psychodynamic literature indicated that the disorder was difficult to treat in that treatment tended to be lengthy, varying from several months to several years, and generalization from the treatment setting to the school was inconsistent. The behavioral studies were generally conducted in the environment in which the mutism occurred and followed a structure of ignoring the nonverbal communications of the child and reinforcing appropriate verbalizations. The procedures were clearly beneficial in relatively short periods of time and at follow-up. The authors concluded that the results must be considered tentative until future studies incorporate more refined methodological procedures.

separation anxiety disorder

During the early preschool years, all children periodically show signs of distress when their parents leave them temporarily. These reactions are normal, and their magnitude is probably dependent on the previous patterns established by the parents. That is, if the child's early history includes only rare instances of being left with a babysitter, for example, then the child may be expected to have a stronger reaction to mother's leaving than if the mother had established a frequent pattern of leaving the child. A child whose previous life has been spent in the company of his or her mother may well be very upset at being left at nursery school or kindergarten for the first time.

In a separation anxiety disorder, the primary feature is excessive anxiety associated with separation from family members or familiar surroundings. This disorder may be manifested by the children's refusal to stay at friends' houses or in a room by themselves or to go to school or camp. They often have problems going to sleep and may experience nightmares. When separation is anticipated, they may develop physical complaints such as headaches, stomach aches, nausea, and vomiting. They tend to have a network of fears involving danger to themselves and their families and fears of animals, monsters, accidents, burglars, and dying. When separated, they may become preoccupied with fears of something terrible happening to themselves or their parents.

Children with separation anxiety disorder tend to come from close-knit, warm families, suggesting that the child may have become too attached or dependent on family members. In many cases, a major life stress precedes the development of the disorder. These life stresses may include moving or changing schools, illness of the child or close relative, or death of a pet or close relative.

Without effective treatment, the disorder may continue for several years. In some cases, the disorder persists into adulthood and may be involved in an adolescent's refusal to go away to college, for example. Treatment procedures will be discussed in the section on phobias.

overanxious disorder

In contrast to the more specific fears in separation anxiety disorder and phobias, overanxious disorder involves excessive anxiety that is *not* focused on a particular situation or object. In overanxious disorder, the child worries about a wide variety of future events and situations. The major theme seems to be a concern about competence, particularly evaluation by others in social, academic, and athletic areas. Physical signs of anxiety, such as headache, lump in the throat, digestive problems, and nausea, are frequently present. The child seems to be unable to relax and has an excessive need for reassurance.

DSM-III reports that this disorder appears to be more common in boys, eldest children, small families, upper socioeconomic groups, and in families in which there is concern about performance even though the child's performance may be adequate or even superior. These factors suggest that the child's emotional behaviors may be side effects from earlier punishment, particularly in home settings in which virtually no performance level was reinforced and nearly all behaviors were criticized as being deficient.

This disorder is probably relatively common, but referral would not be likely to occur unless the child was failing in school or repeatedly seeking medical care without evidence of physical illness. The symptoms may persist into adulthood.

phobias

Until the publication of DSM-III (1980), phobias were one type of neurosis; the term "neurosis" has been deleted from the classification system but will occasionally be used in this section to describe anxiety disorders. Phobias are characterized by extreme fear of specific objects or situations that pose little or no threat in reality. Phobic adults report their recognition of the fact that the feared situation is not harmful. The subjective fear may be expressed as tremor, faintness, nausea, perspiration, and feelings of panic. Behaviorally, phobias are manifested by escape from and avoidance of the feared object or situation.

Fears and phobias are extremely common in children (Bauer, 1976) and are usually more frequent in girls than boys. Because these responses are so common during the developmental period, it is relatively unusual for preschool children to be referred and formally diagnosed as phobic. The most frequent childhood fears are of animals, darkness, and separation from parents. It is only when a fear becomes debilitating or significantly interferes with the child's functioning within the family or school environments that professional help is sought.

Because school phobia has such serious implications psychologically, educationally, and legally, it will be our primary focus in the remaining portion of this section. School phobia is usually defined as refusal to attend school because the child is afraid; this definition discriminates school phobia from truancy in which fear is not a principal component. DSM-III (1980, p. 50) limits the term school phobia to the child being fearful of the school situation; refusing to go to school because of fear to leave home or parents is diagnosed as separation anxiety disorder rather than school phobia. Estimates of the occurrence of school phobia vary depending on the specific definition used (such as number of days absent from school) and the treatment facilities available in the community and have ranged from 1 percent of a psychiatric sample to 8 percent of a school population. School phobia is consistently reported more often for girls than boys and tends to peak in the middle of the elementary school years.

assessment

In contrast to the elaborate assessment devices designed to evaluate adults' fears, the assessment procedures used with children have been relatively unsophisticated. Typically, assessment is conducted through interviews with the child's parents; the content of the interview varies somewhat as a function of the clinician's theoretical persuasion.

The traditional clinician concentrates heavily on the child's history of emotional development and parent-child interactions because school phobia is typically assumed to be an extension of a continuing neurotic condition. The behavioral clinician, on the other hand, is more interested in the present environmental (particularly school) circumstances and the immediate past, beginning with the onset of the school phobia. To obtain this information, the behavioral clinician is more likely to interview the relevant school personnel.

A number of measures have been developed to assess children's fears, but their reliability and validity are not consistently reported (Johnson and Melamed, 1979). Furthermore, the relationship among these measures is largely unknown. There are two types of self-report measures: those that assess anxiety as a trait and those that measure specific fears. An example of the latter type is an eighty-item scale, the Fear Survey Schedule for Children (Scherer and Nakamura, 1968). The items consist of specific fears in the areas of school, home, social, physical, animal, travel, classical phobia, and miscellaneous. The number of fears the child reports is viewed as a measure of chronic anxiety. Melamed and Siegel (1975) have designed the Observer Rating Scale of Anxiety that has twenty-nine behaviors, two of which are "talking about being afraid" and "trembling hands." Several behavior checklists that are completed by someone familiar with the child contain a subset of items related to fear and anxiety. These measures are particularly helpful in research studies and screening programs.

To facilitate the assessment process a number of studies have been conducted that delineate the characteristics of school phobic children and attempt to differentiate subtypes of school phobia. Frequently cited is Hersov's (1960) study that compared the characteristics of three groups of children: (1) school phobia greater than two months duration, (2) school truancy greater than two months duration, and (3) a nonphobic, nontruant control group. Fifteen of the 124 listed characteristics were found to discriminate between school phobics and truants. In comparison to truants, school phobics were described as having more maternal overprotection, eating disturbances, nausea and abdominal pains, sleep disturbances, diagnoses of anxiety reaction, and histories of family neurosis; they were less likely to have absent parents, inconsistent home discipline, bed wetting, juvenile court appearances and conduct problems.

Kennedy (1965) has proposed two subtypes of school phobia on the basis of his research: "Neurotic" and "characterological." The "neurotic" type of school phobic child was more frequently found to be a younger child experiencing a first episode with an acute onset, to be concerned about death and the mother's physical health status, and to have well-adjusted parents with good communication between themselves and with the clinician. The "characterological" type, on the other hand, was an older child manifesting a second, third, or fourth episode after an incipient onset and had parents who were poorly adjusted and evidenced minimal cooperation with the clinician. Kennedy has recommended that close attention should be given to parental and child characteristics during the assessment process, because they may markedly affect the later success of the intervention program and may be important factors in the maintenance of the school phobic behavior.

etiology

There is only indirect evidence suggesting that biological factors may be implicated in the etiology of neuroses in adults, and virtually no studies have examined the possible role of biological variables in childhood neuroses. One family pedigree study has shown a higher rate of neurosis in the blood relatives of neurotics than in nonblood relatives (18 percent versus 3 percent) (Noyes, and others, 1978). Constitutional factors have also been invoked as causal agents; the person who develops a neurotic problem is one who is biologically vulnerable and unable to withstand everyday stresses. While there can be no question that great variability to stress exists, evidence that constitutional vulnerability is a necessary prerequisite for the development of a phobia has not been forthcoming.

In the research literature, most of the attention has been given to two theories emphasizing environmental or psychological factors as causing school phobia: psychoanalytic theory and learning theory. The advocates of psychoanalytic theory propose that school phobia is the product of a basically disturbed personality and disturbed family interactions. Most clinicians continue to support the contention that school phobia represents a form of separation anxiety that is manifested equally by the mother and the child (Johnson, Falstein, Szurek, and Svendsen, 1941). Early clinical investigations suggested that the mother of a school phobic child "unconsciously" teaches her child to fear school by strongly sympathizing with complaints about school. The mother herself views school negatively as an impersonal place and communicates the message that she wishes the child to remain at home. According to the Johnson view, the abnormal dependency relationship between mother and child is passed from generation to generation; that is, the mother of a school phobic child has typically had a poorly resolved dependency relationship with her own mother.

Clinicians have reported additional characteristics of mothers in relationship to their school phobic children. In general, the mothers have been described as being able to provide an adequate psychological environment for their children during the period of infancy when the child is most dependent, but the mother develops a strong identity with the dependent child and tries to gratify the child's every wish. She is unable to deprive the child of any desire and frequently sacrifices her own needs for those of the child. The mother expends much energy toward protecting the child from any physical discomfort or other unpleasant experiences. Normal parenting behaviors involving frustration of the child and discipline cannot be handled because the mother has conflicts with regard to aggression. Ordinary problems experienced by her child outside of the home are magnified in importance by the mother.

In evaluating these descriptions of mothers, it should be kept in mind that the data were collected during and after the diagnostic process, and material may have been selected to reflect the hypotheses of the authors. Perhaps the psychological characteristics of the mother follow rather than precede the episode of school phobia. Why is it that other children in the same family do not experience school phobia? It is also puzzling that many clinicians have not seriously considered the possible role of school environmental stimuli in the etiology of school phobia.

From a learning point of view, several behavior principles are likely to be involved in the development of a school phobia. One principle involves classical conditioning in which the previously neutral school stimuli have been paired with an aversive stimulus that elicits a strong fear or emotional response. A return to school following such a pairing produces fear and anxiety. An operant learning component is also necessary to explain the full range of behaviors presented during school phobia. For example, leaving or avoiding school itself would become strengthened by the concomitant reduction of fear. Thus, excessive aversive stimulation or even one traumatic episode could lead to the development of school phobia. This analysis follows the paradigm used by Watson and Rayner (1920) in their famous study of conditioning Albert to fear a white rat by pairing the rat with a loud noise.

In the case of school phobia, the operant component may become more complex. That is, parents and other relevant people in the child's environment may reinforce the child's negative statements about school, complaints about bad feelings, and staying home from school. It is this aspect of the operant component that is emphasized by the traditional clinicians in their analyses of school phobia. It is also possible for school phobia to be, instead, a fear of leaving home. In this case, similar learning principles would be operating. Having a parent become ill while away at school might result in the child's experiencing anxiety upon the subsequent leaving of home for school. Remaining at home may be reinforced both by the avoidance or alleviation of anxiety and social reinforcement by the ill parent or others.

School phobia cases include a wide variety of stimulus events that may be relevant to the etiology and maintenance of the problem. Some case studies reveal that one or another of the parents has had a history of either real or "imagined" illness and that the child has learned to take on the role of caretaker for the incapacitated parent and has been strongly reinforced for caretaking activities. In a few instances of the author's experiences, the "school phobic" child has had virtually complete responsibility for running the household while ministering to the "ill" parent. Such cases usually involve far more complicated intervention programs than those originating primarily in the school environment.

Fears of leaving home need not be confined to situations of parental illness. Separation from mother, in and of itself, can result in a child's feeling and acting fearful, depending on the child's previous learning history. During the preschool years of most children, the mother is the principal social reinforcer and the mediator for many other reinforcers for the child. When the child becomes frightened, the mother is the one most available for comfort. Thus, separation from her can represent at best the temporary loss of many reinforcers and result in the child's refusal to go to school. Many children exhibit this concern at the beginning of their first school experiences. To the extent that they have had exposure to reinforcers outside of the home, children's initial negative reactions to the school environment are likely to be attenuated.

Because they are so common, emotional responses to initial school entry are not usually considered instances of school phobia. The child who is susceptible to these emotional responses, because a history of reinforcers outside of the home is lacking, is more likely than the child with reinforcers to develop school phobia at a later time unless the school environment subsequently provides adequate reinforcement. In a large classroom the quiet, timid child may be less likely to receive the teacher's attention, particularly if the child's academic abilities are poor. A paucity of reinforcers in the classroom could certainly decrease the child's desire to go to school and is also probably involved in the development of truancy.

Individual differences in responsiveness to environmental occurrences also play a role in determining the child's susceptibility to developing school phobia. A sudden, loud reprimand from a teacher, for example, will elicit a wide range of emotional responses in the various pupils. Some of this variability is no doubt due to innate biological differences, while the remaining portion is dependent on the specific previous experiences of the individual children. The child who has been exposed to frequent, loud reprimands in earlier grades or at home would not be likely to respond in the same way as the child with minimal exposure to such stimuli. In fact, the latter child would be expected to experience a greater emotional response on hearing a reprimand than would the former.

The research literature indicates that, in general, behavior problems are reported significantly more often for boys than girls. Perhaps boys, then, experience more negative social interactions with adults and thus tend to respond less vigorously physiologically to subsequent occurrences. This analysis could account for the higher incidence of school phobia in girls.

treatment

The treatment of school phobia has received a great amount of attention in the clinical and research literature. Traditional clinicians, while specifying that treatment should vary according to the severity and child's internal conflicts, have utilized psychotherapy with the mother and child as the primary therapeutic intervention. Most often, the mother and child are seen by different therapists who maintain close communication with one another. Psychotherapists vary in their recommendations with regard to school attendance. Most of them try to get the child back in school as soon as possible using any method that is less severe than physical coercion, while others have preferred that the child not return to school during treatment. In the latter instance, the child obtains instruction from individual tutoring at home. Recognition has been given to research findings indicating that treatment initiated immediately after the onset of symptoms is much more rapid and successful than treatment that is delayed for weeks or months. Under the latter condition, the phobia may persist for several years. For this reason, clinicians consider school phobia as an emergency referral, and treatment is initiated promptly.

Studies evaluating the effectiveness of psychotherapy with or without hospitalization indicates that about 72 percent of the children return to school. When psychotherapy is combined with pressure for the child to return to school (an example of an extreme case of pressure is threatening court action), about 90 percent of the children return to school. The spontaneous recovery rate for severe cases of school phobia has been estimated at 20 percent (Yates, 1970, p. 154).

In recent years, behavior therapists have reported a number of successful intervention programs with school phobic children. In general, the programs use several behavioral techniques to counteract both the classical and operant components of school phobia. In 1965 Lazarus, Davison, and Polefka reported a case study in which treatment was based on both classical and operant conditioning procedures. The principal therapeutic strategy was *in vivo* desensitization in which the child was exposed to increasingly greater contacts with school by the therapist. For example, the first step in the procedure included the therapist's accompanying the child on a walk from his house to the school on a Sunday afternoon. Later steps included a therapist walking with the child to the schoolyard at 8:30 A.M., entering the classroom after the regular school hours, and remaining in the classroom with other children for increasing periods with the therapist's removing himself from the child's view for increasing lengths of time. During these sessions the therapist socially reinforced any progress made by the child and tried to minimize anxiety by distraction, humor, and getting the child to imagine pleasant events that were then related to school. In addition, the teacher was asked to provide occasions when the child could receive reinforcement. During the later phases of the treatment, comic books and tokens were used as reinforcement for attending school without the therapist's being present. Although the entire treatment program extended over 4½ months, the child was spending a full morning in the classroom within a week and remained in the classroom all day after the next few weeks of treatment.

Kennedy (1965) reported a rapid treatment procedure that was effective in every case; moreover, its success was maintained on long-term follow-up. Kennedy's procedure included emphasis on enlisting the cooperation of all persons in the child's environment, ignoring such complaints by the child as those of fears and pains, forcing school attendance, and counseling the parents about specific procedures. Very little time was spent in therapist-child interaction. Kennedy's great success may have been due in part to the fact that his school phobics were referred within a few days after the initial refusal to go to school. No control group was included in the Kennedy study, but it might be anticipated that the spontaneous recovery in a control group would be somewhat higher than that found for control groups in studies with more severe cases of school phobia. Nevertheless, Kennedy's study may be considered doubly significant, both demonstrating an effective therapeutic program and showing the importance of the earliest possible initiation of therapy.

A comparison of the traditional and behavioral approaches to school phobia reveals a number of similarities. In practice, both of them attempt to decrease the child's anxiety and to arrange environmental contingencies such that the child is reinforced for going to school. Some of the methods by which these attempts are made do vary; for example, the traditional therapist tries to reduce anxiety by encouraging the child to talk about fears during the therapy sessions, while the behavioral clinician seeks the same goal through desensitization and reinforcement for proschool behaviors.

The research literature contains many examples of successful therapeutic interventions for children's fears. Attention is now being directed toward teaching phobic children skills that might have predisposed them to the phobias or that might be deficient because of the longstanding phobias. Ollendick (1979) has suggested that future research examine comprehensive treatment programs that include systematic desensitization, modeling, and operant conditioning. Social skills training in a group therapy format, such as that described by LaGreca and Santogrossi (1980), may also be beneficial.

obsessions and compulsions

Obsessions are characterized by persistent, intrusive, unwanted *thoughts* or urges that the person is unable to control. These thoughts may consist of single words or ideas, or of combinations, that often appear nonsensical to the person experiencing them. The commonly reported experience of a particular tune recurring in one's thought is suggestive of an obsession, but, because it is relatively transient and does not significantly interfere with activities, it would not be classified as one.

Compulsions consist of *behaviors* that are excessively repeated. Compulsive behaviors vary from simple movements to elaborate and complex rituals. Interference with the behavior commonly results in feelings of distress and anxiety. Anxiety is also reported when the person becomes concerned about being unable to control the compulsion.

Many questions still remain about the relationship of obsessions and compulsions. In general, compulsive behaviors are almost always preceded by obsessional thoughts that are preceded by anxiety, but, compulsive behaviors may become relatively autonomous after a long period of practice. Surveys of psychiatric clinic populations reveal that the incidence of obsessive-compulsive neurosis (currently classified as an anxiety disorder in DSM-III) in children is very low, just as it is in adults (from 1 percent to 3 percent of clinical populations). In one survey (Judd, 1965) of 405 children from a clinic population, 34 children were described as having abnormal obsessive-compulsive symptoms, but only 5 of them were considered to be examples of classical obsessive-compulsive neurosis.

assessment and etiology

Diagnosis of obsessive-compulsive disorder is usually made by a psychiatrist on the basis of characteristics described in the DSM-III (1980). Information about the child's symptoms is obtained from interviews with the parents. The child is also interviewed and sometimes observed in diagnostic play sessions. Since compulsive behaviors are more readily observed by adults in the child's environment, children with such behaviors will be referred more often. A child with only obsessional thoughts would be referred depending on the frequency with which such thoughts were reported; thus, there is no reason to assume that referrals reflect the actual incidence of both obsessions and compulsions in the child population.

The Judd (1965) study reported that several characteristics were shared by the five children with obsessive-compulsive neurosis. All of them had superior IQ scores, rigid moral codes, and active fantasy lives. Their symptoms had a sudden onset, and at the time of diagnosis both obsessions and compulsions were present. Their symptoms caused severe disruptions of their adjustment to the environment, and they verbalized guilt feelings. None of the children had a history of sexual trauma. Four out of five of the children had normal personalities before the onset of symptoms, uneventful bowel training, an identifiable precipitating event, a family history of obsessive-compulsive symptoms, and strong ambivalent feelings toward their parents.

Questions have also been raised as to whether the classical form of obsessive-compulsive neurosis occurs in children. Ritualistic behavior tends to occur as a part of the normal developmental process in children and may present significant diagnostic problems. That is, mild compulsions, such as stepping over the cracks in sidewalks, are very common in young children and would not usually be considered indicative of the disorder. The clinician's problem is to determine whether instances of compulsive behavior reflect an underlying psychological problem. The decision is usually based on the extent to which the symptoms interfere with everyday living, the length of time the symptoms have been present, and other characteristics of the child. Other signs of disturbance, such as irritability, worry, tension, and lack of sociability, tend to increase the likelihood that a neurosis would be diagnosed.

The traditional clinician may describe the obsessive-compulsive child as using the defenses of reaction formation, undoing, and isolation. According to Freud, obsessive-compulsive neurosis originates in an unsuccessful solution to the Oedipal complex; the obsessive-compulsive neurosis represents a regression to the anal stage and the concomitant struggles with aggression and cleanliness.

Occasionally, specific thought patterns or behaviors are suggestive of both psychosis and neurosis. In these instances, the child's perception of the thoughts or behaviors guide the diagnosis. Generally, if the child recognizes the thoughts or behaviors as being inappropriate or senseless, the problem is considered neurotic.

Behavioral assessment of children with obsessive-compulsive symptoms also relies on the interview with the parents, which would focus on the stimulus environment in which the excessive thoughts and behaviors occur. An attempt would be made to determine whether external events contributed reinforcement for the reported thoughts and overt behaviors. Since anxiety is often a significant component in the constellation of symptoms, assessment would also include an interview with the child to determine the range of thoughts and acts that are associated with anxiety. An historical event that precipitated the onset of the symptoms might also contribute toward the design of a specific treatment program.

Observational data would also be collected, when possible. When the behaviors occur in the home setting, such data can often be collected by the parents. Future research may consider the possibility of using self-recording techniques with older children. The baseline observation period is also utilized to determine the possibility of association of the obsessive-compulsive behaviors with specific environmental stimuli.

On the basis of research with animals and human adults, several learning models have been developed to account for the genesis of obsessive-compulsive symptoms. One model (derived from the animal literature) suggests that compulsions may be manifested as by-products of situations in which a very difficult learning problem reduces the likelihood of successful performance. That is, compulsions may be instances of traumatic avoidance learning—learning to avoid making a response that is likely to be followed by no reward or by an aversive stimulus. The compulsive behavior is maintained by anxiety-reduction and avoiding the possibility of failure or aversive consequences. Another model suggests that the social consequences (criticism) of obsessive behaviors occur too late to be effective in reducing the behaviors and thus do not successfully compete with the immediate reinforcement that comes from the obsession itself. Criticism, rather, has the effect of producing "guilt" (conditioned autonomic reactions), and the guilt or anxiety initiates avoidance responses. These avoidance responses are manifested in the obsessions.

While it seems likely that obsessions and compulsions continue to occur because of the reinforcing effects of anxiety-reduction, the origin of the specific contents of the obsessions and compulsions remains unclear. Perhaps the content is whatever occurs in the original traumatic situation that diverts the child's attention and thereby reduces anxiety. The content, then, may or may not contain elements derived from the original situation. Virtually no research has examined the role of hereditary or physical factors in the etiology of obsessions and compulsions in children.

In the 1940s several studies suggested that adults with severe obsessive-compulsive symptoms had an increased number of neurological disorders, but more recent data have not confirmed those findings.

treatment

The most common treatment for children's obsessions and compulsions has been individual psychotherapy. With the exception of a collection of case studies by Adams (1973), the clinical research literature specifically describing the treatment of obsessions and compulsions in children is extremely limited. It is generally agreed that the success of therapy depends on the severity of symptoms and ability of the child to tolerate the high level of anxiety engendered by the treatment process. Therapy becomes more difficult in those instances in which the behavior is generally appropriate but is carried out excessively (for example, hand washing). Treatment can also be long and stormy because the therapist must deal with the ambivalent feelings toward adults (including the therapist) that are characteristic of the anal stage.

Several behavioral approaches have been used for intervention programs with adults depending on whether the behavior was judged to represent a conditioned avoidance response or to have become "functionally autonomous" in that a wide range of stimuli, including the original anxiety, were capable of producing the behavior. One approach includes a desensitization program in which the client is gradually prevented from making the compulsive response and increasingly engages in incompatible responses (for example, touching a door knob after increasingly fewer cleaning responses). Other approaches have focused on more direct manipulations of the stimulus antecedents or consequences, such as verbal interruptions or reprimands, assertive training, and active encounters with the avoided object.

Case studies using behavioral approaches to obsessions and compulsions in children are rare. Weiner (1967) described a relatively simple solution to the extensive compulsive rituals of a fifteen-year-old boy. The therapist and client together constructed a list of five rituals and the reasons why the rituals were performed. For each reason, an alternative reason was constructed that could be satisfied by specific and limited motor and verbal responses. For example, repeated checking of a locked drawer was reported as a way of avoiding being sent to Vietnam. The therapist suggested that the drawer be locked and checked to ensure its safety against thieves. Face washing that had been lasting fifteen minutes was reduced to five minutes, which was timed with a stop watch. These instructional and mechanical controls resulted in the gradual disappearance of the boy's compulsions. A seven-month follow-up revealed that he was symptom free, and the parents reported that his current behavior was normal.

While therapists with both psychodynamic and behavioral orientations have published case studies showing improvement in clients with obsessive-compulsive symptoms, a review of the literature on the evaluation of therapy indicates disappointing results. Yates (1970, p. 166-167) concludes that no traditional therapy has been demonstrated to produce significant improvement in these symptoms. Comparable outcome studies with behavior therapy are not yet available.

depression

Historically, little attention has been given to depression in children. Sptiz's (1945, 1946) classic studies describing the symptoms of hospitalized infants stimulated considerable interest in mother-infant separation as well as experimental research on the effects of separating infant monkeys from their mothers. Spitz observed that the hospitalized infants were retarded in intellectual, social, and motor development and called this collection of symptoms, "anaclitic depression." In addition, Spitz noted the following symptoms as well: apprehension, sadness, immobility, listlessness, and apathy. He believed that these symptoms were similar to those found in depressed adults.

Despite Spitz's early work, depression as a childhood psychological disorder has often been omitted from textbooks on child psychopathology probably because many clinicians have had serious doubts that depression or other affective disorders exist in children prior to later adolescence. Hersh (1977) has suggested that our cultural mythology depicting childhood as a period without responsibilities or concerns may be responsible for the relative lack of attention to depression in children in contrast to the substantial research conducted on adult depression during the last thirty years. During recent years, however, there has been an increasing acknowledgement that depression can and does occur in children, but most of the important questions regarding assessment, etiology, and treatment remain to be answered.

Arguments against the use of a formal diagnosis of childhood depression have been presented by Lefkowitz and Burton (1978). Their review of the research literature indicates that normal children tend to have symptoms comparable to those described for depressed children. They further stated that assessment instruments with adequate reliability and validity have not been developed, therefore preventing the longitudinal and cross-sectional research necessary for establishing norms for children of different ages. In their view, until adequate instruments and norms are developed, diagnosis appears to be premature and treatment, particularly medical treatment, possibly harmful.

At the present time childhood depression is diagnosed by clinicians on the basis of information obtained during the interviews with the child and parents. A diagnosis of depression may be made if the child presents any of a wide range of behaviors such as crying, social withdrawal, school failure, physical complaints, aggression, and lack of bladder control. This variation clearly reflects the differing conceptual models of childhood depression. Feelings of sadness are rarely presented clinically without other symptoms; that is, by the time the child has been referred, a number of symptoms are reported. One critical question is which of these symptoms occurs before, after, or simultaneously with the onset of sad feelings. To make the problem of assessment more complicated, a number of clinicians (for example, Glaser, 1968; Cytryn and McKnew, 1974) have maintained the existence of "masked depression"; these clinicians believe that depression in children is "masked" by symptoms that are not typically associated with the problem in adults; such symptoms may include hyperactivity, aggressiveness, delinquency, and school failure.

In reviewing the literature on childhood depression, Kovacs and Beck (1977) maintain that childhood depression is demonstrated by behavioral changes that are similar in type to those manifested in adult depression. All of the studies agree that depressed children show some type of negative cognitive change; most of the studies describe attitudinal-motivational changes as well as disturbances in vegetative (such as, sleep and appetite) and psychomotor (for example, activity) functions. The studies do not, however, uniformly consider a report of "feeling sad" as the primary symptom of childhood depression.

Current research attention is focusing on the development of behavior checklists and rating scales that may be used for screening or identification and the establishment of norms for these instruments in samples of normal school children. Kovacs and Beck (1977) administered the short form of the Beck Depression Inventory (Beck, 1972), originally developed for adults, to a sample of seventh and eighth grade parochial school children. The items describe the following symptoms: sadness, pessimism, sense of failure, dissatisfaction, guilt, self-dislike, self-harm, social withdrawal, indecisiveness, self-image change, work difficulty, fatigability, and anorexia. Based on adult norms, 33 percent of the students were classified as moderately to severely depressed. This high incidence suggests that these depressive symptoms may reflect a normal developmental variation, namely, that adolescents typically check more depression items than do adults. A more recent study (Kashani and Simonds, 1979) found that only 1.9 percent of a sample of seven to twelve year olds met the DSM-III diagnostic criteria for affective disorders, while sadness was reported by 17.4 percent of the children.

A screening or identification instrument, the Peer Nomination Inventory of Depression (PNID), has recently been developed by Lefkowitz and Tesiny (1980). This instrument was administered to fourth and fifth graders who identified peers in response to questions such as "Who doesn't have much fun?" Reliability and validity were judged to be acceptable, and normative data are being collected.

The development of self-report scales for younger children is considerably restricted by their relatively poor reading skills. Therefore, researchers have relied
more on scales that are completed by parents, or teachers, or both. Using the depression scale of the Personality Inventory for Children (Wirt, Lachar, Klinedinst, and
Seat, 1977) that is completed by parents, Kendall, Garten and Leon (1979), from a
sample of 138 children with a mean age of 10.7 years, compared the 21 children
who obtained the highest scores with the 21 children who obtained the lowest
scores on a number of measures. Their results indicated that the depressed children
were rated by both parents and teachers as having more behavior problems than
nondepressed children. The children designated as depressed by their parents
showed a tendency (though statistically not significant) to rate themselves as more
depressed on the Kovacs and Beck (1977) self-report Child Depression Inventory.

At a conference called Depression in Childhood, sponsored by the National Institute of Mental Health in 1975, a subcommittee proposed a set of clinical criteria for
the diagnosis of depression in children (Dweck, Gittleman-Klein, McKinney, and Watson, 1977). Two essential clinical features were described: (1) dysphoria or reports
of feeling sad and (2) an impairment in responding to experiences that were previously rewarding. The impairment has to be apparent across settings and not confined to a specific area of functioning. These clinical features have to be present for
four weeks before the diagnosis can be made. The subcommittee also described
secondary features that may be associated with the essential features: changes in
self-esteem, guilt, personal and general pessimism, and blaming others. The subcommittee recognized that research is needed to determine the role of these features in children of different ages.

There are several issues that future research must resolve. One issue involves the
development of valid assessment instruments. Related to this issue is the choice of a
validity criterion; at what age do children's reports about their own feelings (namely, about sadness) become a critical part of the assessment process? Another issue
involves the identification of the syndrome, the collection of symptoms that occur
together at various ages as distinguished from events and symptoms that are correlated less perfectly with the syndrome and that may either cause depression or
occur as a result of depression. For example, poor school achievement could have
a role in causing depression; on the other hand, depression (from other causes)
could result in a decreased rate of school learning.

etiology

Several etiological models of depression have been developed for adults, and a few
of them are being examined for their relevance to children. It has long been recognized that the loss of a significant person in one's life can result in depression. In
the case of children, significant persons may include parents, siblings, peers, and
other adults, such as caretakers, who have had close relationships with them. Such
loss normally precipitates a period of depression followed by a gradual recovery to

normal functioning; this process is considered to be entirely normal. When the symptoms become prolonged, however, the possibility of other factors affecting the depression must be examined.

In adults, several biological etiologies have been hypothesized for severe depression. Hereditary factors appear to be implicated because the blood relatives of severely depressed persons have a much higher incidence of depression than occurs in the population, and identical twins have a much higher concordance rate than do fraternal twins. Comparable studies with depressed preadolescent children have not been conducted.

Again with severely depressed adults, considerable research has focused on the role of biochemical factors. During the last two decades, increasing evidence has accumulated that depression is related to the level of catecholamines in the brain. These catecholamines regulate the transmission of neural impulses, that is, determine the probability of information being transmitted from one neuron to another in the nervous system. Indirect evidence from the success of biological therapies (for example, drugs) also supports the hypothesis of biological etiologies, at least in the cases of severe depressions. Since preadolescent children almost never present the symptoms of severe depression, these factors may be relatively less important in the etiology of their depression.

Both psychoanalytic and behavioral theories have been used to conceptualize the etiology of depression. Psychoanalytic conceptualization discriminates between grief and melancholia; grief is a normal response to the loss of a love object, while melancholia includes feelings of anger and hostility toward the love object in addition to the depression. Melancholia is also believed to be accompanied by a loss of self-esteem through a process in which the depressed inviduals convert their hostility toward the lost love objects to self-hatred. Because they are so dependent on others for self-esteem, particularly at some developmental stages, children may be likely to show melancholic reactions, but there is still considerable debate among psychoanalytic clinicians about whether children manifest depression in the same ways that adults do. Moreover, the theory has not lent itself to adequate hypothesis testing.

Behavioral views (Ferster, 1973) of the etiology of depression emphasize inadequate or insufficient reinforcement. The reinforcement deficits may originate with the loss of a person who provided reinforcement, poor skills in arranging for positive reinforcement, or environmental changes that are correlated with decreases in reinforcement. Loss of reinforcement could account for the low activity rate observed in depressed people. If generalized, the low activity rate furthermore deprives the person of potential reinforcement from other sources. Other behaviors characteristic of the depressed person, such as complaining and requesting help, are believed to be strengthened or maintained by social attention.

Beck's theory of depression is based primarily on cognitive factors (Kovacs and Beck, 1977). Depressed individuals view events negatively; that is, they view themselves as deficient and inadequate and attribute their bad feelings to defects within themselves. They also perceive their environment as making excessive demands on them and tend to interpret interactions in terms of failure. The negative cognitive patterns are projected to the future in the belief that the current situation and feelings will continue indefinitely.

In Beck's analysis the depressed person's negative cognitions are irrational and do not correspond to reality. Although a particular loss or deprivation may have occurred, the depressed person develops thought patterns that implicate more factors than are, in fact, involved. Once a pervasive attitude of self-blame is developed, other symptoms, such as indecisiveness and increased dependency, may result. Beck's view is that a person's feelings mirror cognitions; in the case of depression, negative cognitions lead to feelings of depression.

Seligman (1975) describes a cognitive model of depression with a basis in learned helplessness and emphasizes the individual's inability to escape or avoid aversive situations. According to Seligman, depression results from the person's *perceiving* that aversive events are going to occur whether or not a response is made. Such perceptions could be based in reality (persistent school failure experiences due to inability) or could be derived from generalized cognitions that failure is due to factors beyond one's control.

treatment

Although biological factors have not been demonstrated to cause childhood depression, medication has nevertheless been used for treatment. Research on the effectiveness of medication for depressed children has produced mixed results. While some findings certainly support continued research in this area, there are no adequate criteria for determining which depressed children will respond favorably to the available medications (Rapaport, 1977).

A study by Weinberg and colleagues (1973) has presented positive results. A sample of depressed children was selected on the basis of particular criteria (decline in school work, sad mood, and verbal statements about low self-esteem) from a group of children referred to an educational diagnostic center. Of the nineteen children treated with medication, eighteen were reported as having moderate or marked improvement. The general concensus among most investigators is that both tricyclic antidepressants and monoamine oxidase (MAO) inhibitors are effective for depressed children. Children with learning disabilities, speech problems, or hyperactivity, however, are likely to be nonresponsive to these medications.

Given that strong arguments have been made against the existence of depression in children and that there has been a lack of consensus with regard to diagnostic criteria, it is not surprising that psychotherapy and behavior therapy outcome studies have not been conducted. There are therapeutic models, successful with depressed adults, however, that may be suitable for children. Some forms of therapy focus on gradually getting the person to be active again (for example, doing small chores and jogging). Cognitive-behavioral therapies combine cognitive restructuring (changing negative self-statements to more realistic evaluations of achievements) and activity assignments.

identity disorder

An identity disorder is characterized by internal distress and uncertainty about one's role in life. It typically begins during late adolescence and is usually resolved by the mid-twenties; it may become chronic and be manifested later by an inability to make commitments to relationships and a career. This disorder appears to have become increasingly common during the past few decades and may be related to the greater number of choices of values and life-styles available to the modern adolescent.

The areas causing distress may include career choice, friendship patterns, religion, moral values, and sexual orientation. The disorder is characterized by an inability to make decisions related to these important areas and a preoccupation with one's self rather than external events. Alienation from the family and other close individuals is common while the person is attempting to resolve these issues of identity. Underachievement in educational and occupational performance may also result. Although psychotherapy has been used as a treatment method for identity disorders, systematic study of its effectiveness has not been conducted.

Conclusions

This chapter has described a broad range of disorders that are believed to be related to anxiety or depression, or both. For most of the disorders, the behavioral symptomology represents an avoidance of the feared object or situation. Levitt's (1971) conclusion that psychotherapy with children classified as neurotic has not been demonstrated to be effective has been upheld by Barrett, Hampe, and Miller (1978) who recognized the lack of adequate research in the interim. Behavior therapy approaches appear to be effective for several of these disorders, such as school phobia and avoidant disorder, but comparable outcome research for the other disorders has not yet been conducted.

Recommended Readings

Adams, P. L., *Obsessive Children*. New York: Penguin, 1973. A description of forty-nine obsessive children.

Freud, A., *Normality and Pathology in Childhood*. New York: International Universities Press, 1965. Describes normal child development and psychopathology within the context of psychoanalytic theory.

Gelfand, D., "Social Withdrawal and Negative Emotional States: Behavior Therapy," in *Handbook of Treatment of Mental Disorders in Childhood and Adolescence*, pp. 330–353. Edited by B. B. Wolman, J. Egan, and A. O. Ross. Englewood Cliffs, N. J.: Prentice-Hall, 1978.

Johnson, S. B., and Malamed, B. G., "Assessment and Treatment of Children's Fears," in *Advances in Clinical Child Psychology*. Vol. 2, pp. 107–139. Edited by B. B. Lahey, and A. E. Kazdin. New York: Plenum, 1979.

disorders
affecting
physical functioning

13

Janet was a fifteen-year-old emaciated girl who had been admitted to a general hospital for diagnosis and treatment of severe weight loss. She was the oldest of three daughters and had no history of significant physical or psychological problems. Her parents described her as having been easy to rear and having done well in her school work. They expressed only a mild complaint about her being perfectionistic and placing high demands on herself. They had become increasingly concerned about her weight loss during the past year. She was not worried about the weight loss and had to be forced to go to the physician who subsequently admitted her to the hospital.

The parents reported that she had never been overweight but that she put herself on a strict diet because she felt that she was too fat. Even after she lost weight, however, she continued to feel "too fat." At family mealtimes, she came to the table but ate only small portions of food.

On a few occasions, she ate a normal amount of food but later went to the bathroom and vomited.

Examination and laboratory tests revealed no physical problems except those caused by the weight loss. Although displeased by being forced to go to a physician and being hospitalized, Janet was a model patient; she was cooperative and cheerful and spent much of her time being physically active and socializing with other patients. While in the hospital, she continued the eating pattern she had at home and continued to lose weight.

In this chapter, we examine disorders of which the primary symptoms affect some aspect of physical functioning. In some instances the disorder involves biological damage and may be life threatening, while in other instances physical functioning is disrupted, but no long-term biological consequences are implicated. Many of these disorders appear to be either initiated or maintained by psychological factors, such as anxiety. Although their etiologies are complex and not well understood, the diagnosis and optimal treatment of these disorders often require the close cooperation of physician and therapist.

eating disorders

Children's eating experiences have received considerable attention from both theorists and practitioners. Psychoanalytic theorists have suggested that early eating experiences and their association with the gratification of oral needs play a significant role in determining later personality characteristics. Disturbances in eating behavior itself have been traced to the inadequate gratification of oral needs. Anna Freud (1965, p. 7) has stated that psychoanalytic investigators have been responsible for the cessation of certain eating disturbances by recommending that feeding and weaning correspond to oral needs.

In comparison with most other animals, the newborn infant is relatively helpless. All of the baby's needs must be met by another person who, in turn, must learn to understand these needs. The newborn infant has had little experience with schedules of feeding, because nutrients have been supplied continuously through the umbilical cord. Neither has the infant had more than accidental experiences with sucking an object. The newborn, thus, has much to learn and much to teach his caregivers about the process of eating and feeding.

Certain standard information about feeding the young infant is usually made available to the new mother, but infants vary greatly in terms of their frequency of eating, the amount ingested at each feeding, and reactions to formulas and milk. Very young infants spend most of their time sleeping; they awake periodically and cry until fed. The average feeding frequency for young infants is every three to four hours. The frequency of awakening tends to be lower for higher birth weight infants, but some normal birth weight infants may awaken as often as every hour or two. Needless to say, parents are eager for the time when they and the infant sleep through the night. Interestingly, the middle of the night feeding is usually the first one the infant "sleeps through."

During the first year of life the frequency of feeding is gradually decreased to three meals a day plus milk at nap and bedtimes. Within three to six months after birth, solid food in the form of strained cereal, egg, meat, fruit, and vegetable begin to be introduced into the child's diet. Foods with more solid consistencies are added toward the end of the first year of life, when the child has several teeth and is learning to drink from a cup.

How and when to wean the infant from the bottle or breast to cup feeding often poses a problem for mothers. Psychoanalytic theory has suggested that weaning, carried out too early or too abruptly, or both, can lead to harmful psychological consequences. Early eating behavior receives a strong contribution from the sucking reflex that is present at birth; the sucking response, however, is greatly refined through learning during the first several months of life. Thus, strong patterns of motor behavior become associated with the eating process. Other forms of ingestion, such as drinking from a cup or eating from a spoon require a number of different motor behaviors. Transferring an infant from one mode of feeding to another should logically proceed in a gradual manner as the child is able to learn the new eating behaviors. Abrupt weaning before the child has acquired the new eating behaviors is likely to cause at least a temporary reduction in the ingestion of food and may be detrimental to health in extreme cases.

Pediatricians recommend that training for drinking from a cup be initiated between eight and twelve months of age, with the bottle being eliminated about the age of one year. Training for self-feeding with a spoon can usually be started at about one year and within a few months the child can feed himself or herself with only minimal spilling. These training tasks take time and patience from the mother, and sometimes hurried mothers postpone the training, continuing to feed the child themselves, and allow bottle feeding to continue for an extended period. Children who remain on the bottle beyond the second year are often subjected to ridicule by adult family members and peers.

While the psychological importance of sucking *per se* has been reiterated in the clinical literature, questions have been raised as to whether its significance has not been overstated. Studies (for example, Davis, Sears, Miller, and Brodbeck, 1948) have shown that infants who were cup fed did not engage in more nonnutritive sucking than those breast or bottle fed. Furthermore, infants who were weaned to the cup early showed fewer signs of frustration than those who were weaned later (Sears and Wise, 1950). These studies suggest that the need to suck is based primarily on learning with greater sucking experience resulting in an increased sucking need.

The introduction of new foods is usually correlated with the weaning process and presents its own problems. Children tend to reject foods that vary greatly from their regular food in either taste or consistency. They push the food out of their mouths or, if forced to eat, will vomit.

One method that is likely to be successful with rejected foods is based on a fading procedure. The mother begins by mixing a small amount of the new food with the familiar food and gradually increases the proportion of new food as long as the child continues to accept the mixture. That is, the familiar food is gradually faded out of the mixture until the new food is accepted by itself.

not eating

Problems related to not eating tend to occur with considerable frequency during infancy and the preschool years. The great majority of children who are brought to the attention of their physicians for refusal to eat are, however, exhibiting typical developmental patterns or are reflecting a learned pattern of behavior.

After the initial learning to suck efficiently and adjustment of formula, the infant becomes an eager eater, usually tripling his birth weight during the first year. During the second through fifth years of life, the rate of weight gain is decreased to about 5 pounds each year. It is typically during the second year of life that parents become concerned about the child's refusal to eat. Eating patterns become more erratic, and weight gain likewise follows an ir-regular pattern. The child's weight may also remain unchanged over a period of months.

Parents are especially prone toward overemphasizing the ingestion of food in certain quantities without realizing that they may be facilitating the development of poor eating habits. If they are unaware of the normal daily fluctuations in appe-tite, they may begin to try a variety of methods, including cajoling, to get the child to eat. Sometimes, the child is not allowed to leave the table until the food is consumed, or the child is required to eat the food from the previous meal before being served the new one. Anger may be freely exhibited through threats and actual punishment. Under these circumstances, the child may learn that refusing to eat results in greater parental attention or that being at the table is an aversive experience.

Parents who have had these types of interactions occasionally need a little assistance in reversing the refusal pattern, but most parents learning on a trial-and-error basis soon realize that their method is not having the desired effect and try another. The physician's advice would probably include an elimination of parental urges and threats. In extreme cases of refusing to eat, the child may be given a preferred food at each meal. The goal is to get the child to eat and associate positive consequences with eating. Once eating has stabilized within normal developmental limits, different foods are gradually added to the daily menu.

It is important to keep in mind that certain other factors may also be involved with refusal of food. Illness of various types may cause a decrease in eating, with the rejection of food sometimes occurring before the illness is manifested. Other factors include fatigue, overstimulation, and inadequate exercise.

Regurgitation of food is frequent in young children, especially infants. Persistent vomiting in the first days or weeks of life may be indicative of an obstruction in the digestive system. Vomiting may also be caused by an excess of swallowed air, overfeeding, allergy, or infections. If all of these factors are ruled out, then consideration is given to the possibility that the vomiting may have a psychogenic origin.

Children vary greatly in their proneness to vomit. Vomiting tends to occur during highly stimulating events, changes in environment, and stressful experiences associated with food. Around the ages of six and seven years, many children experience nausea and vomiting when riding in automobiles. Since vomiting may be elicited in a wide variety of situations, it is relatively easy to see how a broad range of previously neutral stimuli can become conditioned to elicit vomiting. The eating of a particular food and becoming ill while riding in a car may be classically conditioned and result in the avoidance of this food.

DSM-III includes a diagnostic category for a more intense course of vomiting, rumination disorder of infancy. This disorder usually begins between three and twelve months of age. It is characterized by repeated regurgitation of food with resulting weight loss or failure to gain the expected amount of weight. To be diagnosed, the condition has to last at least one month and follow a period of normal eating behavior. This disorder is potentially fatal due to malnutrition.

Physicians tend to prescribe drugs, such as phenobarbital and Thorazine, to treat severe cases of psychogenic vomiting. Behavioral intervention programs have been successful in eliminating vomiting in infants and older retarded children. In one case study, Lang and Melamed (1969) treated an infant who had a normal weight of 17 pounds at six months but whose vomiting had reduced his weight to 12 pounds at nine months. The child was vomiting within ten to fifteen minutes after every meal. The behavior therapy procedures were used because other treatment approaches were ineffective and his life was endangered. Treatment consisted of a brief electric shock to the calf of the infant's leg and a loud tone when vomiting was about to occur. The response to this procedure was rapid; by the sixth session the infant was no longer vomiting. One month after discharge from the hospital he weighed 21 pounds. He continued a normal course of weight gain and social development during the year following treatment, and the procedure did not appear to have any negative consequences.

pica

Pica refers to the persistent ingestion of a nonnutritive substance. The age of onset is usually between twelve and twenty-four months; pica may persist into adolescence. Most young children attempt to consume substances such as sand or grass or, during the teething period, they may chew on their crib rails or other furnishings, and thereby ingest paint and wood. Normally, the child is either easily taught or spontaneously gives up these activities. Children with pica continue to seek out and eat these substances that may be harmful; lead poisoning from paint and blockage of the intestines are possible complications.

Pica is more common among mentally retarded and psychotic children; other predisposing factors may be dietary deficiencies, neglect, and inadequate supervision. Treatment usually consists of careful monitoring of the child and preventing the ingestion as well as providing an appropriate diet.

obesity

Several generations ago, a plump or overweight infant was desirable because the extra weight was viewed as a sign of health. Children at that time were subject to many communicable diseases and infections that today are prevented by immunization or are treated with antibiotics. During the sieges with disease, many children succumbed; those with extra body fat were able to survive the days or weeks with minimal nutrition (due to depressed appetite) and great expenditure of energy to fight the infection.

Obesity is defined as a body weight that is 20 percent or greater than the norm for height and weight or determined by skin fold measurements that estimate subcutaneous fat. At present, being overweight is viewed as being detrimental to health. Overweight infants tend to become overweight children who tend to become overweight adults. Obese adults have shorter life expectancies and have a higher rate of chronic health problems. Research has suggested that the number of fat cells in the body is determined during the preadolescent years, with the overweight child developing more fat cells than a slimmer peer (Brook, Lloyd, and Wolf, 1972). Once these cells are developed, their number is not diminished by dieting, thus perhaps making it more difficult for people with juvenile-onset obesity to reduce effectively. Physicians are now trying to prevent obesity in young children as a way of ensuring healthier adulthood.

Obesity in children is related to a number of factors. Heredity apparently plays a significant role in the probability of being overweight. Heritability for weight is as high as that for height. Studies of twins have shown that identical twins resemble one another more closely in weight than do fraternal twins, whose weight similarity is the same as that for nontwin siblings. These results do not mean that body weight is strictly determined but rather that weight is controlled within certain limits by hereditary factors; the specific weight is still determined by activity level and food intake.

Both activity level and food intake may be affected by psychological factors. Clinicians who work with overweight children have emphasized the mother as the primary agent in the psychological contribution to obesity. Some mothers expect the child to eat unusually large amounts of food, and their children please them by cooperating. Food, in a sense, becomes a substitute for other parental behaviors, such as social attention and affection. During the preschool years the overweight child tends to maintain such a close relationship to the mother that peer relationships are only minimally developed. The mother may continue to dress and bathe the child long after it is necessary. Entering school is a traumatic experience because the child lacks many of the necessary social skills. Disappointments and frustrations are followed by more eating, the child's principal source of comfort.

Obese children are seldom happy children. They may be characterized as dependent and immature, but simultaneously demanding. They tend to be withdrawn with peers or choose playmates who are much younger or older than themselves. Older obese children are often convinced that they are ugly and undesirable.

Not all obese children are overweight from an early age. Obesity can develop as a reaction to traumatic events such as the death of a parent or sibling, birth of a sibling, separation of the parents, personal failures, and illnesses.

Although overeating is the behavior that most clinicians try to control with overweight adults, it appears that *underactivity* may be the more important behavior of overweight children. Research suggests that underactivity is far more prevalent among obese children than is overeating. Perhaps for some children, obesity is initiated by a decrease in activity level with no corresponding decrease in the amount of food eaten. Among the factors that may account for decreases in activity are the traumatic events mentioned earlier, the overweight condition itself, and ridicule from peers.

Treatment of obese children must take into account all of the known factors. First, an increase in exercise is usually prescribed—one hour per day during the week and three hours per day on weekends and vacations. Second, the child is given an individually planned diet high in protein and low in calories. A diet for an adolescent, for example, would have 1,200 calories. A considerable effort is made not to blame the parents or child but rather to emphasize the positive aspects of losing weight. Sometimes, parents have to be given instructions about nutrition and the caloric value of food.

Successful treatment of obese children is very difficult. Individual psychotherapy has not proved effective, but group therapy has shown some promise of success. Group therapy capitalizes on the importance of peer social approval for most children. Behavioral approaches to the treatment of obesity in adults have been well developed (Jeffrey, 1976), but comparable programs for children are only now being evaluated.

bulimia

This disorder is characterized by binge eating that occurs episodically. The food usually has a high caloric content, is sweet, and is eaten very rapidly. The binges are done secretively or as inconspicuously as possible.

Bulimia usually begins during adolescence or early adulthood. The person is aware that the binge eating is abnormal and becomes fearful that the eating cannot be stopped voluntarily. Depression and self-depreciation tend to follow the binges. Binges are usually terminated by abdominal pain, induced vomiting, sleep, or social interruption.

The disorder occurs predominantly in females most of whom are within a normal weight range. Their histories reveal great concern about their weight and repeated attempts to control it, and they have experienced frequent weight fluctuations that are greater than 10 pounds. Obesity is often present in the parents or siblings.

Bulimia tends to be a long-term disorder with the individuals alternating among binges, fasting, and normal eating. In a few instances, there may be alternation between binges and fasting with no normal eating pattern.

anorexia nervosa

The primary features of anorexia nervosa are substantial (25 percent) weight loss, an intense fear of obesity that continues during weight loss, a body image of "feeling fat" that continues during weight loss, and a refusal to eat enough food to maintain body weight. The disorder usually has an onset during adolescence, and it affects females predominantly (Bemis, 1978). Weight loss is accomplished by total reduction of food intake, self-induced vomiting, exercising, and use of laxatives and diuretics.

Most individuals with this disorder deny that they have a problem and resist suggestions that they seek help. They come to medical attention only when the weight loss becomes significant, and other physical problems appear. The physical signs include amenorrhea (in females), hypotension, and other metabolic changes. The disorder is usually manifested in a single episode with a full recovery, but it may be episodic or chronic until death is caused by starvation; the mortality rate has been estimated as between 10 percent and 20 percent.

In some cases, the onset of anorexia nervosa is associated with a stressful life situation. About one-third of the individuals were mildly overweight prior to the onset, and many of them are described as having been overly perfectionistic.

As is evident by the high mortality rate, anorexia nervosa is extremely difficult to treat. By the time these individuals come to the attention of a professional, they are in need of both medical and psychotherapeutic assistance.

Several behavior therapy case studies of anorexia nervosa have reported successful results with adolescents and adults. One of the difficult problems posed in the behavioral treatment of anorexia is finding an effective reinforcer for eating behavior. In one case study, the hospitalized client was placed in a sparsely furnished room, and all privileges, such as visits and television watching were made contingent on eating. Under those circumstances the client began to gain weight; she was later discharged, obtained employment, and remained in good health. A behavioral analysis of several other anorexic clients revealed that they were more active than normal women spending their time at home. For these clients, opportunity to engage in physical activity was made contingent on weight gain and was effective for the initiation and maintenance of rapid increases in weight gain (Blinder, Freeman, and Stunkard, 1970). Reduction of medication (chlorpromazine) was also reported as an effective reinforcer for weight gain in one case study.

After feeding, toilet-training has perhaps been given the greatest attention by the traditional theoreticians and clinicians. According to psychoanalytic theory, the methods of toilet-training can have long-term consequences for later personality characteristics. One assumption is that the child's body products are highly valued by the child and may be given as "gifts" to the mother or withheld as punishment to the mother, or they may be associated with aggression and used as weapons. The dual role of body products is viewed as consistent with the toddler's characteristic ambivalence.

Strong demands by the mother for early and rigid toilet-training may result in a psychological battle between mother and child. The mother's attitudes toward the toilet-training process are believed to result from her own training and its by-productions as manifested in her personality. If, on the other hand, she is able to perceive the child's needs in their ambivalent state and proceed with toilet-training in a sympathetic manner, then the process should be relatively free of stress.

Eventually, with or without strife, the child accepts the mother's standards of cleanliness and internalizes them. Defense mechanisms are developed to guard against the appearance of urges that are in contradiction to mother's standards. Traits such as orderliness, tidiness, punctuality, and reliability are viewed as evidence of these defense mechanisms.

Toilet-training may also be viewed primarily as a learning task in which the mother must develop stimulus control for the elimination responses. Children vary greatly in their progress toward successful toilet-training. In our society, about half of the two-year-olds have bladder control during the day; by the age of four years the figure is 90 percent. Night bladder control is achieved by nearly 70 percent of three-year-olds and 90 percent of eight-year-olds. Bowel control generally comes earlier; nearly 70 percent of two-year-olds and 95 percent of four-year-olds have control of their bowel movements. In general, girls are successfully toilet trained at an earlier age than boys.

During the infancy period, urination and defecation are frequent. As the child matures and the number of daily feedings decreases, there is usually a concomitant reduction in the frequency of elimination episodes. The regularity of these episodes contributes to the ease or difficulty of initiating training. The child who has a regular elimination pattern is easier to train because the mother is able to anticipate the elimination and place the child on the toilet at times when elimination is highly likely. The child who has an irregular pattern is usually placed on the toilet at certain (for example, two-hour) intervals throughout the day. The probability of the child's eliminating is markedly reduced, but it is higher than zero over a number of days or weeks. In addition to regularity of pattern, the mother should be alert to any behavior that precedes elimination; these behaviors might include straining, irritability, or pulling at the diaper. These behaviors can serve as signals to the mother to place the child on the toilet.

Sometimes, the child strongly resists being seated on the toilet. This resistance seems to be due to the novelty of the situation and to conditioned fears. Many young children become fearful when the toilet is flushed or if they lose their balance while on the toilet. The latter problem can be avoided by using a potty chair.

Once the child voids or defecates in the toilet, the mother can use praise or other reinforcers to indicate that she is pleased with the child's performance. Since, to be most effective, reinforcement should occur immediately after the desired response, the mother should remain with the child in the bathroom. Pediatricians suggest that each bathroom trial last only a few minutes, with the mother remaining silent, if there is no result. This suggestion is in contrast to some mothers' methods whereby the child remains on the toilet until he performs. In the latter situation, toilet-training may become aversive to the child and resistance to training increases. If the child shows strong resistance to being placed on the toilet, it is sometimes recommended that toilet training be postponed for two or three weeks. This postponement attempts to capitalize on the young child's short memory.

During the training process, the mother should use a specific word, such as *toilet,* to signify the act of elimination. Each time the child is successful, she can use the word. After the word acquires this specific meaning, she can use the word in the form of a request outside of the bathroom environment. The child gradually learns to use the word, first to describe his own behavior and, second, to indicate his need in an anticipatory manner. Once the child can signal his or her need to use the toilet, the mother can begin to train the child to become independent.

Toilet-training is often a long and arduous experience because the process is started when the child is quite young and lacks many of the prerequisite skills. From the available research, most children have the necessary prerequisite skills to be started on a toilet training program at about two years of age. Several effective toilet training programs (for example, Azrin and Foxx, 1974) are available for parents.

functional enuresis

Functional enuresis is defined in DSM-III as the "repeated involuntary voiding of urine during the day or at night, after an age at which continence is expected, that is not due to any physical disorder" (p. 79). For diagnosis, the child must have at least two events per month between the ages of five and six years and at least one event per month for older children. Thus, children less than five years old could not be diagnosed as having functional enuresis. At age five, the prevalence of functional enuresis is 7 percent for boys and 3 percent for girls, at age ten, 3 percent for boys and 2 percent for girls, and at age eighteen, 1 percent for boys and virtually zero for girls.

The majority of functionally enuretic children have a close relative who has or has had the disorder. Twin studies have shown a higher concordance in identical than in fraternal twins, suggesting a hereditary disposition for the disorder.

Functional enuresis can have multiple psychological effects on the child. The wetting is socially embarrassing, and the child will try to avoid situations, such as camp and overnight stays with friends, that will publicize the problem. Parents and other adults are sometimes severe in their anger and rejection and may punish the child inappropriately. The accumulation of these experiences may lead to poor self-esteem and affect behavior in other areas.

Among the factors that have been implicated in the etiology of functional enuresis are delayed development of the physical structures of the urinary system, delayed or incomplete toilet-training, and psychological stress. The psychological factors may be the child's hospitalization, starting school, or the birth of a sibling. It appears that children who have never had a lengthy period of urinary continence are more likely to have delayed development or inadequate toilet training, whereas psychological stress may be a more important factor when children become enuretic after a period of urinary continence.

Physicians have found that certain medications are useful for helping the school-age child who wets at night. One of these medications, imipramine, has been particularly effective. The child is started on a low dosage given at bedtime, and the dosage is gradually increased until improvement is apparent or the maximum dosage has been reached. The child continues to receive the drug for eight weeks, after which time it is gradually decreased.

One successful home treatment method for night-time enuretics is the "bell and pad" system, which is based on the principles of classical conditioning. The pad, which is wired to a bell, is placed on the child's mattress. When moisture makes contact with the pad, an electrical circuit is completed causing the bell to ring. The ringing bell awakens the child who then uses the toilet. In this paradigm, bladder tension is the conditioned stimulus, and the bell is the unconditioned stimulus for awakening. The pairing of the two stimuli results in the child's eventually awakening in response to the bladder tension alone. The bell and pad system has been quite successful for the majority of enuretic children and works fairly rapidly—within weeks or a few months. Earlier studies had suggested a 30 percent to 40 percent relapse rate within a two-year period after treatment, but subsequent research showed that overlearning to a criterion of fourteen consecutive dry nights greatly decreased the relapse rate (Young and Morgan, 1972).

Psychotherapy was a popular treatment for enuresis when it was believed to be a symptom of an underlying psychological conflict. Current practice relies primarily on the conditioning method and medication; psychotherapy is reserved for the small number of cases in which serious psychological problems are present.

functional encopresis

Functional encopresis is the voluntary or involuntary passage of feces in inappropriate places and is not due to a physical disorder. The child must be four years old before the diagnosis is made. Approximately 1 percent of five-year-olds have this disorder, and it is more common in males and in lower socioeconomic classes. About 25 percent of children with functional encopresis also have functional enuresis. Involuntary encopresis is likely to be associated with constipation. When the incontinence is deliberate, other psychological problems are usually evident.

When encopresis is involuntary or associated with constipation, physicians recommend dietary changes and the daily ingestion of mineral oil. After about a month of regular bowel movements, the mineral oil is gradually discontinued. Occasional use of enemas may also be recommended initially. When encopresis is associated with enuresis, imipramine helps both disorders.

Behavior therapy has been successful with encopretic children. Several case studies describe the achievement of normal bowel movements through the use of positive reinforcement. In these studies, the child is trained to sit on the toilet at designated times until a bowel movement has occurred or for a predetermined number of minutes (for example, five) have elapsed. Bowel movements were highly praised, and tangible rewards were given. No punishment or other consequences occurred if bowel movements did not occur.

Dramatic success was reported by Wright (1973) who had only one failure in over thirty cases. In this study, suppositories were given to the children immediately before breakfast. If the suppositories were not effective, an enema was given at a specific time. Positive reinforcement was given for bowel movements; punishment was used only for soiling. After soiling had not occurred for two weeks, the cathartics were gradually reduced; they were discontinued after eight weeks of daily bowel movements and no soiling.

Some cases of encopresis are viewed as involving serious psychopathology in the child and family (Bemporad, 1978). In such instances with younger children, intervention with the parents may help the problem. Older children may require individual psychotherapy in addition to the parental intervention.

sleep disorders

During the period immediately after birth, the infant sleeps virtually all of the time, waking only to eat. As the infant becomes older, the number of hours each day spent sleeping decreases. Gradually, the child's sleep schedule begins to conform to that of adults. Before the age of three or four years, most children are still taking one or two naps every day and sleeping continuously beginning soon after the evening meal until the next morning. After the naps are discontinued, the evening bedtime hour is gradually moved to later times. It is not until adolescence that the sleeping schedule approximates that of adults.

Parents may encounter problems when the child recognizes the discrepancy between his or her hour of retiring and those of other family members. The child does not want to be left out of any activities by going to sleep. Establishing a sleeping schedule and preparatory activities seems to be a satisfactory arrangement for most parents and children. The schedule must, however, conform to the child's sleeping needs; individual children vary in the amount of sleep they require for optimal functioning, just as adults do. Picking a bedtime solely on the basis of parental convenience is often not successful. Parents sometimes forget that the child's sleeping needs decrease over time and insist on the child's continuing to go to sleep at a time that is more appropriate for a younger child.

When a child resists going to sleep at night, parents are advised to assess sleeping needs in the context of the child's past sleeping history. In addition, they should review the stimulus events that are occurring immediately before bedtime. A child who becomes very activated just before bedtime may have increased difficulties falling asleep. In some families, a sleep problem may develop because the father returns home from work late in the day and plays roughhouse games with the child just before bedtime. Parents can prevent this problem by engaging in more relaxed activities, such as reading stories. Likewise, family members ought not to describe exciting events that are going to occur after the child goes to bed.

The young child typically cries when he does not want to be put to bed, but the older child presents a wide variety of behaviors, such as requests to use the bathroom or to get drinks of water. These behaviors are often an attempt to secure a continued interaction with other people.

Parents who remain in the room or in the same bed until the child falls asleep frequently find themselves repeating that performance weeks and months later. If a child's calls and requests for companionship at bedtime are granted, parental social contacts may serve as reinforcers, thereby strengthening these behaviors.

Sometimes, reluctance to go to sleep is accompanied by emotional responses reflecting fear on the part of the child. Preschool children are particularly prone to the development of fears, and, more often than not, going to sleep is inadvertently associated with a stimulus that elicits fear in the child. Events such as loud, sudden sounds and unfamiliar light patterns coming through the windows are sometimes sufficient for the conditioning of fear to the darkened bedroom. Fear of the dark can often be alleviated by using a night light in the child's room.

Awakening during the night may be initiated by many different events, for example, illness, nightmares, changes in daytime routine, and wetting the bed. Once the rhythmic sleep pattern has been broken, there is a tendency for the child to continue awakening in the night in the absence of the original event.

Almost all children have occasion to wake up during the night, and almost all of them go to their parent's bedroom. Under these circumstances, the child is often taken into the parent's bed. The comfort of being taken into a warm bed has great reinforcing properties and thereby increases the probability of the child's returning to the parent's bedroom on subsequent nights. In some extreme cases, children have been known to sleep with one or both parents over a period of years. Most parents, however, are not interested in sharing their beds with a third person and realize that the child must be returned to his own bed without further strengthening of the child's behavior. Occasionally, a parent accepts the child in bed as a way of preventing sexual relations with the other parent. Single parents who are feeling lonely themselves sometimes allow the child to remain for company.

sleepwalking disorder

The primary characteristics of a sleepwalking disorder are recurring episodes of behaviors that involve leaving the bed and walking without being conscious of the activity or remembering the activities. The episodes usually occur between 30 and 200 minutes after sleep has begun.

The sleepwalking disorder usually begins between the ages of six and twelve years and lasts several years. In the minority of cases, sleepwalking recurs during early adulthood. It has been estimated that between 1 percent and 6 percent of children have the disorder at some time; it is more common among males than females and usually affects more than one member of a family.

Factors related to sleepwalking include seizure disorders, central nervous system infections, and trauma. Individuals with this disorder are more likely to have an episode when they are fatigued, have experienced a stress, or have taken a sedative before going to bed.

The most serious complication with this disorder is accidental injury. Contrary to a popular belief, sleepwalking individuals are not as careful as they would be when awake, even though they are able to see and avoid objects in their path. Parents must take special precautions to be alerted and to prevent injury if their child has this disorder.

sleep terror disorder

Sleep terror disorder refers to recurrent episodes of abrupt awakening from sleep that are initiated by a scream. The individual displays the signs of intense anxiety, such as a frightened expression, rapid breathing, perspiration, and repetitive motor movements; efforts to comfort the person are not successful until the intense agitation subsides; episodes last from one to ten minutes. There is usually no memory of the episode upon awakening in the morning.

As in the sleepwalking disorder, episodes occur between 30 and 200 minutes after sleep onset when dreaming is not usually occurring. The sleep terror disorder usually begins between the ages of four and twelve years and gradually disappears in early adolescence. This disorder is more common in males and affects 1 percent to 4 percent of children at some time. Etiology is unknown, but individuals with the disorder are more likely to have an episode if they are fatigued or under stress or have taken certain antidepressant or antipsychotic drugs. There are no complications as far as the child is concerned, but the episodes are likely to be very stressful to the parents.

stereotyped movement disorders

Although there are a number of movement abnormalities, most of which have been related to neurological problems, the disorders in this category have certain features in common and are considered to be distinguishable from other movement abnormalities. The primary feature of a stereotyped movement disorder is involuntary rapid movement of a functionally related group of skeletal muscles or involuntary production of sounds or words. They are likely to create social problems for the individual and may interfere with normal functioning.

tic disorder

Tics are repetitive, involuntary, rapid movements, the most common of which are eye blinks and other facial tics, but the whole head, torso, or limbs may manifest the movement. The individual may have one or several tics that occur at the same time, sequentially, or independently. Tics are considered to be transient, if their intensity varies and their duration has been at least one month but not longer than one year; they are considered to be chronic, if their intensity does not vary and they have occurred for more than a year.

The onset of transient tics is always during childhood (as early as two years) or early adolescence. Some 12 percent to 24 percent of school-age children have had some history of tics; the disorder is three times more common in boys and is more common in family members of persons who have the disorder.

Tics become worse with stress but may decrease when attention is focused on some activity. They do not occur during sleep. The individual may be able to suppress the tics temporarily.

Because tics have been considered to be evidence of a neurotic process, in the past most of the more severely affected children were probably referred for traditional psychotherapy, but no evaluation of its effectiveness can be determined from the available research. Behavioral therapists have used a procedure called massed practice in which the child voluntarily performs the tic response repeatedly. This procedure has helped some children but is not uniform in its effect.

tourette's disorder

This disorder has the features just described for tics but, in addition, vocal tics are characteristic. These vocal tics may take such forms as clicks, grunts, coughs, or words; the majority of cases has a vocal tic that include verbal obscenities or curse words. The onset of Tourette's disorder may be as early as two years and almost always before thirteen years; in about half of the cases a single tic is the first symptom, and in the other half multiple tics begin to occur simultaneously. The disorder is three times more common in boys, and tics occur more often in family members of persons with the disorder. The disruptive effect of this disorder on home and school activities is severe.

Nothing definitive is known about etiology, but about half of the individuals have some signs of mild neurological abnormalities. The disorder can be lifelong and debilitating, and a variety of treatment approaches have been tried. From the available research, Fernando's (1977) suggestion appears to be the best, namely, a combination of haloperidol (an antipsychotic drug), massed practice, and psychotherapy that is altered to suit the needs of the individuals.

stuttering

Stuttering is one of the more familiar speech disorders, particularly since it is most readily identified. Stuttering may be defined as frequent interruptions of speech production by repetitions of sounds or syllables or by their prolongation, often accompanied by excessive motor behaviors. Repetitions in speech are characteristic of the young preschool child. For the great majority of children, these dysfluencies tend to decrease during the preschool years. While there are great individual differences in the types and amounts of fluency irregularities, certain kinds of irregularities, notably syllable repetitions, are heard more frequently in children who later become diagnosed as stutterers. The differences between potential stutterers and nonstutterers, however, are not great enough to discriminate these groups without considerable error in identification (false positives and false negatives). Perhaps future research with more refined screening techniques will lead to early identification and thus development of prevention strategies.

Because dysfluencies are so common during the preschool years, it is generally believed that speech therapy for stuttering is not indicated during this period. Some parents, however, equate developmental dysfluencies with stuttering and react in a way that exacerbates the speech irregularity. Speech pathologists have suggested that the onset of stuttering in school-age children is most often between two and four years of age, the peak time for developmental dysfluencies.

Stuttering occurs in approximately 1 percent to 2 percent of the school population and has its onset before the age of nine years (Young, 1975). Stuttering occurs about five times as often in males as in females. Both stuttering and other speech problems are frequently found in the families of stutterers. Speech and language delays are commonly reported for stutterers, although their intellectual functioning is otherwise within normal limits. Fine motor coordination is often poor, while gross motor development is within normal limits. Reading and writing difficulties are encountered by a significant number of stutterers and members of their families.

Assessment and etiology. Speech pathologists frequently identify forms of stuttering on the basis of observed or inferred etiological factors, but the available research literature does not provide evidence that different etiological factors produce different stuttering patterns. Thus, at the present time, it would appear more reasonable to diagnose stuttering solely on the basis of behavioral criteria and to continue the search for its causes. A diagnosis of stuttering is made by the speech pathologist after careful assessment of the child's speech and language repertoire. Since stuttering is most often identified in children between the ages of six and twelve years, both teachers and parents are primary referral sources. Speech pathologists employed by the schools provide most of the services for children who stutter. The school pathologist, in contrast to a pathologist in a clinic, has a certain advantage in being able to observe easily the child in the context of various school activities and in having ready access to the teacher. Thus, assessment of the child includes school observation and teacher interviews as well as the testing procedures and speech samples obtained in the office. School pathologists, however, may have greater difficulty obtaining parents' cooperation, thus reducing the amount of information that may be obtained with regard to the child's history and development of the problem.

As with other speech disorders, the assessment procedure includes a hearing test. Stuttering is only rarely associated with hearing loss, although it is occasionally found in conjunction with decreased levels of intellectual functioning. Other findings being equal, a child with a mental age of four years may not receive speech therapy for stuttering for the same reasons that a four-year-old with average intelligence might not. That is, both children have a high probability of "outgrowing" their stuttering behavior.

It is likely that children who stutter have been subjected to numerous instances of psychological stress. Parents and teachers try to correct them, and their peers laugh at them. These reactions from important people in the child's environment are believed by most pathologists to make the problem worse. During the assessment process, the pathologist attempts to evaluate the possible psychological contributions to the problem. It may be assumed that psychological factors increase in importance as the child gets older and experiences more demands and ridicule.

Both organic and psychological factors have been hypothesized to cause stuttering, but research has yet to identify whether stuttering is constitutional or learned (Travis, 1978). Pathologists in the past were taught adherence to a specific, single cause for stuttering. Contemporary teaching, however, advocates an open-minded attitude toward the etiology of stuttering. This attitude has been developed on the basis of the research evidence that contradicts the notion of a single cause. That is, no single factor has been found to be involved in all cases of childhood stuttering.

Van Riper (1972, p. 252) has organized the various points of view concerning the etiology of stuttering into three principal types of theories: constitutional, neurotic, and learned. Most of the available evidence supports a learned, or neurotic, basis for the problem, although a few studies suggest an organic basis for at least some cases. A search for possible neurological mechanisms has been motivated by recent studies in which stuttering has been produced by electrical stimulation of a certain part of the brain in an unanesthetized adult and has been alleviated or eliminated following neurosurgical treatment of other conditions, such as epilepsy, brain tumors, and aneurysms.

In the past, stuttering has been linked to being left-handed or ambidextrous, suggesting a problem related to cerebral dominance. Investigations have also hypothesized an underlying neuromuscular condition that manifests itself in poorly timed nervous impulses to the speech organs. Other researchers have suggested that stutterers may have defects in auditory perception; evidence for this suggestion comes from studies in which delaying the feedback of the person's voice for a fraction of a second has produced behaviors similar to stuttering. Adherence to constitutional factors as being implicated in the etiology of stuttering is further strengthened by its tendency to run in families, the substantial male-female ratio, a higher than expected rate of abnormal EEG patterns, and problems in fine motor coordination.

Many psychiatrists and psychologists believe that stuttering is a symptom reflecting an underlying personality disturbance. These professionals have suggested that stuttering is an external manifestation of repressed wishes to satisfy basic oral or anal needs. The mouth movements of the stutterer have been perceived by some clinicians as a way of prolonging infantile oral activities, while other clinicians have focused on the stutterer's fear of revealing forbidden wishes. These psychoanalytic views were particularly popular during the 1940s and early 1950s and were accepted because many of the *adult* stutterers seen by psychiatrists and psychologists did present serious emotional problems. These views are still held by some practitioners (Rousey, 1978).

Speech pathologists have tended to view stuttering as a learned behavior. Since so many stutterers have reported the onset of the problem during the preschool years, speech professionals have hypothesized that stuttering is a learning extension of the repetitions and nonfluencies that normally occur between the ages of two and four years. This view proposes that the developmental repetitions are inadvertently reinforced by parental attention. Most stuttering patterns are not, however, duplications of developmental speech patterns, which tend to be repetitions of whole words, rather than initial sounds. In addition, environmental stress seems to be highly correlated with stuttering patterns. It has therefore been suggested that stress or frustration is responsible for the initial stuttering pattern. At some period in the child's life, psychological pressure to communicate is strong enough to disrupt the normal flow of speech. Indeed, there are instances reported in the clinical literature of children who changed from fluent speakers to stutterers in a matter of days.

At the present time the model that best fits most child stutterers is a two-factor learning theory, the first component consisting of the classical conditioning of the stuttering response and the second component consisting of additional strengthening through reinforcement contingencies. Other aspects of stuttering behavior, such as avoidance of certain sounds or speech in certain settings, can also be explained by the second component, operant conditioning.

Treatment. Many types of therapy have been used for stuttering, and claims of success have been reported by their proponents. Contemporary pathologists who work with children tend to take an eclectic approach with a primary emphasis on learning principles. During the assessment process the pathologist evaluates the role of environmental stimuli as potential antecedents and consequences of the stuttering behavior. In the case of young (four to eight years of age) stutterers, the pathologist often discovers that the parents are reprimanding the child for stuttering and, in addition, placing substantial demands for the presence or absence of other behaviors. Under these circumstances, the pathologist recommends that the parents reduce their reprimands and other demands. Occasionally, such changes in the home environment rapidly lead to a complete disappearance of the stuttering. Some children have such a low level of frustration tolerance (correlated with high rates of stuttering) that the pathologist may instruct the parents in conditioning procedures whereby the child is taught to cope with gradually increasing amounts of frustration.

In some cases, the parents are not willing or able to follow the speech pathologist's advice to reduce the psychological stresses in the home. If such is the case, the speech pathologist may recommend supplementary psychological help for the parents or child, or for both. Depending on the factors in the specific case, play therapy, role playing, or counseling for the parents may be recommended.

If the reduction of psychological stress in the home is not completely successful in eliminating the stuttering, the speech pathologist embarks on a course of action that emphasizes the increase of fluent speech. One tactic involves demonstrations by the parents and the pathologist of the child's acceptance by them. The acceptance may be manifested in numerous ways, such as giving the child appropriate responsibilities and rewarding successful achievements. In a similar manner, parents and the pathologist begin to reinforce fluent speech and eliminate attention to stuttering differentially.

Of the elementary school-age children who receive help for stuttering, about 75 percent to 85 percent receive that help from speech pathologists employed by the schools. Unfortunately, many of these school speech pathologists have not been well trained to work with elementary school-age stutterers (Williams, 1971, p. 1,073) and attempt to conduct therapy through counseling of the parents, which might be appropriate for the younger child, or with procedures designed for adults. It is generally agreed that children in this age group require direct therapy. Since most school-age stutterers have a history of stuttering lasting several years, they usually present a greater challenge to the pathologist. The stutterer is probably well aware of his or her stuttering and has begun to react to it in several ways. The more the child tenses in order to control or prevent stuttering, the greater the difficulty and unpleasantness of speaking the child experiences. Sometimes, extensive repertoires of superfluous motor movements have developed prior to referral for therapy. Fear of speaking, virtually absent in the young stutterer, becomes more prevalent as the child experiences more and more frustration. At present, there are three principal approaches to treatment of the older child who has stuttered for several years.

One method is through psychotherapy alone. While case studies that describe the reduction and elimination of stuttering through psychoanalysis and psychotherapy have been reported in the clinical literature, speech professionals do not view psychotherapy as a useful approach for the majority of children who stutter.

The second approach for treating the older child is currently used by many of the older speech pathologists. It includes a wide variety of techniques for teaching the stutterer to avoid or prevent the fear that precipitates the stuttering episodes. Every effort is made to convince the stutterer that it is possible to be cured. That is, the pathologist uses strong suggestion to obtain the client's confidence in the therapeutic effectiveness. In addition, breathing and vocalization exercises, as well as gestures and head movements, are utilized to distract the child from the fear of stuttering. In an effort to convince the stutterer that he or she is a normal speaker, the pathologist designs speech situations and forms of communication that are arranged in order of difficulty or the probability of eliciting stuttering. Each level is maintained until fear and stuttering are absent. This form of treatment has resulted in many cures and thus has many proponents. The evidence suggests, however, that generalization to the natural environment may be poor.

The third major treatment approach to stuttering is a method that attempts to deal with all of the factors that increase the probability of stuttering. This approach has been strongly recommended by Van Riper (1972, p. 307), a recognized expert in the area of speech correction. The pattern of treatment may be conceptualized in six phases or tasks: motivation, identification, desensitization, variation, approximation, and stabilization. Starkweather (1973) has presented a behavioral analysis of Van Riper's treatment pattern.

In the motivation phase, the therapist seeks to motivate the client to view the problem realistically and to be willing to invest considerable energy in the therapy program. The therapist provides a totally nonpunitive situation in which stuttering is initially encouraged and confronted directly. When the client stutters, the therapist provides objective evaluations of the behavior. When the client avoids speaking or substitutes other words that are easier to speak, the therapist interprets these behaviors in an accepting manner.

Motivation is encouraged by convincing the client that the therapist's role is primarily that of a guide in a joint venture. Early in treatment the therapist shares the client's problem by repeating the stuttering behaviors and explaining that engaging in the stuttering behaviors helps to understand the client's feelings. This procedure not only facilitates the relationship between the client and the therapist but begins to extinguish some of the emotional responses that were developed by other people's ridiculing the child in the past. The therapist also encourages the client to talk about his or her feelings when stuttering occurs.

During this initial phase the therapist begins to assist the client to discriminate his or her own speech productions. Virtually all stutterers have some fluent speech in addition to both *easy* and *hard* stuttering. Easy stuttering consists of relatively short dysfluencies without accompanying exaggerated motor movements, while hard stuttering consists of a prolonged series of sound repetitions with superfluous movements, such as facial contortions.

The second phase, identification, consists of delineating those factors that are implicated in the client's own stuttering behavior. Knowledge of these factors is obtained by reviewing with the child, parents, and teacher those situations in which stuttering has occurred and what the consequences of stuttering have been. The primary goal in this phase is to provide the client with a realistic and objective understanding of all facets of the stuttering problem.

In the third phase of treatment, desensitization, the goal is to reduce the level of fear associated with speaking and stuttering. This goal is attained through a variety of exercises or assignments in the natural environment. While no formal hierarchy of feared situations is constructed, the pathologist initially chooses activities with relatively low levels of associated fear and progresses to higher levels. The basic idea is to allow the client to experience these situations and discover that it is possible to endure one's own and others' reactions.

The purpose of the fourth stage of treatment, variation, is to attach new responses to the old stimuli and begin to break up the stuttering patterns. Specific exercises are designed in which the client gives a response that is different from the one typically given in that situation. For example, if a child usually lowers his or her head while stuttering, the child may be asked to lift it while speaking in front of a mirror with an observer present.

In the fifth stage of therapy, approximation, operant conditioning techniques are used to shape the client's stuttering behavior, initially toward easy stuttering, and later to nonstuttering. A variety of facilitory stimulus control methods are also employed. One such method would include the pathologist and client stuttering in unison with the pathologist's serving as a model for easier stuttering.

The final phase of treatment, stabilization, is one in which the client's fluent behavior is strengthened and made less vulnerable to environmental stresses. The client is taught to resist conditions that predispose him or her to stutter. One procedure involves having the client read in unison with the pathologist—a task the client can easily do without stuttering. Then the pathologist introduces stuttering into the material being read, while requesting the client to remain fluent. This task is very difficult, and the pathologist is careful to use this exercise as an opportunity for success.

Speech pathologists who work with stuttering children use a variety of techniques, such as role playing, to facilitate generalization outside of the therapy room. The pathologist takes the role of people in the child's environment (for example, parents, teacher) and gives the child practice with "easy" talking. Role playing is followed by conferences with the child, parents, and pathologist during which the child's progress is reviewed, and situations in the home are designated in which the child can practice the easy talking. The parents are instructed to reinforce the child immediately for successes. Similar procedures are followed with the teacher.

conversion disorder (hysterical neurosis, conversion type)

The primary characteristic of a conversion disorder is an involuntary loss of sensory or motor function; blindness, deafness, and paralysis are some of the possible symptoms. Clients usually show a lack of concern about their symptoms. Conversion disorders are diagnosed more frequently in adults than in children; adolescents rather than younger children are typically affected. A diagnosis of hysteria is usually made by a physician who must be able to rule out physical causes, such as neurological abnormalities.

Proctor (1958) has reported on the most extensive study of childhood hysteria. Out of 191 unselected, consecutively diagnosed cases from a North Carolina medical school psychiatric clinic, twenty-five children, or 13 percent, were diagnosed as cases of hysteria. Both sexes were equally represented in contrast to a ratio of two males to one female in the remaining sample. Older children and black children were overrepresented in comparison to the ratios found for the remaining psychiatric cases. Proctor attributed the relatively high incidence of hysteria in his population to factors such as low education, rural living conditions, and poor economic environment, which tend to create primitive and repressive attitudes.

In his analysis of hysteria, Freud suggested that the condition originated from inner conflict that was unsuccessfully repressed; the symptoms represented a return of the repressed conflict. The particular symptoms presented by the client are important in that they are supposed to reflect some part of the original conflict.

In Freud's time, hysteria was seemingly much more common than it is at the present time. It has been suggested that the original higher rate of hysteria was due to child-rearing practices. Child management during the Victorian era emphasized a rigid routine and suppression of emotional expression. There was also a general attitude that preschool children were basically "bad" and required strong measures to convert them into "little adults" by the age of six or seven years. Freud's influence, as well as general societal changes, served to change child-rearing practices markedly toward the other extreme, permissiveness. The subsequent reduction in the occurrence of hysteria is often credited to the increased use of permissiveness in child management.

Proctor's (1958) analysis with respect to etiology follows a psychodynamic model. He suggested that extreme inconsistency between action and word gives rise to the development of hysterical symptoms. Proctor proposed that experiences, such as being exposed to highly emotional religious services emphasizing hellfire and damnation for engaging in certain (for example, sexual) behaviors and simultaneously being witness to these behaviors or having strong wishes to participate in these behaviors may create internal conflict to the degree that hysterical symptoms are manifested. That is, hysteria develops as a result of strong emotional pressures both to engage and not to engage in a particular activity.

As mentioned earlier, specific hysterical symptoms are supposed to serve as clues to the underlying conflict. Hysterical blindness, for example, indicates that the affected person's internal conflict involves something that has been seen. Motor paralysis, in general, would reflect internal conflict about engaging in a particular behavior.

Behavioral clinicians have given little attention to the etiology of hysterical symptoms, perhaps because clients with hysteria have become increasingly uncommon during the short history of behavior therapy and because such clients are typically referred to traditional clinicians. Behavioral hypotheses with regard to the initiation and maintenance of hysterical symptoms can, however, be described. A number of the classical symptoms (for example, blindness, deafness, paralysis) represent behavioral absences in which onset was sudden. In the experimental psychology literature, rapid decreases and elimination of behavior are usually the result of the contingent presentation of an aversive stimulus. Moreover, the learning of behaviors to avoid aversive stimuli is rapid; these avoidance behaviors continue for long periods of time after the last experience with the aversive stimulus. In these situations it has been hypothesized that the avoidance behavior is maintained by the reinforcing effect of anxiety reduction. Thus, learning theory suggests that certain hysterical symptoms are avoidance behaviors, which, in effect, reduce anxiety. These symptoms may, in addition, be further strengthened by other reinforcers, such as social attention.

Suggestions have been made that physical factors may be involved in the etiology of hysteria, but they have been largely ignored. Whitlock (1967) reported that a high percentage of adults with hysteria also presented evidence of organic brain disorder preceding or accompanying the onset of symptoms. Additional research is needed to clarify the role of organic factors in the etiology of hysteria in children.

treatment

Treatment of hysterical neurosis has a long history in the traditional clinical literature. Freud himself worked extensively with adult cases of hysteria and found, like many clinicians after him, that the specific hysterical symptom is relatively easy to cure. Techniques, such as hypnosis and suggestion, seemed to be effective, but the clients had a strong tendency toward developing new symptoms. Freud concluded that only psychoanalysis, which emphasized insight, was capable of producing a lasting cure without symptom substitution. Thus, psychoanalysis and psychoanalytically oriented psychotherapy have become the treatments of choice by most clinicians for children and adolescents with hysterical symptoms. Behavioral clinicians have reported only a few case studies in which hysterical symptoms have been eliminated.

psychosomatic disorders

The term *psychosomatic* has undergone changes in definition during the past few decades. The earlier view was that certain physical problems were primarily or exclusively caused by psychological factors; some of the physical disorders that were so identified were asthma in children and stomach ulcers in adults. Subsequent research began to identify physical factors, such as heredity and abnormal immunity functioning, as strong competitors for the primary etiologies of these physical disorders. This research required an expansion of the definition of psychosomatic to include the contribution of psychological factors as secondary, namely, as making the physical disorder worse or more prolonged. As research has continued, it has become apparent that psychological factors can affect the course of an increasing number of physical disorders, including disorders previously believed to be completely unaffected by psychological factors.

Expansion of the number of physical disorders that involve psychological factors has progressed to the point that practically all of the disorders in this chapter would be considered psychosomatic by some authors. For example, Schaefer, Millman, and Levine (1979, p. ix) in their preface to *Therapies for Psychosomatic Disorders in Children* defined the term, *psychosomatic disorders,* as referring "to any physical conditions that can be initiated, exacerbated, or prolonged by psychosocial factors." Their book includes chapters on cardiovascular system, gastrointestinal system, neuromuscular, central nervous system, skin, and urinary system disorders as well as conversion reactions. In this section of the chapter we will review several of the major psychosomatic disorders not previously covered.

asthma

Asthma is a disorder of the respiratory system in which the person has difficulty getting air in and out of the lungs. This difficulty has been associated with the constriction of the smooth muscles lining the bronchial tubes, and increased secretions in the air passages. These conditions prevent the free exchange of air. The disorder is episodic and produces attacks in which the observable symptoms are coughing, wheezing (noisy breathing), and labored breathing. The person having the attack experiences the sensation of being suffocated and the associated fear.

Asthma is more common in children than adults and affects more boys than girls. For the majority of children with asthma the symptoms subside during or soon after adolescence. Asthma attacks may occur at any time and may range from a few minutes to several hours in duration.

It is generally agreed that genetic factors are significantly involved in the etiology of asthma. Although the underlying mechanisms have not been identified, asthma appears to involve allergic reactions to foods or airborne substances, such as dust and pollen, or to both foods and other substances.

Emotional factors in the etiology of asthma have been given much attention in the psychological literature. A number of studies have shown that asthma attacks can be induced by emotional stress. Other studies have also shown that some asthmatic children improved when they were separated from their families. Psychodynamic formulations suggesting that asthmatics have a certain type of intrapsychic conflict in common have not, however, been corroborated.

The more recent research literature is tending to deemphasize the blaming of mothers for their children's asthma (Gauthier, Fortin, Drapeau, Breton, Gosselin, Quintal, Weisnagel, and Lamarre, 1978) and to explore the role of classical conditioning in which previously neutral or positive stimuli may acquire fear-producing characteristics. It may also be that any stimulus that activates the respiratory system beyond a particular threshold could precipitate an asthma attack in a constitutionally vulnerable child.

Many forms of treatment have been tried with asthmatics. Drugs, such as bronchodilators and steroids, are particularly effective for the rapid relief of symptoms. Of the psychological therapies, the behavioral types have demonstrated the most promise. One of the earlier behavioral studies showed that relaxation training was effective in increasing the peak expiratory flow rates in asthmatic children (Alexander, Miklich, and Hershkoff, 1972). Subsequently, Hock, Rodgers, Reddi, and Kennard (1978) found that a relaxation program involving seven to nine forty-minute weekly sessions significantly lowered attack rates in adolescent male asthmatics and improved their pulmonary functioning (the amount of air force-fully exhaled in one second). However, four weeks after training was terminated, only an improved pulmonary functioning was maintained. Biofeedback training to decrease airway resistance (five to eight fifty-minute sessions) and ten sessions dur-ing which the subjects were told to relax and continue the biofeedback training during induced mild asthma episodes served to decrease asthma attacks during a one-year period (Khan, 1977).

ulcerative colitis

Ulcerative colitis is a chronic inflammation of the large intestine that is manifested by abdominal pain, diarrhea, and damage to the intestinal lining resulting in bleed-ing and mucous discharge. The available data suggest that genetic factors are in-volved in the etiology of ulcerative colitis; however, both its onset and recurring episodes have been associated with emotional stress. The emotional stressors for children are believed to be excessive demands for achievement or inconsistent de-mands by parents that are impossible to satisfy. Being reared under these condi-tions leads to feelings of insecurity, distrustfulness, and low self-esteem.

Finch and Hess (1962) in a study of the psychological characteristics of seven-teen children with ulcerative colitis concluded that successful therapy requires a cooperative team of specialists for the simultaneous intervention at both the physi-cal and psychological levels. The psychotherapist of this team should provide a comfortable, secure, and nonpunishing relationship to allow the child more free-dom to express aggressive and hostile feelings. Vandersall (1978) suggests that psychotherapists be prepared to work nonjudgmentally with the family and the child, be willing to stay with the client for a long period of time, and be accepting of small gains in insight and personality reorganization.

seizures

Seizures refer to a wide variety of symptoms that are caused by abnormal electrical rhythms in the brain. *Epilepsy* is a general term that is frequently used interchange-ably with seizures. Seizures, or epilepsy, are diagnosed on the basis of an EEG that can often identify the part of the brain affected by the abnormal electrical rhythms. The site of the abnormal activity usually determines the types of symptoms that are manifested. These symptoms may range from loss of consciousness and involun-tary movements of the whole body to very brief interruptions of activity without obvious behavioral signs. Some seizures appear to be wholly the result of abnormal electrical activity, while others require particular environmental conditions before they occur.

Historically, medications such as Dilatin have been used in the treatment of seizures; successful control of seizures through medication is achieved in about 75 percent of the cases. Seizures have also been treated with psychotherapy (Gott-schalk, 1953) and increasingly with behavior therapy. Ince (1976) reported a case of a twelve-year-old boy with a four-year history of recurrent seizures and secondary anxiety problems. Therapy consisted of first removing the anxiety through relaxation training and then using this training whenever the onset of a seizure was anticipated. Treatment was conducted one hour a week for three months with one booster session at six months while the boy was at camp. A nine-month follow-up after therapy termination revealed that no seizures had occurred. Mostofsky (1978) has reviewed the role of psychological interventions, such as psychotherapy, reinforcement, desensitization, and biofeedback, for developing a better understanding of epileptic disorders.

Conclusions

It is becoming increasingly evident that psychological and environmental factors can affect virtually any sensory, motor, and organ system including the central nervous system. In some instances, family histories support a genetic vulnerability hypothesis, and adverse psychological factors may serve to worsen these disorders. For other disorders, the etiology is unclear, but psychological intervention has nevertheless proved helpful.

Recommended Readings

Doleys, D. M., "Assessment and Treatment of Enuresis and Encopresis in Children." in *Progress in Behavior Modification*. Vol. 6. Edited by M. Hersen, R. M. Eisler, and P. M. Miller. pp. 85–121. New York: Academic Press, 1978.

Schaefer, C. E., Millman, H. L., and Levine, G. F., *Therapies for Psychosomatic Disorders in Children*. San Francisco: Jossey-Bass, 1979. Contains condensations of professional articles on a wide range of children's problems that are related to physical functioning.

prevention

14

Although our understanding of children's developmental and behavior problems is far from satisfactory, it is possible to describe a number of identification and screening procedures that may lead to the prevention or early treatment of some of these problems. In some instances, the knowledge of specific etiological factors and the methodology for their assessment have been necessary prerequisites for the design of effective intervention programs; this situation is particularly true for physically based disorders. In other instances, intervention may be successful even when etiology is unknown or vaguely conceptualized. Knowledge of etiological factors, although not necessary for successful treatment, may eventually lead to more efficient and, therefore, less costly intervention programs.

Discovery of etiological factors depends, to a large extent, on assessment methods and criteria for diagnostic classification that, in turn, depend on normative information. In general, more has been learned about the etiology of behavior disorders that are precisely defined and reliably assessed than about those with definitions that allow for considerable clinical judgment.

Caplan (1964) has described three levels of prevention: (1) Primary prevention refers to the reduction of new cases of behavior disorders; (2) secondary prevention involves a reduction in the duration or severity, or both aspects, of behavior disorders; and (3) tertiary prevention includes attempts to reduce long-term consequences of disability, such as institutionalization, or to prevent the disability from becoming worse. Both secondary and tertiary prevention may also be conceptualized as treatment programs because a behavior disorder has already been identified. Some behavior problems, however, do not necessarily result in later disorders but only identify the child as having a higher risk for a later disorder. Thus, in some instances, it is not clear whether a particular program is indeed primary or secondary for the individuals participating in it.

In this chapter, we review the methods and programs that have been designed to prevent children's behavior problems and developmental disabilities. Included in this review will be some of the methods and criteria for identifying children who have an above average risk for developing behavior disorders. The focus will be on primary and secondary prevention because most of the programs described as tertiary prevention have been covered in the treatment sections of previous chapters.

primary prevention

Primary prevention programs include a wide variety of medical and educational procedures. These programs may occur before and during pregnancy as well as during the child's developmental years.

prior to pregnancy

A number of educational programs that affect people's behavior prior to the conception of children may be described as examples of primary prevention. For example, providing school children with information about *nutrition* that improves their eating behavior can have positive effects both on them and children subsequently born to them. Similarly, primary prevention would include any program that improves the health status of future parents; avoidance of exposure to radiation, drugs, and other environmental substances that have adverse effects on general health or the reproductive system in particular can decrease the incidence of developmental problems in their offspring.

Immunization programs during the developmental period either eliminate or greatly reduce the probability of women's experiencing infectious diseases during pregnancy that may be harmful to the unborn child. Correcting or controlling health-related problems prior to pregnancy may also serve to improve the physical and behavioral status of subsequently born children. Examples of such problems are hypertension and obesity.

A variety of educational programs have considerable potential for decreasing the incidence of behavior problems and developmental disabilities. Convincing adolescents to postpone pregnancy until the optimal age range and insuring that they have the birth control information to do so is one of society's current challenges. Many parents of adolescents do not want to teach their children about birth control (or have them taught by others) even though it is known that contemporary adolescents have become more sexually active than those of previous generations. Prevention of adolescent pregnancy has far greater implications than those based on the age of the mother alone. Adolescent parents have greater difficulty providing adequate physical and psychological environments for their children. In many cases, their education and occupational training have been prematurely curtailed by the pregnancy and responsibility for child care; in addition, some of their own psychological needs continue to be unmet, and feelings of intense frustration with inadequate coping skills are more likely to develop. These factors have been associated with child abuse.

Educating young people before the occurrence of pregnancy (preparents) about the realities of rearing children may have some influence on their choices. Many adolescents have unrealistic, romantic views about parenthood; having one's own child is sometimes seen as an optimal way to ensure being loved or to have status. Although child development courses are offered in many high schools, they have generally not been designed to have the impact we are discussing here; in addition, they are taken by relatively few (usually female) students.

Effective education for preparents may need to involve all students of both sexes and may need to start early in puberty. Such a program would reflect the fact that both males and females are responsible for children before as well as after birth. Furthermore, education about sexuality as well as about sexual activity and the responsibilities of parenthood may reduce the high incidence of misinformation currently given to sexually active teenagers.

Still another educational program oriented toward primary prevention is genetic counseling. Informing potential parents that they have a high probability of bearing an abnormal child can effect their decision to initiate pregnancy or to undergo testing during pregnancy. Although genetic counseling is usually done after a genetically determined abnormality has already occurred in the family, it will probably be increasingly used for advising persons who have been identified as carriers through screening tests.

during pregnancy and after birth

Primary prevention during pregnancy includes educating the prospective parents to avoid substances and situations that may harm the fetus. Physicians usually have the primary responsibility for prescribing the best possible diet, exercise, and weight gain guidelines. They also communicate the importance of not ingesting drugs and medications without carefully monitoring and minimizing the pregnant woman's intake of alcohol and caffein.

Primary prevention may also be considered to include abortion when it is based on the risk that the child will be born with an abnormality known to have a significant negative effect on behavior or development, or both. Induced abortion is a topic associated with much social disagreement; some people feel that all induced abortion is wrong, others feel that it is acceptable under certain circumstances, such as rape and conditions that are life threatening to the mother, and still others feel that termination of a pregnancy is a decision that should be made only by the pregnant woman. Thus, society has not yet agreed that it is preferable to prevent the birth of an abnormal child.

Technology for identifying fetuses with certain abnormalities is available. Amniocentesis involves the withdrawal of a small amount of amniotic fluid surrounding the fetus during the fourth month of pregnancy and subjecting the cells (sloughed from the fetus) in this fluid to either laboratory testing or chromosomal analysis, or both. The procedure is a reliable and accurate technique for identifying many of the known genetic abnormalities, such as Down syndrome (O'Brien, 1971). Amniocentesis is currently recommended only when the fetus is known to be at risk, such as in cases in which the mother is over thirty-five years old or the couple has already had a child with a genetic disorder. Large-scale studies are showing that amniocentesis can be a safe procedure for both the mother and the fetus.

Amniocentesis is also being done in the pregnancies of diabetic women. Tests on the fluid can assess the maturity of the fetus's respiratory system; therefore, physicians can now choose the best time to induce the labor of diabetic women— a time that minimizes the complications of birth due to the baby's large size and simultaneously reduces the probability of respiratory distress due to immaturity. Tests that detect carriers of certain genetic abnormalities, such as phenylketonuria, are available, but most couples currently being tested have already had an affected child or are otherwise known to be at risk. For example, it is estimated that one in thirty Ashkenazic Jews is a carrier for Tay-Sachs disease, which leads to mental retardation and an early death, and screening programs for carriers have been initiated in many communities. If both parents are found to be carriers, each pregnancy can be monitored with amniocentesis.

Another technological advance has been the use of ultrasound (sound waves) to examine the infant *in utero*. Ultrasound can be used to estimate the fetus's weight and to assess the physical proportions of the fetus. The information obtained from the ultrasound procedure is somewhat comparable to that obtained from X rays, but ultrasound does not have the dangers of radiation. Physicians use the information to determine whether the baby can be naturally delivered or requires a Caesarean delivery. Thus, ultrasound could become a routine screening test for assessing the fetus's size and other physical characteristics.

Public service programs on radio and television and articles in popular magazines may also be described as primary prevention; they sometimes serve as the only source of information that prospective parents have prior to becoming involved with a physician. These sources of information may continue to have primary prevention functions after birth as well. They may persuade parents to maintain the optimal immunization schedule and to avoid the injuries due to accidents through the use of seat restraints in automobiles and by removing poisonous substances from the child's access.

There is enormous potential in the education of parents for the prevention of children's behavioral, emotional, and developmental problems. Teaching parents about the relationships between their behaviors and their children's behaviors and the behavior principles that govern these relationships can avoid many of the situations in which parents inadvertently strengthen behaviors that they do not want their children to have.

Much prevention is determined by the values of parents, in particular, and society at large. That is, parents vary in terms of the amount of effort they are willing to contribute toward prevention of future problems. How many smoking parents stop smoking when they are informed that their smoking increases the probability of their own child's becoming a smoker in addition to being exposed to the health hazards of living in a smoker's environment during the developmental years? How much organized social effort has there been to modify children's television programming after research findings showed a relationship between watching televised aggression and the amount of aggressive behavior in children? How many parents actually monitor the television shows that their children watch? To the extent that parents are unable or unwilling to control their children's environment, their children's behavior will be influenced by others.

For those psychological problems that are conceptualized as due to specific skill deficits, programs that develop those skills may be considered to be primary prevention. For example, Spivack and Shure (1974) developed a social problem-solving curriculum for four-year-old Head Start children that was presented to teachers who taught the children over a ten-week period (five to twenty minutes a day). The children who received this program were superior to control children in their social problem-solving skills at the end of the program and during the kindergarten year. A reduction in maladjustment was found to be related to gains in social problem-solving skills. Similar programs for older children have also been effective (see, for example, Allen, Chinsky, Larcen, Lochman, and Salinger, 1976).

Primary prevention also includes any program that identifies children known to be at risk for psychological problems because an adverse event has occurred in their lives, and carries out intervention procedures to reduce the incidence of such problems. For example, research is currently being conducted to examine the effectiveness of school- and home-based intervention programs in improving the psychological status of children whose parents have been divorced (Stolberg, 1980). Children who already have significant psychological problems are not included in the study but are referred to mental health agencies.

Secondary prevention is based on the ability to identify children with behavioral and developmental problems during the early stages of their manifestation. Behavioral and developmental problems vary widely in terms of the earliest age at which they can be reliably detected. Problems that are associated with physical abnormalities tend to be identified at earlier ages. For example, the physical characteristics associated with Down syndrome are apparent at birth and are predictive of later mental retardation. We have not yet identified behavioral indicators at birth that can predict with the same level of accuracy later psychological problems. In recent years, more attention has been given to the training of professionals and the designing of screening instruments to detect the child who is likely to have significant problems. Researchers have been examining the effectiveness of intervention programs in reducing the severity of or, in some instances, eventually eliminating these problems.

Devising effective methods for predicting children's behavioral and developmental problems is an important prerequisite for prevention programs. Screening methods that identify children as high risk when they are not (false positives) or that do not identify children who have significant problems (false negatives) are wasteful of resources in the former case and inefficient in the latter case. In addition, since psychological problems become manifest continuously throughout the developmental period, screening devices must reflect changes in predictability that occur as a function of age. In general, the behavior of young children is less predictable (reliable) than that of older children.

methods for identifying high-risk children

Tests for genetic disorders. Inexpensive tests are available for the detection of some of the recessive genetic abnormalities, such as phenylketonuria and galactosemia; many newborn infants are currently receiving these tests with the result that the behavior disorders associated with these conditions can be largely prevented by feeding the children special diets. Children suspected of having a chromosomal anomaly on the basis of physical characteristics may have a chromosomal assay test performed. If an abnormality is detected, the parents can receive further testing and be advised through genetic counseling of the probability of having another affected child. Amniocentesis would also be recommended.

Demographic screening. Since a number of pregnancy and labor complications have been associated with an increased risk to the child's life and development, such factors could be used to identify children who would then receive closer monitoring with physical and behavioral examinations. Although the data are available, no systematic approach to identifying high-risk children on the basis of pregnancy complications has been devised. Scurletis and Headrick (1976), however, have constructed from population data a list of questions to identify women of childbearing age who have high risk for fetal, neonatal, and postnatal death:

1. What is your age?
2. How many years of education have you completed?
3. What is your marital status?
4. How many pregnancies have you had?
5. Have you had a previous fetal death?
6. Have you had a previous child born alive who is now dead?

Physical examination of the child. Medical care for the child after birth may also reduce risk and provide an opportunity for early intervention. Good medical care includes periodic physical examination of the child and immunization shots against diseases. Most parents are reasonably conscientious about visits to the physician for inoculations during the first year or two, but there is reason to believe that many children are not properly immunized because they have not received booster shots. Moreover, relatively few children are being examined on a regular basis when they are well. That is, physicians typically see children only when they are ill. This situation certainly diminishes the possibility of physicians' validly assessing behavioral development. Good medical care should also include assessment of the family's nutritional status, periodic vision and hearing screening tests, and alertness for possible cases of child abuse or neglect.

The value of medical care in secondary prevention depends greatly on physicians' training in normal and abnormal child development and behavior. Because family practitioners and pediatricians are the only professionals to have regular access to children before they enter school, they currently have much of the potential for providing secondary prevention programs for young children. Physicians' training and interests in children's behavior and development have been inadequate until recent years; changing patterns in medical care and a decreased incidence in acute illnesses in children have served to shift more attention toward chronic illnesses and behavioral or developmental problems. It is now possible for many physicians to receive the necessary specialized training during their residencies. Clinical child psychologists are being asked to join the faculties of pediatrics departments to provide some of this training.

Behavioral screening procedures. The development of reliable and valid screening tests for identifying high-risk children is in an early stage of refinement. Most of the available, valid, psychological tests for children require administration by a trained professional and an hour or more in administration time, both of which requirements currently preclude their use as screening instruments. An ideal screening instrument can be administered by a variety of professionals and paraprofessionals with minimal training in testing; it takes fifteen to thirty minutes to administer and requires a minimal amount of materials and cooperation from the child (which allows the mother to report the presence or absence of certain behaviors in the child's natural environment). Having adequate screening tests, however, will not guarantee that they will be used. Their use depends greatly on society's commitment to children in general and to children with behavior disorders in particular.

Tests for the newborn. Several tests for neonates have been devised and offer some potential for identifying high risk infants. One of the earliest tests was devised by Graham, Matarazzo, and Caldwell (1956) and revised by Rosenblith (1961). The Graham-Rosenblith test contains items that evaluate maturation, irritability, muscle tonus, and vision. A longitudinal study of a large number of infants who had been administered the Graham-Rosenblith revealed that certain findings during the neonatal period are prognostic for later developmental problems. For example, newborns with marked hypersensitivity to light had developmental problems throughout the first four years of life. In addition, infants who showed marked discrepancies in muscle tonus between the upper and lower halves of the body also performed poorly on almost all eight-month and four-year ratings and tests. While many other correlational relationships between items on the Graham-Rosenblith scale and later measures (for example, activity level, physical development, mental development, fine and gross motor development, social emotional development, mental age, motor age) were obtained, they were "not sufficiently strong to have much practical value" (Rosenblith, 1975, p. 170).

Brazelton (1974) has developed a behavioral test that evaluates the neonate's organized responses to a variety of environmental events. Examples of the test items are: Response decrease to repeated visual stimuli: Orienting response to animate visual-examiner's face: Cuddleness – responses to being cuddled by the examiner; Self-quieting activity – attempts to console self and control state. Each of the twenty-six behavioral items is rated on a 9-point scale. Tronick and Brazelton (1975) report that, while the Brazelton Scale is comparable to a standard neurological test for detecting neonates who will be classified as "suspect-abnormal" at age seven (80 percent vs. 87 percent success rate), it is superior in its lower rate of classifying, as "suspect/abnormal," children who are normal at age seven. The children included in the "suspect/abnormal" category at age seven had a variety of behavior disorders; mental retardation, specific reading difficulties, speech disorders, motor disorders, as well as a number of neurological abnormalties.

Newborn test findings can easily be obscured by factors such as the infant's awake-asleep state, medications given to the mother during labor and delivery, and birth weight. Tronick and Brazelton (1975) suggest that decisions about the infant's status be based on repeated evaluations during the neonatal period, since many infants are capable of rapid recovery from physical stresses and will not show behavioral residues at an older age.

Infant and preschool tests. While a number of screening tests have been devised for use with infants and preschool children, few of them have been subjected to the necessary reliability and validity studies. Among the available tests, the Denver Developmental Screening Test (DDST) (Frankenburg and Dodds, 1970) has perhaps received the most research attention, and findings indicate that the DDST is reliable and valid (Erickson, 1976). However, it has not yet been demonstrated as an accurate *predictor* of children's development disorders. Its high correlation with developmental and intelligence tests suggests that children who perform very poorly on DDST during the early years will have a high probability of developmental disorders at later ages.

It must be concluded that, although we have a list of factors and screening tests that can identify high-risk children, we are still some distance from being able to make accurate predictions about individual children. Our screening devices appear to be inefficient in that they are not capable of identifying at an early age all children who will later have serious behavior disorders, and they may identify as "abnormal" a disproportionate number of children who will later have no behavior disorders. The former situation is understandable in view of the fact that certain abnormalities may not manifest themselves at the earlier ages and that certain environmental factors are cumulative and do not manifest themselves in behavior at the earliest ages. The latter situation is scientifically problematic and indicates that a significant number of infants with initially poor physical or behavioral status, or both, apparently "recover." When the variables related to their recovery are identified, the information will likely contribute toward more efficient screening devices and effective prevention programs.

In the evaluation of an intervention program, the typical study compares the behaviors of the group receiving the intervention with behaviors of a control group drawn from the same population. If both groups contain sizable portions of children who would have improved spontaneously (without intervention), the findings of the study would be diminished or, at least, be obscured. Moreover, the most successful intervention programs to date have been intensive and long term and, therefore, very expensive; it can be expected that funding for the implementation of such programs would likely be given for only those children who have a very high probability of developing behavior disorders.

Very little research has been done on the feasibility of using parent or teacher ratings, or ratings from both, as initial screening procedures for identifying high-risk children. An initial attempt has been reported by Frankenburg and associates (1976) who devised the Denver Prescreening Developmental Questionnaire (PDQ) to identify children who should be screened with the DDST. Knobloch and associates (1979) describe the validity of parental reporting of infant development on their questionnaire (based on items from the Gesell Developmental and Neurological Evaluation) as high and describe their instrument as the most accurate and useful screening questionnaire to date.

Tests for school-age children. It is possible that many children of school age are not receiving treatment services simply because they have not been identified as needing such services. As mentioned in earlier chapters, most children are identified as a result of individual referrals by concerned parents, teachers, or physicians. Such a system, however, may lend itself to the underidentification of certain problems and the overidentification of other problems. The implementation of screening programs in the schools could be expected to identify a high percentage of children with behavior disorders. A screening program for school children would be likely to include tests of general intellectual functioning, school achievement, speech and language, and a behavior problem checklist. Children identified through a screening procedure could then be referred for more thorough assessment procedures. Although research has been conducted on the reliability and validity of screening tests for specific behavior disorders, few attempts have been made to design comprehensive screening instruments that could be implemented in the schools.

An exemplary screening program for children over four years of age is being conducted by the Permanent Medical Group at the Kaiser Foundation Hospital in San Francisco (Allen and Shinefield, 1969). This screening program requires about 1½ hours and includes a wide range of physical tests and measures. The behavioral component includes tests of intellectual, visual-motor, and specific learning abilities. In addition, a behavior inventory completed by the parent evaluates sensorimotor development, communication skills, social interactions, and a variety of other behaviors. The data are computer-analyzed, and interpretation of the results is given to the parents within a month.

screening, identification, and prevention programs

The emphasis up to the present time has been on the early identification and treatment of children at high risk for deficits in general intellectual functioning and language delay. The development of screening devices for some of the other behavior disorders has probably been hampered by a lack of concensus on the criteria for diagnosis of the disorders and a general lack of information about which early behaviors might be precursors for the disorder. In the case of infantile autism, much of the necessary information for devising a screening test is available, but its very low rate or occurrence in the population (therefore requiring the examination of very large numbers of children in order to identify an adequate sample of children with the condition) has likely deterred investigators from conducting the requisite longitudinal studies.

Early identification of children who are at risk or who display behavior disorders is probably not possible without the implementation of large-scale screening programs that examine children repeatedly at specific ages beginning at birth. The particular instruments and ages of examination could be selected on the basis of current information and continuously refined as additional data are collected.

One example of a proposed age sequence would be the following: six months, eighteen months, three years, five years, end of first grade (seven years), end of third grade (nine years) end of sixth grade (twelve years), and end of ninth grade (fifteen years). These ages can be justified in terms of their representing important milestones or being optimal as far as program planning is concerned. By six months, the infant typically can sit alone, can pick up small objects, repeat syllables such as "mama" and "dada," and the infant exhibits a variety of social behaviors. By eighteen months, the child should walk alone and drink from a cup, have a small vocabulary of single words, and respond to a variety of verbal requests. By this age, most children with severe problems in the motor, intellectual, language, and social areas can probably be identified. Intervention programs begun during the first eighteen months of life have also been very effective.

At three years of age, the child can jump, walk up stairs, play ball, name many common objects, combine words in sentences, and put on clothing. The five year screening would probably shift the focus toward skills that are necessary for school performance. Given the subsequent importance of school experiences, later screenings should probably be timed on the basis of particular grades rather than chronological age. Screening near the end of the school year provides adequate time during the remaining school year and following summer for follow-up assessment and intervention program planning, if necessary.

preschool children

Secondary prevention or early intervention programs focusing on children's developmental and behavioral problems began to be explored during the 1960s at about the same time that Project Head Start was begun. Virtually all of the approximately one hundred longitudinal studies and program evaluations have focused on the preschool child. The studies initiated earlier involved relatively brief interventions with older preschool children, while subsequent studies have focused on infant programs conducted for longer periods of time. While there are some notable differences among the programs, they can all be described as planned "stimulation" programs. That is, the environment is arranged to provide the best possible learning opportunities for the child who is given considerable social attention for accomplishments.

Many of the earlier programs, in effect, removed children from their home environments for most of the daytime hours. Subsequent programs have explored other possibilities including teaching the mother to implement some or all aspects of the programs.

These early intervention programs have received mixed reviews. The earlier studies with older preschool children tended to report no effects or small positive effects that "washed out" within a year or two. The more recent studies that focused on infants for longer time periods with more structured programs have reported far more success, particularly when the children's parents were actively involved in the program (Goodson and Hess, 1978).

school-age children

The prevention programs for school-age children have been oriented more toward behavior problems than toward developmental problems and have included parental training, surrogate families, and school-based intervention.

Several behaviorally oriented parent-instruction programs have been implemented, but very little is known about their effectiveness. Parents are generally provided with instruction on behavior management procedures through lectures and films. After there is assurance that the parents know the behavior principles and their correct application, they are supervised in their treatment of the child's behavior problem. Patterson and his colleagues (1975) have developed such a program for aggressive boys that has had demonstrated success.

The Achievement Place program described in Chapter 11 is an example of a prevention program utilizing surrogate families. These surrogate families comprise a specially trained couple, the teaching parents, and about six youths who are at high risk for institutionalization because they have engaged in illegal behavior. This program has been implemented on a large scale and has had a positive review both in terms of lower recidivism rates and lower costs compared with institutionalization.

School-based prevention programs offer a considerable potential, but only a few have been developed in spite of a large research literature describing successful single case intervention. The Rochester Project, developed by Cowen and his associates (1975), identified first grade children as having problems or potential programs in adjustment. The prevention program included teachers' in-service education, availability of mental health consultants to teachers, after school group meetings for the children, and parents' groups focusing on child rearing during the first three grades. Reporting on the results for 215 children, Cowen, Gesten, and Wilson (1979) found improvements on all of their measures. One methodological problem, however, was that the ratings were done by persons (teachers, aides, and professionals) who were involved with the program. Comparison of the treatment group with a control group showed significantly greater improvement for the experimental group on about half of the variables measured.

It appears that the more specifically focused prevention programs may have greater success. Hops and Cobb (1973) designed a program to teach elementary school children "academic survival-skills," such as attending to the teacher, volunteering answers, and looking at one's own work. Teachers are trained to implement the program that has been found to be helpful in preventing academic underachievement.

Conclusions

The possibility of preventing a substantial percentage of behavioral and developmental problem cases has become increasingly feasible. Identification of etiological factors, genetic counseling, prenatal diagnosis, and early postnatal physical and behavioral assessment all contribute toward a reduction in the number of cases or the severity of children's behavior disorders, or both. Considerably more effort needs to be directed toward the prevention of behavior problems that initially manifest themselves during the school-age years.

Recommended Readings

Brown, B., ed., *Found: Long-Term Gains from Early Intervention.* Boulder, Colo.: Westview Press, 1978.

Field, T. M., Sostek, A. M., Goldberg, S., and **Shuman, H. H.,** eds., *Infants Born at Risk.* New York: SP Medical and Scientific Books, 1979. Chapters 19, 20, and 21 on intervention programs.

Gelfand, D. M., and **Hartman, D. P.,** "The Prevention of Childhood Behavior Disorders," in *Advances in Clinical Child Psychology,* Vol. 1, pp. 361–395. Edited by B. B. Lahey, and A. E. Kazdin New York: Plenum, 1977.

references

Abramowitz, C. V., "The effectiveness of group psychotherapy with children," *Archives of General Psychiatry,* 33 (1976), 320-326.

Achenbach, T.M., *Developmental Psychopathology.* New York: Ronald Press, 1974.

—— "The Child Behavior Profile: I. Boys aged 6-11," *Journal of Consulting and Clinical Psychology,* 46 (1978), 478-488.

——, **and Edelbrock, C.S.,** "The Child Behavior Profile: II. Boys Aged 12-16 and Girls Aged 6-11 and 12-16," *Journal of Consulting and Clinical Psychology,* 47 (1979), 223-233.

Ackerman, N. W., *The Psychodynamics of Family Life.* New York: Basic Books, 1958.

Adams, P.L., *Obsessive Children.* New York: Penguin Books, 1973.

Adler, A., *The practice and Theory of Individual Psychology.* New York: Harcourt, Brace, 1927.

Alexander, A., Miklich, D., and **Hershkoff, H.,** "The immediate effects of systematic relaxation training on peak expiratory flow rates in asthmatic children," *Psychosomatic Medicine,* 34 (1972), 388-394.

Alexander, D., Ehrhardt, A. A., and **Money, J.**, "Defective figure drawing, geometric and human, in Turner's syndrome," *Journal of Nervous and Mental Disease,* 142 (1966), 161–167.

Allen, C. M., and **Shinefield, H.R.,** "Pediatric multiphasic program: Preliminary description," *American Journal of Diseases in Children,* 118 (1969), 459–472.

Allen, F. H. *Psychotherapy with Children.* New York: Norton, 1942.

Allen, G. J., Chinsky, J. M., Larcen, S. W., Lochman, J. E., and **Salinger, H. V.,** *Community Psychology and the Schools: A Behaviorally Oriented Multi-level Preventive Approach.* Hillsdale, N.J.: Laurence Erlbaum Associates, 1976.

Allen, K. E., Hart, B., Buell, J. S., Harris, F. R., and **Wolf, M. M.,** "Effects of Social Reinforcement on Isolate Behavior of a Nursery School Child," *Child Development,* 35 (1964), pp. 511–518.

Alpern, G. C., and **Boll, T. J.,** *Developmental Profile.* Indianapolis, Ind.: Psychological Development Publications, 1972.

American Academy of Pediatrics: Committee on Adolescence, Statement on Teenage Pregnancy, *Pediatrics,* 63 (1972), 795–797.

American Psychiatric Association, *Diagnostic and Statistical Manual of Mental Disorders* (3rd ed.). Washington, D.C.: American Psychiatric Association, 1980.

American Psychological Association, "APA-Approved Doctoral Programs in Clinical, Counseling, and School Psychology: 1980, " *American Psychologist,* 35 (1980), 1116–1118.

Ames, L. B., Metraux, R. W., and **Walker, R. N.,** *Adolescent Rorschach Responses* (rev. ed.). New York: Brunner/Mazel, 1971.

Ames, L. B., Metraux, R. W., Rodell, J. L., and **Walker, R. N.,** *Child Rorschach Responses* (rev. ed.). New York: Brunner/Mazel, 1974.

Anthony, E. J., "A Group of Murderous Mothers," *Acta Psychotherapeutica,* 7, Supplement, (1959), pp. 1–6.

———,"The Behavior Disorders of Childhood," in *Carmichael's Manual of Child Psychology.* Vol. 2, pp. 667–764. Edited by P. H. Mussen. New York: John Wiley, 1970.

Arthur, G., *The Arthur Adaptation of the Leiter International Performance Scale.* Los Angeles: Western Psychological Services, 1952.

Axelrod, S., Hall, R. V., Weis, L., and **Rohrer, S.,** "Use of Self-Imposed Contingencies to Reduce the Frequency of Smoking Behavior," in *Self-Control: Power to the Person,* pp. 77–85. Edited by M. J. Mahoney and C. E. Thorensen. Monterey, Calif.: Brooks/Cole, 1974.

Axline, V. M., *Play Therapy.* Boston: Houghton Mifflin, 1947.

Ayllon, T., Layman, D., and **Kandel, H. J.,** "A Behavioral-Educational Alternative to Drug Control of Hyperactive Children," *Journal of Applied Behavior Analysis,* 8 (1975), pp. 137–146.

Ayllon, T., and **Rosenbaum, M. S.,** "The Behavioral Treatment of Disruption and Hyperactivity in School Settings," in *Advances in Clinical Psychology.* Vol. 1, pp. 85–118. Edited by B. B. Lahey, and A. E. Kazden. New York: Plenum, 1977.

Azrin, N. H., and **Armstrong, P. M.,** "The Mini-Meal—A Method of Teaching Eating Skills to the Profoundly Retarded," *Mental Retardation,* 11 (1973), pp. 9–13.

Azrin, N. H., and **Foxx, R. M.,** *Toilet Training in Less than a Day.* New York: Simon & Schuster, 1974.

Azrin, N. H., and **Holz, W. C.,** "Punishment," in *Operant Behavior: Areas of Re-*

search and Application, pp. 380–447. Edited by W. K. Honig. Englewood Cliffs, N. J.: Prentice-Hall, 1966.

Babson, S. G., and **Phillips, D. S.,** "Growth and Development of Twins Dissimilar in Size at Birth," *New England Journal of Medicine,* 289 (1973), pp. 937–940.

Bachara, G. H., and **Laba, J. N.,** "Learning Disabilities and Juvenile Delinquency," *Journal of Learning Disabilities,* 11 (1978), pp. 242–246.

Baer, D. M., and **Sherman, J. A.,** "Reinforcement Control of Generalized Imitation in Young Children," *Journal of Experimental Child Psychology,* 1 (1964), pp. 37–49.

Baloh, R., Sturm, R., Green, B., and **Gleser, G.,** "Neuropsychological Effects of Asymptomatic Increased Lead Absorption: A Controlled Study," *Archives of Neurology,* 32 (1975), pp. 326–330.

Bandura, A., "Influence of Models' Reinforcement Contingencies on the Acquisition of Imitative Responses," *Journal of Personality and Social Psychology,* 1 (1965), pp. 589–595.

——, *Principles of Behavior Modification.* New York: Holt, Rinehart and Winston, 1969.

Bandura, A., Ross, D., and **Ross, S. A.,** "Transmission of Aggression through Imitation of Aggressive Models," *Journal of Abnormal and Social Psychology,* 63 (1961), pp. 575–582.

——, "Imitation of Film-Mediated Aggressive Models," *Journal of Abnormal and Social Psychology,* 66 (1963a), pp. 3–11.

——, "Vicarious Reinforcement and Imitation Learning," *Journal of Abnormal and Social Psychology,* 67 (1963b), pp. 601–607.

Baratz, J. C., "Language and Cognitive Assessment of Negro Children: Assumptions and Research Needs," *ASHA,* 11 (1969), pp. 87–91.

Barrett, C. L., Hampe, I. E., and **Miller, L. C.,** "Research on Child Psychotherapy," in *Handbook of Psychotherapy and Behavior Change* (2nd ed.), pp. 411–435. Edited by S. L. Garfield and A. E. Bergin. New York: John Wiley, 1978.

Barton, E. S., Guess, D., Garcia, E., and **Baer, D. M.,** "Improvement of Retardates' Mealtime Behaviors by Timeout Procedures Using Multiple Baseline Techniques," *Journal of Applied Behavior Analysis,* 3 (1970), pp. 77–84.

Bauer, D. H., "An Exploratory Study of Developmental Changes in Children's Fears," *Journal of Child Psychology and Psychiatry,* 17 (1976), pp. 69–74.

Bayley, N., *Bayley Scales of Infant Development Manual.* New York: Psychological Corporation, 1969.

Beck, A. T., "Measuring Depression: The Depression Inventory," in *Recent Advances in the Psychology of the Depressive Illnesses,* pp. 299–302. Edited by T. A. Williams, M. M. Katz, and J. A. Shield. Washington: U. S. Government Printing Office, 1972.

Beery, K. D., *Developmental Test of Visual-Motor Integration Administration and Scoring Manual.* Chicago: Follett Educational Corporation, 1967.

Bell, J., "On Rubella in Pregnancy," *British Medical Journal,* 1 (1959), pp. 686–688.

Bellak, L., *The Thematic Apperception Test, the Children's Apperception Test, and the Senior Apperception Technique in Clinical Use* (3rd ed.). New York: Grune & Stratton, 1975.

Bellak, L., and **Bellak, S. S.,** *Children's Apperception Test.* Larchmont, N.Y.: C.P.S. Co., 1949.

Belmont, L., "Birth Order, Intellectual Competence, and Psychiatric Status," *Journal of Individual Psychology,* 33 (1977), pp. 97-103.

Belsky, J., and **Steinberg, L. D.,** "The Effects of Day Care: A Critical Review," *Child Development,* 49 (1978), pp. 929-949.

Bemis, K. M., "Current Approaches to the Etiology and Treatment of Anorexia Nervosa," *Psychological Bulletin,* 85 (1978), pp. 593-617.

Bemporad, J. R., "Encopresis," in *Handbook of Treatment of Mental Disorders in Childhood and Adolescence,* pp. 161-178. Edited by B. B. Wolman, J. Egan, and A. O. Ross. Englewood Cliffs, N. J.: Prentice-Hall, 1978.

Bender, L., "Twenty Years of Clinical Research on Schizophrenic Children with Special Reference to Those under Six Years of Age," in *Emotional Problems of Early Childhood,* pp. 503-515. Edited by G. Caplan. New York: Basic Books, 1955.

———, "Treatment in Early Schizophrenia," *Progress in Psychotherapy,* 5 (1960), pp. 177-184.

Bennett, S., and **Klein, H. R.,** "Childhood Schizophrenia: 30 Years Later," *American Journal of Psychiatry,* 122 (1966), pp. 1,121-1,124.

Bereiter, D., "An Academic Preschool for Disadvantaged Children: Conclusions from Evaluation Studies," in *Preschool Programs for the Disadvantaged,* pp. 1-21. Edited by J. Stanley. Baltimore, Md.: Johns Hopkins University Press, 1972.

Bereiter, D., and **Engelmann, S.,** *Teaching Disadvantaged Children in the Preschool.* Englewood Cliffs, N. J.: Prentice-Hall, 1966.

Berger, M. J., and **Goldstein, D. P.,** "Impaired Reproductive Performance in DES-Exposed Women," *Obstetrics and Gynecology,* 55 (1980), pp. 25-27.

Berman, A., and **Siegal, A.** "A Neuropsychological Approach to the Etiology, Prevention, and Treatment of Juvenile Delinquency," in *Child Personality and Psychopathology.* Vol. 3. Edited by A. Davids. New York: John Wiley, 1976.

Berman, J. L., and **Ford, R.,** "Intelligence Quotients and Intelligence Loss in Patients with Phenylketonuria and Some Variant States," *Journal of Pediatrics,* 77 (1970), pp. 764-770.

Bernard, R. M., "Shape and Size of the Female Pelvis," *Edinburg Medical Journal, Transactions of the Edinburg Obstetrical Society,* 59 (1952), pp. 1-16.

Bettelheim, B., *The Empty Fortress.* New York: Free Press, 1967.

Bijou, S. W., "A Functional Analysis of Retarded Development," in *International Review of Research in Mental Retardation.* Vol. 1, pp. 1-19. Edited by N. R. Ellis. New York: Academic Press, New York, 1966.

Bijou, S. W., and **Peterson, R. F.,** "Functional Analysis in the Assessment of Children," in *Advances in Psychological Assessment.* Vol. 2, pp. 63-78. Edited by P. McReynolds. Palo Alto, Calif.: Science and Behavior Books, 1971.

Birch, H. G., and **Gussow, J. D.,** *Disadvantaged Children: Health, Nutrition, and School Failure.* New York: Harcourt Brace Jovanovich, Inc., 1970.

Birch, H. G., Richardson, S. A., Baird, D., Horobin, G., and **Illsley, R.,** *Mental Subnormality in the Community: A Clinical and Epidemiological Study.* Baltimore, Williams & Wilkins, 1970.

Birnbrauer, J. S., Wolf, M. M., Kidder, J. D., and **Tague, C. E.,** "Classroom Behavior in Retarded Pupils with Token Reinforcement," *Journal of Experimental Child Psychology,* 2 (1965), pp. 219-235.

Blau, T. H., "Diagnosis of Disturbed Children," *American Psychologist,* 34 (1979), pp. 969-972.

Blinder, B. J., Freeman, D. M., and Stunkard, A. J., "Behavior Therapy of Anorexia Nervosa: Effectiveness of Activity as a Reinforcer of Weight Gain," *American Journal of Psychiatry*, 126 (1970), pp. 1,093–1,098.

Bond, G. L., and Tinker, M. A., *Reading Difficulties: Their Diagnosis and Correction* (2nd ed.). Englewood Cliffs, N. J.: Prentice-Hall, 1967.

Bondy, A., and Erickson, M. T., "Comparison of Modeling and Reinforcement Procedures in Increasing Question-Asking of Mildly Retarded Children," *Journal of Applied Behavior Analysis*, 9 (1976), p. 108.

Böök, J., Nicktern, S., and Gurenberg, E., "Cytogenetical Investigation in Childhood Schizophrenia," *Acta Psychiatrica Scandinavica*, 39 (1963), pp. 309–325.

Bornstein, P. H., Bridgwater, C. A., Hickey, J. S., and Sweeney, T. M., "Characteristics and Trends in Behavioral Assessment: An Archival Analysis," *Behavioral Assessment*, 2 (1980), pp. 125–133.

Bowes, W. A., Brackbill, T., Conway, E., and Steinschneider, A., "Obstetrical Medication and Infant Outcome: A Review of the Literature," *Monographs of the Society for Research in Child Development*, 35, no. 137 (1970).

Bowlby, J., *Maternal Care and Mental Health*. Geneva: World Health Organization, 1952.

Brazelton, T. B., *Neonatal Behavioral Assessment Scale*. Philadelphia: Lippincott, 1973.

Brazelton, T. B., *Neonatal Behavioral Assessment Scale*. London: Spastics International Medical Publications, 1974.

Broden, M., Hall, R. V., and Mitts, B., "The Effect of Self-Recording on the Classroom Behavior of Two Eighth-Grade Students," *Journal of Applied Behavior Analysis*, 4 (1971), pp. 191–199.

Brook, C. G., Lloyd, J. K., and Worf, O. H., "Relation between Age of Oneset of Obesity and Size and Number of Adipose Cells," *British Medical Journal*, 28 (1972), pp. 25–27.

Brown, J. L., "Prognosis from Presenting Symptoms of Preschool Children with Atypical Development," *American Journal of Orthopsychiatry*, 30 (1960), pp. 382–390.

——, "Follow-Up of Children with Atypical Development (Infantile Psychosis)," *American Journal of Orthopsychiatry*, 33 (1963), pp. 855–861.

Brown, N. A., Goulding, E. H., and Fabro, S., "Ethanol Embryotoxicity: Direct Effects on Mammalian Embryos in Vitro," *Science*, 206 (1979), pp. 573–575.

Burchard, J. D., "Systematic Socialization: A Programmed Environment for the Habilitation of Antisocial Retardates," *Psychological Record*, 17 (1967), pp. 461–476.

Butler, E. W., "Personality Dimensions of Delinquent Girls," *Criminologica*, 3 (1965), pp. 7–10.

Butler, N. R., Goldstein, H., and Ross, E. M., "Cigarette Smoking in Pregnancy: Its Influence on Birth Weight and Perinatal Mortality," *British Medical Journal*, 28 (1972), pp. 127–130.

Cameron, J. R., "Parental Treatment, Children's Temperament, and the Risk of Childhood Behavioral Problems," *American Journal of Orthopsychiatry*, 47 (1977), pp. 568–576.

Campbell, M., and Small, A. M., "Chemotherapy," in *Handbook of Treatment of Mental Disorders in Childhood and Adolescence*, pp. 9–27. Edited by B. B. Wolman, J. Egan, and A. O. Ross. Englewood Cliffs, N. J.: Prentice-Hall, 1978.

Cantwell, D., "Genetics of Hyperactivity. *Journal of Child Psychology and Psychiatry,* 16 (1975), pp. 181–197.

Cantwell, D. P., Baker, L., and Rutter, M., "Families of Autistic and Dysphasic Children," *Archives of General Psychiatry,* 36 (1979), pp. 682–687.

Cantwell, D. P., Russell, A. T., Mattison, R., and Will, L., "A Comparison of DSM-II and DSM-III in the Diagnosis of Childhood Psychiatric Disorders. I. Agreement with Expected Diagnosis," *Archives of General Psychiatry,* 36 (1979), pp. 1,208–1,213.

Caplan, B., *Principles of Preventive Psychiatry.* New York: Basic Books, 1964.

Casler, L., "Maternal Deprivation: A Critical Review of the Literature," *Monographs of the Society for Research in Child Development,* 26, no. 2, (1961).

Cattell, P., *The Measurement of Intelligence of Infants and Young Children.* New York: Psychological Corporation, 1940.

Chess, S., "Autism in Children with Congenital Rubella," *Journal of Autism and Childhood Schizophrenia,* 1 (1971), pp. 33–47.

——, "Follow-Up Report on Autism in Congential Rubella," *Journal of Autism and Childhood Schizophrenia,* 7 (1977), pp. 69–81.

Chess, S., Korn, S., and Fernandez, P., *Psychiatric Disorders of Children with Rubella.* New York: Brunner/Mazel, 1971.

Christiansen, K. O., "A Preliminary Study of Criminality among Twins," in *Biosocial Basis of Criminal Behavior,* pp. 89–108. Edited by S. A. Medrick and K. O. Christiansen. New York: Gardner Press, 1977a.

——, "A Review of Studies of Criminality among Twins," in *Biosocial Basis of Criminal Behavior,* pp. 45–88. Edited by S. A. Medrick and K. O. Christiansen. New York: Gardner Press, 1977b.

Clarizio, H. F., and McCoy, G. F., *Behavior Disorders in School-Aged Children.* Scranton, Conn.: Chandler, 1970.

Clements, S. D., "Minimal Brain Dysfunction in Children," *NINDB Monograph,* no. 3. U.S. Department of Health, Education, and Welfare, 1966.

Coffey, V. P., and Jessop, W. J. E., "Maternal Influenza and Congenital Deformities," *Lancet,* 2 (1959), pp. 935–938.

Cohen, H. L., and Filipczak, J., *A New Learning Environment.* San Francisco: Jossey-Bass, 1971.

Cohen, M. M., Hirschhorn, K., Verbo, S., Frosch, W. A., and Groeschel, M. M., "The Effect of LSD-25 on Chromosomes of Children Exposed in Utero," *Pediatric Research,* 2 (1968), pp. 486–492.

Cohen, R. L., and Netley, C., "Cognitive Deficits, Learning Disabilities, and WISC Verbal-Performance Consistency," *Developmental Psychology,* 14 (1978), pp. 624–634.

Cohen, S., and Przybycien, C. A., "Some Effects of Sociometrically Selected Peer Models on the Cognitive Styles of Impulsive Children," *Journal of Genetic Psychology,* 124 (1974), pp. 213–220.

Conners, C. K., "Pharmacotherapy of Psychopathology in Children," in *Psychopathological Disorders in Childhood.* Edited by H. Quay and J. S. Werry. New York: John Wiley, 1972.

——, "Psychotropic Drug Treatment of Children," in *Clinical Psychopharmacology,* pp. 86–102. Edited by J. C. Bernstein. Littleton, Mass.: PSG Publishing Company, 1978.

Cowen, E. L., Gesten, E. L., and **Wilson, A. B.**, "The Primary Mental Health Project (PMHP): Evaluation of Current Program Effectiveness," *American Journal of Community Psychology,* 7 (1979), pp. 293–303.

Cowen, E. L., Trost, M. A., Lorion, R. P., Dorr, D., Izzo, L. D., and Isaacson, R. V., *New Ways in School Mental Health: Early Detection and Prevention of School Maladaptation.* New York: Behavioral Publications, 1975.

Creak, M., "Schizophrenic Syndrome in Childhood: Progress Report of a Working Party." *British Medical Journal,* 2 (1961), pp. 889–890.

——, "Childhood Psychosis: A review of 100 Cases," *British Journal of Psychiatry,* 109 (1963), pp. 84–89.

Cronbach, L. J., "Five Decades of Public Controversy over Mental Testing," 30 *American Psychologist,* (1975), pp. 1–14.

Cytryn, L., and McKnew, D. H., "Factors Influencing the Changing Clinical Expression of the Depressive Process in Children," *American Journal of Psychiatry,* 131 (1974), pp. 879–881.

Dahlstrom, W. B., Welsh, G. S., and Dahlstrom, L. E., *An MMPI Handbook* (rev. ed.). Vol. 1. Minneapolis, Minn.: University of Minnesota Press, 1972.

——, *An MMPI Handbook* (rev. ed.). Vol. 2. Minneapolis, Minn.: University of Minnesota Press, 1975.

Dalterio, S., and Bartke, A., "Perinatal Exposure of Cannabinoids Alters Male Reproductive Function in Mice," *Science,* 205 (1979), pp. 1420–1422.

Darley, F. L., Fay, W. H., Newman, P. W., Rees, N., and Siegel, G. M., eds., *Evaluation of Assessment Techniques in Speech Pathology.* Reading, Mass.: Addison-Wesley, 1979.

Darlington, R. B., Royce, J. M., Snipper, A. S., Murray, H. W., and Lazar, I., "Preschool Programs and Later School Competence of Children from Low-Income Families," *Science,* 208 (1980), pp. 202–204.

Davids, A., DeVault, S., and Talmadge, M., "Anxiety, Pregnancy, and Childbirth Abnormalities," *Journal of Consulting Psychology,* 25 (1961), pp. 74–77.

Davis, H. V., Sears, R. R., Miller, H. C., and Brodbeck, A. J., "Effects of Cup, Bottle, and Breast Feeding on Oral Activities of Newborn Infants," *Pediatrics,* 2 (1948), pp. 549–558.

DeMyer, M., Barton, S., Alpern, G., Kimberlin, C., Allen, J., Yang, E., and Steele, R., "The Measured Intelligence of Autistic Children," *Journal of Autism and Childhood Schizophrenia,* 4 (1974), pp. 42–60.

DeMyer, M. K., Pontius, W., Norton, J. A., Barton, S., Allen, Jr., and Steele, R., "Parental Practices and Innate Activity in Normal, Autistic, and Brain-Damaged Infants," *Journal of Autism and Childhood Schizophrenia,* 2 (1972), pp. 49–66.

Despert, J. L., "Schizophrenia in Children," *Psychiatric Quarterly,* 12 (1938), pp. 366–371.

DeWitt, K. N., "The Effectiveness of Family Therapy," *Archives of General Psychiatry,* 35 (1978), pp. 549–564.

Diagnostic and Statistical Manual of Mental Disorders (3rd ed.). American Psychiatric Association, 1980.

Dishotsky, N. I., Loughman, W. D., Mogar, R. E., and Lipscomb, W. R., "LSD and Genetic Damage," *Science,* 172 (1971), pp. 431–440.

Dollard, J., Doob, L. W., Miller, N. E., Mowrer, O. H., and Sears, R. R., *Frustration and Aggression.* New Haven, Conn.: Yale University Press, 1939.

Douglas, C. P., "Prenatal Risks," in *Risks in the Practice of Modern Obstetrics* (2nd ed.), pp. 1–33. Edited by S. Aladjem. St. Louis: Mosby, 1975.

Drillien, C. M., "The Incidence of Mental and Physical Handicaps in School-Age Children of Very Low Birth Weight," *Pediatrics,* 27 (1961), pp. 452–464.

Dunn, L. M., *Peabody Picture Vocabulary Test Manual.* Minneapolis, Minn.: American Guidance Service, 1959.

——, *Expanded Manual for the Peabody Picture Vocabulary Test.* Minneapolis, Minn.: American Guidance Service, 1965.

Dunn. L. M., and Markwardt, F. C., *Peabody Individual Achievement Test.* Circle Pines, Minn.: American Guidance Service, 1970.

Dweck, C. S., Gittelman-Klein, R., McKinney, W. T., and Watson, J. S., "Summary of the Subcommittee on Clinical Criteria for Diagnosis of Depression in Children," in *Depression in Childhood: Diagnosis, Treatment, and Conceptual Models,* pp. 153–154. Edited by J. G. Schulterbrandt and A. Raskin. New York: Raven Press, 1977.

Ebbs, J. H., Tisdall, F. F., and Scott, W. A., "The Influence of Prenatal Diet on the Mother and Child," *The Milbank Memorial Fund Quarterly,* 20 (1942), pp. 35–36.

Egeland, B., Breitenbucker, M., and Rosenberg, D., "Prospective Study on the Significance of Life Stress in the Etiology of Child Abuse," *Journal of Counseling and Clinical Psychology,* 48 (1980), pp. 195–205.

Ehrlich, C. H., Shapiro, E., Kimball, B. D., and Huttner, M., "Communication Skills in Five-Year-Old Children with High Risk Neonatal Histories," *Journal of Speech and Hearing Research,* 16 (1973), pp. 522–529.

Eisenberg, L., "The Epidemiology of Reading Retardation and a Program for Preventive Intervention," in *The Disabled Reader,* pp. 3–19. Edited by J. Money. Baltimore: Johns Hopkins University Press, 1966.

Eisenson, J., *Aphasia in Children.* New York: Harper & Row, Pub., 1972.

Erickson, M. L., *Assessment and Management of Developmental Changes in Children,* pp. 174–175. St. Louis: Mosby, 1976.

Erickson, M. T., "Relationship between Psychological Attitudes During Pregnancy and Complications of Pregnancy, Labor, and Delivery," *Proceedings of the American Psychological Association,* 1 (1965), pp. 213–214.

——, "Intelligence: Prenatal and Preconception Environmental Influences," *Science.* 157 (1967), p. 1,210.

——, "MMP Comparisons between Parents of Young Emotionally Disturbed and Organically Retarded Children," *Journal of Consulting and Clinical Psychology,* 32 (1968a), pp. 701–706.

——, "The Predictive Validity of the Cattell Infant Intelligence Scale for Young Mentally Retarded Children," *American Journal of Mental Deficiency,* 72 (1968b), pp. 728–733.

——, "Risk Factors Associated with Complications of Pregnancy, Labor, and Delivery," *American Journal of Obstetrics and Gynecology,"* (1971), pp. 658–662.

Erikson, E. H., *Childhood and Society* (2nd ed., rev.). New York: W. W. Norton, & Co., Inc., 1963.

Eron, L. D., "Prescription for Reduction of Aggression," *American Psychologist,* 35 (1980), pp. 244–252.

Eron, L. D., Huesmann, L. R., Lefkowitz, M. M., and Walder, L. O., "Does Television Violence Cause Aggression?" *American Psychologist,* 27 (1972), pp. 253–263.

Eron, L. D., Walder, L. O., and **Lefkowitz, M. M.,** *Learning of Aggression in Children.* Boston: Little, Brown, 1971.

Esman, A. H., "The Primal Scene: A Review and a Reconsideration," *Psychoanalytic Study of the Child,* 28 (1973), pp. 49–81.

Exner, J. E., *The Rorschach: A Comprehensive System.* New York: John Wiley, 1974.

Eysenck, H. J., "Personality Tests," in *Recent Progress in Psychology,* pp. 118–159. Edited by **T. H. Fleming.** London: J. & A. Churchill, 1959.

Farber, B., "Effects of a Severely Mentally Retarded Child on Family Integration," 24 no. 2 (1959). *Monographs of the Society for Research in Child Development.*

——, "Family Organization and Crisis: Maintenance of Integration in Families with a Severely Mentally Retarded Child," 25, no. 1 (1960). *Monographs of the Society for Research in Child Development.*

Fechter, J. V., Jr., "Modeling and Environmental Generalization By Mentally Retarded Subjects of Televised Aggressive or Friendly Behavior," *American Journal of Mental Deficiency,* 76 (1971), pp. 266–267.

Feingold, B., *Why Your Child Is Hyperactive.* New York: Random House, 1975.

Fernando, S., "Six Cases of Gilles de la Tourette's Syndrome," *British Journal of Psychiatry,"* 128 (1976), pp. 436–441.

Ferster, C. B., "Positive Reinforcement and Behavioral Deficits of Autistic Children," *Child Development,* 32 (1961), pp. 437–456.

——, "A Functional Analysis of Depression," *American Psychologist,* 28 (1973), pp. 857–869.

Feshbach, S., Aggression, in *Carmichael's Manual of Child Psychology.* Vol. 2, pp. 159–260. Edited by P. H. Mussen. New York: John Wiley, 1970.

Finch, S. M., and **Hess, J. H.,** "Ulcerative Colitis in Children," *American Journal of Psychiatry,* 118 (1962), pp. 819–826.

Finch, A. J., Wilkinson, M. D., Nelson, W. M., and **Montgomery, L. E.,** "Modification of an Impulsive Cognitive Tempo in Emotionally Disturbed Boys," *Journal of Abnormal Child Psychology,* 3 (1975), pp. 49–52.

Finucci, J.M., Guthrie .T., Childs, A.L., Abbey, H., and **Childs, B.,** "The Genetics of Specific Reading Disability," *Annals of Human Genetics,* 40 (1976), pp. 1–23.

Fish, B., "Pharmacotherapy for Autistic and Schizophrenic Children," in *Autism: Diagnosis, Current Research and Management.* Edited by E. R. Ritvo. Jamaica, N.Y.: Spectrum Publ., 1976.

Fish, B., Shapiro, T., Campbell, M., and **Wile, R.,** " A Classification of Schizophrenic Children under Five Years," *American Journal of Psychiatry,* 124 (1968), pp. 1,415–1,423.

Folstein, S., and **Rutter, M.,** "Infantile Autism: A Study of 21 Twin Pairs," *Journal of Child Psychology and Psychiatry,* 18 (1977), pp. 297–321.

Foxx, R.M., and **Azrin, N.H.,** "Restitution: A Method of Eliminating Aggressive-Disruptive Behavior of Retarded and Brain Damaged Patients," *Behaviour Research And Therapy,* 10 (1972), pp. 15–27.

Frankenburg, W. K., and **Dodds, J. B.,** *Denver Developmental Screening Test.* Denver, Colo.: University of Colorado Medical Center, 1970.

Frankenburg, W. K., van Doornick, W. J., Liddell, T. N., and **Dick, N. P.,** "The Denver Prescreening Developmental Questionnaire (PDQ)," *Pediatrics,* 57 (1976), pp. 744–753.

Frazier, T. M., Davis, G. H., Goldstein, H., and **Goldberg, I. D.,** "Cigarette Smoking and Prematurity: A Prospective Study," *American Journal of Obstetrics and Gynecology,* 81 (1961), pp. 988–996.

Freud, A., *The Ego and the Mechanisms of Defense.* Translated by Cecil Baines. New York: International Universities Press, 1946a (originally published 1936).

——, *The Psychoanalytic Treatment of Children.* London: Imago Publishing Company, 1946b.

——, *Normality and Pathology in Childhood.* New York: International Universities Press, 1965.

——, "The Infantile Neurosis: Genetic and Dynamic Considerations," *Psychoanalytic Study of the Child,* 26 (1971), pp. 79–90.

Freud, S., "Three Essays of the Theory of Sexuality," in *Standard Edition of the Complete Psychological Works of Sigmund Freud,* Vol. 7, pp. 125–243. London: Hogarth Press, 1953 (originally published 1905).

——, *Analysis of a Phobia in a Five-Year-Old boy.* London: Hogarth Press, 1955 (originally published 1909).

——, "Inhibition, Symptoms, and Anxiety," in *Standard Edition of the Complete Psychological Works of Sigmund Freud,* Vol. 20, pp. 77–174. London: Hogarth Press, 1959 (originally published 1926).

Frostig, M., and **Horne, D.,** *The Frostig Program for the Development of Visual Perception.* Chicago, Ill.: Follett, 1964.

Frostig, M., Lefever, D. W., and **Whittlesey, J. R. B.,** *The Marianne Frostig Developmental Test of Visual Perception.* Palo Alto, Calif.: Consulting Psychology Press, 1964.

Fuller, J.L., and **Scott, J.P.,** "Heredity and Learning Ability in Infrahuman Mammals," *Eugenics Quarterly,* 1 (1954), pp. 28–43.

Fuller, J. L., and **Thompson, W. R.,** *Foundations of Behavior Genetics,* pp. 132–222. St. Louis: Mosby, 1978.

Fuller, P. R., "Operant Conditioning of a Vegetative Human Organism," *American Journal of Psychiatry,* 62 (1949), pp. 587–590.

Galton, F., *Hereditary Genius.* London: Macmillan, 1869.

Garber, H., and **Heber, F. R.,** "The Milwaukee Project," in *Research to Practice in Mental Retardation,* Vol. 1, pp. 119–127. Edited by P. Mittler. Baltimore, Md.: University Park Press, 1977.

Garcia, E. E., and **DeHaven, E. D.,** "Use of Operant Techniques in the Establishment and Generalization of Language: A Review and Analysis," *American Journal of Mental Deficiency,* 79 (1974), pp. 169–178.

Gauthier, Y., Fortin, C., Drapeau, R., Breton, J., Gosselin, J., Quintal, L., Weisnagel, J., and **Lamarre, A.,** "Follow-Up Study of 35 Asthmatic Preschool Children," *Journal of the American Academy of Child Psychiatry,* 17 (1978), pp. 679–694.

Gehman, I. H., and **Matyas, R. P.,** "Stability of the WISC and Binet Tests," *Journal of Consulting Psychology,* 20 (1956), pp. 150–152.

Gibbons, D. C., *Delinquent Behavior.* Englewood Cliffs, N.J.: Prentice-Hall, 1970.

Gibson, H. B., "Early Delinquency in Relation to Broken Homes," *Journal of Child Psychology and Psychiatry,* 10 (1969), pp. 195–204.

Gillingham, A., and **Stillman, B. W.,** *Remedial Training for Children with Specific Disability in Reading, Spelling and Penmanship* (6th ed.). Cambridge, Mass.: Educators Publishing Service, 1960.

Gittelman-Klein, R., "Overview of Clinical Psychopharmacology in Childhood

Disorders," in *Clinical Psychopharmacology,* pp. 103–120. Edited by J. G. Bernstein. Littleton, Mass.: PSG Publishing Co., 1978.

Glaser, K., "Masked Depression in Children and Adolescents," *Annual Progress in Child Psychiatry and Child Development,* 1 (1968), pp. 345–355.

Glueck, S., and **Glueck, E.,** *Unraveling Juvenile Delinquency.* New York: Commonwealth Fund, 1950.

——, *Predicting Delinquency and Crime.* Cambridge, Mass.: Harvard University Press, 1959.

——, *Deliquents and Nondelinquents in Perspective.* Cambridge, Mass.: Harvard University Press, 1968.

——, *Toward a Typology of Juvenile Offenders.* New York: Grune & Stratton, 1970.

Goldfarb, W., "The Effects of Early Institutional Care on Adolescent Personality: Rorschach Data," *American Journal of Orthopsychiatry,* 14 (1944), pp. 441–447.

——, *Childhood Schizophrenia.* Cambridge, Mass.: Harvard University Press, 1961.

——, "Childhood Psychosis," in *Carmichael's Manual of Child Psychology* (3rd ed.), Vol. 2, pp. 765–830. Edited by P. H. Mussen. New York: John Wiley, 1970.

Goldfarb, W., Goldfarb, N., and **Pollack, R. C.,** "Treatment of Childhood Schizophrenia: A Three-Year Comparison of Day and Residential Treatment," *Archives of General Psychiatry,* 14 (1966), pp. 119–128.

Goldstein, A. C., Auerbach, V. H., and **Grover, W. D.,** "Normal Development in an Infant of a Mother with Phenylketonuria," *Journal of Pediatrics,* 82 (1973), pp. 489–491.

Goldstein, H., Moss, J. W., and **Jordan, L. J.,** *The Efficacy of Special Class Training on the Development of Mentally Retarded Children.* Urbana, Ill.: University of Illinois, 1965.

Goldstein, R., Landau, W. M., and **Kleffner, F. R.,** "Neurological Assessment of Deaf and Aphasic Children," *Transactions of the American Otological Society,* 46 (1958), pp. 122–136.

Goodson, B. D., and **Hess, R. D.,** "The Effects of Parent Training Programs on Child Performance and Behavior," in *Found: Long-Term Gains from Early Intervention,* pp. 37–78. Edited by B. Brown. Boulder, Colo.: Westorew, 1978.

Gottesfeld, H., "Professionals and Delinquents Evaluate Professional Methods with Delinquents," *Social Problems,* 13 (1965), pp. 45–59.

Gottesman, I. I., "Schizophrenia and Genetics," in *The Nature of Schizophrenia,* pp. 59–69. Edited by L. C. Wynne, R. L. Cromwell, and S. Matthysse. New York: John Wiley, 1978.

Gottesman, I. I., and **Shields, J. A.,** "A Critical Review of Recent Adoption, Twin, and Family Studies of Schizophrenia: Behavioral Genetic Perspectives," *Schizophrenia Bulletin,* 2 (1976), pp. 360–401.

Gottschalk, L. A., "Effects of Intensive Psychotherapy on Epileptic Children," *American Medical Association Archives of Neurology and Psychiatry,* 70 (1953), pp. 361–384.

Graham, F. K., Ernhart, C. B., Craft, M., and **Berman, P. W.,** "Brain Injury in the Preschool Child: Some Developmental Considerations," *Psychological Monographs,* 77, no. 10 and 11 (1953).

Graham, F. K., Ernhart, C. B., Thurston, D., and **Craft, M.,** "Development Three Years after Perinatal Anoxia and Other Potentially Damaging Newborn Experiences," *Psychological Monographs,* 76, no. 3 (1962).

Graham, F. K., Matarazzo, R. G., and **Caldwell, B. M.,** "Behavioral Differences between Normal and Traumatized Newborns: II. Standardization, Reliability and Validity," *Psychological Monographs,* 70, no. 21 (1956).

Granger, J. A., and **Wanberg, L. D.,** "The Conjoint Structured Interview in Child Guidance Evaluations," *American Journal of Orthopsychiatry,* 36 (1967), pp. 310–311.

Gregg, N. M., "Congenital Cataract following German Measles in the Mother," *Transactions of the Opthamological Society of Australia,* 3 (1941), pp. 35–46.

Grossman, H. J., ed., *Manual on Terminology and Classification in Mental Retardation.* Washington, D. C.: American Association of Mental Deficiency, 1977.

Group for the Advancement of Psychiatry, "Psychopathological Disorders in Childhood: Theoretical Considerations and a Proposed Classification," 6, no. 62 (1966), pp. 173–343.

Guilford, J. P., "Three Faces of Intellect," *American Psychologist,* 14 (1959), pp. 469–479.

Gully, K. J., and **Hosch, H. M.,** "Adaptive Behavior Scale: Development as a Diagnostic Tool via Discriminant Analysis," *American Journal of Mental Deficiency,* 83 (1979), pp. 518–523.

Gunzburg, H. C., "Psychotherapy," in *Mental Deficiency: The Changing Outlook,* pp. 708–728. Edited by A. M. Clarke and A. D. B. Clarke. New York: Fue Press, 1975.

Gurman, A. S., and **Kniskern, D. P.,** "Research on Marital and Family Therapy: Progress, Perspective, and Prospect," in *Handbook of Psychotherapy and Behavior Change,* pp. 817–901. Edited by S. L. Garfield and A. E. Bergin. New York: John Wiley, 1978.

Guthrie, R. D., and **Wyatt, R. J.,** "Biochemistry and Schizophrenia: A Review of Childhood Psychosis," *Schizophrenia Bulletin,* no. 12 (1975), pp. 18–32.

Hall, P. K., and **Tomblin, J. B.,** "A Follow-Up Study of Children with Articulation and Language Disorders," *Journal of Speech and Hearing Disorders,* 43 (1978), pp. 227–241.

Hall, R. V., Axelrod, S., Foundopoulos, M., Shelman, J., Campbell, R. A., and **Cranston, S. S.,** "The Effective Use of Punishment to Modify Behavior in the Classroom," *Educational Technology,* 11 (1971), pp. 24–26.

Hallahan, D. P., and **Cruickshank, W. M.,** *Psychoeducational Foundations of Learning Disabilities.* Englewood Cliffs, N. J.: Prentice-Hall, 1973.

Harrell, R. F., Woodyard, E., and **Gates, A. I.,** *The Effects of Mother's Diets on the Intelligence of Offspring.* New York: Teachers College, Columbia University, 1955.

Hathaway, S. R., and **McKinley, J. C.,** *Minnesota Multiphasic Personality Inventory* (rev. ed.). New York: Psychological Corporation, 1951.

Heber, R., and **Garber, H.,** "The Milwaukee Project: A Study in the Use of Family Intervention to Prevent Cultural Familial Mental Retardation," in *Exceptional Infant: Assessment and Intervention,* Vol. 3, pp. 399–433. Edited by B. Z. Friedlander, G. M. Sterritt, and G. E. Kirk. New York: Brunner/Mazel, 1975.

Hellmuth, J., ed., *Exceptional Infant.* Vol. 1. New York: Brunner/Mazel, 1967.

Heron, W. T., "The Inheritance of Brightness and Dullness in Maze Learning Ability in the Rat, *"Journal of Genetic Psychology,* 59 (1941), pp. 49–59.

Herrenkohl, L. R., "Prenatal Stress Reduces Fertility and Fecundity in Female Offspring," *Science,* 206 (1979), pp. 1,097–1,099.

Hersh, S. P., "Epilogue: Future Considerations and Directions," in *Depression in*

Childhood Diagnosis, Treatment, and Conceptual Models, pp. 147–149. Edited by J. G. Schulterbrandt and A. Raskin. New York: Raven, 1977.

Hersov, L. A., "Persistent Non-Attendance at School," *Journal of Child Psychology and Psychiatry*, 1 (1960), pp. 130–136.

Heston, L. L., "Psychiatric Disorders in Foster Home Reared Children of Schizophrenic Mothers," *British Journal of Psychiatry*, 12 (1966), pp. 819–825.

Heston, L. L., and Denny, D., "Interactions between Early Life Experience and Biological Factors in Schizophrenia," in *The Transmission of Schizophrenia*, pp. 363–376. Edited by D. Rosenthal and S. Kety. Elmsford, N.Y.: Pergamon Press, 1968.

Hetherington, E. M., Stouwie, R. J., and Ridberg, E. H., "Patterns of Family Interaction and Child-Rearing Attitudes Related to Three Dimensions of Juvenile Delinquency," *Journal of Abnormal Psychology*, 78 (1971), pp. 160–176.

Himelstein, P., "Review of the Slosson Intelligence Test," in *The Seventh Mental Measurements Yearbook*, pp. 765–766. Edited by O. K. Buros. Highland Park, N. J.: Gryphon Press, 1972.

Hock, R., Rodgers, C., Reddi, C., and Kennard, D., "Medico-Psychological Interventions in Male Asthmatic Children: An Evaluation of Physiological Change," *Psychosomatic Medicine*, 40 (1978), pp. 210–215.

Hops, H., and Cobb, J. A., "Survival Behaviors in the Educational Setting: Their Implications for Research and Intervention," in *Behavior Change: Methodology, Concepts, and Practice*. Edited by L. A. Hamerlynck, L. C. Handy, and E. J. Mash. Champaign, Ill.: Research Press, 1973.

Horney, K., *The Neurotic Personality of Our Time*. New York: W. W. Norton and Co., Inc., 1937.

Horrocks, J. E., *Assessment of Behavior*. Columbus, Ohio: Charles E. Merrill, 1964.

Huschka, M., "Psychopathological Disorders in the Mother," *Journal of Nervous and Mental Disease*, 94 (1941), pp. 76–83.

Illingworth, R. S., and Birch, L. B., "The Diagnosis of Mental Retardation in Infancy: A Follow-Up Study," *Archives of Disease in Childhood*, 34 (1959), pp. 269–273.

Ince, L. P., "The Use of Relaxation Training and a Conditioned Stimulus in the Elimination of Epileptic Seizures in a Child: A Case Study," *Journal of Behavior Therapy and Experimental Psychiatry*, 7 (1976), pp. 39–42.

International Statistical Classification of Diseases, Injuries and Causes of Death (9th rev. ed.). Geneva: World Health Organization, 1978.

Irvine, E. E., "Children in Kibbutzim: Thirteen Years After," *Journal of Child Psychology and Psychiatry*, 7 (1966), pp. 167–178.

Itard, J., *The Wild Boy of Aveyron*. Translated by G. and M. Humphrey. Englewood Cliffs, N.J.: Prentice-Hall, 1962.

Jacobs, P. A., and Strong, J. A., "A Case of Human Intersexuality Having a Possible XXY Sex-Determining Mechanism," *Nature*, 183 (1959), pp. 302–303.

Jacobson, C. B., and Berlin, C. M., "Possible Reproductive Detriment in LSD Users," *Journal of the American Medical Association*, 222 (1972), pp. 1,367–1,373.

Jastak, J. F., and Jastak, S. R., *The Wide Range Achievement Test* (rev. ed.). Wilmington, Del.: Guidance Associates of Delaware, 1976.

Jayasekara, R., and Street, J., "Parental Age and Parity in Dyslexic Boys," *Journal of Biosocial Science*, 10 (1978), pp. 255-261.

Jeffrey, D. B., "Behavioral Management of Obesity," in *Behavior Modification: Principles, Issues, and Applications,* pp. 394–413. Edited by W. E. Craighead, A. E. Kazdin, and J. J. Mahoney. Boston: Houghton Mifflin, 1976.

Johnson, A. M., Falstein, E. I., Szurek, S. A., and Svendsen, M., "School Phobia," *American Journal of Orthopsychiatry,* 11 (1941), pp. 702–711.

Johnson, S. B., and Melamed, B. C., "The Assessment and Treatment of Children's Fears," in *Advances in Clinical Child Psychology,* Vol. 2, pp. 107–139. Edited by B. B. Lahey and A. E. Kazdin. New York: Plenum, 1979.

Jondorf, W. R., Maickel, R. P., and Brodie, B. B., "Inability of Newborn Mice and Guinea Pigs to Metabolize Drugs," *Biochemical Pharmacology,* 1 (1958), pp. 352–354.

Jones, K. L., Smith, D. W., Ulleland, C. N., and Streissguth, A. P., "Pattern of Malformation in Offspring of Chronic Alcoholic Mothers," *Lancet,* 1 (1973), pp. 1,267–1,271.

Jones, M. C., "The Elimination of Children's Fears," *Journal of Experimental Psychology,* 7 (1924), pp. 383–390.

Judd, L. L., "Obsessive-Compulsive Neurosis in Children," *Archives of General Psychiatry,* 12 (1965), pp. 136–143.

Judd, L. L., and Mandell, A. J., "Chromosome Studies in Early Autism," *Archives of General Psychiatry,* 18 (1968), pp. 450–457.

Kagan, J., "Reflection-Impulsivity: The Generality and Dynamics of Conceptual Tempo," *Journal of Abnormal Psychology,* 71 (1966), pp. 17–24.

Kalakar, H. M., Kinoshita, J. H., and Donnell, G. N., "Galactosemia: Biochemistry, Genetics, Pathophysiology and Developmental Aspects," *Biology of Brain Dysfunction,* 1 (1973), 31–88.

Kallam, S. G., Ensminger, M. E., and Turner, R. J., "Family Structure and the Mental Health of Children," *Archives of General Psychiatry,* 34 (1977), pp. 1,012–1,022.

Kallmann, F. J., "Genetics of Psychoses," *American Journal of Human Genetics,* 2 (1950), pp. 385–390.

Kallmann, F. J., and Roth, B., "Genetic Aspects of Preadolescent Schizophrenia," *American Journal of Psychiatry,* 112 (1956), pp. 599–606.

Kanner, L., "Autistic Disturbances of Affective Contact," *Nervous Child,* 2 (1943), pp. 217–250.

——, "To What Extent Is Early Infantile Autism Determined by Constitutional Inadequacies?" *Association for Research in Nervous and Mental Disease,* 33 (1954), Research Publications, pp. 378–385.

——, "Emotionally Disturbed Children: A Historical Review," *Child Development,* 33 (1962), 97–102.

Kaplan, A. H., "Joint Parent-Adolescent Interview as a Parameter in the Psychoanalysis of the Younger Adolescent," *Journal of Nervous and Mental Disease,* 148 (1969), pp. 550–558.

Kashami, J., and Simonds, J. F., "The Incidence of Depression in Children," *American Journal of Psychiatry,* 136 (1979), pp. 1,203–1,205.

Kaufman, A. S., and Waterstreet, M. A., "Determining a Child's Strong and Weak Areas of Functioning on the Stanford-Binet: A Simplification of Sattler's SD Method," *Journal of School Psychology,* 16 (1978), pp. 72–78.

Kaufman, I., Frank, T., Friend, J., Heins, L. W., and Weiss, R., "Success and Failure in the Treatment of Childhood Schizophrenia," *American Journal of Psychiatry,* 118 (1962), pp. 909–913.

Kaufman, K. R., and **Katz-Garris, L.,** "Epilepsy, Mental Retardation, and Anticonvulsant Therapy," *American Journal of Mental Deficiency,* 84 (1979), pp. 256–259.

Kawi, A. A., and **Pasamanick, B.,** "Prenatal and Paranatal Factors in the Development of Childhood Reading Disorders," *Monographs of the Society for Research in Child Development,* 24, no. 4 (1959).

Kazdin, A. E., "Methodological and Assessment Considerations in Evaluating Reinforcement Programs in Applied Settings," *Journal of Applied Behavior Analysis,* 6 (1973), pp. 517–531.

Keat, D. B., "A Reinforcement Survey Schedule for Children," *Psychological Reports,* 35 (1974), pp. 287–293.

——, *Multimodal Therapy with Children,* Elmsford, N.Y.: Pergamon Press, 1979.

Kelley, T. L., Madden, R., Gardner, E. F., and **Rudman, H. C.,** *The Stanford Achievement Test.* New York: Harcourt Brace Jovanovich, Inc., 1964.

Kellogg, C., Tervo, D., Ison, J., Parisi, T., and **Miller, R. K.,** "Prenatal Exposure to Diezepam Alters Behavioral Development in Rats," *Science,* 207 (1980), pp. 205–207.

Kempe, R. S., and **Kempe, C. H.,** *Child Abuse.* Cambridge, Mass: Harvard University Press, 1978.

Kendall, P. C., and **Finch, A. J.,** "A Cognitive-Behavioral Treatment for Impulsivity: A Group Comparison Study," *Journal of Consulting and Clinical Psychology,* 46 (1978), pp. 110–118.

——, "Developing Nonimpulsive Behavior in Children: Cognitive Behavioral Strategies for Self Control," in *Cognitive-Behavioral Interventions: Theory, Research, and Procedures,* pp. 37–79. Edited by P. C. Kendal and S. D. Hollon. New York: Academic Press, 1979.

Kendall, P. C., Garten, J., and **Leon, G. R.,** "An Investigation of Depression in Children." Paper presented at the American Psychological Association meeting, New York, September, 1979.

Kennedy, W. A., "School Phobia: Rapid Treatment of Fifty Cases," *Journal of Abnormal Psychology,* 70 (1965), pp. 285–289.

Kessen, W., Haith, M. M., and **Salapatek, P. H.,** "Human Infancy: A Bibliography and Guide," in *Carmichael's Manual of Child Psychology,* Vol. 1, pp. 287–445. Edited by P. H. Mussen. New York: John Wiley, 1970.

Kessler, J., *Psychopathology of Childhood.* Englewood Cliffs, N.·J.: Prentice-Hall, 1966.

Kestenbaum, C. J., "Child Psychosis: Psychotherapy," in *Handbook of Treatment of Mental Disorders in Childhood and Adolescence,* pp. 354–384. Edited by B. B. Wolmen, J. Egan, and A. O. Ross. Englewood Cliffs, N. J.: Prentice-Hall, 1978.

Khan, A., "Effectiveness of Biofeedback and Counterconditioning in the Treatment of Bronchial Asthma," *Journal of Psychosomatic Research,* 21 (1977), pp. 97–104.

Kinsbourne, M., and **Caplan, P. J.,** *Children's Learning and Attention Problems.* Boston: Little, Brown, 1979.

Kirigin, K. A., Wolf, M. M., and **Phillips, E. L.,** "Achievement Place: A Preliminary Outcome Evaluation," in *Progress in Behavior Therapy with Delinquents,* pp. 118–145. Edited by J. S. Stumphauzer. Springfield, Ill.: Chas. C. Thomas, 1979.

Klebanoff, L. B., "Parental Attitudes of Mothers of Schizophrenic, Brain-Injured and Retarded, and Normal Children," *American Journal of Orthopsychiatry,* 29 (1959), pp. 445–454.

Klein, A. E., "Reliability and Predictive Validity of the Slosson Intelligence Test for Pre-Kindergarten Pupils," *Educational and Psychological Measurement,* 38 (1978), pp. 1,211–1,218.

Knobloch, H., Stevens, F., Malone, A., Ellison, P., and Risemberg, H., "The Validity of Parental Reporting of Infant Development," *Pediatrics,* 63 (1979), pp. 872–878.

Koegel, R. L., and Rincover, A., "Treatment of Psychotic Children in a Classroom Environment: I. Learning in a Large Group," *Journal of Applied Behavior Analysis,* 7 (1974), pp. 45–59.

Kolstoe, O. P., *Teaching Educable Mentally Retarded Children.* New York: Holt, Rinehart and Winston, 1970.

Köng, E., "Very Early Treatment of Cerebral Palsy," In *The Results of Treatment in Cerebral Palsy.* Edited by J. M. Wolf, Springfield, Ill.: Chas. C. Thomas, 1969.

Korner, A. R., "The Effect of Infants' State, Level of Arousal, Sex, and Ontogenetic Stages on the Caregiver," in *The Effect of the Infant on its Caregiver,* pp. 105–121. Edited by M. Lewis and L. A. Rosenblum. New York: John Wiley, 1974.

Kovacs, M., and Beck, A. T., "An Empirical-Clinical Approach toward a Definition of Childhood Depression," in *Depression in Childhood: Diagnosis, Treatment, and Conceptual Models,* pp. 1–25. Edited by J. G. Schulterbrandt and A. Raskin. New York: Raven Press, 1977.

Kratochwill, T. R., Brody, G. H., and Piersel, W. C., "Elective Mutism in Children," in *Advances in Clinical Child Psychology,* Vol. 2, pp. 193–240. Edited by B. B. Lahey and A. E. Kazdin. New York: Plenum, 1979.

Krill, D. F., "Family Interviewing as an Intake Diagnostic Method," *Social Work,* 13 (1968), pp. 56–63.

LaGreca, A. M., and Santogrossi, D. A., "Social Skills Training with Elementary School Students: A Behavioral Group Approach," *Journal of Consulting and Clinical Psychology,* 48 (1980), pp. 220–227.

Lambert, N. M., Windmiller, M., Cole, L., and Figuerva, R. A., "Standardization of a Public School Version of the AAMD Adaptive Behavior Scale," *Mental Retardation,* 13 (1975), pp. 3–7.

Lang, P. J., and Melamed, B. G., "Avoidance Conditioning Therapy of an Infant with Chronic Ruminative Vomiting: Case Report," *Journal of Abnormal Psychology,* 74 (1969), pp. 1–8.

La Vor, M., and Harvey, J., "Headstart, Economic Opportunity, Community Partnership Act of 1974," *Exceptional Children,* 42 (1976), pp. 227–230.

Lazarus, A. A., ed, *Multimodal Behavior Therapy.* New York: Springer, 1976.

Lazarus, A. A., and Abramovitz, A., "The Use of 'Emotive Imagery' in the Treatment of Children's Phobias," *Journal of Mental Science,* 108 (1962), pp. 191–195.

Lazarus, A. A., Davison, G. C., and Polefka, D. A., "Classical and Operant Factors in the Treatment of School Phobia," *Journal of Abnormal Psychology,* 70 (1965), pp. 225–229.

Lee, L. L., *Developmental Sentence Analysis: A Grammatical Assessment Procedure for Speech and Language Clinicians.* Evanston, Ill.: Northwestern University Press, 1974.

Lefkowitz, M. M., and Burton, N., "Childhood Depression: A Critique of the Concept," *Psychological Bulletin,* 85 (1978), pp. 716–726.

Lefkowitz, M. M., and Tesiny, E. P., "Assessment of Childhood Depression," *Journal of Consulting and Clinical Psychology,* 48 (1980), pp. 43–50.

Lejeune, J., Gautier, M., and Turpin, R., "Le monogolisme: premier example d' aberration autosomique humaine," *Annales de Genetique*, 1, no. 41 (1959).

Leland, H., and Smith, D. E., *Play Therapy with Mentally Subnormal Children.* New York: Grune & Stratton, 1965.

Leonard, M. F., Landy, G., Ruddle, F. H., and Lubs, H. A., "Early Development of Children with Abnormalities of the Sex Chromosomes: A Prospective Study," *Pediatrics*, 54 (1974), pp. 208-212.

Lesser, S. R., "Psychoanalysis with Children," in *Manual of Child Psychopathology*, pp. 847-864. Edited by B. B. Wolman. New York: McGraw-Hill, 1972.

Levitt, E. E., "Research on Psychotherapy with Children," in *Handbook of Psychotherapy and Behavior Change*, pp. 474-494. Edited by A. E. Bergin and S. L. Garfield. New York: John Wiley, 1971.

Levy, D., "Release Therapy in Young Children," *Psychiatry*, 1 (1938), pp. 387-390.

Lewis, H., *Deprived Children.* London: Oxford University Press, 1954.

Lewis, M., and Rosenburg, L. A., eds., *The Effect of the Infant on Its Caregiver.* New York: John Wiley, 1974.

Lilienfeld, A. M., Pasamanick, B., and Rogers, M., "Relationship between Pregnancy Experience and the Development of Certain Neuropsychiatric Disorders in Childhood," *American Journal of Public Health*, 45 (1955), pp. 637-643.

Lindquist, E. F., and Hieronymus, A. N., *Iowa Tests of Basic Skills Manuals.* Boston: Houghton Mifflin, 1955-56.

Lindsley, O. R., "Characteristics of the Behavior of Chronic Psychotics as Revealed by Free-Operant Conditioning Methods," *Diseases of the Nervous System*, 21 (Monograph Supplement) (1960), pp. 66-78.

Linehan, M., "Content Validity: Its Relevance to Behavioral Assessment," *Behavioral Assessment*, 2 (1980), pp. 147-159.

Lipman, R. S., "The Use of Psychopharmacological Agents in Residential Facilities for the Retarded," in *Psychiatric Approaches to Mental Retardation*, pp. 387-398. Edited by F. J. Menolascino. New York: Basic Books, 1970.

Little, V. L., and Kendall, P. C., "Cognitive-Behavioral Interventions with Delinquents: Problem-Solving, Role-Taking, and Self-Control," in *Cognitive-Behavioral Interventions*, pp. 81-114. Edited by P. C. Kendall and S. D. Hollon. New York: Academic Press, 1979.

Lorenz, K., *On Aggression.* New York: Harcourt Brace Jovanovich, Inc., 1966.

Lovaas, O. I., Berberich, J. P., Perloff, B. F., and Schaeffer, B., "Acquisition of Imitative Speech by Schizophrenic Children," *Science*, 151 (1966), pp. 705-707.

Lovaas, O. I., Koegel, R., Simmons, J. Q., and Stevens-Long, J., "Some Generalization and Follow-Up Measures on Autistic Children in Behavior Therapy," *Journal of Applied Behavior Analysis*, 6 (1973), pp. 131-166.

Lovaas, O. I., Young, D. B., and Newsom, C. D., "Childhood Psychosis: Behavioral Treatment." in *Handbook of Treatment of Mental Disorders in Childhood and Adolescence*, pp. 385-420. Edited by B. B. Wolman, J. Egan, and A. O. Ross. Englewood Cliffs, N. J.: Prentice-Hall, 1978.

Lubs, H. A., and Walknowska, J., "New Chromosomal Syndromes and Mental Retardation," in *Research to Practice in Mental Retardation*, Vol. 3, pp. 55-70. Edited by P. Mittler. Baltimore, Md.: University Park Press, 1977.

Lykken, D. T., "The Diagnosing Zygosity in Twins," *Behavior Genetics*, 8 (1978), pp. 437-473.

Maccoby, E. E., and Jacklin, C. H., *The Psychology of Sex Differences.* Stanford,

Calif.: Stanford University Press, 1974.

Macfarlane, J. W., Allen, L., and **Honzik, M. P.,** *A Developmental Study of the Behavior Problems of Normal Children between Twenty-One Months and Fourteen Years.* Berkeley, Calif.: University of California Press, 1954.

MacMillan, D. L., Jones, R. L., and **Aloia, G. F.,** "The Mentally Retarded Label: A Theoretical Analysis and Review of Research," *American Journal of Mental Deficiency,* 79 (1974), pp. 241–261.

MacMillan, D. L., Jones, R. L., and **Meyers, C. E.,** "Mainstreaming the Mildly Retarded: Some Questions, Cautions and Guidelines," *Mental Retardation,* 14 (1976), pp. 3–10.

Magrab, P. R., and **Johnson, R. B.,** "Mental Retardation," in *Child Development and Developmental Disabilities,* pp. 241–257. Edited by S. Gabel and M. T. Erickson. Boston: Little, Brown, 1980.

Mallick, S. K., and **McCandless, B. R.,** "A Study of Cartharsis of Aggression," *Journal of Personality and Social Psychology,* 4 (1966), pp. 591–596.

Massimo, J. L., and **Shore, M. F.,** "The Effectiveness of a Comprehensive Vocationally Oriented Psychotherapeutic Program for Adolescent Delinquent Boys," *American Journal of Orthopsychiatry,* 33 (1963), pp. 634–642.

Matthews, H. B., and **der Brucke, M. G.,** "'Normal Expectancy' in the Extremely Obese Pregnant Woman," *Journal of the American Medical Association,* 110 (1938), pp. 554–559.

Mattison, R., Cantwell, D. P., Russell, A. T., and **Will, L.,** "A Comparison of DSM-II and DSM-III in the Diagnosis of Childhood Psychiatric Disorders. II. Interrater Agreement," *Archives of General Psychiatry,* 36 (1979), pp. 1,217–1,223.

McCarthy, D., "McCarthy Scales of Children's Abilities," New York: Psychological Corporation, 1972.

McCorkle, L. W., Elias, A., and **Bixby, F. L.,** *The Highfields Story.* New York: Holt, Rinehart and Winston, 1958.

McKusick, V. A., and **Ruddle, F. H.,** "The Status of the Gene Map of the Human Chromosomes," *Science,* 196 (1977), pp. 390–405.

McLeod, J., "Educational Underachievement: Toward a Defensible Psychometric Definition," *Journal of Learning Disabilities,* 12 (1979), pp. 322–330.

McMillan, M. M., "Differential Mortality by Sex in Fetal and Neonatal Deaths," *Science,* 204 (1979), pp. 89–91.

Meichenbaum, D., "Teaching Children Self-Control," in *Advances in Clinical Child Psychology,* Vol. 2, pp. 1–33. Edited by B. B. Lahey and A. E. Kazdin. New York: Plenum, 1979.

Meichenbaum, D. H., and **Goodman, J.,** "Training Impulsive Children To Talk To Themselves," *Journal of Abnormal Psychology,* 77 (1971), pp. 115–126.

Melamed, B., and **Siegel, L.,** "Reduction of Anxiety in Children Facing Hospitalization and Surgery by Use of Filmed Modeling," *Journal of Consulting and Clinical Psychology,* 43 (1975), pp. 511–521.

Merton, R. K., *Social Theory and Social Structure,* pp. 131–160. New York: Free Press, 1957.

Meyers, D. I., and **Goldfarb, W.,** "Studies of Perplexity in Mothers of Schizophrenic Children," *American Journal of Orthopsychiatry,* 31 (1961), pp. 551–564.

Mikkelsen, M., and **Stene, J.,** "Genetic Counselling in Down's Syndrome," *Human Heredity,* 20 (1970), pp. 457–464.

Milgram, N. A., "IQ Constancy in Disadvantaged Negro Children," *Psychological Reports,* 29 (1971), pp. 319-326.

Milkovich, L., and Van Den Berg, B. J., "Effects of Prenatal Meprobamate and Chlordiazepoxide Hydrochloride on Human Embryonic and Fetal Development," *New England Journal of Medicine,* 291 (1974), pp. 1,268-1,271.

Miller, L. C., "School Behavior Checklist: An Inventory of Deviant Behavior for Elementary School Children," *Journal of Consulting and Clinical Psychology,* 38 (1972), pp. 134-143.

——, *School Behavior Checklist.* Los Angeles: Western Psychological Services, 1977.

Miller, W. B., "Lower-Class Culture as a Generating Milieu of Gang Delinquency," *Journal of Social Issues,* 14 (1958), pp. 5-19.

Millman, R. B., "Drug and Alcohol Abuse," in *Handbook of Treatment of Mental Disorders in Childhood Adolescence,* pp. 238-267. Edited by. B. B. Wolman, J. Egan, and A. O. Ross. Englewood Cliffs, N. J.: Prentice-Hall, 1978.

Minuchin, S., *Families and Family Therapy.* Cambridge, Mass.: Howard University Press, 1974.

Mischel, W., *Personality and Assessment.* New York: John Wiley, 1968.

——, "On the Interface of Cognition and Personality," *American Psychologist,* 34 (1979), pp. 740-754.

Montagu, M. F. A., *Prenatal Influences.* Springfield, Ill.: Thomas, 1962.

Moreno, J. L., "Group Method and Group Psychotherapy," *Sociometry Monographs,* no. 5 (1946).

Morrison, T. L., and Newcomer, B. L., "Effects of Directive vs. Nondirective Play Therapy with Institutionalized Mentally Retarded Children," *American Journal of Mental Deficiency,* 79 (1975), pp. 666-669.

Mostofsky, D., "Epilepsy: Returning the Ghost to Psychology," *Professional Psychology,* 9 (1978), pp. 87-92.

Mumpower, D. L., "Sex Ratios Found in Various Types of Referred Exceptional Children," *Exceptional Children,* 36 (1970), pp. 621-622.

Murray, H. A., *Thematic Apperception Test.* Cambridge, Mass.: Harvard University Press, 1943.

Neal, M., "The Relationship between a Regimen of Vestibular Stimulation and the Developmental Behavior of the Premature Infant," *Dissertation Abstracts International,* 30, no. 10 (1970).

Nelson, W. M., Finch, A. J., and Hooke, J. F., "Effects of Reinforcement and Response Cost on Cognitive Styles in Emotionally Disturbed Boys," *Journal of Abnormal Psychology,* 84 (1975), pp. 426-428.

Newcomer, B. L., and Morrison, T. L., "Play Therapy with Institutionalized Mentally Retarded Children," *American Journal of Mental Deficiency,* 78 (1974), pp. 727-733.

Newland, T. E., and Smith, P. A., "Statistically Significant Differences between Subtest Scaled Scores on the WISC and the WAIS," *Journal of School Psychology,* 5 (1967), pp. 122-127.

Ney, P., Palvesky, E., and Markely, J., "Relative Effectiveness of Operant Conditioning and Play Therapy in Childhood Schizophrenia," *Journal of Autism and Childhood Schizophrenia,* 1 (1971), pp. 337-349.

Nickerson, G., and MacDermot, P. N., "Psychometric Evaluation and Factors

Affecting the Performance of Children Who Have Recovered from Tuberculous Meningitis," *Pediatrics,* 27 (1961), pp. 68–82.

Nielsen, J., "Klinefelter's Syndrom and the XYY Syndrome," *Acta Psychiatrica Scandinavica,* 45, Supplementum 209 (1969).

Nihara, K., Foster, R., Shellhaas, M., and **Leland, H.,** *AAMD Adaptive Behavior Scale, 1975 Revision Manual.* Washington, D. C.: American Association of Mental Deficiency, 1975.

Niswander, K. R., and **Gordon, M.,** *The Women and Their Pregnancies,* Vol. 1. Philadelphia: Saunders, 1972.

Northern, J. L., and **Downs, M. P.,** *Hearing in Children* (2nd ed.). Baltimore, Md.: Williams & Wilkins, 1978.

Noyes, A., *Modern Clinical Psychiatry* (3rd ed.). Philadelphia: Saunders, 1948.

Noyes, R., Clancy, J., Crowe, R., Hoenk, P. R., and **Slymen, D. J.,** "The Familial Problems of Anxiety Neurosis," *Archives of General Psychiatry,* 35 (1978), pp. 1,057–1,062.

Nunnally, J., "Research Strategies and Measurement Methods for Investigating Human Development," in *Life-span Developmental Psychology,* pp. 87–109. Edited by J. R. Nesselroade and H. W. Reese. New York: Academic Press, New York, 1973.

O'Brien, J. S., "How We Detect Mental Retardation before Birth," *Medical Times,* 99, no. 2 (1971), pp. 103–108.

O'Leary, K. D., Kaufman, K. F., Kass, R. E., and **Drabman, R. S.,** "The Effects of Loud and Soft Reprimands on the Behavior of Disruptive Students," *Exceptional Children,* 37 (1970), pp. 145–155.

O'Leary, K. D., and **O'Leary, S. G.,** *Classroom Management: The Successful Use of Behavior Modification* (2nd ed.). Elmsford, N.Y.: Pergamon Press, 1977 (originally published 1972).

O'Leary, K. D., Pelham, W. E., Rosenbaum, A., and **Price, G. H.,** "Behavioral Treatment of Hyperkinetic Children," *Clinical Pediatrics,* 15 (1976), pp. 510–515.

O'Leary, S. G., and **Dubey, D.,** "Applications of Self-Control Procedures by Children: A Review," *Journal of Applied Behavior Analysis,* 12 (1979), pp. 449–465.

O'Leary, S. G., and **Pelham, W. E.,** "Behavior Therapy and Withdrawal of Stimulant Medication with Hyperactive Children," *Pediatrics,* 61 (1978), pp. 211–217.

Oldridge, O. A., and **Allison, E. E.,** "Wechsler Preschool and Primary Scale of Intelligence," *Journal of Educational Measurement,* 5 (1968), pp. 347–348.

Ollendick, T. H., "Fear Reduction Techniques with Children," in *Progress in Behavior Modification,* Vol. 8, pp. 127–168. Edited by M. Hersen, M. R. Eisler, and P. M. Miller. New York: Academic Press, New York, 1979.

Orton, J. L., "The Orton-Gillingham Approach," in *The Disabled Reader,* pp. 119–145. Edited by J. Money. Baltimore, Md.: Johns Hopkins University Press, 1966.

Orton, S. T., "Specific Reading Disability-Strephosymbolia," *Journal of the American Medical Association,* 90 (1928), pp. 1,095–1,099.

——, *Reading, Writing and Speech Problems in Children.* New York: W. W. Norton & Co., Inc., 1937.

Otis, A. S., and **Lennon, R. T.,** *Otis-Lennon Mental Ability Test.* New York: Harcourt Brace Jovanovich, Inc., 1969.

Owen, F. W., "Dyslexia-Genetic Aspects," in *Dyslexia: In Appraisal of Current Knowledge*, pp. 267-284. Edited by A. L. Benton and D. Pearl. New York: Oxford University Press, 1978.

Palmer, J. O., *The Psychological Assessment of Children.* New York: John Wiley, 1970.

Patterson, G. R., Reid, J. B., Jones, R. R., and Conger, R. E., *A Social Learning Approach to Family Intervention.* Eugene, Ore.: Castalia, 1975.

Penrose, L. S., "Mutation," in *Recent Advances in Human Genetics*, pp. 1-18. Edited by L. S. Penrose. Boston: Little, Brown, 1961.

Pettit, J. M., and Helms, S. B., "Hemispheric Language Dominance of Language-Disordered, Articulated-Disordered, and Normal Children," *Journal of Learning Disabilities*, 12 (1979), pp. 71-76.

Phillips, E. L., "Achievement Place: Token Reinforcement Procedures in a Home-Style Rehabilitation Setting for 'Pre-Delinquent' Boys," *Journal of Applied Behavior Analysis*, 1 (1968), pp. 213-223.

Plomin, R., and Rowe, D. C., "A Twin Study of Temperament in Young Children," *Journal of Psychology*, 97 (1977), pp. 107-113.

Polk, K., and Schaefer, W. E., *Schools and Delinquency.* Englewood Cliffs, N. J.: Prentice-Hall, 1972.

Pollack, M., and Woerner, M. G., "Pre- and Perinatal Complications and 'Childhood Schizophrenia': A Comparison of Five Controlled Studies," *Journal of Child Psychology and Psychiatry*, 7 (1966), pp. 235-242.

Pollin, W., "A Possible Genetic Factor Related to Psychosis," *American Journal of Psychiatry*, 128 (1971), pp. 311-317.

Pollin, W., Stabenau, J. R., Mosher, L., and Tupin, J., "Life History Differences in Identical Twins Discordant for Schizophrenia," *American Journal of Orthopsychiatry*, 36 (1966), pp. 492-509.

Porter, R. B., and Cattell, R. B., *Children's Personality Questionnaire.* Champaign, Ill.: IPAT, 1963.

Potter, E. L., "Twin Zygosity and Placental Form in Relation to the Outcome of Pregnancy," *American Journal of Obstetrics and Gynecology*, 87 (1963), pp. 566-577.

Powell, J., and Rockinson, R., "On the Inability of Interval Time Sampling to Reflect Frequency of Occurrence Data," *Journal of Applied Behavior Analysis*. 11 (1978), pp. 531-532.

Powers, M. H., "Clinical and Educational Procedures in Functional Disorders of Articulation," in *Handbook of Speech Pathology and Audiology*, pp. 877-910. Edited by L. E. Travis. Englewood Cliffs, N. J.: Prentice-Hall, 1971.

Prechtl, H. F. R., "Neurological Sequelae of Prenatal and Paranatal Complications," in *Determinants of Infant Behavior*, pp. 45-48. Edited by B. M. Foss. New York: John Wiley, 1961.

Premack, D., "Reinforcement Theory," in *Nebraska Symposium on Motivation*, pp. 123-180. Edited by D. Levine. Lincoln, Neb.: University of Nebraska Press, 1965.

Proctor, J. T., "Hysteria in Childhood," *American Journal of Orthopsychiatry*, 28 (1958), pp. 394-406.

Quay, H. C., "Classification," in *Psychopathological Disorders of Childhood* (2nd ed.) pp. 1-42. Edited by H. C. Quay and J. S. Werry. New York: John Wiley, 1979.

——, "Dimensions of Personality in Deliquent Boys as Inferred from the Factor Analysis of Case History Data," *Child Development*, 35 (1964), pp. 479-484.

——, and **Peterson, D.R.**, *Behavior Problem Checklist.* Champaign, Ill.: Children's Research Center, University of Illinois, 1967.

Rabin, A. I., and **McKinney, J. P.**, "Intelligence Tests and Childhood Psychopathology," in *Manual of Child Psychopatnology.* Edited by B. B. Wolman. New York: McGraw-Hill, 1972.

Rainer, J. D., "Heredity and Character Disorders," *American Journal of Psychotherapy,* 33 (1979), pp. 6–16.

Rank, B., "Intensive Study and Treatment of Preschool Children Who Show Marked Personality Deviations, or 'Atypical Development' and Their Parents," in *Emotional Problems of Early Childhood,* pp. 491–501. Edited by G. Caplan. New York: Basic Books, 1955.

Rank, O., *The Trauma of Birth.* New York: Brunner-Mazel, 1952.

Rapaport, J. L., "Pediatric Psychopharmacology and Childhood Depression," in *Depression in Childhood: Diagnosis, Treatment, and Conceptual Models,* pp. 87–100. Edited by J. G. Schulterbrandt and A. Raskin. New York: Raven, 1977.

Rapaport, J. L., Buchsbaum, M. S., Lahn, T. P., Weingartoner, H., Ludlow, C., and **Mikkelsen, E. J.**, "Dextroamphetamine: Cognitive and Behavioral Effects in Normal Prepubertal Boys," *Science,* 199 (1978), pp. 560–562.

Ricks, D. F., and **Berry, J. C.**, "Family and Symptom Patterns that Precede Schizophrenia," in *Life History Research in Psychopathology,* pp. 31–50. Edited by M. Roff and D. F. Ricks. Minneapolis, Minn.: University of Minnesota Press, 1970.

Rimland, B., *Infantile Autism.* New York: Appleton-Century-Crofts, 1964.

——, "Infantile Autism: Status and Research," in *Child Personality and Psychopathology,* Vol. 1, pp. 137–167. Edited by A. Davids. New York: John Wiley, 1974.

Risley, T. R., "The Effects and Side Effects of Punishing the Autistic Behaviors of a Deviant Child," *Journal of Applied Behavior Analysis,* 1 (1968), pp. 21–34.

Roche, A. F., Lipman, R. S., Overall, J. E., and **Hung, W.**, "The Effects of Stimulant Medication on the Growth of Hyperkinetic Children," *Pediatrics,* 63 (1979), pp. 847–850.

Rorschach, H., *Psychodiagnostics: A Diagnostic Test Based on Perception* (4th ed.). New York: Grune & Stratton, 1942.

Rosen, B. M., Bahn, A. K., and **Kramer, M.**, "Demographic and Diagnostic Characteristics of Psychiatric Clinic Patients in the U.S.A., 1961," *American Journal of Orthopsychiatry,* 34 (1964), pp. 455–468.

Rosenblith, J., "The Modified Graham Behavior Test for Neonates: Test-Retest Reliability, Normative Data and Hypotheses for Future Work," *Biology of the Neonate,* 3 (1961), pp. 174–192.

Rosenblith, J.F., "Prognostic Value of Neonatal Behavior Tests," in *Exceptional Infant: Assessment and Intervention,* Vol. 3, pp. 157–172. Edited by B. Z. Friedlander, G. M. Sterritt, and G. E. Kirk. New York: Brunner/Mazel, 1975.

Rosenthal, D., "Three Adoption Studies of Heredity in the Schizophrenic Disorders," *International Journal of Mental Health,* 1 (1972), pp. 63–75.

——, **Wender, P. H., Kety, S. S., Welner, J.**, and **Schulsinger, F.**, "The Adopted-Away Offspring of Schizophrenics," *American Journal of Psychiatry,* 128 (1971), pp. 307–311.

Ross, A. O., "The Issue of Normality in Clinical Child Psychology," *Mental Hygiene,* 47 (1963), pp. 267–272.

——, *Psychological Disorders of Children.* New York: McGraw-Hill, 1974.

Ross, A. O., Lacey, H. M., and Parton, D. A., "The Development of a Behavior Checklist for Boys," *Child Development,* 36 (1965), pp. 1,013–1,027.

Ross, D. M., and Ross, S. A., *Pacemaker Primary Curriculum.* Belmont, Calif.: Fearon Publishers, 1974.

Rourke, B. P., "Neuropsychological Research in Reading Retardation: A Review," in *Dyslexia,* pp. 140–171. Edited by A. L. Benton and D. Pearl. New York: Oxford University Press, 1978.

Rousey, C. L., "Speech Disorders," in *Handbook of Treatment of Mental Disorders in Childhood and Adolescence,* pp. 185–201. Edited by B. B. Wolman, J. Egan, and A. E. Ross. Englewood Cliffs, N.J.: Prentice-Hall, 1978.

Routh, D. K., and Schroeder, C. S., "Standardized Playroom Measures as Indices of Hyperactivity," *Journal of Abnormal Child Psychology,* 4 (1976), pp.199–207.

Rubinstein, E. A., "Television and the Young Viewer," *American Scientist,* 66 (1978), pp. 685–693.

Rutter, M., "Parent-Child Separation: Psychological Effects on the Children," *Journal of Child Psychology and Psychiatry,* 12 (1971), pp. 233–260.

Rutter, M., and Bartak, L., "Causes of Infantile Autism: Some Considerations from Recent Research," *Journal of Autism and Childhood Schizophrenia,* 1 (1971), pp. 20–32.

——, "Special Education Treatment of Autistic Children: A Comparative Study. II. Follow-Up Findings and Implications for Services," *Journal of Child Psychology and Psychiatry,* 14 (1973), pp. 241–270.

——, and Newman, S., "Autism—A Central Disorder of Cognition and Language," in *Infantile Autism: Concepts, Characteristics and Treatment.* Edited by M. Rutter. London: Churchill-Livingstone, 1971.

Safer, D. J., and Allen, R. P., "Factors Influencing the Suppressant Effects of Two Stimulant Drugs on the Growth of Hyperactive Children," *Pediatrics,* 51 (1973), pp. 660–667.

Satir, V., *Conjoint Family Therapy: A Guide to Theory and Technique.* Palo Alto, Calif.: Science and Behavior Books, 1964.

Satir, V., Stachowiak, J., Taschman, H. A., Tiffany, D. W., Cohen, J. I., Robinson, A. M., and Ogburn, K. C., *Helping Families to Change.* New York: Jason Aronson, 1975.

Sattler, J. M., *Assessment of Children's Intelligence.* Philadelphia: Saunders, 1974.

Scarr-Salapatek, S., "Race, Social Class, and I.Q.," *Science,* 174 (1971), pp. 1,285–1,295.

Schaefer, C. E., Millman, H. L., and Levine, G. F., *Therapies for Psychosomatic Disorders in Children.* San Francisco: Jossey-Bass, 1979.

Schaefer, W. E., and Polk, K., "Recommendations," in *Schools and Deliquency,* pp. 239–277. Edited by K. Polk and W. E. Schafer. Englewood Cliffs, N. J.: Prentice-Hall, 1972.

Scharfman, M. A., "Psychoanalytic Treatment," in *Handbook of Treatment of Mental Disorders in Childhood and Adolescence,* pp. 47–69. Edited by B. B. Wolman, J. Egan, and A. O. Ross. Englewood Cliffs, N. J.: Prentice-Hall, 1978.

Scheer, E. M., *Radical Nonintervention: Rethinking the Delinquency Problem.* Englewood Cliffs, N. J.: Prentice-Hall, 1973.

Scherer, M., and Nakamura, C., "A Fear Survey Schedule for Children (FSS-FC): A Factor Analytic Comparison with Manifest Anxiety (CMAS)," *Behavior Research and Therapy,* 6 (1968), pp. 173–182.

Schmauk, F.J., "Punishment, Arousal, and Avoidance Learning in Sociopaths," *Journal of Abnormal Psychology,* 76 (1970), pp. 325–335.

Schopler, E. and Reichler, R.J. (Eds.) *Child Development, Deviations, and Treatment.* New York: Plenum, 1976.

Scurletis, T.D., Headrick-Haynes, M., Turnbull, C.D., and Fallon, R., "Comprehensive Developmental Health Services: A Concept and a Plan," in *Intervention Strategies for High Risk Infants and Young Children.* Edited by T. D. Tjossem. Baltimore, Md.: University Park Press, 1976.

Sears, R.R., Maccoby, E.E., and Levin, H., *Patterns of Child Rearing.* New York: Harper & Row, Pub., 1957.

Sears, R.R., and Wise, G.M., "Relation of Cup Feeding in Infancy to Thumbsucking and the Oral Drive," *American Journal of Orthopsychiatry,* 20 (1950), pp. 123–138.

Seligman, M.E.P., *Helplessness: On Depression, Development, and Death.* San Francisco, Calif.: W. H. Freeman and Company Publishers, 1975.

Sever, J.L., "Infectious Agents and Fetal Disease," in *Fetal Growth and Development.* Edited by H. A. Waisman and G. R. Kerr. New York: McGraw-Hill, 1970.

Shaywitz, B. A., Cohen, D. J., and Bowers, M. B., "CSF Monoamine Metabolites in Children with Minimal Brain Dysfunction: Evidence for Alteration of Brain Dopamine," *Journal of Pediatrics,* 90 (1977), pp. 67–71.

Sheldon, W.H. *Varieties of Delinquent Youth.* New York: Harper & Row, Pub., 1949.

Shinn, M., "Father Absence and Children's Cognitive Development," *Psychological Bulletin,* 85 (1978), pp. 295–324.

Shore, M. F., Massimo, J. L., Kisielewski, B. A., and Moran, J. K., "Object Relations Changes Resulting from Successful Psychotherapy with Adolescent Delinquents and Their Relationship to Academic Performance," *Journal of the American Academy of Child Psychiatry,* 5 (1966), pp. 93–104.

Simpson, W.J. "A Preliminary Report on Cigarette Smoking and the Incidence of Prematurity," *American Journal of Obstetrics and Gynecology,* 73 (1957), pp. 808–815.

Slater, E., "Psychiatry," in *Clinical Genetics,* Chapter 18, pp. 332–349. Edited by A. Sorsby. London: Butterworth, 1953.

Slavson, S.R., and Schiffer, M., *Group Psychotherapies for Children.* New York: International Universities Press, 1975.

Sloan, W., *Lincoln-Oseretsky Motor Development Scale.* Chicago: C. H. Stoelting, 1955.

Slosson, R.L., *Slosson Intelligence Test for Children and Adults.* New York: Slosson Educational Publications, 1963.

Smith, C.A., "Effects of Maternal Undernutrition upon the Newborn Infant in Holland (1944–45)," *Journal of Pediatrics,* 30 (1947), pp. 229–243.

Sontag, L.W., and Wallace, R.F., "The Effect of Cigaret Smoking during Pregnancy upon the Fetal Heart Rate," *American Journal of Obstetrics and Gynecology,* 29 (1935), pp. 77–83.

Spache, G.D., *Spache Diagnostic Reading Scales.* Monterey, Calif.: California Test Bureau, 1963.

Spearman, C., "General Intelligence Objectively Measured and Determined," *American Journal of Psychology,* 15 (1904), pp. 201–293.

Sperry, B., Ulrich, D. N., and **Staver, N.,** "The Relation of Motility to Boys' Learning Problems," *American Journal of Orthopsychiatry,* 28 (1958), pp. 640–646.

Spitz, R. A., "Hospitalism: An Inquiry into the Genesis of Psychiatric Conditions in Early Childhood," *Psychoanalytic Study of the Child,* 1 (1945), pp. 53–64.

——, "Anaclitic Depression," *Psychoanalytic Study of the Child,* 2 (1946), pp. 313–342.

Spivak, G., and **Shure, M. B.,** *Social Adjustment of Young Children.* San Francisco: Jossey-Bass, 1974.

Sprague, R. L., and **Sleator, E. K.,** "Methylphenidate in Hyperkinetic Children: Differences in Dose Effects on Learning and Social Behavior," *Science,* 198 (1977), pp. 1,274–1,276.

Staats. A., *Learning, Language, and Cognition.* New York: Holt, Rinehart and Winston, 1968.

Stacey, M., Dearden, R., Pill, R., and **Robinson, D.,** *Hospitals, Children and Their Families.* London: Routledge and Kegan Paul, 1970.

Starkweather, C. W., "A Behavioral Analysis of Van Riperian Therapy for Stutterers," *Journal of Communication Disorders,* 63 (1973), pp. 273–291.

Stein, Z., Susser, M., Saenger, G., and **Marolla, F.,** "Nutrition and Mental Performance," *Science,* 179 (1972), pp. 708–713.

Stevens-Long, J., and **Lovaas, O. I.,** "Research and Treatment with Autistic Children in a Program of Behavior Therapy," in *Child Personality and Psychopathology,* Vol. 1, pp. 169–203. Edited by A. Davids. New York: John Wiley, 1974.

Stewart, M., Pills, F., Craig, W., and **Dieruf, W.,** "The Hyperactive Child Syndrome," *American Journal of Orthopsychiatry,* 36 (1966), pp. 861–867.

Stolberg, A., *Primary Prevention of Psychopathology in Children of Divorce,* NIMH Research Grant Proposal, 1980.

Stott, D. H., "Follow-Up Study from Birth Effects of Prenatal Stresses," *Developmental Medicine and Child Neurology,* 15 (1973), pp. 770–787.

Strauss, A. A., and **Kephart, N. C.,** "Behavior Differences in Mentally Retarded Children Measured by a New Behavior Rating Scale," *American Journal of Psychiatry,* 96 (1940), pp. 1,117–1,123.

Strauss, A. A., and **Lehtinen, L. E.,** *Psychopathology and Education of the Brain-Injured Child.* New York: Grune and Stratton, 1947.

Sugar, M., "At-Risk Factors for the Adolescent Mother and Her Infant," *Journal of Youth and Adolescence,* 5 (1976), pp. 251–270.

Sullivan, E. T., Clark, W. W., and **Tiegs, E. W.,** *California Test of Mental Maturity,* Monterey, Calif.: California Test Bureau, 1957.

Sullivan, H. S., *Clinical Studies in Psychiatry.* New York: W.W. Norton & Co., Inc., 1956.

Taft, J., *The Dynamics of Therapy in a Controlled Relationship.* New York: Macmillan, 1933.

Talkington, L. W., Hall, S. M., and **Altman, R.,** "Use of Peer Modeling Procedure with Severely Retarded Subjects on a Basic Communication Response Skill," *Training School Bulletin,* 69 (1973), pp. 145–149.

Terman, L. M., and **Merrill, M. A.,** *The Stanford-Binet Intelligence Scale: Manual for the Third Revision.* Boston: Houghton Mifflin, 1960.

Teuber, H., "Mental Retardation after Early Trauma to the Brain," in *Physical Trauma as an Etiological Agent in Mental Retardation,* pp. 7–28. Edited by C. R.

Angle and E. A. Bering. Washington, D. C.: U.S. Government Printing Office, 1970.

Thomas, A., and Chess, S., *Temperament and Development.* New York: Brunner/Mazel, 1977.

Thomas, A., Chess, S., and Birch, H. G., *Temperament and Behavior Disorders in Children.* New York: New York University Press, 1968.

Thompson, W. R., "Influence of Prenatal Maternal Anxiety on Emotionality in Young Rats," *Science,* 125 (1957), 698–699.

Thomson, A. M., "Maternal Stature and Reproductive Efficiency," *Eugenics Review,* 51 (1960), pp. 157–162.

Thorndike, R. L., *The Concepts of Over- and Under-Achievement.* New York: Teachers College, Columbia University, 1963.

——, *Stanford-Binet Intelligence Scale: 1972 Norms Tables.* Boston: Houghton Mifflin, 1973.

Thorpe, L. P., "Appraising Personality and Social Adjustment," *Educational Bulletin of the California Test Bureau,* no. 11. Monterey, Calif.: California Test Bureau, 1945.

Thorpe, L. P., Clark, W. W., and Tiegs, E. W., *California Test of Personality.* Monterey, Calif.: California Test Bureau, 1953.

Thurston, D., Graham, F. K., Ernhart, C. B., Eichman, F. L., and Craft, M., "Neurologic Status of Three-Year-Old Children Originally Studied at Birth," *Neurology,* 10 (1960), pp. 680–690.

Thurstone, L. L., *Primary Mental Abilities.* Chicago: University of Chicago Press, 1938.

Tjio, J., and Levan, A., "The Chromosome Number of Man," *Hereditas,* 42, no. 1 (1956).

Travis, L. E., "The Cerebral Dominance Theory of Stuttering: 1931–1978," *Journal of Speech and Hearing Disorders,* 43 (1978), pp. 278–281.

Tronick, E., and Brazelton, T. B., "Clinical Uses of the Brazelton Neonatal Behavioral Assessment," in *Exceptional Infant: Assessment and Intervention,* Vol. 3, pp. 137–156. Edited by B. Z. Friedlander, G. M. Sterritt, and G. E. Kirk. New York: Brunner/Mazel, 1975.

Truax, C. B., and Mitchell, K. M., "Research on Certain Therapist Interpersonal Skills in Relation to Process and Outcome." in *Handbook of Psychotherapy and Behavior Change,* pp. 299–344. Edited by A. E. Bergin and S. L. Garfield. New York: John Wiley, 1971.

Tryon, R. C., "Genetic Differences in Maze-Learning in Rats," in *Intelligence: Its Nature and Nurture, National Society for the Study of Education Yearbook,* pp. 111–119. Edited by G. M. Whipple. 1, no. 39 (1940).

Vanderheiden, G., and Grilley, K., eds., *Nonvocal Communication Techniques and Aids for the Severely Physically Handicapped.* Baltimore, Md.,: University Park Press, 1975.

Vandersall, T. A., "Ulcerative Colitis," in *Handbook of Treatment of Mental Disorders In Childhood and Adolescence,* pp. 144–152. Edited by B. B. Wolman, J. Egan, and A. O. Ross. Englewood Cliffs, N. J.: Prentice-Hall, 1978.

Van Riper, C., *Speech Correction: Principles and Methods* (5th ed.). Englewood Cliffs, N. J.: Prentice-Hall, 1972.

Van Wagenen, R. K., Meyerson, L., Kerr, N. J., and Mahoney, K., "Field Trials of a New Procedure for Toilet Training," *Journal of Experimental Child Psychology,* 8 (1969), pp. 147–159.

Vellutino, F. R., Steger, B. M., Meyer, S. C., Harding, C. J., and Niles, J. A., "Has the Perceptual Deficit Hypothesis Led Us Astray? *Journal of Learning Disabilities,* 10 (1979), pp. 375–385.

Verville, E., *Behavior Problems of Children.* Philadelphia: Saunders, 1967.

Volkart, E. H., "Bereavement and Mental Health," in *Explorations in Social Psychiatry.* Edited by A. H. Leighton, J. A. Clausen, and R. N. Wilson. New York: Basic Books, 1957.

Vorhees, C. V., Brunner, R. L., and Butcher, R. E., "Psychotropic Drugs as Behavioral Teratogens," *Science,* 205 (1979), pp. 1,220–1,225.

Wahler, R. G., and Cormier, W. H., "The Ecological Interview: A First Step in Outpatient Child Behavior Therapy," *Journal of Behavior Therapy and Experimental Psychiatry,* 1 (1970), pp. 279–289.

Wahler, R. G., House, A. E., and Stembaugh, E. E., *Ecological Assessment of Child Problem Behavior.* Elmsford, N.Y.: Pergamon Press, 1976.

Waldrop, M. F., Bell, R. Q., McLaughlin, B., and Halverson, C. F., "Newborn Minor Physical Normalities Predict Short Attention Span, Peer Aggression, and Impulsivity at Age 3," *Science,* 199 (1978), pp. 563–565.

Wallston, B., "The Effects of Maternal Employment on Children," *Journal of Child Psychology and Psychiatry,* 14 (1973), pp. 81–95.

Watson, J. B., and Rayner, R., "Conditioned Emotional Reactions," *Journal of Experimental Psychology,* 3 (1920), pp. 1–14.

Watson, J. D., and Crick, F. H. C., "A Structure for Deoxyribose Nucleric Acid," *Nature,* 171 (1953), pp. 737–738.

Webb, C. E., and Siegenthaler, B. M., "Comparison of Aural Stimulation Methods for Teaching Speech Sounds," *Journal of Speech and Hearing Disorders,* 22 (1957), pp. 264–270.

Weber, W. W., "Survival and Sex Ratio in Trisomy 17–18," *American Journal of Human Genetics,* 19 (1967), pp. 369–377.

Wechsler, D., *Manual for the Wechsler Intelligence Scale for Children.* New York: Psychological Corporation, 1949.

——, *Manual for the Wechsler Preschool and Primary Scale of Intelligence.* New York: Psychological corporation, 1967.

——, *Manual for the Wechsler Intelligence Scale for Children–Revised.* New York: Psychological Corporation, 1974.

——, "Intelligence Defined and Undefined: A Relativistic Appraisal," *American Psychologist,* 30 (1975), pp. 135–139.

Weinberg, W., Rutman, J., Sullivan, L., Penick, E. C., and Dietz, S. G., "Depression in Children Referred to an Educational Diagnostic Center: Diagnostic and Treatment," *Journal of Pediatrics,* 83 (1973), pp. 1,065–1,072.

Weiner, I. B., "Behavior Therapy in Obsessive-Compulsive Neurosis: Treatment of an Adolescent Boy," *Psychotherapy,* 4 (1967), pp. 27–29.

Weiss, G., and Hechtman, L., "The Hyperactive Child Syndrome," *Science,* 205 (1979), pp. 1,348–1,354.

Weiss, G., Kruger, E., Danielson, U., and Elman, M., "Effect of Long-Term Treatment of Hyperactive Children with Methylphenidate," *Canadian Medical Association Journal,* 112 (1975), pp. 159–165.

Wenar, C., Ruttenberg, B. A., Dratman, M. L., and Wolf, E. G., "Changing Autistic Behavior: The Effectiveness of Three Milieus," *Archives of General Psychiatry,* 17 (1967), pp. 26–35.

Wepman, J., *Wepman Test of Auditory Discrimination.* Chicago: Language Research Associates, 1958.

Werner, E. E., Honzik, M. P., and Smith, R. S., "Prediction of Intelligence and Achievement at Ten Years from Twenty Months Pediatric and Psychologic Examinations," *Child Development,* 39 (1968), pp. 1,063–1,075.

Werry, J. S., "Childhood Psychosis," in *Psychopathological Disorders of Childhood,* pp. 173–233. Edited by H. C. Quay and J. S. Werry. New York: John Wiley, 1972.

Werry, J. S., and Quay, H. C., "Observing the Classroom Behavior of Elementary School Children," *Exceptional Children,* 35 (1969), pp. 461–467.

Whitlock, F. A., "The Etiology of Hysteria," *Acta Psychiatrica Scandinavica,* 43 (1967), pp. 144–162.

Wiener, G., "Psychologic Correlates of Premature Birth: A Review," *Journal of Nervous and Mental Disease,* 134 (1962), pp. 129–144.

Wiener, G., Rider, R. V., Oppel, W. C., Fischer, L. K., and Harper, P. A., "Correlates of Low Birth Weight: Psychological Status at Six to Seven Years of Age," *Pediatrics,* 35 (1965), pp. 434–444.

Williams, C. D., "The Elimination of Tantrum Behavior by Extinction Procedures," *Journal of Abnormal and Social Psychology,* 59 (1959), p. 269.

Williams, D. E., "Stuttering Therapy for Children," in *Handbook of Speech Pathology and Audiology,* pp. 1,073–1,093. Edited by L. E. Travis. Englewood Cliffs, N.J.: Prentice–Hall, Inc., 1971.

Wilson, R. S., "Synchronies in Mental Development: An Epigenetic Perspective," *Science,* 202 (1978), pp. 939–948.

Windle, W. F., ed., *Neurological and Psychological Deficits of Asphyxia Neonatorium.* Springfield, Ill.: Chas. C. Thomas, 1958.

Winick, M., *Malnutrition and Brain Development.* New York: Oxford University Press, 1976.

——, *Human Nutrition: A Comprehensive Treatise, Volume 1: Pre- and Postnatal Development.* New York: Plenum, 1979.

Winick, M., and Rosso, P., "Effects of Malnutrition on Brain Development." *Biology of Brain Dysfunction,* 1 (1973), pp. 301–317.

Wing, L., ed., *Early Childhood Autism,* (2nd ed.). Elmsford, N. Y.: Pergamon Press, 1976.

Wirt, R. D., Lachar, D., Klinedinst, J., Seat, P. D., and Broen, W. E., *The Personality Inventory for Children.* Los Angeles: Western Psychological Services, 1977.

Witkin, H. A., and others, "XYY and XXY Men: Criminality and Aggression," *Science,* 193 (1976), pp. 547–555.

Wolf, L. C., and Whitehead, P. C., "The Decision to Institutionalize Retarded Children: Comparison of Individually Matched Groups," *Mental Retardation,* 13 (1975), pp. 3–7.

Wolking, W. D., Quast, W., and Lawton, J. J., "MMPI Profiles of Parents of Behaviorally Disturbed Children and Parents from the General Population," *Journal of Clinical Psychology,* 22 (1966), pp. 39–48.

Woolman, M., *The Progressive Choice Reading Program.* Washington, D.C.: Institute of Educational Research, 1962.

World Health Organization, *International Classification of Diseases* (9th rev. ed.). New York: WHO, 1978.

Wright, L., "Handling the Encopretic Child," *Professional Psychology,* 4 (1973), pp. 137–144.

Wright, S. W., Tarjan, G., and **Eyer, L.,** "Investigation of Families with Two or More Mentally Defective Siblings: Clinical Observations," *American Journal of Diseases of Children,* 97 (1959), pp. 445-456.

Wyke, M. A., ed., *Developmental Dysphasia.* New York: Academic Press, New York, 1978.

Yarrow, L. J., "Separation from Parents During Early Childhood," in *Review of Child Development Research,* Vol. 1, pp. 89-136. Edited by M. L. Hoffman and L. W. Hoffman. New York: Russell Sage, 1964.

Yarrow, M. R., Campbell, J. D., and **Burton, R. V.,** "Recollections of Childhood: A Study of the Retrospective Method," *Monographs of the Society for Research in Child Development,* 35, no. 5 (1970).

Yates, A. J., *Behavior Therapy.* New York: John Wiley, 1970.

Yoder, P., and **Forehand, R.,** "Effects of Modeling and Verbal Cues upon Concept Acquisition of Nonretarded and Retarded Children," *American Journal of Mental Deficiency,* 78 (1974), pp. 566-570.

Young, G. C., and **Morgan, R. T.,** "Overlearning in the Conditioning Treatment of Enuresis: A Long-Term Follow-Up Study," *Behavior Research and Therapy,* 10 (1972), pp. 419-420.

Young, M. A., "Onset, Prevalence, and Recovery from Stuttering," *Journal of Speech and Hearing Disorders,* 40 (1975), pp. 49-58.

Zigler, E., "The Retarded Child as a Whole Person," in *The Experimental Psychology of Mental Retardation,* pp. 231-322. Edited by D. K. Routh. Chicago: Aldine, 1973.

Zigler, E., and **Trickett, P. K.,** "IQ, Social Competence, and Evaluation of Early Childhood Intervention Programs," *American Psychologist,* 33 (1978), pp. 789-798.

Zubin, J., Iron, L. D., and **Schumer, F.,** *An Experimental Approach to Projective Techniques.* New York: John Wiley, 1965.

Zussman, J. U., "Relationship of Demographic Factors to Parental Discipline Techniques," *Developmental Psychology,* 14 (1978), pp. 685-686.

author index

Sears, R. R., 95, 234, 275
Seat, P. D., 32, 269
Seguin, 155
Seligman, M. E. P., 271
Serer, J. L., 150
Shapiro, E., 218
Shapiro, T., 178
Shaywitz, B. A., 226
Sheldon, W. H., 235, 237
Shellhaas, M., 142
Sherman, J. A., 129
Shinefield, H. R., 308
Shinn, M., 89
Shore, M. F., 241
Shure, M. B., 303
Siegal, A., 235
Siegel, G. M., 218
Siegel, L., 258
Sieganthaler, B. M., 219
Simmons, J. B., 184, 185
Simonds, J. F., 268
Simpson, W. J., 75
Skinner, B. S., 119
Slater, E., 63
Slavson, S. R., 109
Sleator, E. K., 226
Sloan, W., 195
Slosson, R. L., 25
Slyman, D. J., 259
Small, A. M., 114
Smith, C. A., 67
Smith, D. E., 163
Smith, D. W., 74, 151
Smith, P. A., 194
Smith, R. S., 141
Snipper, A. S., 159
Sontag, L. W., 75
Spache, G. D., 29, 30
Spearman, C., 139
Sperry, B., 199
Spitz, R. A., 87, 253, 267
Spivak, G., 303
Sprague, R. L., 226
Staats, A., 204
Stabenau, J. R., 178
Stacey, M., 90
Stachowiak, J., 111, 117
Starkweather, C. W., 292
Staver, N., 199
Steele, R., 172, 176
Steger, B. M., 202
Stein, Z., 150
Steinberg, L. D., 87
Steinschneider, A., 73

Stembaugh, E. E., 59, 97
Stene, J., 147
Stevens, F., 307
Stevens-Long, J., 184, 185
Stewart, M., 225
Stillman, B. W., 201
Stolberg, A., 303
Stott, D. H., 151
Stouwie, R. J., 233
Street, J., 198
Streissguth, A. P., 74, 151
Strong, J. A., 148
Stunkard, A. J., 280
Sturm, R., 226
Sugar, M., 90
Sullivan, E. T., 28
Sullivan, H. S., 94
Sullivan, L., 271
Susser, M., 150
Sweeney, T. M., 40

Taft, J., 107
Tague, C. E., 162
Talkington, L. W., 161
Talmadge, M., 76
Tarjan, G., 62
Taschman, H. A., 111, 117
Terman, L., 19, 20, 21
Tervo, D., 73
Tesiny, E. P., 268
Teuber, H., 152
Thompson, W. R., 65, 75
Thomson, A. M., 67
Thorndike, R. L., 20, 193
Thorpe, L. P., 32
Thurston, D., 77
Thurstone, L. L., 139
Tiegs, E. W., 28, 32
Tiffany, D. W., 111, 117
Tijo, J., 61
Tinker, M. A., 193
Tisdall, F. F., 66
Tomblin, J. B., 217
Travis, L. E., 289
Truax, C. B., 241
Tupin, J., 178
Turnbull, C. D., 304
Turner, R. J., 88
Turpin, R., 61, 146

Ulleland, C. N., 74, 151
Ulrich, D. N., 199

VandenBerg, B. J., 151
Vanderheiden, G., 217
Vandersall, T. A., 297
VanRiper, C., 289, 292
VanWagenen, R. K., 161
Vellutino, F. R., 202
Verbo, S., 74
Verville, E., 90
Volkart, E. H., 89
Vorhees, C. V., 73

Wahler, R. G., 43, 59, 97
Walder, L. O., 238
Walknowska, J., 146
Wallace, R. F., 75
Wallston, B., 90
Wanberg, L. D., 15
Waterstreet, M. A., 21
Watson, J. B., 99, 118, 119, 260
Watson, J. D., 61
Watson, J. S., 269
Webb, C. E., 219
Weber, W. W., 148
Wechsler, D., 19, 21, 23
Weinberg, W., 271
Weiner, I. B., 266
Weingartoner, H., 227
Weis, L., 124
Weisnagel, J., 296
Weiss, G., 224, 225, 226, 227
Weiss, R., 182
Welner, J., 177
Welsh, G. S., 31
Wenar, C., 181
Wender, P. H., 177
Wepman, J., 195
Werner, E. E., 141
Werry, J. S., 52, 168
Whitehead, P. C., 156
Whitlock, F. A., 295

Whittlesey, J. R. B., 194
Wiener, G., 78, 151
Wile, R., 178
Wilkinson, M. D., 135
Will, L., 37
Williams, C. D., 97
Williams, D. E., 291
Wilson, A. B., 310
Wilson, R. S., 63
Windle, W. F., 77
Windmiller, M., 144
Winick, M., 67
Wirt, R. D., 32, 269
Wise, G. M., 275
Witkin, H. A., 235
Woerner, M. G., 178
Wolf, E. G., 181
Wolf, L. C., 156
Wolf, M. M., 162, 244, 255
Wolking, W. D., 96, 180
Woodyard, E., 67
Woolman, M., 202
Worf, O. H., 278
Wright, L., 284
Wright, S. W., 62
Wyatt, R. J., 175
Wyke, M. A., 214

Yang, E., 172
Yarrow, L. J., 87
Yarrow, M. R., 45
Yates, A. J., 176, 267
Yoder, P., 161
Young, D. B., 185, 186
Young, G. C., 283
Young, M. A., 288

Zigler, E., 155, 159
Zubin, J., 33
Zussman, J. U., 83

subject index